Original Buddhist Sources

Original Buddhist Sources

A Reader

CARL OLSON

RUTGERS UNIVERSITY PRESS

NEW BRUNSWICK, NEW JERSEY, AND LONDON

LIBRARY OF CONGRESS CATALOGING-IN-PUBLICATION DATA

Olson, Carl.
   Original Buddhist sources : a reader / Carl Olson.
      p.   cm.
   Includes bibliographical references and index.
   ISBN 0-8135-3563-8 (hardcover : alk. paper) — ISBN 0-8135-3564-6 (pbk. : alk. paper)
1. Buddhist literature—Translations into English. I. Title.
   BQ1012.057 2005
   294.3'8—dc22

2004016358

A British Cataloging-in-Publication record for this book is available from the British Library

Manufactured in the United States of America

Thanks to Andy, Jo, Jake, Millie, John, and all the
Haspels for many wonderful family memories.

CONTENTS

PREFACE AND ACKNOWLEDGMENTS

This anthology is divided into two major parts: Theravāda and Mahāyāna forms of Buddhism. The former is often referred to as southern Buddhism, whereas the latter is often called northern Buddhism because it includes the regions of Tibet, China, and Japan. Due to limits of length, there are no selections from such Buddhist countries as Thailand, Myanmar (formerly Burma), Korea, or Vietnam. Buddhists in these countries often used many of the texts included in this reader, although they also developed their own texts. Each part will be introduced by an introductory essay about the literature with the context of Buddhist history, but the major focus will be on the selected readings. The first part of the anthology, concentrating on the Theravāda tradition, is arranged chiefly according to the basic teaching of the Buddha from the perspective of this major division of Buddhism. The second part is arranged largely according to the different schools of Mahāyāna Buddhism. This anthology is designed to allow instructors to select their own set of readings and to use the text to fit their teaching style, intentions, and goals for their course by offering instructors a rich selection of primary source material. In contrast to other anthologies of primary source readings in Buddhism, it includes selections on previously neglected topics such as ethics, monastic regulations, the role of women, and hagiographic literature.

The wide-ranging selection of Buddhist primary sources in this reader is intended to supplement an accompanying text about the religious tradition published by Rutgers University Press entitled *The Different Paths of Buddhism: A Narrative-Historical Introduction*. The features of the religious tradition that are emphasized by the introductory text also help to explain the structure of this anthology and some of the selections. More detailed historical background and discussion of the thought of specific figures and schools of Buddhism can be obtained there. Although the two volumes are intended to be used in tandem, it is also possible to use them separately. It is my conviction that no introductory text can replace the primary sources. To truly understand any religious tradition with a substantial body of literature a student must intellectually struggle with and grasp the primary sources, although the introductory text helps a student place the primary sources into a wider sociohistorical context.

Translations not otherwise credited are by the editor of this volume.

I want to thank the former editor of the Social Sciences and Religion Division of Rutgers University Press, David Myers, for his enthusiastic embrace of this book and its companion volume. My appreciation also extends to the current editor, Kristi Long, and her assistant, Adi Hovav. On the path to publication, Kristi has made some helpful suggestions for improving the text, for which I am grateful. This anthology originated during my fellowship at Clare Hall, University of Cambridge. The staff, fellows, and ducks on the River Cam contributed to my adventure in many rewarding ways. My time in Cambridge was made possible by our former Dean Lloyd Michaels and President Richard Cook, who granted me the Teacher-Scholar Chair in the Humanities that provided me the leisure time to begin compiling these writings. I want to thank the bodhisattva in my life, Peggy, my colleagues, and the many students that have studied Buddhism with me over many years.

Original Buddhist Sources

Introduction

It is generally agreed among scholars that an extraordinary and charismatic man lived around the sixth to fifth centuries B.C.E. in India. He was distressed by the fundamental problems of human existence; he discovered a solution to these problems, spent his life teaching others, established a monastic community that preserved and expounded his teachings to future generations, and died at around the age of eighty. We have no idea what he looked like, but we have a general notion about the content of his message, although there is no way to be certain about the precise words that he uttered during his lifetime. Ironically, there is no evidence that he wrote anything, but a substantial literature evolved after his death. Much of this literature claims to capture his actual teachings, preserved in an oral tradition for a couple of centuries before they were written down on pieces of bark, palm leaves, or other available material.

The religious message contained in this literature is not very complicated, because the Buddha provides some simple summaries of his basic teachings. These basic summaries were called the *Dhamma* (Sanskrit: *dharma*). The first summary of his teaching and analysis of human existence is embodied in the Four Noble Truths: (1) all life is suffering; (2) ignorant craving is the cause of suffering; (3) the attainment of *nibbāna* (Sanskrit: *nirvāṇa*) ends suffering; (4) and the Eightfold Path is the means of attaining the goal. This path is an interdependent way of wisdom, ethical or moral action, and meditation. The other shorthand summary of the Buddha's teachings is contained in the three marks of existence: (1) impermanence due to dependent origination and the cycle of causation, (2) suffering, (3) and non-self. Due to the fact that everything within the world is subject to the cycle of causation, there is nothing within the empirical realm that is permanent. Moreover, there is nothing permanent about the self, ego, or soul to which humans can cling. The Buddha's basic teaching is that it is important to cut out one's love of self, which functions as a means of keeping us confined to this realm of suffering, cyclic causation, ignorance, rebirth, and suffering. The Buddha's teachings are intended to carry a person to a nonempirical realm beyond the cycle of causation and rebirth, freedom from ignorant craving, and liberation from suffering. This transcendent state of *nibbāna,* which represents the exact opposite of the characteristics of the world, can only be achieved while one is alive, although an enlightened person gains a permanent state of liberation after death.

The basic message of the Buddha was delivered during the sixth century B.C.E. in northwestern India. During this period, Brahmin priests, their complex sacrificial system, and polytheistic religion characterized the major orthodox form of religion. This was a period of profound political, social, and economic change. India was moving toward a more urban life; iron tools enabled people to cultivate more land and support a larger population; and the development of a monetary system improved economic circumstances, while political change was marked by a shift toward monarchies and empires. When the Buddha delivered his message, he was one of numerous wandering teachers, with various messages. Although the message of the Buddha was presented within a context of change and competition, his followers sought to preserve his teachings unaltered in their memories and dispense them orally to listeners. After the death of the Buddha, tradition credited a series of councils for establishing the authenticity of the authoritative teachings and discipline of the founder.

Buddhism was able to thrive, find stability, and to expand within the social, political, and cultural context created by the Mauryan Dynasty (322–183 B.C.E.), which advocated religious tolerance and support for many religious groups. King Aśoka, who converted to Buddhism late in his life, gave royal support for the teachings. He encouraged the expansion of the religion by sending missionaries to other countries of South Asia and the East. The mission to the island of Sri Lanka in the third century B.C.E. initiated the southern expansion of Buddhism, whereas its journey over the Silk Road played a pivotal role in its spread northward and eastward through Central Asia and into China. From the Chinese mainland, Buddhism spread to Korea and then to Japan.

Scripture, Canon, and Interpretation

Whereas the Abrahamic religions of Judaism, Christianity, and Islam attribute their sacred scriptures to divine revelation, Buddhism traces the origin of its scripture to the personal intuitive insights of a human being. Within the Indian cultural context during the lifetime of the Buddha, the leaders of Vedic religion, which was dominated by high-caste Brahmins, conceived of their sacred literature as originating in an eternal realm of truth that provided inspiration to individual priestly poets. This was a realm beyond the deities of the Vedic pantheon. The Vedic priests taught that the Vedic scriptures originated as primal sound that was personified as the deity Vāc and not as a written word. In contrast to the Vedic religion, Buddhist scripture emerged from the words of a human being, who based his discourses upon his personal and direct experience of what he grasped as reality. In contrast to the Abrahamic religious traditions in which the truth is given directly from a theistic deity to a mediator of some kind (such as an angel) or a human recipient (such as a prophet), the Buddha discovered the truth by himself. Over a period of time, the discourses of the Buddha became a body of doctrine that could be used as a teaching device and guide for followers. The discourses of the Buddha were memorized by followers, orally transmitted from one generation of adherents to another, and eventually became a written body of scripture. As the historical Buddha became more revered and exalted in the minds and hearts of his followers, his words became a sacred body of literature.

There is nothing divinely unique about Buddhist scriptures because they did not appear only once in history. From the Buddhist perspective, they are facts about the nature of human existence and the world, and not the revelation of some deity. This lack of uniqueness should not be construed as a negative characteristic. Rather, the Buddhists have tended to place the teachings of the Buddha within a broader context in that the discourses of the Buddha, which were based on his personal religious quest and discovery, had occurred repeatedly during the lives of previous Buddhas. The historical Buddha merely rediscovered that which was known by prior enlightened beings. Thus the achievement of the historical Buddha represented an awareness of an eternal body of truths that had also been realized by prior figures. This teaching is always present as a realized possibility for others. Furthermore, the long line of sequential teaching by Buddhas of the past means that enlightenment is not merely an ever-present possibility but is also an actuality. The possibility and actuality of enlightenment suggests that there is always the possibility of a newer awakening to the eternal truth that can take place within the Buddhist community. Moreover, it suggests that a sacred Buddhist text possesses no intrinsic value in and of itself. It is only valuable if someone uses it as a guide. Once such a person attains enlightenment, the sacred text can be abandoned and even rejected because it has no further utility.

The Buddhist attitude toward the scriptures is grounded in an understanding of language, which is viewed as an impermanent human product. A basic Buddhist philosophical presupposition is that everything within the world is impermanent. The impermanent and nonabsolute nature of language means that its does not have an enduring structure or metaphysical status. Lacking any intrinsic importance, words are only valuable in an instrumental way—their value resides in their ability to accomplish something. They are comparable to a teacher who helps a person attain liberation by being instructive. The informative function of scripture is connected to mental activities such as concept formation, readings; it is studied for information, knowledge, and guidance.

Another way in which words can function is performative: the recitation of words makes something happen. The ritual repetition of the *Pāṭimokkha* (monastic regulations) periodically by Theravāda monks is an example of the performative function of scripture: it unites the members of the monastery into a brotherhood. The performative nature of mantras can function for liturgical purposes, and they can also be continually recited as a devotional practice or as a way to maintain concentration during periods of meditation. Along with Christianity and Confucianism, Buddhism tends to stress the informative over the performative function of scripture.

Moreover, whereas Sanskrit is the sacred language of Hinduism, Arabic of Islam, and Hebrew of Judaism, there is no single sacred language for Buddhism. As Buddhism spread, it used the languages of various different cultures: Pāli (in Sri Lanka), Tibetan, Sanskrit, Chinese, Korean, Japanese, and others. Beliefs about the impermanent nature of language and lack of a divine revelation probably formed the context for allowing many languages for Buddhist scriptures without compromising their authenticity or authority.

What gives the Buddhist canon its authority? A canon comprises the official writings of a religious tradition. From a cross-cultural perspective, a canon can be considered closed, as in the case of Islam. In the Muslim tradition, the revelation to the prophet Muhammad ended with his life, and it was accepted as the final perfect revelation. As in the case of Judaism, there can be levels of the canon. Within the context of Judaism, these levels were formed by Talmudic, legal, ritual, and exegetical commentary. In order for a religious literature to reach canonical status, there must be a strong social dimension of consensus in the formation of scripture. Buddhism reached a social consensus by a series of learned councils.

Buddhist literature, as has been said, grew from the direct experience of a human being, shared by teaching others. These instructive discourses were memorized by followers and preserved in personal memory. In fact, oral reciters specialized in the memorization of a particular subject. This oral teaching tradition was maintained for a couple of centuries until Buddhist elders met in councils and decided to preserve the teachings and transform them into a more permanent and written form. This process included making decisions about what was authentic and trustworthy. The major criterion for inclusion into the canon was whether a discourse could be traced directly to the Buddha or to a genuine witness or two.

A canon of sacred scripture can contain many different genres of literature. In the Theravāda Buddhist tradition, it is possible to find philosophical discourse, poetry, chronicle, stories, parables, pedagogical discourse, oaths, history, legend, biography, myth, hymns, law, and apocalyptic speculation. It is not as easy to find oracle, divination, prayers, proverbs, ritual procedures, or theology in Theravāda literature, although this does not mean that some examples of these literary genres could not be discovered. What is important for Buddhism is that scripture played a significant role during the centuries after the establishment of a written literary tradition, which itself developed after the career of the Buddha. Buddhist scripture served as a medium for the propagation of the religion for those who entered monastic life, although oral communication continued to play an important role as monks and nuns shared the message of the Buddha with often illiterate lay people. The accepted canonical literature also operated to maintain and regulate the religion. The Theravāda canon was substantially closed by the early fifth century c.e., which was about the period when the monk Buddhaghoṣa compiled his commentaries in Sri Lanka. The closing of the canon was associated with the process of political struggle among three monastic groups of Theravāda Buddhists in Sri Lanka.

Even before the canon was formed, Buddhists raised the issue of correct interpretation of scriptures. It was not, however, until the second or first century B.C.E. that a systematic attempt was made to devise a procedure for the art of hermeneutics, in a text entitled *The Guide* (*Nettippakaraṇa*). According to this text, the Buddha referred to his Dhamma (teaching) as something positive at its beginning, middle, and end. In other words, the Buddha insisted that his teaching possessed consistency and clarity from its beginning to its end. This suggests that the Dhamma was guided by the Buddha to accomplish particular purposes. Furthermore, Buddhists assumed that the Dhamma was an immeasurably unique teaching grounded in transcendent wisdom, which goes beyond empirical truth and reason. Moreover, the basic nature of the Dhamma influences the process of interpretation because its own meaning and phrasing are inherent in it. This means that the teaching itself embodies a structure that makes interpretation possible and shapes any such interpretation. This is similar to having an internal interpretative guideline within the teaching itself.

The Dhamma also possesses multiple forms and levels. It is incumbent upon the interpreter to seek the internal coherence and consistency within a text in order to understand it. If the method of interpretation must be based on the inherent structure and intention of the Dhamma, interpretation must mirror the Dhamma itself. This means, for instance, that any interpretation that contradicts the three marks of existence (that is, all life is suffering, everything is impermanent, and non-self) is incorrect. The nature of the Dhamma necessarily requires interpreting the Dhamma in terms of itself. This suggests that the Buddha becomes the interpreter of his own teachings. More specifically, the meaning of the Dhamma points to the purpose or goal, which is identified with nibbāna. This implies that any genuine interpretation brings forth the basic intention of the teachings, points to the goal of nibbāna, and demonstrates the way that the teaching is interrelated with other parts.

In order to accomplish an interpretation, the *Guide* provides guidelines (*nayā*) for dealing with concerns that involve meaning (*attha*) and phrasing (*byañjana*) of a passage. The three guidelines for determining the meaning of a text involve grasping its truth. The guidelines are based on nine pairs of root terms that represent the text's essence. There is one positive and negative term in each pair: negative or unprofitable types of roots would include greed, hate, and delusion, whereas profitable roots would be the opposites.

The initial meaning guideline is called "conversion of relishing." This helps to explain how root terms like desire and ignorance apply to people with desire and "inadequate temperaments," and how they can be counteracted by positive root terms. What is called "lion's play" represents the second meaning guideline. This guideline correlates four "useful" and "useless" root terms with four types of people: lustful, hateful, dull, and intelligent. The third meaning guideline represents three types of people in terms of their knowledge: those with brief knowledge, those with expanded knowledge, and those hardly guidable.

With respect to phrasing, a person can interpret a passage by using the sixteen modes of conveying (*hārā*). The purpose of these modes is to discern the "fitness" or "correctness of meaning" of a phrase that is in accord with the essence of Dhamma. The essence of the Dhamma includes the core elements of the Four Noble Truths, dependent origination, and delusion. An interpretation is thus acceptable if it corresponds with these central notions. An interpreter uses categories to penetrate to the essence of a text by correlating the phraseology with central concepts from the Dhamma. Monkeys jumping from one branch to another, grabbing at fruit of a tree, can be interpreted, for example, as a metaphor for human greed and attachment that leads to further suffering, which is a fundamental truth of the teaching. Although phrasing reveals that the Buddha delivered his teaching according to the level of understanding of the audience, and although there are sixteen different ways of analyzing a text, the purpose of phrasing is to show an interpreter how to reduce texts to their principal factors. In summary, phrasing calls attention to the unity beneath the diversity within a text, whereas the meaning evokes its singularity and unity. This method of interpretation represents the Theravāda Buddhist's version of the hermeneutical circle well known in the West.

PART I

Selections from the
Theravāda Tradition

Introduction to Theravāda Buddhist Literature

During the formative period of the historical evolution of Buddhism, the literature was organized into two "baskets": Vinaya-piṭaka (basket of monastic discipline), and Sutta-piṭaka (basket of discourses). The term *piṭaka* (basket) connotes a container used to hold items. According to tradition, this occurred at the first council at Rājagṛha, the capital of Magadha, immediately following the Buddha's death around 486 B.C.E., when monks met to recite from memory the words of the Buddha. In order to assure accuracy, the monks chanted the remembered teachings in unison. The teaching (Dhamma) of the Buddha was called *āgama* (literally, that which has been transmitted). After a period of oral transmission from teacher to disciple, the teachings were collected and organized into *suttas* (threads or texts) and *gāthās* (verses). The root derivation of the term *sutta* (Sanskrit: *sūtra*) connotes the warp of a woven cloth. This suggests that the teachings were made into phrases that could be memorized, just as verses could. Around second century B.C.E., a third basket was added called the Abhidhamma-piṭaka (basket of additional teachings), thus creating the "three baskets" (tipiṭaka) of Buddhist teachings. Before these three collections were written, oral reciters preserved them by means of memorization, each specializing in a particular subject matter.

The basket of monastic discipline contains the rules and precepts that guide monastic life. This basket is divided into three major categories: *Sutta-vibhanga*, *Khandhaka,* and *Parivāra.* The first category consists of the *Pāṭimokkha* and its 227 rules, which are arranged according to the degree of seriousness of the offense. The *Pāṭimokkha* developed from a simple confession of faith made by monks and nuns into a basic monastic code used to guarantee proper monastic behavior. After it became established, it functioned as a monastic liturgy. Monks and nuns periodically chanted these rules within their respective communities as entire groups. This type of group activity worked to unify the communities and functioned as a reminder of the rules that bound them together. The group reciting of the *Pāṭimokkha* occurred twice a month in connection with fast days (*poṣadha*) that were historically connected to the religious significance of the new and full moon days in ancient Indian religion. Certain literary features were added to the text as it evolved, including introductory and concluding verses that praised monastic virtue and discipline. An introduction (*nidāna*) to the text functioned to summon the monastic community together and served as a means to conduct the proper confessional procedure. Finally, after each category of violations, the text contained an interrogatory procedure with the purpose of determining violators of the monastic code and distinguishing the pure from the impure members.

The *Sutta-vibhanga* can be literally translated as "analysis of a sutta" (thread or text); the text in this case is the *Pāṭimokkha*. There are four parts to each item in the *Sutta-vibhanga*. The initial part contains a narrative or narratives that present actual human circumstances for a particular rule. Second, there is the actual rule. Then there is a commentary on each term of the rule. It concludes with a narrative which indicates any mitigating circumstances that provide exceptions to the rule. It might also relate any changes that could be made in the punishment. This last aspect suggests the beginning of some flexibility in the monastic code. Flexibility is also evident with the use of terms such as grave offense, light offense, or an offense of improper conduct. This introduction of elasticity probably reflects the historical development of the *Pāṭimokkha* into a fixed and closed body of rules. When new rules became inadmissible to the code of conduct, monastic communities discovered that they needed some suppleness to be able to respond properly to new incidents that were without precedent in the established code.

In contrast to the *Sutta-vibhanga,* the *Khandhaka* represents a broader body of rules that serves as a supplement to the basic rules of the *Pāṭimokkha*. The

Khandhaka also deals with broader issues of communal disharmony and actions by the larger monastic order, along with procedures for the ceremonial life of the community and regulations for dealing with a schism or the threat of a split within the order. It includes more mundane issues like the use of shoes and leather objects, proper and improper clothing, correct and incorrect behavior during probationary periods, procedures for settling disputes, and rules specifically for nuns. Finally, the third major category in the basket is the *Parivāra,* which is collection of auxiliary texts of different dates and origin.

The discourses of the Buddha are contained in the Sutta-piṭaka. Besides its connection to the metaphor of weaving, the term *sutta* refers to the thread or thong of leather or string used to hold the pages of a text together. In this metaphorical sense, the sutta suggests something that binds pages of a discourse together. A sutta follows a specific form that commences with the words "Thus have I heard. At one time. . . ." This introduction is followed by the location of the discourse, which is followed in turn by a list of names of those in the audience. It concludes with the sermon of the Buddha. This basic format evokes the circumstances after the death of the Buddha, when monks gathered to share and recite from memory the sermons that they had heard and could remember. The disciples were concerned about transmitting accurately the teachings of their enlightened master. Because of this, the sutta literature tends to move in the direction of becoming dogmatic, that is, inflexible and authoritarian. This did not mean that the disciples were concerned with proving or verifying statements made by the Buddha. Any person listening to the message embodied within a discourse could either accept or reject it.

The suttas tend to be repetitive. This feature reflects the original oral nature of the Buddhist teachings. Repetition helped disciples memorize them. A reader will also discover a wide variety of figures of speech in the texts, such as similes, metaphors, examples based on lived experiences, and analogies. In fact, it is possible to identify original texts by their length because shorter texts grew over a period of time as monks added to them.

The Sutta-piṭaka texts are arranged according to length. Among the five major collections of these texts are the long sayings (*Dīgha-nikāya*), middle-length sayings (*Majjhima-nikāya*), works connected by their contents (*Saṃyutta-nikāya*), texts arranged by numerical groupings of items (*Aṅguttara-nikāya*) in an ascending order culminating with a list of eleven things, and a collection of minor works (*Khuddaka-nikāya*). This Pāli canon became fixed and closed by 100 B.C.E.

With respect to the collection of minor works (about whose authenticity Buddhist scholars have disagreed), the Sri Lankan collection includes fifteen works with a postcanonical status. These texts include the *Udāna* (solemn utterances of the sage), the popular *Dhammapada* (stanzas on the teaching), *Sutta-nipāta* (collection of texts), *Vimāna-vatthu* (narratives of heavenly palaces), *Peta-vatthu* (narratives about ghosts), *Niddesa* (exposition), *Jātaka* tales about the former lives of the Buddha, and others. The *Jātaka* tales function as paradigms for the religious tradition, depicting and stressing basic religious practices and virtues. It was common for monks to share these entertaining stories with the laity and use them to impart religious lessons. Another important text in this category is the *Itivuttaka*, which is a collection of discourses that begin "Thus has been said by the Lord." The *Theragāthā* gives a reader a glimpse into the lives of monks, whereas the *Theragāthā* presents a look at the lives and poetry of nuns. Selections from the latter are included in chapter 10 of this volume.

In addition to these texts, the Theravāda tradition also includes faith-inspiring biographies of the religious deeds of a person, called *avadāna* (legend) that were added to the body of literature, although they are noncanonical. Embodied within the narratives of such individuals, there are abstract religious notions and concerns, illustrations of the operation of acts of merit, and attention to values such as faith and devotion. The biographical narratives refer simultaneously to the past and present in a wide variety of cultural and linguistic contexts. These narratives have both cultural value as entertaining tales and didactic value as illustrations of an exemplary style of life. They also mediate between the real and the ideal. A good example of such literature is the *Aśokāvadāna* of the second century C.E. by an unknown author, which focuses on the famous Buddhist king and benefactor of the religion, Aśoka. Two other examples are the *Divyāvadāna*, an anthology of Buddhist legends, and the *Avadānaśataka*, a collection of one hundred narratives. These texts should be distinguished from the history or lineages portrayed in a chronicle (*vaṃsa*), which concentrates on the sacred genealogy of a country, a particular Buddhist sect, or a holy object. A primary example of a chronicle is the *Mahāvaṃsa,* a fifth-century chronicle of the island of Sri Lanka.

The final basket to be added to the Pāli canon was the Abhidhamma-piṭaka. The prefix *abhi* means above. This prefix suggests what is beyond or superior to the Dhamma (doctrine/teaching) that it is analyzing. The term *abhidhamma* implies that it possesses more authority than the explanations to be discovered in the suttas themselves. The scholastic analysis of material from the Sutta-piṭaka was thought to embody "understanding of the teachings" or "analysis of the teachings." This basket of frequently technical literature probably originated from lists of doctrinal topics that were used to collect and preserve concepts and teachings of the Buddha from a variety of diverse viewpoints.

The Pāli-language Abhidhamma tradition consists of seven books, which the Sri Lankan tradition believes the Buddha taught in a spiritual body to his deceased mother in a heavenly realm. This filial legend enabled the Therav̄adins a chance to give an account of the time lapse between the prior baskets and the appearance of this literature. Another legend from the *Aṭṭlasālinī,* a work attributed to the monk Buddhaghosa, relates the transmission of the Abhidhamma from the Buddha to his disciples. At the Anotatta Lake located in the Himalayan Mountains, the Buddha taught Abhidhamma to the monk Śāriputra, who took responsibility for organizing the texts and transmitting them to disciples. It is wise to look beyond this pious fiction to the efforts of learned elders.

When the Buddha is depicted teaching after his death he is represented with a nonphysical body called a "mentally created body." It enables a person to appear and teach in a spiritualized form to another person in a dream or vision. By teaching in such a way, the Buddha is credited with providing an analysis of mental and bodily factors in the first book of this collection, called the *Dhammasangaṇi* (Enumeration of Dhammas). According to Buddhist tradition, this text was recited at the Second Council held around 386 B.C.E. Even though it is probably the oldest Abhidhamma text, it also contains later material that scholars date to the second century B.C.E. The five aggregates (*khandhas*), fetters, causation, meditation, and kinds of knowledge are topics examined by the *Vibhanga* (a term that means analysis). The five aggregates are identified as matter, feelings or sensations, perceptions, mental constituents, and consciousness. This text is considered to complement the *Dhammasangaṇi* and to be contemporary with it. The style of the *Vibhanga* assumes a question-and-answer format.

Another Abhidhamma work accepted by the Theravāda tradition is the *Kathāvattu* (Points of Controversy). This text is a polemical work intended to support an orthodox position against views of rival schools. Hence it consists of a series of debates over disputed points of doctrine, including the existence of a person, whether disciples also possess powers of the Buddha, whether a layperson can become a perfected being, and the issue of liberation. Some scholars date this text to around 240 B.C.E., during Aśoka's reign. Belonging to the same historical period as the *Abhidhamma* texts already mentioned is the *Puggalapaññatti* (Description of Human Types). This text examines various kinds of personality such as lustful, hateful, and delusional types.

Included in the collection of Abhidhamma texts is the *Dhātukathā* (Discourse on Elements). Various scholars differ with respect to its date, which may be first century B.C.E. The text proposes fourteen modes of analysis for some 105 topics. It also offers an analysis of common principles and characteristics of the modes proposed. It covers such topics as the factors of five aggregates and senses, elements, truth, causation, and powers attained by monks by means of meditation. In contrast to the *Dhātukathā,* the *Yamaka* (Book of Pairs) provides more precise analysis of ambiguous terms. This book's title reflects the contents of the text: it consists of paired questions on the distribution of terms in a proposition. The answers to these questions indicate whether the term covers all the members of the class it denotes, whether it covers some of them, or whether it focuses on none of them. The questions consider topics such as matter, sensation, consciousness, and other subjects. Finally, the *Paṭṭhāna* (Conditional Relations) is a broad discussion of causation that dates to around the time of the composition of the *Yamaka* in the first century C.E. The text also discusses the conditions of the relations among the items identified in the other Theravāda Abhidhamma texts.

Besides the Abhidhamma-piṭaka in Pāli of the Theravāda tradition, there are also collections in Sanskrit and Tibetan of the Sarvāstivāda school and a Chinese translation of the *Dharmaguptaka,* which became part of the Mahāyāna literary tradition.

After the establishment of the *Tipiṭaka,* (triple basket), learned monks wrote commentaries on the texts. During the fifth century C.E., the monk Buddhaghoṣa consolidated, for instance, previous commentaries, and he wrote five commentaries on the Nikāya texts. This great Buddhist scholar also composed several works on the Abhidhamma literature. He gained great authority in the Pāli canon for his scholarly efforts with such texts as the *Path of Purification* (*Visuddhimagga*) and his extensive commentaries on canonical texts. This monk earned the status of the voice of orthodoxy for the Sri Lankan tradition. Other Buddhist scholars followed in the footsteps of Buddhaghoṣa with their own commentaries.

In addition to the three baskets, other works gained a postcanonical status. *Questions of King Milinda* (*Milindapañha*) reflects a philosophical-religious dialogue between a king and a learned Buddhist monk named Nāgasena. This work was compiled in north India around the third century C.E. Other works of note are the *Discourse on the Traditions* (*Peṭakopadesa*), and *The Guide* (*Nettippakaraṇa*). The former text was composed around 150 B.C.E., and it begins by explaining the Four Noble Truths, discusses marks of truth, and presents a scheme for classifying various types of passages, texts, and categories. *The Guide* falls into the same literary genre as the *Discourse on the Traditions.* With a date of composition around the second or first century B.C.E., it represents an early hermeneutical work, as previously discussed. In fact, it is the earliest attempt to solve problems associated with interpreting the teachings correctly.

As Buddhism developed, it divided into many different sects over differences related to issues of monastic regulation and doctrine. These various schisms would often create a new recension of the body of literature. In order to simplify a complicated history, there evolved a shorthand way to refer to two major divisions of Buddhism: Theravāda and Mahāyāna. The first part of this anthology contains selections of literature from the former tradition, whereas the second half contains selections from the latter. The Theravāda tradition is often called the southern tradition because it includes such countries as Sri Lanka, Cambodia, Burma, and Thailand, whereas Mahāyāna is called the northern school because it includes such countries as Tibet, China, Vietnam, Korea, and Japan. The literature of the southern tradition was preserved chiefly in the Pāli language of Sri Lanka, while the northern school embraced texts composed in Sanskrit before these works were translated into Tibetan, Chinese, Japanese and other languages.

Because Theravāda forms a single religious tradition that is spread over several countries with a common view of the literature and its message, this anthology will focus on central issues connected to the teachings of the Buddha such as his discourse on causality, the Four Noble Truths, non-self, nibbāna, meditation, and ethics. Before offering selections on such topics, the volume gives some examples of the former lives of the Buddha from the *Jātaka* tales and the narrative of the Buddha's life. It also contains selections concerning monastic regulations, narratives about women, and finally examples of hagiographic literature.

The second part of the book covers aspects of Mahāyāna Buddhism. Because this tradition lacks a unified perspective and comprises a vast body of literature composed over a wide geographical area, this second part surveys examples of important texts before turning to examine the literature of particular schools. Selections from the Mādhyamika school and the Yogācāra school are available from Sanskrit texts. Thus the presence of these schools in China and Tibet is not covered. With respect to Tibet, this volume focuses on the strong Tantric influence on this culture. Selections from Tantric texts will provide readers with a more informed understanding of the types of Buddhist literature. The readings on China focus on indigenous schools: Hua-yen, T'ien t'ai, Pure Land, and Ch'an. With respect to the readings on Japanese Buddhism, a reader will find selections from the Pure Land and Zen traditions. Finally, this volume concludes with selections of hagiographic literature and narratives about women within the Mahāyāna tradition.

1

Jātaka Tales
(Former Lives of the Buddha)

Before considering the biography of the Buddha, it is necessary to examine some examples of the former lives of the Buddha. In line with the traditional Buddhist belief in the notion of karma (action) and rebirth (*saṃsāra*), the historical Buddha is thought to have passed through many prior modes of existence before being born as Siddhārtha, a prince who would attain enlightenment. Because of his numerous previous lives, the historical Buddha is not considered unique (unlike the depiction of Jesus in early Christian scriptures) in the sense of being a single historical occurrence. There have been Buddhas before Siddhārtha, and there will be such figures in the future. The only future figure mentioned by the Pāli canon, however, is Metteya (Sanskrit: Maitreya), who will become the final person of the five Buddhas of this eon. The number of previous Buddhas before Siddhārtha depends on the text that is consulted. The *Mahāpadāna Sutta* describes seven Buddhas, the *Buddhavaṃsa* provides a list of twenty-four Buddhas of the past, and other texts give even higher numbers. Even though the Buddha is a plural figure, the path of Buddhism is singular and grounded in the experience of a single person. This forms the background for understanding the *Jātaka* narratives.

The *Jātaka* tales date to the historical period of the Buddha, which gives these tales a rich antiquity. Evidence for their antiquity can be traced to the Sutta-piṭaka body of literature, where the Buddha refers to three accomplishments that are indicative of the attainment of enlightenment. A major achievement is the ability to remember all one's previous modes of existence. The ability to remember previous lives provides a firm credible epistemological foundation for others to believe in such a possibility. This is, of course, already anticipated by and grounded in the culturally accepted doctrine of rebirth.

The *Jātaka* tales all follow a similar format that begins with a short story that reflects the present by recalling a situation during which the Buddha recounted the story. The second phase consists of a tale of the past, which represents the *Jātaka* itself. Finally, the Buddha concludes the narrative by identifying certain characters as himself and others in a previous birth. In these narratives, the Buddha is depicted as an animal, human, or a deity, and he acts within a context without the presence of an historical Buddha. In these narratives he cultivates a virtue that prefigures one that he will prefect when he becomes Gotama, the historical Buddha. Among these virtues are selfless giving, truth, renunciation, moral rectitude, determination, equanimity, and friendliness.

The Pāli rendition of the *Jātaka* tales is entitled the *Jātakaṭṭhakathā*, and it dates to around the period of the fifth or fourth century c.e. In imitation of the historical Buddha, monks retold these stories to ordinary villagers and city dwellers in order to communicate the Buddhist message and provide an entertaining respite from ordinary social duties. It is possible to find archeological evidence of the importance of these tales by looking at great stone stūpas (funerary mounds) erected by the second century b.c.e. Carved onto these stone monuments are sculptured depictions of various rebirth stories that functioned as visual libraries for ordinary people without the ability to read the narratives.

Selections from the *Matakabhatta Jātaka* (no. 18)

Once upon a time when Brahmadatta ruled in Benares, a Brahmin who was a Vedic expert in literature and a world-famous instructor was reminded to offer a Feast for the Dead. He had a goat fetched and said to his pupils, "My sons, give this goat a purifying bath at the river, place a garland around its neck, give it some grain to eat, groom it, and return with it."

Agreeing with the request, they took the goat to the river. There they bathed and groomed it, and set it on the river bank. The goat, becoming aware of its ethical actions in previous lifetimes became overjoyed at the thought that now it would be freed from all its suffering, and laughed aloud with abandon. Then the goat thought about the ethical consequences for the Brahmin when he sacrificed it. Feeling compassionate for the Brahmin, the goat wept loudly. "Friend goat," said the young Brahmins, "since your voice expressed both laughter and weeping, what made you laugh and what made you weep?"

"Ask me these questions before your master."

Accompanying the goat, they came to their master and told him of the animal's reaction. After hearing their story, the master asked the goat why it laughed and why it wept. Thereupon the animal, recalling its former modes of existences, replied to the Brahmin: "In the past, Brahmin, I, like you, was also a Brahmin versed in the texts of the Vedas, and I, to offer a Feast for the Dead, killed a goat for my offering. By killing a single goat, I have had my head cut off five hundred times with the exception of one time. This is my five hundredth and last birth; and I laughed aloud when I reflected that on this precise day I should be freed from my suffering. On the other hand, I wept when I reflected about my punishment for killing a goat and was now being freed from my misery, while you, as a penalty for your violence, would be doomed to lose your head like me, five hundred times. Thus it was out of compassion for you that I wept." The Brahmin replied, "Fear not, goat. I will not kill you." "What is this you say, Brahmin?" asked the goat. "Whether you kill me or not, I cannot escape death today." "Do not fear, goat; I will protect you." "Brahmin, your protection is meager compared to the force of my evil deeds."

Setting free the goat, the Brahmin said to his disciples, "Do not allow anyone to kill this goat"; and accompanied by the young men, he closely followed the animal. When the goat was set free, it extended its neck to eat the leaves of a bush growing near the top of a rock. At that very moment a thunderbolt struck the rock; it broke off a chunk that hit the goat on its outstretched neck and severed its head. And people gathered to witness the aftermath.

In those days the bodhisattva had been born a tree-fairy in that very spot. By means of his supernatural powers, he now seated himself cross-legged in mid-air while the crowd watched him. He thought to himself, "If these creatures only knew the result of doing evil, perhaps they would desist from killing," and with his melodious voice he taught them the truth with this stanza:

If people knew that the penalty would be
Birth unto sorrow, living things would cease
From taking life. Strict is the slayer's fate.

Thus did the bodhisattva preach the truth, frightening his hearers with the fear of hell. After hearing him, people were so terrified at the fear of hell that they quit killing life. And after establishing the people in the ethical precepts through his preaching the truth to them, the bodhisattva passed away to fare according to his deeds. The people, too, remained steadfast in the teaching of the bodhisattva and spent their lives in charity and other good works, so they were reborn into the city of the gods.

Mudulakkhana Jātaka (no. 66)

Once upon a time when Brahmadatta ruled in Benares, the bodhisattva was born into a rich Brahmin family in Kāśi. When he matured and finished his education, he renounced worldly desires, and turned to a life of solitude. He went to live alone in the Himalayas. After completion of preliminary modes of meditation, he gained the higher knowledges and the ecstatic trance states; and he lived his life in the bliss of religious insight.

Lacking necessary food, he went to Benares, where he assumed his quarters in the king's pleasure grove. Next day, meeting his daily needs, he collected his red suit of bark, threw over his shoulder a black antelope's skin, knotted his tangled locks in a coil on the top of his head, and carried two baskets from a yoke on his neck; he went begging. Arriving at the palace gates, his demeanor impressed the king, who invited him to enter. Thus the ascetic was seated on an impressive couch and fed abundantly the finest food. After he thanked the king, he was invited to assume a place to live. The ascetic accepted the offer, and for sixteen years he lived in the pleasure grove, exhorting the king's household, and ate the king's food.

There came a time when the king had to suppress a revolt on the borders of his land. But before he started, he instructed his queen, whose name was Kind-heart, to attend to the needs of the holy man. Thus, the bodhisattva continued to frequent the palace.

One day Queen Kind-heart prepared a meal for the bodhisattva. When he did not arrive she retired to her own bathroom. After bathing in perfumed water, she dressed herself beautifully, lay down, and awaited his arrival on a small couch within the spacious chamber.

Waking from his trance state and noticing that it was late, the bodhisattva decided to fly to the palace. Hearing the rustling of his bark-robe, the queen sat up quickly to receive him. In her rush to rise, her dress slipped down, revealing her body to the ascetic as he entered the window. Upon seeing her naked, he continued to gaze for the sheer sake of pleasure on the marvelous beauty of the queen in violation of moral precepts. Lust was ignited within him; he was like a tree cut down by an axe. At once he lost all insight, and he became like a crow with its wings clipped. Standing and holding his food, still trembling with desire, he made his way from the palace to his hut in the pleasure grove, and placed it down beneath his wooden couch. Thereupon, he lay for seven entire days a prey to hunger and thirst, enslaved by the queen's loveliness with his heart overcome with lust.

On the seventh day, the king returned from pacifying the revolt on his border. After passing in solemn procession around the city, he entered his palace. Then, wishing to see the ascetic, he made his way to the pleasure grove, and there in the hut found the bodhisattva lying on his couch. Assuming that the holy man had been ill and having the hut cleaned out, the king asked, as he stroked the sufferer's feet, what afflicted him. "Sire, my heart is enslaved by lust; that is my sole ailment." "Lust for who?" "For Kind-heart, sire." "The queen is yours because I give her to you," said the king. Then he accompanied the ascetic to the palace, and asking the queen to array herself in all her splendor, gave her to the bodhisattva. But, as he was giving her away, the king secretly encouraged the queen to try hard to save the holy man.

"Fear not. Sire," said the queen; "I will save him." Thus the queen and the ascetic left the palace. But when they passed through the great gate, the queen said that they must have a house in which to live, and he was directed to return to ask the king for one. So he returned to the king to ask for a house in which to live, and the king gave them a dilapidated building that passers-by used as a toilet. The ascetic took the queen to this building. But she vehemently refused to enter it due to its filthy condition.

"What am I to do?" he cried. "Why, clean it," she replied. And she sent him to the king for a shovel and a basket, forced him to remove all the filth and dirt, and plaster the walls with cowdung, which he had to fetch. After this was completed, she made him get a bed, a stool, a rug, a water-pot, and a cup, sending him for only one item at a time. Next, she sent him to retrieve water and a thousand other things. He began to get the water, filled up a water-pot, and set out the water for the bath, and made the bed. And, as he sat with her upon the bed, she grabbed him by his whiskers and drew him toward her until they were face to face, saying, "Have you forgotten that you are a holy man and a Brahmin?" Thereupon, he came to his senses after his interval of senseless foolishness.

When he returned to his senses he thought to himself how, growing weaker, his fatal craving would condemn him later to the future states of punishment. "This very day," he cried, "I will return this woman to the king and fly to the mountains!" He stood with the queen before the king and said, "Sire, I do not desire your queen any longer; and it was only for her that cravings were awakening within me" . . . Soon his lost power of insight came back to him. Arising from the earth and sitting in the air, he preached the truth to the king; and without touching earth he passed through the air to the Himalayas. He never came back to human ways; but he developed love and charity until, with insight intact, he was reborn in the realm of Brahma.

Javasakuṇa Jātaka (no. 308)

Once upon a time when Brahmadatta reigned in Benares, the bodhisattva was reborn as a woodpecker in the Himalaya region. Now a lion, while eating his prey, got a bone stuck in his throat. His throat became so swollen that he could not consume any more food, and he was afflicted with severe pains. Then the woodpecker, searching for food, saw the lion from his perch on a branch, and asked, "Friend, what ails you?" The lion told him the problem, and the bird said, "I will take the bone out of your throat, friend, but I dare not put my head into your mouth because of fear that you might eat me." "Do not be afraid, friend; I will not eat you. Just save my life."

"All right," said the bird, and ordered the lion to lie down upon his side. Then it thought: "Who knows if I can trust this creature?" And to prevent him from closing his mouth, the bird fixed a stick between the upper and lower jaws of the lion and then, putting its head into the lion's mouth, dislodged the bone with its beak. The bone fell out and disappeared. And then the woodpecker withdrew its head from the lion's mouth, knocked out the stick with its beak and, hopping away, it sat on a branch.

The lion recovered from his malaise, and one day was devouring a wild buffalo that he had killed. The woodpecker thought to himself: "I will now test the lion," and perching on a branch above the lion's head, it conversed with him and uttered the following stanza:

> As much kindness within me reside,
> To you, my lord, did I demonstrate;
> To me in turn, I humbly pray,
> Do you bestow a small favor.

Upon hearing this, the lion responded with another stanza:

> To trust your head to a lion's jaw,
> A creature of tooth and claw,
> To dare such a deed and be living still,
> Is proof enough of my good will.

The woodpecker on hearing this responded with this stanza:

> From the base ingrate do not hope to obtain,
> The due recompense for kind service rendered;
> Refrain from bitter thought and angry word
> But avoid the presence of the ingrate.

With these words, the woodpecker flew away.

Sasa Jātaka (no. 316)

Once upon a time when Brahmadatta reigned in Benares, the bodhisattva was reborn as a young rabbit and lived in a forest. On one side of this forest was the base of a mountain, on another side a river, and on the third side a rural village. The rabbit had three friends—a monkey, a jackal, and an otter. These four wise creatures lived together, and each animal got its food by it own means. At night they again came together. By means of his wisdom, the rabbit preached the truth to his three companions, teaching about the necessity of giving, observation of the moral law, and observance of holy days. They accepted his teaching, and each animal dispersed to his own part of the forest and lived there.

As time went by, the bodhisattva, observing the moon at the time, knew that the next day would be a fast day. He addressed his three companions, "tomorrow is a fast day. Let all three of you assume the moral precepts, and observe the holy day. Beings who observe moral precepts find that almsgiving brings a great reward. Therefore, feed any beggars that you encounter with your own food." They readily agreed, and lived within their own place of residence.

Early the next day, the otter went to seek his prey and went down to the bank of the Ganges River. Now it occurred that a fisherman caught seven red fish. Stringing them together on a line, he buried them in the sand on the river's bank. And then he went down stream, to catch more fish. The otter smelled the buried fish, dug them up, and pulled them out crying aloud three times, "Does anyone own these fish?" And not seeing any owner, he grasped the line with his teeth and laid the fish in the forest where he lived, intending to eat them later. And then he lay down, thinking how virtuous he was! The jackal also went to find food, and discovered in the hut of a field-watcher two items, a lizard and a container of milk-curd. And after crying aloud three times, "To whom do these belong?" and not finding an owner, he took the items to his own dwelling, thinking, "In due course I will eat them," and he reclined, reflecting on his virtue.

The monkey also entered the clump of trees, and gathering a bunch of man-goes placed them in his part of the forest, intending to eat them later, and he lay down, thinking that he was virtuous. The bodhisattva came out, intending to graze on the kuśa grass, and as he lay in the forest, a thought occurred to him: "It is impossible for me to offer grass to any beggars that may appear, and I have no oil, rice, or other foods. If any beggar asks, I shall have to give him my own flesh to eat." At this splendid display of virtue, Sakka's [Indra's] white marble throne became hot. Upon reflection, Sakka discovered the cause and resolved to put the rabbit to a test. He arrived wet and stood before the otter's dwelling place, dis-guised as a Brahmin, and being asked why he stood there, he replied, "Wise Sir, if I could get something to eat, after keeping the fast, I could perform all my priestly duties." The otter replied, "Very well, I will give you some food." . . .

Next he went to the jackal, and when asked by him why he stood there, he gave the same answer. The jackal, too, readily promised him some food. . . . Then he went to the monkey, and when asked why he was standing there, he answered as previously. The monkey readily offered him some food. . . .

And he went to the wise rabbit, and on being asked by him why he stood there, he made the same reply. Upon hearing the request, the bodhisattva was very delighted, and said, "Brahmin, you have done well in coming to me for food. This day I shall grant you a boon that I have never granted before, but you shall not break the moral precept by taking animal life. Go, friend, and when you have piled together wooden logs, and kindled a fire, come and inform me, and I will sacrifice myself into the midst of the flames, and when my body is roasted, you can eat my flesh and still meet your priestly duties." . . .

On the words of the rabbit, Sakka caused a heap of burning coals to appear by means of his miraculous power, and he came and told the bodhisattva. Rising from his bed of kuśa grass and coming to the place, he shook himself three times in order to eject any insects within his fur so that they would escape death. Then offering his whole body as a free gift he leaped up, and like a royal swan landing on a cluster of lotuses, in an ecstatic condition he fell on the heap of burning coals. But the flames failed to burn even the hairs on his body, and it was as if he had entered a frozen place. Then he addressed Sakka in these words: "Brahmin, the fire you have lit is cold. It failed to heat even the hairs on my body. What is the meaning of this?" "Wise sir," he replied, "I am no Brahmin. I am Sakka, and I have come to test your virtue." The bodhisattva said, "If not only you, Sakka, but all the inhabitants of the world were to try me in this matter of almsgiving, they would not find me unwilling to give," and with this the bodhisattva uttered a cry of exultation similar to a lion's roar. Then, Sakka said to the bodhisattva, "O wise rabbit, may your virtue be known throughout a whole eon." And squeezing the mountain to extract its essence, he drew the sign of the rabbit on the moon. And after depositing the rabbit on a bed of young kuśa grass in the same wooded part of the forest, Sakka returned to his palace in heaven.

Source: *Jātaka together with Its Commentary,* edited by V. Fausböll, 6 volumes (London, 1877–1896).

2

Life of the Buddha

The three baskets (tipiṭaka) of the Pāli Buddhist canon offer a reader an incomplete biography of the historical Buddha. In the *Acchariyabbhutadhamma Sutta* of the *Majjhima Nikāya* and the *Mahāpadāna Sutta* of the *Dīgha Nikāya*, for example, one can recognize an early tendency to mythologize the life of the Buddha. Such early accounts tend to focus on his attainment of enlightenment, death, and passing into final nibbāna. After his death, the literary vacuum was filled by noncanonical renditions of the Buddha's life, although these accounts are partly dependent on the earlier narratives.

There are five such texts worth mentioning. The *Mahāvastu* (Great Account) is a narrative that belongs to the Lokottaravādin subsect of the Mahāsāmghika school of Buddhism. An example of a text related to the Sarvāstivadin school of Buddhism is the *Lalitavistara* (Detailed Account of the Sports). The *Nidānakathā* (Connected Story) is credited to the monk named Buddhaghoṣa, an eminent Theravādin scholar and exegete, and forms an introduction to the Pāli *Jātaka* narratives. The *Abhiniṣkramaṇa Sūtra* (Discourse of the Great Renunciation) is a work connected to the Dharmaguptaka school. Finally, the *Buddhacarita* (Acts of the Buddha) is a text attributed to Aśvaghoṣa, a first-century C.E. poet. Aśvaghoṣa based his work on the Pāli canon *Nidānakathā*. This present volume uses the text by Aśvaghoṣa to tell the birth and enlightenment narratives. For the death narrative of the Buddha, this chapter turns to the account in the *Mahāparinibbāna Sutta* of the *Dīgha Nikāya*.

These biographical accounts of the Buddha represent sacred narratives for the Buddhist faithful. Although the biography relates a story of the past, it continues to refer simultaneously to the present, which encompasses a variety of linguistic and cultural contexts. The sacred biography of the Buddha not only embodies abstract religious concepts but also functions as a paradigmatic model for religious practice and potential source of motivation for individual Buddhists. It thus has didactic value as a means of illustrating exemplary patterns of behavior and moral practice. Buddhists have accepted the sacred biography of the Buddha for centuries on faith.

Birth of the Buddha

There was a king of the unconquerable Śākyas, named Śuddhodana, of the race of Ikṣvāku in power. He was virtuous and beloved of his people, like the moon in autumn. That counterpart of the deity Indra had a queen, a veritable Śacī, whose beauty corresponded to his might. In beauty like a lotus, firm like the earth, she was called Mahāmāyā, by her resemblance to the incomparable illusion. This ruler of men, playing with his queen, enjoyed the sovereign glory of Vaiśravaṇa. Devoid of any impurity, she became pregnant, just as knowledge united with mental concentration bears fruit. Before she conceived, she saw in a dream a white elephant entering her body, but she felt no pain.

When the infant was born, he appeared to be descended from the sky because he did not come into the world through the portal of life; and, since he had purified his being through many ages, he was not born ignorant but fully conscious. With his luster and steadfastness, he appeared like the young deity descended on earth. . . . He . . . walked seven steps with such firmness that his feet were raised unwavering and straight and his strides were long and firm. And looking to the four quarters with the demeanor of a lion, he uttered a truth statement: "I am born for enlightenment for the benefit of the world; this is my last birth in the phenomenal world." Two streams of water, as lucid as moon rays and possessing virtue, one hot, one cold, poured forth from the sky and fell on his gracious head, refreshing his body. . . . At his birth the earth, supporting the king of mountains, trembled like a ship subjected to strong winds; and from the cloudless sky there fell a shower perfumed with sandalwood along with blue and red lotuses. . . .

When the famous Brahmins, learned and eloquent, heard about these omens and reflected upon them, then with their faces shining with wonder and exultation they said to the king, who was equally fearful and joyful: "On earth men desire for their peace of mind nothing more than a son. As this light of yours is the light of your race, rejoice and enjoy a feast today. Therefore in all steadfastness reject anxiety and be happy because your race will certainly flourish. Your infant son is the leader of those who are overcome by the suffering of the world. According to the signs found on this excellent one, the brilliance of gold and the radiance of light, he will undoubtedly become either an enlightened being or a world ruler. Should he desire to become a king, then by his might and law he will lead all kings on earth, as the light of the sun stands as the leader of all constellations. Should he desire salvation and retire to the forest, then by his knowledge and truth he will overcome all creeds and stand on the earth, like Meru King of mountains among all high places." . . .

The king took the prince, as he lay on his nurse's lap, and showed him to the asetic. Then the ascetic saw the marks on the child. The soles of his feet were marked with a wheel, the fingers and toes were webbed, and a whorl of hair was located between his eyebrows, while his testicles were withdrawn like those of an elephant. The ascetic understood the reason that the king was troubled by the thought of misfortune and said: "Do not let your mind, O king, be disturbed; what I have said is not to be doubted." The king replied, "My concern is not entirely focused on him, but I am distressed due to my own disappointment, since my time to depart from life has arrived just when he is born who shall discover the means, so difficult to find, of destroying rebirth. For he will renounce the kingdom in his detachment to worldly pleasures, and, through difficult struggles grasping the final truth, he will shine like a sun to dispel the darkness of delusion in the world with his knowledge." . . .

When queen Māyā saw the vast power of her son, like that of a divine seer, she was unable to withstand the joy that it caused her. Then she went to heaven to dwell there. Then the queen's sister, who equaled her in majesty, affection, and tenderness, raised the prince, who was like a descendent of divine beings, as if he were her own son. . . .

He matured and was duly initiated. And it took only a few days to learn the sciences, whereas their mastery usually requires many years. Because the king of the Sākyas had heard from the great ascetic, Asita, that the prince's goal would be liberation, he feared that he would go to the forest, and therefore he exposed the prince to sensual pleasures. . . . There the women delighted him with their soft voices, charming flattery, sexual excitements, sweet laughter, curving of the eye-brows. and sidelong glances. Then, becoming a captive to the women, who were skilled in the art of love and sexual seduction, he did not move from the palace to the outside world, just as someone who has won heaven by his merit does not descend to earth from the heavenly realm. . . .

Then, in due time, the fair-bosomed and famous Yaśodharā gave birth to the off-spring of Śuddhodana, a son named Rāhula (fetter). . . . Then the ruler of the earth . . . rejoiced at the birth of a grandson as much as he had rejoiced at the birth of a son.

Renunciation of the World

Then the king learned about the intentions of his son, and directed a pleasure excursion to be worthy of his love and status and his son's youth. And thinking that the young mind of the prince might be disturbed by what he saw, he forbade the appearance of any afflicted people on the royal highway. Then with the utmost care they cleared away on all sides of the highway those who were maimed, deformed, old, sick, and the wretched, and transformed the royal high-way into something magnificent. Then, when the road had been made beautiful, the prince, after being given permission, descended at the right time in full splendor along with well-trained attendants from the heights of the palace, and approached the king. Thereupon the tearful ruler of the earth gazed long at his son and kissed him on the head; and he bid him farewell, but out of affection he continued to think of him. Then the prince mounted a golden chariot, to which were harnessed four well-trained horses with golden gear with a skillful and reli-able driver. . . .

And very slowly he entered the royal highway, which was covered with the halves of blue lotuses shaped with eyes wide open with excitement, as all around the citizens watched him. . . .

The deities of the pure abode . . . created the illusion of an old man in order to incite the king's son to renounce his home. Then the prince recognized that the old man was senile and misshapen, and different from younger men. With his gaze steadily focused on the old man and his interest stimulated, he asked the charioteer: "Good charioteer, who is this man with white hair, supporting himself with a staff, with his eyes covered by wrinkles, and bent limbs? Is this some con-dition due to a transformation, or is this his original state, or is it due to mere chance?" When the charioteer heard these questions, the very same deities caused him to become confused, so, that, unaware of his error, he told the prince something he should have withheld: "Old age, it is called, that which has transformed him—the destroyer of beauty, the ruin of vigor, the origin of sorrow, the grave of pleasure, the destroyer of memory, the enemy of the senses. . . . At these words, the king's son, a bit apprehensive, questioned the charioteer thus, "Will this evil fall on me also?" Then the charioteer said to him: "Inevitably by force of time, my young lord became aware of the end of his life. Men are aware that old age destroys beauty and yet they seek beauty." Since his mind was purified by his intentions in prior forms of existence and his good merit accumulated through countless ages, he was mentally disturbed at hearing about old age. . . .

At the request of his master's son, the driver turned back the chariot. Then, the prince returned to the palace, but he was captive to anxiety and everything seemed empty to him. He was unable to find relief in the palace because he concentrated on the subject of old age. Therefore, with the permission of the king, he went out again, with everything arranged as it was previously.

Thereupon, the same deities created a man with a body afflicted by disease, and the son of Śuddhodana saw him, and gazing on him, he said to the charioteer: "Who is this man with swollen stomach and body that heaves with his panting? His shoulders and arms are weak, and his limbs are emaciated and pale. He calls out pitifully 'mother,' as he leans on another for support." Then the charioteer replied to him, "God sir, it is the mighty misfortune called disease, developed in full force from the disorder of the humors, that has transformed this once competent man through an uncontrollable condition." Thereupon, the king's son looked at the man compassionately and asked, "Is this evil peculiar to him, or is the danger of disease common to all humans?" Then, the charioteer replied, "Prince, this evil is shared by all. Even though humans eat well, they are oppressed yet by disease and racked by pain." Upon hearing this truth, he became mentally disturbed and trembled like the reflection of the moon on rippling water; and he piteously uttered these words softly: "This is the calamity of disease for humankind. The world knows it and is not alarmed. The ignorance of human beings is widespread, and they live within the shadow of disease." . . .

When the king learned the reason for his son's return, he felt himself already abandoned by his son. And he merely reprimanded the officer in charge of clearing the road, and angry though he was, imposed no severe punishment on him. And he further increased his son's sensual pleasures, hoping that his son would be held captive by the restlessness of his senses and not leave the king. But when his son refrained from seeking pleasure in the women's quarters, objects of sense, sounds, and the rest, then he directed another excursion outside with the thought that it might cause a change of mood. . . .

Then the royal highway was decorated and guarded with especial care; and the king changed the charioteer and chariot and sent the prince forth. Then, as the king's son was traveling, those same deities created a dead man, so that only the charioteer and the prince could see the corpse being carried along. Thereupon, the king's son asked the charioteer, "Who is being carried along there by four men followed by a group of dejected people? He is dressed handsomely and yet they wail for him." Then the driver's mind was overcome by the deities of the pure abode and, though it should have remained secret, he explained this matter to the lord and humankind: "This is someone or other, lying without intellect, senses, breath, and qualities, unconsciousness and akin to an inert log or bundle of grass. He was raised and cherished with loving care and now he is being abandoned." Hearing the driver's reply, he was slightly startled and said, "Is this law of human existence particular to this man, or is such the destiny of all creatures?" Then the driver replied to him, "This is the final destination for all creatures. Death is inevitable for all in the world, be one of low, middle, or high status." . . .

While this passionless state of mind grew within him, there appeared a man in mendicant's clothes unseen by others. The king's son asked him, "Tell me, who are you?" To this question he explained to him, "O bull among men, I am a renouncer, who in fear of birth and death have left the household life for the sake of liberation. Since the world is subject to death, I desire liberation and seek a higher incorruptible stage. I look equally on kinsman and stranger, and attachment to and detachment from objects of sense that no longer affect me. I dwell wherever I happen to be, at the base of a tree or in a deserted temple, on a hill or in the forest, and I wander without attachment or expectations in search of the highest good, accepting any alms that I receive." After saying this, he ascended upward to the sky before the prince's sight; for he was a heavenly being who in that form had seen other Buddhas and had encountered him to gain his attention. . . .

Then with the gait of the king of beasts, he approached his father in the midst of his body of ministers . . . prostrating himself with folded hands, he said, "O king, graciously grant me permission. I wish to become a renouncer to seek liberation; for separation is inevitable for me." Hearing his words, the king quivered with emotion . . . and responded, "Give up this resolve. Devote yourself for the present to the duties of a householder." . . . The son replied to his father: "If this is not possible, then I am not to be stopped; for it is not right to restrain a man, wishing to escape from a house that is being consumed by fire." . . .

Thereupon, the deities of the pure abode, aware of his resolve, suddenly caused the women to fall asleep, laying with distorted limbs . . . others laying in immodest attitudes, snoring, and tossing about their arms. Others looked ugly, lying unconscious like corpses, with their ornaments and garlands askew, the buttons of their dresses undone, and motionless eyes revealing the whites of their eyes. Another lay as if sprawling drunk, with her mouth wide open oozing saliva out, and with her limbs spread out so as to reveal the private parts of her body. Her beauty was gone, her form was distorted. . . . When the king's son saw the young women lying in these different ways and looking so loathsome with their uncontrolled movements, though ordinarily their forms were beautiful, their speech pleasant, he became disgusted. . . .

He awoke the charioteer, the quick-footed Chandaka, and instructed him thus: "Quickly bring the horse Kanthaka; I desire to depart hence today to reach deathlessness. . . . The city gatehouses, which were closed with heavy bars and which could not easily forced open even by elephants, opened quietly on their own as the king's son passed by.

Defeat of Māra and Enlightenment

When the great sage, heir of the royal line sat down, after vowing to become liberated, they rejoiced, but Māra, and enemy of genuine law, trembled. He is called the deity of the shiny weapon and also the flower-arrowed weapon because he is connected to the passions, an enemy of liberation. His three sons, named Caprice, Mirth, and Wantonness, and his three daughters, named Discontent, Delight, and Desire, asked why he was mentally depressed, and he responded to them thus: "The sage, protected by his vow and drawing a bow of resolution with the arrow of wisdom, sits over there, desiring to conquer my realm; hence my mental despondency. For if he succeeds in overcoming me and expounds to the world the path to liberation, then will my realm become empty, like that of the Videha king when he strayed from ethical conduct. While he has not yet attained spiritual insight and is still within my sphere of influence, I shall proceed to break his vow, like the swollen waters of a river breaking an embankment." . . . It is ignoble for a well-born person of royal background to practice asceticism." . . .

Despite these words, the sage of the Śākyas showed no concern and did not change his position; this caused Māra to bring forward his sons and daughters, and to discharge an arrow at him. Then Māra issued instructions to his raging army of demons to terrify the sage. Thereupon, the army attempted to destroy his steadfastness with their numerous powers. . . . The rock, trees, and axes that were discharged rose into the sky, and remained suspended in the sky, like the various rays of the evening clouds. Another demon threw a blazing log as large as a mountain above him; as soon as it was thrown, it hung suspended in the sky, and it burst into a hundred fragments through the sage's magical power. . . . The shower of hot coals scattered, giving off sparks at the base of the tree of enlightenment. They were transformed into a shower of red lotus petals by means of universal loving-kindness on the part of the best of sages. And the Sākya sage, embracing his resolution like a kinsman, did not stir from his posture in spite of these various afflictions and bodily and mental distress, which were directed at him. . . . Then Māra's demonic army fled in every direction, its spirit dissipated, its effort rendered useless, its rocks, logs, and trees scattered everywhere, like a hostile army whose leader has been slain by the foe. . . . Then, after defeating Māra's army by his steadfastness and tranquillity, the master of trance entered into a deep trance in order to obtain knowledge of ultimate reality. And after gaining complete control over all the methods of trance, he recalled in the first watch the succession of his previous births . . . but in the second watch he, whose energy was peerless, gained the supernatural divine eyesight, becoming the most insightful person alive. Then with that completely purified supernatural eyesight he saw the entire world, as it were in a spotless mirror. His compassion increased as he witnessed the passing and rebirth of all creatures according to their lower or higher actions. Those living beings with sinful actions passed to the sphere of misery, while others with good deeds won a place in the triple world. The former were reborn in dreadful hells and were woefully tormented with sufferings of many types. Some were made to drink red-colored molten iron; others were impaled howling on a red-hot iron pillar. Some were boiled with heads downward like metal in iron cauldrons; others were miserably broiled on large burning red-hot coals. Some were devoured by fierce horrible dogs with iron teeth, others by the iron beaks like crows of iron. . . .

Then as the third watch passed that night, the best meditator concentrated in the true nature of this world. . . . Penetrating to the core of truth, he grasped that old age and death are produced when there is birth. . . . With his supernatural eyesight, he saw that active being proceeds from action, not from a creator, or from nature, or from a self, or without a cause. . . . Thereupon, the sage focused his mind on determining the origin of existence. Then he witnessed that the origin of existence was due to the cycle of causation. . . .

During the fourth watch at dawn, everyone and everything was still, the great seer reached the stage that knows no causal change, the state of omniscience. When, as the Buddha, he knew this truth, the earth moved like a woman inebriated from wine, the quarters of the universe brightly revealed Siddhas (accomplished ones), and mighty drums resounded in the sky. . . . Then for seven days, free from the discomfort of a body, he sat, gazing into his own mind, his eyes never blinking. The sage fulfilled his intention, reflecting to himself that he had obtained liberation. Then the sage, who had understood the principle of causation and was firmly fixed in the system of non-self, awakened himself and, filled with immense compassion, he gazed on the world with his enlightened eye for the sake of its tranquillity. Seeing that the world was lost in false views, vanity, and gross passions, seeing also that the doctrine of liberation was very subtle, he focused his mind on remaining immobile.

Then remembering his former promise, he vowed to teach about how to reach tranquillity. . . . Then wishing to preach tranquillity in order to dispel the darkness of ignorance, as the rising sun does darkness, Gautama proceeded to the sacred city . . . of Kāśi in order to convert the world.

Source: *Aśvaghosa's Buddhacarita,* edited by E. H. Johnston (Delhi: Motilal Banarsidass, 1936; reprint 1972), 1–161.

Death of the Buddha

Now Cunda, the worker in metals, heard that the Exalted One had come to Pava, and was staying there in his Mango Grove.

And Cunda the metal worker went to the place of the Lord, and saluting him took his seat respectfully to one side. And when he was thus seated, the Lord instructed, inspired, incited, and gladdened him with religious discourse.

Then he said: "May the Lord do me the honor of taking his meal together with his order of monks at my house tomorrow?" And the Lord signified his consent by silence.

Then seeing that the Lord had consented, Cunda the metal worker rose from his seat and bowed before the Lord, and keeping him on his right hand as he passed him, departed.

At the end of the night, Cunda prepared his dwelling-place along with sweet rice and cakes, and a quantity of truffles. And he announced the time to the Lord, saying: "Lord, the time, has come, and the meal is ready."

And the Lord dressed himself early in the morning, and took his bowl, and went with the monks to the dwelling-place of Cunda. When he arrived he seated himself on a prepared seat, and said: "Serve the truffles you have made ready, Cunda, and serve the other food of the sweet rice and cakes to the monks." "Even so, Lord!" said Cunda in assent to the Lord.

Now the Lord addressed Cunda and said: "Whatever truffles, Cunda, are left over you should bury them in a hole. I see no one, Cunda, on earth nor in Māra's realm, nor in Brahma's heaven, no one among ascetics, Brahmins, among gods, and men, who, when they have eaten it, could properly digest them except a Tathāgata." "Even so, Lord!" said Cunda in assent to the Lord. Having buried whatever truffles remained in a hole, he went to where the Lord was, saluted him, and sat down to one side. And when he was seated, the Lord instructed, inspired, incited, and gladdened Cunda with religious discourse. And the Lord then rose from his seat and departed.

Now when the Lord had eaten the meal prepared by Cunda, he became very sick with bloody dysentery, and with sharp pains akin to death. But the Lord, mindful and clearly aware, bore it without complaint. . . .

Now the Lord said to the venerable Ānanda: "It may be, Ānanda, that some of you might think: 'The teaching of the master has ended, we have no teacher any more!' But it is not like this, Ānanda, that you should regard it. The teachings and the rules of the Order, which I have set forth and laid down for you all, let them, after I am gone, be your teacher."

"Ānanda! When I am gone, do not address one another in the way in which monks have previously addressed each other with the term 'friend.' A younger monk should be addressed by an elder with his name, or his family name, or the term 'friend.' But an elder should be addressed by a younger brother as 'Lord' or as 'Venerable Sir.'

"When I am gone, Ānanda, let the Order abolish all the minor precepts.

"After I am gone, Ānanda, let the higher penalty be imposed on the monk Channa."

"But what, Lord, is the higher penalty?" "Let Channa say whatever likes. The monks should neither speak to him, nor instruct him, nor admonish him."

Then the Lord addressed the monks, and said: "It may be, monks, that there may be doubts or uncertainty about the Buddha, or the Dhamma, or the path, or the method. Inquire, monks, freely. Do not reproach yourselves afterward thinking: 'Our teacher was face-to-face with us, and we failed to ask the Lord when we were face-to-face with him.' And when he had thus spoken the monks were silent. And again the second and the third time the Lord repeated his words to the monks, and said: "Perhaps, monks, there may be doubts or uncertainty in thoughts of some monks about the Buddha, or the doctrine, or the path, or the method. Monks, inquire freely. Do not reproach yourselves afterward thinking: 'Our teacher was face-to-face with us, and we could not bring ourselves to inquire of the Lord when we were face-to-face with him.'" And even the third time the monks were silent. Then the Lord addressed the monks, and said: "It may be, monks, that you put no questions out of reverence for the teacher. Let one friend communicate to another." And when he had thus spoken the monks were silent.

And the venerable Ānanda said to the Lord: "It is wonderful, Lord, and how marvelous! I believe that in this whole assembly there is not one monk who has any doubt or uncertainty about the Buddha, or the doctrine, or the path, or the method!" It is from faith that you have spoken, Ānanda! But the Tathāgata knows for certain that in this whole assembly of monks there is not one brother who has any doubt or uncertainty about the Buddha, or the doctrine, or the path, or the method! For even the most backward, Ānanda, of all these five hundred monks is a stream-enterer and is not capable of falling into a state of suffering, and is assured of attaining enlightenment.

Then the Lord addressed the monks, and said: "Behold now, brethren, I exhort you, saying: 'Decay is inherent in all conditioned things! Work out your salvation with diligence!'" These were the last words of the Tathāgata!

Then the Lord entered into the first stage of trance. And rising out of the first stage, he passed into the second. And rising out of the second, he passed into the third. And rising out of the third stage, he passed into the fourth. And rising out of the fourth stage of trance, he entered into the state of mind to which the infinity of space is alone present. And passing out of the mere consciousness of the infinity of space, he entered into the state of mind to which the infinity of thought is alone present. And passing out of the mere consciousness of the infinity of thought, he entered into a state of mind to which nothing at all is specifically present. And passing out of the consciousness of no specific object, he entered into a state between consciousness and unconsciousness. And passing out of this state, he entered into a state in which the consciousness both of sensations and of ideas had completely passed away.

Then the venerable Ānanda said to the venerable Anuruddha: "O my lord, O Anuruddha, the Lord is dead!"

"No! Brother Ānanda, the Lord is not dead. He has entered into that state in which both sensations and ideas have ceased!"

Then the Lord, passing out of the state in which both sensations and ideas have ceased, entered into the state between consciousness and unconsciousness. And passing out of the state between consciousness and unconsciousness, he entered into the state of mind to which nothing at all is specifically present. And leaving the consciousness of no special object, he entered into the state of mind to which the infinity of thought is alone present. And leaving the consciousness of the infinity of thought, he entered into the state of mind to which the infinity of space is alone present. And leaving the consciousness of the infinity of space, he entered into the fourth stage of trance. And leaving the fourth stage, he entered into the third. And leaving the third stage, he entered into the second. And leaving the second, he entered into the first. And leaving the first stage of trance, he entered into the second. And passing out of the second stage, he entered into the third. And passing out of the third stage, he entered into the fourth stage of trance. And leaving the last stage of trance, he immediately expired.

When the Lord died there was, at the moment of his death, a mighty earthquake, terrible and awe-inspiring, accompanied by thunder.

Then the venerable Anuruddha exhorted the monks, and said: "Enough, my friends! Weep not, neither lament! Has not the Lord formerly declared this to us that it is in the very nature of all things near and dear unto us, that we must divide ourselves from them, leave them, separate ourselves from them? How then, monks, can this be possible—that whereas anything born, brought into being, and organized, contains within itself the inherent necessity of dissolution—how then can this be possible that such a being should not be dissolved?"

Source: *Mahāparinibbāna Suttanta* of the *Dīgha Nikāya* [Long Discourses of the Buddha], volume 2, edited by T. W. Rhys Davids and J. Estlin Carpenter (London: Pali Text Society, 1903; reprint London: Luzac, 1966), 154–162.

3

Teachings of the Buddha:
Causality

Before turning to the Four Noble Truths of the Buddha, it is important to examine the basic presuppositions of his thought. The process of causation was a topic upon which the Buddha meditated for a considerable amount of time early in his career. He discovered that causation functions as the ground of the universal nature of suffering. The Buddha depicted causation as a cyclical, ceaseless chain that conditioned or produced everything except nibbāna, which is absolute freedom from the cycle of causation. The Buddha's theory of causation represents a compromise between the extremes of self-causation (eternalism) and external causation (annihilationism). He was critical of the philosophies behind many of the ancient Hindu Upaniṣad texts, which were being taught in his time—a philosophy that equates the immortal self with being and eternity. These texts with their philosophy of an eternal self serve as examples of the teaching of self-causation. The Buddha criticized this type of philosophy for being a metaphysical postulate and an extreme view because it asserts an unobservable entity. The opposite position is represented by the Materialists, whom the Buddha criticized because their position denied the efficacy of human exertion and established an external principle that caused human pleasure and pain. This type of position, also called annihilationism, postulates the possible destruction of life and a denial of rebirth. Even though the Buddha's understanding of causation signifies a "middle way" between two extremes, it is nevertheless all-encompassing because everything is subject to the chain of causation. This position rules out any accidental occurrences in the world, demonstrates the interconnectedness of all phenomena, and is directly connected to the truth.

The prevalence of causation in the Buddha's teaching implies an impersonal aspect of the natural world in the sense that there is no personal god guiding the process. Moreover, even though there is constant change in the world, this does not mean that there is a prevailing state of chaos. The Buddha identifies stability with the process of change and not with the stability of things, because nothing is exempt from the cycle of causation. In other words, the cycle of causation is one thing of which we can be certain. The teaching of causation suggests that the world comprises an interconnected and interdependent process of change. As part of the teaching of causation, the notion of karma suggests, however, that the universe is morally constructed. The doctrine of karma teaches that one's present condition is a result of one's past actions. Nonetheless, one is free to make good or poor choices in the present. The Buddha is saying that humans shape their destiny by the decisions that they make during life, and these decisions influence their future modes of existence.

The first selection is from a text in the *Dīgha Nikāya*. This text depicts the monk Ānanda asserting that causation is simple. In response, the Buddha proceeds to explain its complexity and importance. The second selection is taken from the *Milindapañha* (Questions of King Milinda), which is a dialogue between a Buddhist monk named Nāgasena and King Milinda, who is identified by many as Menandros or Menander, an Indo-Greek monarch who ruled around 155–130 B.C.E. in the Punjab region of northern India. In comparison to the Nikāya literature that can be dated between the fifth to the third centuries B.C.E., the *Milindapañha* dates to around the first century C.E. Besides serving as a compendium of doctrine, the value of this text is related to its clarity with respect to discussing difficult topics by using various literary devices such as metaphors and similes.

Selection from the *Mahānidāna Suttanta*
(The Great Discourse on Causation)

Thus have I heard. The Lord was dwelling among the Kurus. There is a township in that country called Kammāsadamma. And the venerable Ānanda came to Lord, bowed in salutation before him, and took a seat on one side, and he said to the Lord: "It is wonderful, Lord, and marvelous that whereas this doctrine of dependent origination is very deep and looks so profound, it seems as clear as clear can be to me!

"Do not say so, Ānanda, do not say so! This dependent origination is profound and also appears deep. It is through not understanding, not penetrating it, that this generation has become a tangled mass, like a ball of string, like unto coarse grass and rushes, unable to overcome states of bad destiny, woe, ruin, and continual rebirth.

"If Ānanda, you were asked: 'Is old age and death due to a particular cause?' you should say: 'It is.' If asked: 'What is the cause of old age and death?' you should say: 'Birth is the cause of old age and death.'

"If Ānanda, you were asked: 'Is birth due to a particular cause?' you should say, 'It is.' And if asked: 'From what cause is birth?' you should say, 'Becoming is the cause of birth.'

"If Ānanda, you were asked: 'Is becoming due to a particular cause?' you should say, 'It is.' If asked: 'From what cause is becoming?' you should say, 'Grasping is the cause of becoming.'

"If Ānanda, you were asked: 'Is grasping due to a particular cause?' you should say, 'It is.' If asked: 'From what cause is grasping?' you should say: 'Craving is the cause of grasping?'

"If Ānanda, you were asked: 'Is craving due to a particular cause?' you should say: 'It is.' If asked: 'From what cause is craving?' you should say, 'Sensation is the cause of craving.'

"If Ānanda, you were asked: 'Is sensation due to a particular cause?' you should say, 'It is.' If asked: 'From what cause is sensation?' you should say, 'Contact is the cause of sensation.'

"If Ānanda, you were asked: 'Is contact due to a particular cause?' you should say, 'It is.' If asked: 'From what cause is contact?' you should say: 'Name-and-form is the cause of contact.'

"If Ānanda, you were asked: 'Is name-and-form due to a particular cause?' you should say, 'It is.' And to the question: 'From what cause is name-and-form?' you should say, 'Consciousness is the cause of name-and-form.'

"Thus then is it, Ānanda, that consciousness, with name-and-form as its cause; name-and-form, with consciousness as its cause; contact, with name-and-form as its cause; sensation, with contact as its cause; craving, with sensation as its cause; grasping, with craving as its cause; becoming, with grasping as its cause; birth, with becoming as its cause; old age and death, with birth as its cause; grief, lamentation, pain, sorrow, and despair, all come into being. This is arising of the entire mass of suffering.

"I have said: 'Birth is the cause of old age and death.' This is the way that it is to be understood. If there is no birth of any kind anywhere—that is of gods, godhood, gandhabbas, of yakkhas, goblins, humans, quadrupeds, birds, or insects—if there is no birth of all these beings, then, there being no birth whatever, owing to this cessation of birth, could old age and death appear?"

"There would not, Lord."

"Therefore, Ānanda, that is just the causal ground, that is the basis for the condition of old age and death, namely, birth.

"I have said: 'Becoming is the cause of birth.' If there were absolutely no becoming of any sentient, formed or formless being, then there being no becoming whatever would there, owing to this cessation of becoming, could there be any appearance of birth?"

"There would not, Lord."

"Therefore, Ānanda, that is the ground, that is the basis, the genesis, the cause of birth, namely, becoming.

"I have said: 'Grasping is the cause of becoming.' If there were no grasping of any kind by any one, no grasping at the things of sense, no grasping through speculative opinions, no grasping after rule and ritual, no grasping through theories of soul—then there being no grasping whatever, would there, owing to this cessation of grasping, could there be any appearance of becoming?"

"No, Lord."

"Therefore, Ānanda, that is just the ground the basis, the genesis, the cause of becoming, to wit, grasping.

"I have said: 'Craving is the cause of grasping.' If there were no craving of any kind whatever—that is to say, no craving for sights, sounds, odors, tastes, tangibles, or ideas—then there being no craving whatever, would there, owing to this cessation of craving, could there be any appearance of grasping?"

"No, Lord."

"Therefore, Ānanda, just that is the ground, that is the basis, the genesis, the cause of grasping, namely, craving."

"I have said: 'Sensation is the cause of craving.' If there were no sensation of any kind, that is to say, no sensations born of impressions received by way of sight, hearing, smell, taste, touch, or imagination—then there being no sensation whatever, would there, owing to this cessation of sensation could there be any appearance of craving?"

"No, Lord."

"Therefore, the basis, the genesis, the cause of craving is, namely, sensation.

"Thus it is, Ānanda, that craving comes into being because of sensation, seeking because of craving, gain because of seeking, decision because of gain, desire and passion because of decision, attachment because of desire and passion, possession because of attachment, avarice because of possession, guarding of possessions because of avarice, and many a bad and wicked state of things arising from guarding possessions—blows and wounds, strife, disputes, arguments, quarreling, slander and lies."

Source: *Mahānidāna Suttanta* [The Great Discourse on Causation] of the *Dīgha Nikāya*, volume 2, edited by T. W. Rhys Davids and J. Estlin Carpenter (London: Pali Text Society, 1903; reprint London: Luzac, 1966), 55–59.

Selection from the *Milindapañha*
(Questions of King Milinda)

The king said: "Revered Nāgasena, what is the root of past (saṃsāric) time, of future time, what the root of present time?"

"The root is ignorance; conditioned by ignorance are the karmic formations, conditioned by the karmic formations is consciousness, conditioned by consciousness is name-and-form, conditioned by name-and-form are the six (sensory) fields, conditioned by the six (sensory) fields is sensory contact, conditioned by sensory contact is feeling, conditioned by feeling is craving, conditioned by craving is grasping, conditioned by grasping is becoming, conditioned by becoming birth, conditioned by birth there come into existence old age and dying, grief, sorrow, suffering, lamentation, and despair. Thus the earliest moment of this entire time cannot be demonstrated."

"You are clever, revered Nāgasena."

The king said: "Revered Nāgasena, you assert that the earliest moment cannot be shown. Create a simile for that."

"As, sire, a man might plant a small seed on to the earth, and a shoot springing from that and gradually growing, developing and maturing might produce fruit; and then taking a seed from that fruit, he might plant it again, and a shoot springing from that and gradually growing, and maturing might yield fruit—is there thus an end of this series?"

"No, sir."

"Even so, sire, the earliest moment of time cannot be shown either."

"Make a further simile."

"As, sire, an egg comes from a hen and a hen from an egg and an egg from an hen, is there thus an end of this series?"

"There is not, sir."

"Even so, sire, the earliest moment of time cannot be shown either."

"Make a further simile." The Elder drew a circle on the ground and asked King Milinda: "Is there an end to this circle, sire?"

"There is not, sir."

"Even so, sire, are those cycles that are spoken of by the Lord: 'Visual consciousness arises because of eye and material shapes, the meeting of the three is sensory impingement; conditioned by sensory touch is feeling; conditioned by feeling is craving; conditioned by craving is kamma; vision is born again from kamma'; is there thus an end of this series?"

"There is not, sir."

"And auditory consciousness arises because of ear and sounds. . . . And mental consciousness arises because of mind and mental objects; the meeting of the three is sensory impingement; conditioned by sensory impingement is feeling; conditioned by feeling is craving; conditioned by craving is kamma; mind is born again from kamma'; is there thus an end of this series?"

"There is not, sir."

"Even so, sire, the earliest moment of this time cannot be demonstrated either."

"You are clever, revered Nāgasena."

The king said: "Revered Nāgasena, you say that the earliest point cannot be shown, what is this earliest moment?"

"This earliest moment, sire, is that which is the past."

"Revered Nāgasena, you say that the earliest moment cannot be shown, cannot that every earliest moment be shown?"

"Some can be shown, some cannot be shown."

"Which can be shown, revered sir, which cannot be shown?"

"Previously, there was no ignorance anywhere or in any way—this earliest moment cannot be known; what had not been came into existence and, having been, dissolved, can this earliest moment be known?"

"Revered Nāgasena, if what had not been came into existence and, having been, dissolved, would it not 'go home,' cut off from both (modes)?"

"If, sire, (ignorance) 'goes home,' cut off from both (modes), is it possible for it, cut off from both (modes), to increase?"

"Yes, it is able to increase."

"I, revered sir, am not asking that question, but whether it is possible for it to increase from a moment at which it was transmitted."

"Yes, it is able to increase."

"Make a simile." The Elder repeated the simile of a tree, saying: "The aggregates are the seeds of this whole mass of suffering."

"You are clever, revered Nāgasena."

The king said: "Revered Nāgasena, are there any karmic formations that are produced?"

"Yes, sire, there are karmic formations that are produced."

"Which are they?"

"When there is an eye and when there are material shapes there is visual consciousness; when there is visual consciousness there is sensory contact on the eye; when there is sensory contact on the eye there is feeling; when there is feeling there is craving; when there is craving there is grasping; when there is grasping there is (continued) becoming; when there is (continued) becoming there is birth; when there is birth there come into existence old age and dying, grief, sorrow, suffering, lamentation and despair. Thus is the origination of this mass of pain. But, sire, when there is not eye or material shapes there is no visual consciousness when there is not visual consciousness there is no sensory contact on the eye; when there is not sensory contact on the eye there is no feeling, stopping of this whole mass of pain."

"You are clever, revered Nāgasena." . . .

The king said: "Revered Nāgasena, where does wisdom dwell?"

"Nowhere, sire."

"Well then, revered Nāgasena, there is no wisdom."

"Where does the wind dwell, sire?"

"Nowhere, revered sir."

"Well then, sire, there is no wind."

"You are clever, revered Nāgasena."

The king said: "Revered Nāgasena, you referred to 'circling-on'; what is this circling-on?"

"Sire, what is born here dies here; having died here it arises elsewhere; being born there, there it dies; having died there it arises elsewhere. Such, sire, is circling-on."

"Make a simile."

"Suppose, sire, some man, having eaten a ripe mango, should plant the stone and a large mango tree should grow from it and yield fruit; and that the man, having eaten a ripe mango from it too, should plant the stone and a large mango tree should grow from it too and yield fruit. In this way no end to those trees can be seen. Even so, sire, what is born here dies here; having died here it arises elsewhere; being born there, there it dies; having died there it arises elsewhere. Such, sire, is circling-on."

"You are clever, revered Nāgasena."

Source: *Milindapañho: Being Dialogues between King Milinda and the Buddhist Sage Nāgasena*, edited by V. Trenckner, volume 1 (London: Williams and Norgate, 1880), 49–52.

4

Teachings of the Buddha:
Four Noble Truths

From the viewpoint of the Buddhist tradition, the Four Noble Truths originated with the insight of the Buddha into the nature of human existence. These basic truths are valuable because they not only embody the truthful insights of a very wise human being but they also function as a practical summary of the fundamental message of the Buddha that he learned by means of his own efforts. After stating the initial truth that all life is suffering, the second truth identifies the origin of misery as ignorant craving. If one places the First Noble Truth about suffering into the context of the Buddha's understanding of the cycle of causation, which affirms that everything is subject to causation and everything is interdependent, the initial truth can be characterized as realistic and should not be construed as pessimistic. The third truth gives a practitioner the promise that suffering can be terminated by achieving nibbāna, whereas the final truth presents the Noble Eightfold Path as the means of achieving the goal of enlightenment. This path weaves together eight interconnected steps that embody elements of wisdom, moral and ethical behavior, and meditation.

When reading this chapter it is important to be aware that the Buddha's message extended beyond the confines and inhabitants of India. His message was universal. In other words, it was offered as the truth that was relevant for all human beings regardless of their culture and historical time period. An aspect of his teaching worthy of attention was that its basic thrust was not simply theoretical but was also practical, in the sense that it was intended to enable a person to overcome suffering.

This chapter contains selections from two Pāli texts that give a reader a good idea of how the Buddha gave instructions about these basic truths. A reader will notice in the first selection the Buddha urging his listeners to avoid extremes and to follow a middle path. The Buddha also enumerates various kinds of suffering. A reader will notice that the Buddha is speaking from personal experience. The second discourse occurs at a different location, at which the Buddha speaks more about the middle path.

Selections from the *Saccamyuttasutta* (Connected Discourses on the Truths)

Thus have I heard: Once the Blessed One was dwelling near Benares, at Isipatana, in the Deer-Park. Then the Exalted One thus addressed a group of five monks:

"Monks, these two extremes should not be followed by one who has gone forth as a wanderer. What two? They are the pursuit of sense pleasures, vulgar practice of villagers, ignoble practice, unprofitable; and the pursuit of self-mortification, which is painful, ignoble, and unprofitable. By avoiding these two extremes, the Tathāgata has awakened to the middle path which gives rise to insight, which gives rise to knowledge, which leads to calm, direct knowledge, to enlightenment, to nibbāna.

And what, monks, is that middle path which gives insight that leads to nibbāna?

It is this Noble Eightfold Path, namely: right view, right intention, right speech, right action, right living, right effort, right mindfulness, right concentration. This, monks, is that middle path, which gives insight, gives knowledge, which leads to calm, to direct knowledge, to enlightenment, to nibbāna.

Now this, monks, is the noble truth about suffering: Birth is suffering, aging is suffering, sickness is suffering, death is ill; likewise is sorrow, grief, woe, lamentation, and despair. To be related with things that we dislike, to be separated from things that we like—that also is suffering. Not to get what one wants is also suffering. In brief, the five aggregates, which are based on grasping, is suffering.

Now this, monks, is the noble truth about the arising of suffering: It is craving that leads to rebirth, along with the delight and the lust longingly now here, now there: namely, the craving for sensual pleasure, the craving for rebirth, the craving for extinction. Such, monks, is the noble truth about the arising of suffering.

And this, monks, is the noble truth about the cessation of suffering: It is the utter passionless cessation of the giving up, the forsaking, release from, absence of longing for this craving.

Now this, monks, is the noble truth about the way that leads to the cessation of suffering: It is this Noble Eightfold Path, to wit: right view, right aim, right speech, right action, right living, right effort, right mindfulness, right concentration. . . .

This is the noble truth of suffering, concerning things previously unheard, there arose in me vision, insight, understanding, wisdom, and light.

This noble truth about suffering is to be understood thus: concerning things unheard before, there arose in me vision, insight, understanding, wisdom, and light.

This noble truth about suffering has been understood: thus, monks, concerning things unlearnt before, there arose in me vision, insight, understanding, wisdom, and light.

Again, monks, at the thought of this noble truth about the arising of suffering, concerning things unheard before, there arose in me vision, insight, understanding, wisdom, and light.

This arising of suffering is to be put away, concerning things unheard before . . . there arose in me light.

This arising of suffering has been put away, concerning things unheard before . . . there arose in me light.

Again, monks, at the thought of this noble truth about the cessation of suffering, concerning things unlearnt before . . . there arose in me light.

This ceasing of ill must be realized, concerning things unlearnt before . . . there arose in me light.

This noble truth about the cessation of suffering has been realized, concerning things unheard before . . . there arose in me light.

Again, monks, at the thought of this noble truth about the path leading to the cessation of suffering, concerning things unlearnt before . . . there arose in me light.

This noble truth about the practice leading to the cessation of suffering must be cultivated, concerning things unheard before . . . there arose in me light.

This noble truth about the path leading to the cessation of suffering has been cultivated, concerning things unheard before there arose in me vision, insight, understanding, wisdom, and light.

So long, monks, as my knowledge and insight of these Four Noble Truths as they are in their three phases and twelve aspects were not quite purified, I did not claim to have awakened in this world with its gods, Māras, Brahmās, among the hosts of recluses and brahmins, of gods and humans; there was one enlightened with supreme enlightenment.

But, monks, so soon as my knowledge and insight of these phases and twelve aspects of the noble truths, in their essential nature, was purified, then, monks, I was assured about enlightenment with regard to the world and its gods, Māras, Brahmās, and with regard to the hosts of recluses and brahmins, of gods and humans. The knowledge and insight have arisen in me so that I know: Certain is the mind's liberation. This is my last birth. There is no more becoming for me."

Thus spoke the Lord, and the five monks were glad and rejoiced at the words of the Blessed One.

Source: "Saccamyuttasutta" [Connected Discourses on the Truths] in the *Samyutta-Nikāya of the Sutta-pitaka*, Part 5, edited by M. Leon Feer (London: Pali Text Society, 1898; reprint, London: Luzac, 1960), 419–422.

Selections from *Mahācattārīsakasutta*
(Discourse on the Great Forty)

Thus have I heard: On one occasion the Lord was staying near Sāvatthī in the Jeta Grove in Anāthapindika's monastery. The Lord addressed the monks: "Monks." "Revered One," these monks replied. The Lord spoke thus: "I will teach you, monks, the noble right concentration with its supports and accompaniments. . . .

"Therein, monks, right view comes first. And how, monks, does right view come first? If one comprehends that wrong view is wrong view and comprehends that right view is right view, this is his right view. And what, monks, is a wrong view? There is nothing given, no thing offered, nothing sacrificed; there is no fruit or result of good and bad deeds; there is not this world, there is not a world beyond; there is no mother or father; there are no beings reborn; there are not in the world recluses and brahmins who have realized by direct knowledge and assert this world and the other world. This, monks, is a wrong view.

"And what, monks, is right view? Now, I, monks, say that right view is twofold. There is the right view that has cankers, partaking of merit, that ripens attaching to rebirth. There is, monks, the right view that is noble, without cankers, super-mundane, a component of the path. And what, monks, is the right view that has cankers, partaking of merit, that ripens attaching to rebirth? There is the results of gift . . . offering . . . sacrifice; there is fruit and result of good and bad deeds; there is this world and the other world; there is mother and father; there are spontaneously reborn beings; there are in the world virtuous recluses and brahmins . . . who have realized them and the other world by direct knowledge and assert this world and the other world. This, monks, is a right view that has cankers, is on the side of merit, and ripens attaching to rebirth.

"And what, monks, is the right view that is noble, without cankers, supermundane, a component of the way? The wisdom, its major faculty, its power, the component of enlightenment that is investigation into things, the right view that is a component of the way in one who, by developing the noble way, is of noble thought, without cankers thought, conversant with the noble way—this, monks, is a right view that is noble, without-cankers, supermundane, a component of the way.

"Whoever makes an effort to abandon wrong views and attain right views—that is his right effort. Mindfully, one abandons wrong views; mindfully, one enters the right view and abides in it. This is one's right mindfulness. Thus these three things circle round and follow after right view, that is to say: right view, right effort, right mindfulness. As to this, monks, right view comes first. And how, monks, does right view come first? If one comprehends that wrong intention is wrong intention and comprehends that right intention is right intention, that is one's right view. And what, monks, is wrong intention? Intention for sense-pleasures, for ill-will, for harming. This, monks, is wrong intention. And what, monks, is right intention? Now I, monks, say that right intention is twofold. There is the right intention that has cankers, partaking of merit, and ripens with attaching to rebirth. There is, monks, the right intention that is noble, without cankers, supermundane, a factor of the way. And what, monks, is the right intention that has cankers, is on the side of merit, and ripens unto attachment? It is the intention for renunciation, intention for non-ill-will, and intention for nonharming. This, monks, is right intention that . . . ripens unto attachment.

"And what, monks, is the right intention that is noble, without cankers, supermundane, a component of the way? Whatever, monks, is reasonable, initial thought, intention, an activity of mental absorption, mental concentration, developing the noble way, is of noble thought, of thought without cankers, and is developing the noble path—this, monks, is right intention that is noble, without cankers, supermundane, a component of the way.

"Whoever strives for the riddance of wrong intention, for the attainment of right intention, that is his right effort. Mindfully, one abandons wrong intention;

mindfully one enters on right intention and abides in it. That is his right mind-fulness. Thus these three things circle round and follow right intention, that is: right view, right effort, and right mindfulness.

"Therein, monks, right view comes first. And how, monks, does right view come first? If one comprehends that wrong speech is wrong speech and compre-hends that right speech is right speech, this is his right view. And what, monks, is wrong speech? It is lying, slanderous speech, harsh speech, and gossip. This, monks, is wrong speech. And what, monks, is right speech? Now, I say that right speech is twofold. There is the right speech that has cankers, is meritorious, that ripens unto attachment to rebirth. There is the right speech that is noble, with-out cankers, supermundane, a component of the way. And what, monks, is the right speech that . . . ripens unto attachment to rebirth? It is abstaining from lying, abstaining from slanderous speech . . . harsh speech . . . gossiping. This is the right speech that has cankers, is on the side of merit that ripens unto attach-ment to rebirth.

"And what, monks, is the right speech that is noble, without cankers, super-mundane, a component of the way? Whatever, monks, is abstention from the four kinds of verbal misconduct and develops the pure way is of noble thought, of thought without cankers, and is conversant with the way—this, monks, is right speech that is noble, without cankers, supermundane, a component of the way.

"Whoever makes effort to abandon wrong speech and attain right speech, that is his right effort. Mindfully, one gets rid of wrong speech; mindfully, one enters right speech, abides in it. That is his right mindfulness. Thus these three things circle round and follow after right speech, that is to say: right view, right effort, and right mindfulness.

"In addition to this, monks, right view comes first. And how, monks, does right view come first? If one comprehends that wrong action is wrong action and comprehends that right action is right action, that is his right view. And what, monks, is wrong action? Killing creatures, taking what has not been given, mis-conduct in sense-pleasures. This, monks, is wrong action. And what, monks, is right action? Now, I, monks, say that right action is twofold. There is the right action that has cankers, is meritorious, that ripens unto attachment to rebirth. There is, monks, the right action that is noble, without cankers, supermundane, a component of the way. And what, monks, is the right action that . . . ripens unto attachment to rebirth? It is, monks, abstaining from killing creatures, abstaining from stealing, abstaining from misconduct in the sense-pleasures. This, monks, is the right action that has cankers, is meritorious, and ripens unto attachment.

"And what, monks, is the right action that is noble, without cankers, super mundane, a component of the way? Whatever, monks, is abstention from, refraining from, avoidance of, restraint from the three ways of bodily misconduct, by developing the noble way, being of pure thought, being of without-cankers thought, and being conversant with the way—this, monks, is right action that is noble, without cankers, supermundane, a factor of the way.

"Whoever makes effort to abandon wrong action and to attain right action, that is his right effort. Mindfully, one abandons wrong action; mindfully, one enters right action and abides in it. That is one's right mindfulness. Thus these three things circle round and follow after right action, that is to say: right view, right effort, and right mindfulness.

"As to this, monks, right view comes first. And how, monks, does right view come first? If one comprehends that wrong mode of livelihood is wrong mode of livelihood and comprehends that right mode of livelihood is right mode of livelihood, that is one's right view. And what, monks, is the wrong mode of livelihood? It is trickery, cajolery, insinuation, dissembling, and rapacity. This, monks, is the wrong mode of livelihood. And what, monks, is the right mode of livelihood? Now, I say that the right mode of livelihood is twofold. There is the right mode of livelihood that has cankers, is meritorious, that ripens unto attachment to rebirth. There is the right mode of livelihood that is noble, without cankers, supermundane, a component of the path. And what, monks, is the right mode of livelihood that . . . ripens unto attachment to rebirth? Herein, monks, a pure disciple, abandoning a wrong mode of livelihood, earns his living by a right mode of livelihood. . . .

"And what, monks, is the right mode of livelihood that is noble, without cankers, supermundane, a component of the way? The abstention from, refraining from, avoidance of, restraint from a wrong mode of livelihood in one who, by developing the noble way, is of noble thought, of thought without cankers, and is familiar with the way—this, monks, is the right mode of livelihood that is noble, without cankers, supermundane, a feature of the way.

"Whoever makes an effort to abandon a wrong mode of livelihood, for the attainment of a right mode of livelihood, that is his right effort. Mindfully, he gets rid of a wrong mode of livelihood; mindfully, one enters on a right mode of livelihood, and abides in it. This is his right mindfulness. Thus these three things circle round and follow after right mode of livelihood, that is to say: right view, right effort, and right mindfulness.

"Therein, monks, right view comes first. And how does right view come first? Right intention, monks, proceeds from right view; right speech proceeds from right purpose; right action proceeds from right speech; right mode of livelihood proceeds from right action; right effort proceeds from right mode of livelihood; right mindfulness proceeds from right effort; right concentration proceeds from right mindfulness; right knowledge proceeds from right concentration; deliverance proceeds from right knowledge. Thus the path of the disciple is possessed of eight components, the perfected one's of ten components.

"Therein, monks, right view comes first. And how, monks, does right view come first? Wrong view is abolished in one of right view; and those various evil unwholesome states that arise conditioned by wrong view are abolished in him; and various skilled things conditioned by right view come to development and fulfillment. Wrong intention is abolished in one of right purpose; and those various unwholesome states that arise conditioned by wrong intention are abolished in him; and various skilled things conditioned by right purpose come to development and fulfillment. Wrong speech, monks, is abolished in one of right speech. . . . Wrong action, monks, is abolished in one of right action. . . . Wrong mode of livelihood, monks, is abolished in one of right mode of livelihood. . . . Wrong effort, monks, is abolished in one of right effort. . . . Wrong mindfulness, monks, is worn away in one of right mindfulness. . . . Wrong concentration, monks, is abolished in one of right concentration. . . . Wrong knowledge, monks, is abolished in one of right knowledge. . . . Wrong freedom, monks, is abolished in one of right deliverance; and those various unwholesome states that arise conditioned by wrong deliverance are abolished in him; and various skilled things conditioned by right freedom come to development and fulfillment. So, monks, there are twenty features on the side of skill, twenty on the side of unskilled. The discourse on Dhamma pertaining to the Great Forty that has been set rolling cannot be stopped by a recluse or brahmin, a god, Māra, Brahmā, or by anyone in the world. Monks, whatever recluse or brahmin should think that this discourse on Dhamma pertaining to the Great Forty should be censured and rejected, ten ways of speaking from the standpoint of Dhamma give grounds for censuring him here and now: if the worthy one censures right view, then those recluses and brahmins who are of wrong view are the worthies to be honored, the worthies to be extolled. If the worthy one censures right thought, then those recluses and brahmins who are of wrong thought are the worthies to be honored, to be extolled; if the worthy one censures right speech . . . right action . . . right mode of livelihood . . . right effort . . . right mindfulness . . . right concentration . . . right knowledge . . . right freedom, then those recluses and brahmins who are of wrong speech . . . wrong freedom are the worthies to be honored, to be extolled. Monks, whatever recluse or brahmin should think that this discourse on Dhamma pertaining to the Great Forty should be censured and rejected, these ten ways of speaking from the standpoint of Dhamma give grounds for censuring him here and now. Monks, even teachers from Okkala, Vassa, and Bhañña, deniers of cause, deniers of the effect of cause, affirmers of nihilism, would think that the discourse on Dhamma about the Great Forty should not be censured and rejected. What is the reason for this? The fear of blame, of attack, and reproach are the reasons."

Thus spoke the Lord. The monks were delighted and rejoiced in what the Lord had said.

Source: "Mahācattārīsakasutta" [Discourse on the Great Forty] of the *Majjhima Nikāya* [Middle-Length Sayings], volume 3, edited by Robert Chalmers (London: Pali Text Society, 1899; reprint London: Luzac, 1960), 71–78.

5

Teachings of the Buddha:
Non-self

In ancient India, some thinkers argued for the existence of an immortal self that is reborn from one mode of life to another depending on its karma, as in the texts of the Upaniṣads. Within such a context, the notion of non-self represents a unique feature of the Buddha's teachings. This feature of his message must be understood in terms of his conviction that there is nothing permanent in the phenomenal world. To be attached to a self reflects both a condition of ignorance and bondage to the cycle of suffering. Thus it is essential to become free from any attachment to the notion of an enduring self. It is useful to note that a seeker of enlightenment does not bring himself or herself into contact with nibbāna, because there is, strictly speaking, no permanent self with which to accomplish this. It is more accurate to understand the seeker as attaining nibbāna by realizing and validating the fact that there is no self.

The first selection of this chapter makes it clear that the self is merely a convenient label that we attribute to a group of continually changing aggregates. This selection also assists a reader to grasp that a self is nothing more than a human construct. The second selection shows that there are many different ways of understanding and defining the self. The basic message is that it is preferable not to get ensnared with theories.

Selection from the *Milindapañha*
(Questions of King Milinda)

King Milinda approached the venerable Nāgasena; having approached, he exchanged greetings with the venerable Nāgasena; and, having exchanged greetings of friendliness and courtesy, he sat down at a respectful distance. And the venerable Nāgasena reciprocated the greeting, gladdening the heart of the king. And Milinda asked the venerable Nāgasena:

"How is your reverence known? What is your name, revered sir?"

"I am known as Nāgasena; fellow monks address me sire, as Nāgasena. But although (my) parents gave the name of Nāgasena, Sūrasena, Vīrasena, or Sīhasena, yet it is but a general term, designation, and a common usage. For there is no permanent person present here."

Then King Milinda spoke thus: "Let the five hundred Bactrian Greeks and the eighty thousand monks hear me: 'This Nāgasena says: There is no permanent person present. Is it now possible to approve of that?'" And King Milinda spoke thus to the venerable Nāgasena: "If, revered Nāgasena, a person is not present, who then is it that gives you the necessities of cloth for robes, almsfood, lodgings, and medicines for the sick? Who is it that makes use of them? Who is it that lives righteously, practices meditation, realizes the ways, the fruits, nibbāna? Who is it that kills a living thing, steals, who follows one's sense-pleasures, speaks lies, drinks liquor, and who commits the fivefold action that results in bad consequences? Therefore, there is no merit, there is no demerit, there is neither doer nor maker of good or evil deeds and no consequences of such actions. If, revered Nāgasena, someone killed you there would be no act of murder. Also, revered Nāgasena, you have no teacher, no preceptor, no ordination. If you say, 'Fellow monks address me, sire, as Nāgasena,' what here is Nāgasena? Is it, revered sir, that the hairs of the head are Nāgasena?"

"O no, sire."

"That the hairs of the body are Nāgasena?"

"O no, sire."

"That the nails . . . teeth, skin, flesh, sinews, bones, marrow, kidneys, heart, liver, membranes, spleen, lungs, intestines, mesentery, stomach, excrement, bile, phlegm, pus, blood, sweat, fat, tears, watery fluid, saliva, mucus, joint fluid, urine, or the brain are Nāgasena?"

"O no, sire."

"Is Nāgasena material form, revered sir?"

"O no, sire."

"Is Nāgasena feeling . . . perception . . . the habitual tendencies? Is Nagasena consciousness?"

"O no, sire."

"But then, revered sir, is Nāgasena material form, feeling, perception, habitual tendencies, and consciousness?"

"O no, sire."

"But then, revered sir, is there Nāgasena apart from material form, feeling, perception, habitual tendencies and consciousness?"

"O no, sire."

"Though I, revered sir, am asking you repeatedly, I do not see this Nāgasena. Nāgasena is only an empty sound, revered sir. For who here is Nāgasena? You, revered sir, are speaking a falsehood. There is no Nāgasena."

Then the venerable Nāgasena spoke thus to King Milinda: "You, sire, are a noble delicately nurtured in accordance with your noble status. If you, sire, walk at noontime on the dry ground and hot sand, trampling on sharp gravel and pebbles and sand, your feet would hurt you, your body would experience pain, your thought would be impaired, and tactile consciousness would arise, accompanied by anguish. Now, did you come on foot or in a chariot?"

"I, revered sir, did not come on foot, I came in a chariot."

"If you, sire, came by chariot, show me the chariot. Is the pole the chariot, sire?"

"O no, revered sir."

"Is the axle the chariot?"

"O no, revered sir."

"Are the wheels the chariot?"

"O no, revered sir."

"Is the body of the chariot the chariot . . . is the flag-staff of the chariot the chariot . . . is the yoke the chariot . . . are the reins the chariot . . . is the goad the chariot?"

"O no, revered sir."

"But then sire, is the chariot the pole, the axle, the wheels, the body of the chariot, the flag-staff of the chariot, the yoke, the reins, the goad?"

"O no, revered sir."

"But then, sire, is there a chariot apart from the pole the axle, the wheels, the body of the chariot, the flag-staff of the chariot, the yoke, the reins, the goad?"

"O no, revered sir."

"Though I, sire, am asking you repeatedly, I do not see any chariot. Chariot is only an empty sound. What is the chariot in which you arrived? You, sire, are speaking an untruth, a lying word. There is no chariot. You, sire, are the chief king in the whole of India. Of whom are you afraid that you lie? Let the five hundred worthy Bactrian Greeks and the eighty thousand monks listen to me: This King Milinda speaks thus: I have come by chariot. When asked to explain the nature of the chariot, he is unable to produce the chariot. Is it suitable to agree to that?"

When this had been said, the five hundred Bactrian Greeks, applauding the venerable Nāgasena spoke thus to King Milinda: "Now do you, sire, speak if you can. Then King Milinda spoke thus to the venerable Nāgasena:

"I, revered Nāgasena, am not telling a lie because of the pole, axle, wheels, body of a chariot, flag-staff of a chariot, yoke, reins, and goad; that 'chariot' exists as a denotation, designation, as a common usage, as a mere name."

"Very good, the king understands a chariot. Even so is it for me, sire, because of head hair and because of body hair . . . and because of the brain and because of material form and feeling and perception and the habitual tendencies and consciousness that 'Nāgasena' exists as a denotation, designation, as a common term, or merely as a name. But according to the highest meaning the person is not present."

Source: *Milindapañho: Being Dialogues between King Milinda and the Buddhist Sage Nāgasena*, volume 1, edited by V. Trenkner (London: Williams and Norgate, 1880), 34–38.

Selection from the *Mahānidānasutta* (Great Discourse on Origination)

"Now with declarations concerning the self, Ānanda, how do people explain it? Either the self is declared to have form and to be minute, saying: 'My self has form and is minute.' Or the self is declared to have form and to be boundless, in the words: 'My self has form and is boundless.' Or the self is declared to be formless and minute, saying: 'My self is formless and minute.' Or the self is declared to be formless and unlimited, saying: 'My self is formless and unlimited.'

"And in each case, Ānanda, he who makes the claim, makes it with regard either to the present life, or to the next life, thinking: 'My self not being like that, I will refashion it.' That being so, Ānanda, we have said enough about the case of one who is given to the theories that the soul has form and is minute, . . . has form and is unlimited, and so on.

"In so many ways, Ānanda, are claims made concerning the self.

"And in what ways, Ānanda, do people explain the nature of the self? Some claim the self does not have form and is minute, in the previous formula, or the self is not declared to have form and to be limitless, in the previous formula, or the self is not declared to be formless and minute, in the previous formula, or the self is not declared to be formless and limitless, in the previous formula.

"And in each case, Ānanda, he who refrains from making the claim, does not make it with regard either to the present life, or to the next life, nor is it his idea: 'My self not being like that, I will refashion it into that likeness.' That being so, Ānanda, we have given enough attention to the case about those who do not accept theories respecting the form and dimensions of the self.

"In so many ways, Ānanda, is there a refraining from assertions concerning the self."

Source: "Mahānidānasutta" [Great Discourse on Origination] from the *Dīgha-Nikāya* [Long Discourses of the Buddha], volume 2, edited by T. W. Rhys Davids and J. Estlin Carpenter (London: Pali Text Society, 1903; reprint London: Luzac, 1966), 64–66.

6

Teachings of the Buddha:
Nibbāna

The Theravāda Buddhist understanding of nibbāna is not comparable to a personal, omnipotent, omniscient, and loving God, as is found in various monotheistic traditions. Nibbāna is also not the original cause of the universe, which means that it is not a creative power. Nibbāna is not something that can be intellectually grasped by reason, as is developed in the rational arguments of monotheistic theologians. It is more accurate to understand nibbāna as being beyond change and conditioning associated with the empirical world and the cycle of time.

The selections in this chapter point to the fact that language is inadequate for expressing the nature and experience of nibbāna, even though it is expressed both negatively and positively. In the final analysis, it is unthinkable and incomprehensible.

Nibbāna is something that must be existentially experienced by a person in order to grasp it. After experiencing it, a person cannot conceptualize it and cannot represent it in any way, as one can for a thing. Nonetheless, the experience of nibbāna brings an end to ignorant craving, delusion, greed, and the process of causation. This profound experience also terminates the representational model of thinking. Nibbāna is the exact opposite to the ever-changing nature of the world. The two selections chosen for this chapter make these points clear.

Selection from the *Cūlamālunkyasutta*
(The Shorter Discourse to Mālunkyāputta)

Then, while the venerable Mālunkyāputta was emerging from solitary meditation toward evening, he approached the Lord; having greeted the Lord, he sat down at a respectful distance. As he was sitting down at a respectful distance, the venerable Mālunkyāputta spoke to the Lord: "Now, revered sir, as I was meditating in solitary seclusion, the following thought arose to me: 'Those speculative views that are not explained, set aside, or ignored by the Lord: The world is eternal, infinite, the self is the same as the body; if the world is finite . . . or if that the Tathāgata exists and after death does not exist, then I will renounce the training and return to secular life.' If the Lord knows that the world is eternal, let the Lord explain to me that the world is eternal. If the Lord knows that the world is not eternal, let the Lord explain to me that the world is not eternal. If the Lord does not know whether the world is eternal or whether the world is not eternal, then, not knowing, not seeing, this would be honest, namely, to say: 'I do not know, I do not see.' . . . If the Lord does not know whether the Tathāgata neither is nor is not after dying, then, not knowing, not seeing, this would be honest, namely to say: 'I do not know, I do not see.' "

"But did I ever say to you, Mālunkyāputta: 'Come Mālunkyāputta, travel the holy path under me and I will explain to you either that the world is eternal or that the world is not eternal . . . or that the Tathāgata neither is nor is not after dying?"

"No, revered sir."

"Or did you speak thus to me: 'I, revered sir, will lead the holy life under the Lord, if the Lord will explain to me either that the world is eternal or that the world is not eternal . . . or that the Tathāgata neither is nor is not after dying?' "

"No, revered sir."

"So it is agreed, Mālunkyāputta, that neither did I say: 'Come Mālunkyāputta, lead the holy life under me and I will explain to you either that the world is eternal or that the world is not eternal . . . or that the Tathāgata neither is nor is not after dying;' and that neither did you say: 'I, revered sir, will lead the holy life under the Lord, if the Lord will explain to me either that the world is eternal . . . or that the Tathagata neither is nor is not after dying.' This being so, foolish man, who are you that you are abandoning?

"Whoever, Mālunkyāputta, should speak thus: 'I will not lead the holy life under the Lord until the Lord explains to me whether the world is eternal or whether the world is not eternal . . . or whether the Tathāgata neither is nor is not after dying,' and meanwhile that person would die. Suppose, Mālunkyāputta, a man were wounded by an arrow that was thickly smeared with poison, and his friends, relations, his companions and kin, were to procure a physician to treat him. He might say: 'I will not draw out this arrow until I know whether the man who wounded me is a noble, Brahmin, merchant, or worker.' He might say: 'I will not let the surgeon extract this arrow until I know the name and clan of the man who wounded me.' He might say: 'I will not let the surgeon extract this arrow until I know whether the man who wounded me was tall or short or average in height.' He might say: 'I will not let the surgeon extract this arrow until I know whether the man who wounded me was black, deep brown, or golden skinned.' He might say: 'I will not let the surgeon extract this arrow until I know whether the man who wounded me was from what village, market town, or city.' He might say: 'I will not have this arrow extracted until I know about the bow from which I was wounded: whether it was a spring-bow or a cross-bow.' He might say: 'I will not have this arrow extracted until I know about the bow-string from which I was wounded: whether it was of fiber, reed, sinew, hemp, or bark.' He might say: 'I will not have this arrow extracted until I know of the shaft by which I was wounded: whether it was of reeds of this kind or that.' He might say: 'I will not have this arrow extracted until I know what kind of feathers were on the shaft from which I was wounded: whether those of a vulture, heron, hawk, peacock, or some other bird.' He might say: 'I will not have this arrow extracted until I know what type of sinews encased the shaft from which I was wounded: whether those of a cow or buffalo or deer or monkey.' He might speak thus: 'I will not have this arrow extracted until I know about the arrow by which I was pierced: whether it was an hoof-tipped, curved, barbed, calf-toothed arrow, or some other kind.' Mālunkyā-putta, this man would die, and this world would still not be known to him. In the same way, Mālunkyāputta, whoever should say: 'I will not lead the holy life under the Lord until the Lord explains to me either that the world is eternal or that the world is not eternal . . . or that the Tathāgata neither is nor is not after dying,' this man would die, Mālunkyāputta, and that would still remain unexplained to him by the Tathāgata.

"The living of the holy life, Mālunkyāputta, could not be said to depend on the view that the world is eternal. Nor could the living of the holy life, Mālun-kyāputta, be said to depend on the view that the world is not eternal. Whether there is the view that the world is eternal or whether there is the view that the world is not eternal, there is birth, there is aging, there is dying, there are grief, sorrow, suffering, lamentation and despair, the suppression of which I encourage in the present. . . . The living of the holy life, Mālunkyāputta, could not be said to depend on the view that the Tathāgata neither is nor is not after dying. Whether there is the view that the Tathāgata both is and is not after dying, or whether, Mālunkyāputta, there is the view that the Tathāgata neither is nor is not after dying, there is birth, there is aging, there is dying, there are grief, sorrow, suffering, lamentation, and despair, the suppression of which I encourage in the present.

"Wherefore, Mālunkyāputta, understand as not explained what I have not explained, and understand as explained what has been explained by me. And what, Mālunkyāputta, has not been explained by me? That the world is eternal has not been explained by me, Mālunkyāputta; that the world is not eternal . . . that the world is an ending thing . . . that the world is not an ending thing . . . that the life-principle and the body are the same . . . that the life-principle is one thing and the body another thing . . . that after dying the Tathāgata is . . . is not . . . both is and is not. . . neither is nor is not has not been explained by me, Mālunkyāputta. And why, Mālunkyāputta, has this not been explained by me? It is because it is not connected with the goal, is not fundamental to the holy life, and is not conducive to rejecting, nor to dispassion, stopping, calming, direct knowledge, awakening, to nibbāna. Therefore, I, Mālunkyāputta, have not explained it. And what I, Mālunkyāputta, have explained? 'This is anguish' has been explained by me, Mālunkyāputta. 'This is the arising of suffering' has been explained by me. 'This is the stopping of suffering' has been explained by me. 'This is the course leading to the stopping of suffering' has been explained by me. And why, Mālunkyāputta, has this been explained by me? It is because it is connected with the goal, is fundamental to the holy life, and is conducive to rejecting dispassion, stopping, calming, direct knowledge, awakening, and nibbāna. Therefore, it has been explained by me. Wherefore, Mālunkyāputta, understand as not explained what has not been explained by me, and understand as explained what has been explained by me."

Thus spoke the Lord. Delighted, the venerable Mālunkyāputta rejoiced in what the Lord declared.

Source: "Cūlamālunkyasutta" [The Shorter Discourse to Mālunkyāputta] in the *Majjhima-Nikāya* [Middle Length Sayings], volume 1, edited by V. Trenckner (London: Pali Text Society, 1888; reprint London: Luzac, 1964), 427–432.

Selections from the *Milindapañha*
(Questions of King Milinda)

The King said: "Revered Nāgasena, is there the Buddha?"

"Yes, there is the Lord."

"But is it possible, Nāgasena, to point to the Buddha and say that he is either here or there?"

"The Lord has attained final nibbāna in the element of nibbāna that has no substrate remaining that could result in another birth. It is not possible to point to the Lord and say that he is either here or there."

"Make a simile."

"What do you think about this, sire? When the flame of a large fire has gone out, is it possible to point to that flame and say that it is either here or there?"

"O no, revered sir, that flame has stopped, it has vanished."

"Even so, sire, the Lord has attained final nibbāna in the element of nibbāna that has no substrate remaining for another birth. It is not possible to point to the Lord who has gone and say that he is either here or there; but, sire, it is possible to point to the Lord by means of the body of Dhamma, for Dhamma, sire, was taught by the Lord."

"You are clever, revered Nāgasena." . . .

"Revered Nāgasena, what you said about space is correct: that it is born neither of kamma nor of cause nor of physical change. But in many a hundred ways, revered Nāgasena, did the Lord indicate to disciples the path to the realization of nibbāna, and then you say: Nibbāna is not born of cause?"

"It is true, sire, that in many a hundred ways did the Lord indicate to disciples the path to the realization of nibbāna; but he did not indicate a cause for the arising of nibbāna."

"Here we, revered Nāgasena, are entering from darkness into greater darkness, we are entering from a jungle into a deeper jungle, we are entering from a thicket into a denser thicket, inasmuch as there is indeed a cause for the realization of nibbāna, though there is no cause for its arising. If, Nāgasena, there be a cause for the realization of nibbāna, well then, one would require a cause also for the arising of nibbāna. Just Nāgasena, as there is the father of a child, for that reason one would expect also a father of the father; inasmuch as there is the teacher of a pupil, for that reason one would expect also a teacher of the teacher; inasmuch as there is seed for a plant, for that reason one would expect also a seed for the seed. Even so, Nāgasena, if there be a cause for the realization of nibbāna, for that reason one would require a cause also for the arising of nibbāna. Inasmuch as there is a top to a tree or creeper, we could conclude that there is also a middle portion and a root. Even so, Nāgasena, if there be a cause for the realization of nibbāna, for that reason one would expect a cause also for the arising of nibbāna."

"Nibbāna, sire, is producable, therefore a cause for the arising of nibbāna has not been declared."

"Please, Nāgasena, giving me a reason, convince me by an argument so that I may know: That while there is a cause for the realization of nibbāna, there is no cause for the arising of nibbāna."

"Well then, sire, give me an attentive ear, listen closely and I will tell you the reason for this. Would a man, sire, with his natural strength, be able to climb the Himalaya, a king of mountains?"

"Yes, revered sir."

"But would that man, sire, with his natural strength be able to bring the Himalaya, a king of mountains, here?"

"O no, revered sir."

"Even so, sire, it is possible to point out the path for the realization of nibbāna, but impossible to show a cause for the origin of nibbāna. Would it be possible for a man who with his natural strength to cross the great ocean in a ship to reach the farther shore?"

"Yes, revered sir."

"But would it be possible, sire, for that man with his natural strength to bring the other shore of the great ocean here?"

"O no, revered sir."

"Even so, sire, it is possible to indicate the path for the realization of nibbāna, but impossible to show a cause for the origin of nibbāna. For what reason? Because of the unconstructedness of the Dhamma."

"Revered Nāgasena, is nibbāna unconstructed?"

"Yes, sire, nibbāna is unconstructed; it is not made by anything. One cannot say of nibbāna, sire, that it has arisen, or that it has not arisen, or that it is possible to arise, or that it is past, future, or present, or that it is knowable by the eye, ear, nose, tongue, or the body."

If, revered Nāgasena, nibbāna has neither arisen nor not arisen nor is arisable, is not past or future or present, nor knowable by the eye, ear, nose, tongue, or body, well then, revered Nāgasena, you indicate nibbāna as a Dhamma that does not exist."

"Nibbāna exists, sire. Nibbāna is knowable by the mind. A noble disciple, practicing rightly, with a purified mind, free, straight, without obstructions, and desireless can see nibbāna."

"But, revered sir, what is this nibbāna like? Convince me by reasons about this that can be illustrated by similes."

"Is there, sire, what is called wind?"

"Yes, revered sir."

"Please, sire, show the wind by means of its color or form or whether it is thin or thick, long or short."

"It is not possible, Nāgasena, for the wind to be demonstrated. For the wind does not lend itself to being grasped by the hands or being touched. But yet that 'wind' exists."

"If it is not possible, sire, for the wind to be demonstrated, there is no such thing."

"I know, Nāgasena, that there is wind, I am convinced of it, but I am not able to demonstrate the wind."

"Even so, sire, nibbāna is, though it is not possible to point out nibbāna either by color or form."

"It is good, Nāgasena. Well demonstrated is the simile, convincing the argument. Thus it is, therefore do I accept it: There is nibbāna." . . .

Nibbana Is without a Counterpart

"Revered Nāgasena, you keep on talking about nibbāna, but is it possible by simile, argument, cause, or method to indicate the shape, form, age, or size of this nibbāna?"

"Without a counterpart, sire, is nibbāna, and it is not possible by simile, argument, cause, or method to point out the shape, configuration, age, or size of nibbāna."

"But, I, revered Nāgasena, do not agree that by simile, argument, cause, or method, the shape, configuration, age, or size of nibbāna can be given. Explain this to me."

"Let it be, sire; I will convince you of this by asking: Is there, sire, what is called the great ocean?"

"Yes, revered sir, there is this great ocean."

"But if someone asked you, sire, how much water was in the great ocean or how many beings live in the great ocean, would you, sire, be able to answer him?"

"If someone were to ask me, sir, how much water was in the great ocean or how many beings lived in the great ocean, I would say: 'My good fellow, this is not a question you should ask me, this is not a question to be asked by anyone, this is a question to be rejected. The great ocean has not been analyzed by natural scientists, and it is not possible to estimate the amount of water in the great ocean or the number of those beings that live there.' Thus would I, sire, reply to him."

"But why would you, sire, reply thus about the great ocean? Should you not rather count and tell him how much water is in the great ocean and how many beings live in the great ocean?"

"It is not possible, revered sir. That is a question beyond one's ability."

"As, sire, it is not possible to determine the amount of water in the great ocean, even though it exists, nor the number of beings whose abode is there, even so, sire, it is impossible by simile, argument, cause, or method to indicate the shape, form, age, or size of nibbāna, although it does exist. Even if a person of psychic power, sire, a master of one's own mind, were to count the amount of water in the great ocean and the number of beings living there, not even that person of psychic power who had attained mastery over the mind would be able by simile, argument, cause, or method to indicate the shape, form, age, or size of nibbāna.

"And listen to an additional explanation, sire. It is said: 'It is not possible by simile, argument, cause, or method to indicate the shape, configuration, age, or size of nibbāna, even though it exists.' Among the gods, sire, are there gods belonging to an incorporeal class?"

"Yes, revered sir, it has been heard that among the gods are some belonging to an incorporeal class."

"But is it possible, sire, by simile, argument, cause, or method to indicate the shape, form, age, or size of these gods who belong to an incorporeal class?"

"No, revered sir."

"Well then, sire, there are no gods belonging to an incorporeal class."

"There are, revered sir, gods belonging to an incorporeal class though it is not possible by simile, argument, cause, or method to indicate their shape, form, age, or size."

"As, sire, it is not possible by simile, argument, cause, or method to point out the shape, form, age, or size of the gods belonging to an incorporeal class, even though they exist, even so, sire, it is not possible by simile, argument, cause, or method to indicate the shape, form, age, or size of nibbāna, although it does exist."

"Revered Nāgasena, let stand the assertion that nibbāna is entirely blissful but that it is not possible by simile, argument, cause, or method to point out its shape, form, age, or size."

Source: *Milindapañho: Being Dialogues between King Milinda and the Buddhist Sage Nāgasena,* edited by V. Trenkner (London: Williams and Norgate, 1880), 268–271; 315–319.

7

Teachings of the Buddha:
Meditation

From the perspective of the Buddha, meditation functions as the key that unlocks the door of liberation from the cycle of causation and suffering. The practice of meditation gives one an insight into reality and gives one certainty. Meditation is nonreducible to subjectivity, rationality, objectivity, logical inferences, or empirical knowledge. In short, it is the medicine needed to cure a person suffering from the sickness of the cycle of suffering and rebirth.

The first selection from Pāli primary sources discusses the importance of mindfulness with respect to the body, feeling, and mental objects. It gives a reader insight into early Buddhist attitudes toward the human body, the practice of cemetery contemplations of the body, and the seven factors of enlightenment. The second selection discusses overcoming the five hindrances and enumerates the levels of meditation.

Selection from the *Satipattānasutta*
(Discourse on the Applications of Mindfulness)

Thus have I heard: At one time, the Lord was living among the Kuru people in a town that was called Kammāssadhamna. There the Lord addressed the monks saying: "Monks." "Revered one," these monks responded. The Lord said this:

"There is a direct way, monks, for the purification of beings, for the overcoming of sorrow and lamentation, for the disappearance of suffering and misery, for attaining the right path, for realizing nibbāna, namely, the four foundations of mindfulness. What are the four?

"Herein, monks, a monk abides contemplating the body in the body, ardent, fully conscious of it, mindful of it, having control over covetousness and grief for the world; he abides contemplating feelings in the feelings, ardent, fully conscious of them, mindful of them, having control over covetousness and grief in the world; he abides contemplating the mind in the mind, ardent, fully conscious of it, mindful of it, having control over covetousness and grief in the world; he abides contemplating the mental objects in the mental objects, ardent, fully conscious of them, mindful of them, having control over the covetousness and grief in the world.

"And how, monks, does a monk abide contemplating the body in the body? Herein, monks, a monk gone to the forest, to the root of a tree, or to an empty place, sits down cross-legged, holding his back erect, and establishes mindfulness in front of him. Mindful he breathes in, mindful he breathes out. While he is breathing in a long breath, he comprehends, 'I am breathing in a long breath'; or breathing out a long breath, he comprehends, 'I am breathing out a long breath'; or while he is breathing in a short breath, he comprehends, 'I am breathing in a short breath'; or while he is breathing out a short breath, he comprehends, 'I am breathing out a short breath.' He trains himself, thinking: 'I shall breathe in experiencing the whole body.' He trains himself, thinking: 'I shall breathe out experiencing the whole body.' He trains himself, thinking: 'I shall breathe in calming the activity of the body.' He trains himself, thinking: 'I shall breathe out calming the activity of the body.' . . .

"In this way, monks, he abides contemplating the body in the body internally, or he fares along contemplating the body in the body externally, or he abides contemplating the body in the body internally and externally. Or he abides contemplating the origination of the body, or he abides contemplating dissolution of the body, or he abides contemplating the origination and dissolution of the body. Or, mindfully thinking, 'There is the body,' his mindfulness is established precisely to the extent necessary just for basic knowledge and mindfulness, and he abides independently, not grasping anything in the world. It is thus too, monks, that a monk abides contemplating the body in the body.

"And again, monks, a monk, when he is walking, comprehends, 'I am walking'; or when he is standing still, comprehends, 'I am standing still'; or when he is sitting down, comprehends, 'I am sitting down'; or when he is lying down, comprehends, 'I am lying down.' So that however his body is disposed he comprehends that it is like that. Thus he abides contemplating the body in the body internally, or he abides contemplating the body in the body externally, or he abides contemplating the body in the body internally and externally. Or he abides contemplating the origination of the body, or he abides contemplating the dissolution of the body, or he abides contemplating the origination and dissolution of the body. Or, thinking, 'There is the body,' his mindfulness is established precisely to the extent necessary just for basic knowledge, just for remembrance, and he abides independently, not grasping anything in the world. It is thus too, monks, that a monk abides contemplating the body in the body.

"And again, monks, a monk, when he is setting out or returning is one acting with full awareness; when he is looking in front or looking around . . . when he is flexing or stretching out his limbs . . . when he is carrying his outer robe and bowl . . . when he is eating, drinking, chewing, tasting . . . when he is defecating or urinating . . . when he is walking, standing, sitting, asleep, awake, talking, silent, he is one acting in full awareness. Thus he abides contemplating the body in the body internally, or he abides contemplating the body in the body externally, or he abides contemplating the body in the body internally and externally. Or he abides contemplating the origination of the body, or he abides contemplating dissolution of the body, or he abides contemplating the origination and dissolution of the body. Or, thinking, 'There is the body,' his mindfulness is established precisely to the extent necessary just for basic knowledge, just for remembrance, and he abides independently, not grasping anything in the world. It is thus too, monks, that a monk abides contemplating the body in the body.

"And again, monks, a monk reflects on precisely this body itself full of various impurities, from the soles of the feet up and down from the top of the head: 'There is connected with this body head hair, body hair, nails, teeth, skin, flesh, sinews, bones, marrow, kidneys, heart, liver, membranes, spleen, lungs, intestines, stomach, excrement, bile, phlegm, pus, blood, sweat, fat, tears, grease, saliva, mucus, joint oil, urine.'

"Monks, it, is like a double bag that is full of various kinds of grain such as hill-rice, red rice, beans, peas, sesame, white rice; and a man with good eyesight, pouring them out, and reviewed it thus: 'That's hill-rice, that's red rice, that's beans, that's peas, that's sesame, that's white rice.' Even so, monks, does a monk reflect on precisely this body itself full of various impurities, from the soles of the feet up and down from the top of the head: 'There is connected with this body head hair . . . urine.' Thus he abides contemplating the body in the body internally . . . and he abides independently, not grasping anything in the world. It is thus too, monks, that a monk abides contemplating the body in the body.

"And again, monks, a monk reflects on this body according to how it is placed or disposed in respect of the elements, thinking: 'In this body there is the element of extension, the element of cohesion, the element of heat, the element of motion.' Monks, even as a skilled butcher, or his apprentice, having killed a cow and sits displaying its carcass at a crossroads, even so, monks, does a monk reflect on this body itself according to how it is placed or disposed in respect of the elements, thinking: 'In this body there is the element of extension, the element of cohesion, the element of heat, the element of motion.' Thus he abides contemplating the body in the body internally . . . , externally, and both internally and externally and he abides independently, not grasping anything in the world. It is thus too, monks, that a monk abides contemplating the body in the body.

"Again, monks, as a person might see a corpse discarded in a cemetery, dead for one, two, or three days, swollen, discolored, decomposed. A monk compares his body thinking: 'This body, too, is of the same nature; it will become like that; it is not exempt from that fate.' It is in this way that a monk abides . . . not grasping anything in the world. It is thus too, monks, that a monk fares along contemplating the body in the body.

"Again, monks, a monk might see a body discarded in a cemetery, being devoured by crows, ravens, vultures, wild dogs, jackals, or by various kinds of worms; a monk compares this body with his, thinking: 'This body too is of the same nature, it will become like that; it is not exempt from that fate.' It is in this way that a monk abides . . . not grasping anything in the world. It is thus too, monks, that a monk abides contemplating the body in the body.

"Again, monks, as a monk might see a body discarded in a cemetery, a skeleton with flesh and blood, attached by sinews; . . . or fleshless but blood-bespattered, sinew-bound; . . . or fleshless, a skeleton smeared with blood, attached by sinews; . . . or disconnected bones scattered in all directions: here a hand bone, there a foot-bone, here a leg-bone, there a rib, here a hip-bone, there a backbone, here the skull; he compares this same body with it. . . . It is in this way that a monk abides . . . not grasping anything in the world. It is thus too, monks, that a monk abides contemplating the body in the body.

"Again, monks, a monk might see a body discarded in a cemetery: the bones bleached white and the color of sea-shells . . . a heap of dried up bones more than a year old . . . the rotten bones reduced to dust; he compares this same body with it, thinking: 'This body, too, is the same nature, it will become like that; it is not exempt form that fate.' Thus he abides contemplating the body in the body internally, or he abides contemplating the body in the body externally, or he abides contemplating the body in the body internally and externally. Or he abides contemplating the origination of the body, or he abides contemplating dissolution of the body, or he abides contemplating the origination and dissolution of the body. Or, thinking, 'There is the body,' his mindfulness is established precisely to the extent necessary just for basic knowledge, just for remembrance, and he abides independently, not grasping anything in the world. It is thus too that a monk abides contemplating the body in the body.

"And how, monks, does a monk abide contemplating the feelings as feelings? Herein, monks, while he is experiencing a pleasant feeling he comprehends: 'I am experiencing a pleasant feeling'; while he is experiencing a painful feeling he comprehends, 'I am experiencing a painful feeling'; while he is experiencing a feeling that is neither painful nor pleasant he comprehends: 'I am experiencing a feeling that is neither painful nor pleasant.' While he is experiencing a pleasant feeling with respect to material things . . . with respect to non-material things he comprehends, 'I am experiencing a pleasant feeling in regard to nonmaterial things'; while he is experiencing a painful feeling in regard to material things . . . with respect to nonmaterial things he comprehends, 'I am experiencing a painful feeling with respect to nonmaterial things'; while he is experiencing a feeling that is neither painful nor pleasant with respect to material things . . . with respect to nonmaterial things he comprehends, 'I am experiencing a feeling that is neither painful nor pleasant with respect to nonmaterial things.' Thus he abides contemplating the feelings as the feelings internally, or he abides contemplating the feelings as the feelings externally, or he abides contemplating the feelings as the feelings internally and externally. Or he abides contemplating the origination of the feelings, or he abides contemplating dissolution of the feelings, or he abides contemplating the origination and dissolution-things of the feelings. Or, thinking, 'There is feeling,' his mindfulness is established precisely to the extent necessary just for basic knowledge, just for remembrance, and he abides independently, not grasping anything in the world. It is thus, monks, that a monk abides contemplating feelings as the feelings.

"And how, monks, does a monk abide contemplating mind as the mind? Herein, a monk knows intuitively the mind with attachment as a mind with attachment; he knows intuitively the mind without attachment as a mind without attachment . . . the mind with hatred as a mind with hatred . . . the mind without hatred an a mind without hatred . . . the mind with delusion as a mind with delusion . . . the mind without delusion as a mind without delusion . . . the mind that is contracted as a mind that is contracted . . . the mind that is distracted as a mind that is distracted ... the mind that has become exalted as a mind that has become exalted . . . a mind that has not become exalted as a mind that has not become exalted . . . the mind with some other mental state superior to it as a mind with some other mental state superior to it . . . the mind with no other mental state superior to it as a mind with no other mental state superior to it . . . the mind that is composed as a mind that is composed . . . the mind that is not composed as a mind that is not composed . . . the mind that is freed as a mind that is liberated . . . the mind that is not liberated as a mind that is not liberated. Thus he abides contemplating the mind in the mind internally, or he abides contemplating the mind in the mind externally, or he abides contemplating the mind in the mind internally and externally. Or he abides contemplating the origination of the mind, or he abides contemplating dissolution of the mind, or he abides contemplating the origination and dissolution of the mind. Or, thinking, 'There is mind,' his mindfulness is established precisely to the extent necessary just for basic knowledge, just for remembrance, and he abides independently, not grasping anything in the world. It is thus that a monk abides contemplating mind as the mind.

"And how does a monk abide contemplating mental objects as mental objects? Herein, monks, a monk abides contemplating mental objects as mental objects from the point of view of the five hindrances. And how, monks, does a monk abide contemplating mental objects as mental objects from the point of view of the five hindrances? Herein, monks, when a subjective desire for sense-pleasures is present, a monk comprehends that he has a desire for sense-pleasures; or when a subjective desire for sense-pleasures is not present he comprehends that he has no subjective desire for sense-pleasures. And insofar as there develops an increase of desire for sense-pleasures that had not previously arisen, he comprehends that; and insofar as there comes to be a getting rid of desire for sense-pleasures that has developed, he comprehends that. And insofar as there develops no future uprising of desire for the sense-pleasures that have been overcome, he comprehends that. Or when ill-will is subjectively present he comprehends that he has ill-will. . . . Or when sloth and torpor are subjectively present he comprehends that he has sloth and torpor. . . . Or when restlessness and worry are subjectively present he comprehends that he has restlessness and worry. . . . Or when doubt is present subjectively he comprehends that he has doubt; when doubt is not present, subjectively he comprehends that he has no objective doubt. And insofar as there is a development of doubt that had not arisen before, he comprehends that; and insofar as there is overcoming of doubt that has arisen, he comprehends that, and insofar as there is in the future no uprising of the doubt that has been overcome, he comprehends that. It is thus that he abides contemplating mental objects as mental objects internally, or he abides contemplating mental objects as mental objects externally or he abides contemplating mental objects as mental objects internally and externally. Or he fares along contemplating the origination of mental objects, or he abides contemplating the dissolution of mental objects, or he abides contemplating the origination and dissolution of mental objects. Or thinking 'There are mental objects,' his mindfulness is established precisely to the extent necessary just for basic knowledge, just for remembrance, and he abides independently, not grasping anything in the world. It is thus that a monk abides contemplating mental objects in mental objects from the point of view of the five hindrances.

"Again, monks, a monk abides contemplating mental objects as mental objects from the point of view of the five groups of grasping. And how does a monk abide contemplating mental objects as mental objects from the point of view of the five groups of grasping? Herein a monk thinks, 'Such is material shape, such is the arising of material shape, such is the setting of material shape; such is feeling, such the arising of feeling, such the setting of feeling; such is perception, such the arising . . . such the setting of perception; such are the tendencies, such the arising . . . such the setting of the tendencies; such is consciousness, such the arising of consciousness, such the setting of consciousness.' It is in this way that he abides contemplating mental objects as mental objects internally, or he abides . . . contemplating the origination and dissolution of mental objects. Or, thinking, 'There are mental objects,' his mindfulness is established precisely to the extent necessary just for basic knowledge, just for remembrance, and he fares along independently, not grasping anything in the world. It is thus that a monk abides contemplating mental objects as mental objects from the point of view of the five groups of grasping.

"Again a monk abides contemplating mental objects as mental objects from the point of view of the six internal and external sense-bases. And how does a monk abide contemplating mental objects as mental objects from the point of view of the six internal and external sense-bases? Herein, a monk comprehends the eye, and he comprehends forms, and he comprehends the fetter that arises dependent on both, and he comprehends the uprising of the fetter not arisen before, and he comprehends the getting rid of the fetter that has arisen, and he comprehends the nonuprising in the future of the fetter that has been abandoned. And he comprehends the ear . . . and he comprehends sounds . . . and he comprehends the nose, and he comprehends smells . . . and he comprehends the tongue, and he comprehends flavors . . . and he comprehends the body, and he comprehends tactile objects . . . and he comprehends the mind, and he comprehends mental objects, and he comprehends the fetter that arises dependent on both, and he comprehends the uprising of the fetter that had not arisen before, and he comprehends the getting rid of the fetter that has arisen, and he comprehends the nonarising in the future of the fetter that has been abandoned. It is in this way that he abides contemplating mental objects as mental objects internally, or he abides contemplating mental objects as mental objects externally, or he abides contemplating mental objects as mental objects internally and externally. Or he abides contemplating the origination of mental objects. . . . Or, thinking, 'There are mental objects . . . he abides independently of and not grasping anything in the world. It is thus that a monk abides contemplating mental objects as mental objects from the perspective of the six internal and external sensebases.

"And again, monks, a monk abides contemplating mental objects as mental objects from the point of view of the seven enlightenment factors. And how does a monk abide contemplating mental objects as mental objects from the perspective of the seven links in awakening? Herein, when the enlightenment factor is present internally he comprehends that he has internally the mindful enlightenment factor; when the mindful enlightenment factor is not internally present he comprehends that he has not internally the mindful enlightenment factor. And insofar as there is an uprising of the link the mindful enlightenment factor that had not previously developed, he comprehends that; and insofar as there is a completion of mental development of the developed mindful enlightenment factor, he comprehends that. When the mindful enlightenment factor that represents the investigation of mental objects is present internally . . . and insofar as there is completion by mental development of the uprisen mindful enlightenment factor that is investigation of mental objects, he comprehends that. When the mindful enlightenment factor that is energy is present internally . . . insofar as there is completion by mental development of the uprisen mindful enlightenment factor that is energy, he comprehends that. When the mindful enlightenment factor that is trance is present internally, . . . When the mindful enlightenment factor that is serenity is present internally, . . . When the mindful enlightenment factor that is concentration is present internally, . . . When the mindful enlightenment factor that is equanimity is present internally, he comprehends that he has the mindful enlightenment factor that is equanimity; when the mindful enlightenment factor that is equanimity is not present internally, he comprehends that he has not the mindful enlightenment factor that is equanimity. And insofar as there is an uprising of the mindful enlightenment factor that is equanimity that had not uprisen before, he comprehends that; and insofar as there is completion by mental development of the uprisen link in awakening that is equanimity, he comprehends that. It is in this way that he abides contemplating mental objects as mental objects . . . both internally and externally. Or he expects either final present knowledge or, if there is any trace remaining, the state of nonreturning. . . . Whoever, monks, should thus develop these four applications of mindfulness for seven months, one of two fruits can be expected for him: either final present knowledge, or, if there is any trace remaining, the state of nonreturning. Monks, let alone the seven months. Whoever should thus develop these four applications of mindfulness for six months, five months, four months, three months, two months, for one month, for half a month. . . . Monks, let alone the half month. Whoever should thus develop these four applications of mindfulness for seven days, one of two fruits is to be expected for him: either final present knowledge or, if there is any trace remaining, the state of nonreturning.

"What has been spoken in this way has been spoken in reference to this: 'There is this direct path for the purification of beings, for the overcoming of sorrows and grief, for the disappearance of sufferings and miseries, for the attainment of the right path, for realizing nibbāna, namely, the four factors of mindfulness.'"

Thus spoke the Lord. Delighted, these monks rejoiced in what the Lord had said.

Source: "Satipattānasutta" [Discourse on the Applications of Mindfulness] in the *Majjhima-Nikāya* [Middle Length Sayings], volume 1, edited by V. Trenckner (London: Pali Text Society, 1888; reprint London: Luzac, 1964), 55–62.

Selection from *Cūlahattipadopanasutta*
(The Shorter Discourse on the Simile of the Elephant's Footprint)

"Possessing this pure body of moral virtue and pure control of the sense faculties, and this pure mindfulness and clear consciousness, he resorts to a remote place in a forest, at the root of a tree, on a mountain, in a wilderness, in a hillside cave, in a cemetery, in a jungle thicket, the open space, or on a heap of straw. Returning from begging after his meal, he sits down cross-legged, holding the back erect, establishing mindfulness rising up before him. Abandoning covetousness for the world, he lives with a mind free of coveting; he purifies the mind of coveting. Abandoning ill-will, he lives benevolent in mind and compassionate for the welfare of all living beings; he purifies the mind of the taint of ill-will and hatred. Abandoning sloth and torpor, he lives free of sloth and torpor; perceiving the light, mindful, and clearly conscious, he purifies the mind of sloth and torpor. Abandoning restlessness and worry, he lives calmly with a peaceful mind; he purifies the mind of restlessness and worry. Abandoning doubt, he lives beyond doubt; unperplexed about wholesome states, he purifies his mind of doubt.

"Having abandoned these five hindrances, which are defilements of the mind that weaken intuitive wisdom, aloof from pleasures of the senses, aloof from unwholesome states of mind, he enters upon and abides in the first meditation, which is accompanied by initial thought and discursive thought, aloofness, rapturous and joyful. This, brahmin, is called the Tathāgata's footprint, and what is marked and slashed by the Tathāgata. But not yet does the pure disciple come to fulfillment, thinking: 'The fully Self-awakened One is the Lord; the Dhamma is well taught by the Lord; the Order is practicing the way.'

"Again, brahmin, a monk by allaying initial and sustained thought, his mind subjectively tranquilized and fixed on one point, enters on and abides in the second meditation, which is devoid of initial and sustained thought, is born of concentration, and is rapturous and joyful. This too, brahmin, is called the Tathāgata's footprint, and what is marked and slashed by the Tathāgata. But not yet does the noble disciple come to fulfillment thinking: 'The fully Self-awakened One is the Lord; the Dhamma is well taught by the Lord; the Order is practicing the way.'

"Again, brahmin, a monk, by the fading out of trance, dwells in equanimity, attentive, and fully conscious, and experiences that joy of which the noble ones say: 'Joyful lives he who has equanimity and is mindful,' and he enters on and abides in the third meditation. This too, brahmin, is called the Tathāgata's footprint, and what is marked and slashed by the Tathāgata. But not yet does the noble disciple come to fulfillment, thinking: 'The fully Self-awakened One is the Lord; well taught is Dhamma by the Lord; the Order is practicing the way.'

"Again, brahmin, a monk, by abandoning joy, anguish, and his former pleasures and sorrows, enters upon and abides in the fourth meditation, which has neither pain nor joy, and which is entirely purified by equanimity and mindfulness. This too, brahmin, is called the Tathāgata's footprint, and what is marked and slashed by the Tathāgata. But not yet does the noble disciple arrive at fulfillment, thinking: 'The fully Self-awakened One is the Lord; well taught is Dhamma by the Lord; the Order is practicing the way.'

"Thus with the mind composed, purified, bright, unblemished, without defilement, malleable, fixed, and immovable, he directs his mind to the knowledge and recollection of former modes of existence. . . . Thus he remembers his many former modes of existence in all their detail. This too, brahmin, is called the Tathāgata's footprint, and what is marked and slashed by the Tathāgata. But not yet does the noble disciple come to fulfillment, thinking: 'The fully Self-awakened One is the Lord; well taught is Dhamma by the Lord; the Order is practicing the way.'

"Thus with the mind composed, purified, bright, unblemished, without defilement, malleable, fixed, and immovable, he directs his mind to the knowledge of passing away and arising of beings. With the divine eye, purified and surpassing that of humans, he sees beings dying and being reborn. . . . Thus with the divine eye, purified and surpassing that of humans, does he see beings dying and being reborn, he comprehends that beings are mean, excellent, foul, fair, in a good birth, in a bad birth, according to the consequences of their deeds. This too, brahmin, is called the Tathāgata's footprint, and what is marked and slashed by the Tathāgata. But not yet does the noble disciple come to fulfillment, thinking: 'The fully Self-awakened One is the Lord; well taught is Dhamma by the Lord; the Order is practicing the way.'

"Thus with the mind composed, purified, bright, unblemished, without defilement, malleable, fixed, immovable, he directs his mind to the knowledge of the destruction of the cankers . . . he comprehends as it really is: 'This is the course leading to the stopping of the cankers.' This too, brahmin, is called the Tathāgata's footprint, and what is marked and slashed by the Tathāgata. But not yet does the noble disciple come to fulfillment, thinking: 'The fully Self-awakened One is the Lord; well taught is Dhamma by the Lord: the Order is practicing the way.'

"When he knows and sees thus, the mind is freed from the canker of sense-pleasures, and the mind is freed from the canker of becoming, and the mind is freed from the canker of ignorance. When he is liberated, the knowledge dawns that he is free, and he comprehends: 'Destroyed is birth, brought to a close is the holy life, done is what was to be done, there is no more being reborn.' This too, brahmin, is called the Tathāgata's footprint, and what is marked and slashed by the Tathāgata. It is at this point, brahmin, that the noble disciple comes to fulfillment, thinking: 'The fully Self-awakened One is the Lord; well taught is Dhamma by the Lord; the Order is practicing the way.' At this point, brahmin, the simile of the elephant's footprint is complete in detail." . . .

Source: Cūlahattipadopanasutta [The Shorter Discourse on the Simile of the Elephant's Footprin] in the *Majjhima-Nikāya* [Middle Length Sayings], volume 1, edited by V. Trenckner (London: Pali Text Society, 1888; reprint London: Luzac, 1964), 181–184.

8

Teachings of the Buddha:
Ethical Issues and Virtues

As a cursory examination of the Noble Eightfold Path makes clear, the path was intended to transform a person mentally, emotionally, and ethically. The Buddha was convinced that acting ethically purified wisdom and that ethical and moral behavior are purified by wisdom. On a practical level, a dramatic transformation was required for a person to achieve enlightenment. Likewise, an enlightened person would behave exactly like a morally and ethically good person. This suggests that moral and ethical behavior partially paves the path to enlightenment and is also a product of enlightenment.

As the first selection of this chapter implies, ethical behavior and virtues are not divine commandments to act in a way according to objective and rigid values that cannot be transgressed. Not only did the Buddha allow for moral and ethical flexibility but he also intended that moral and ethical behavior become a means to help us understand and achieve a genuinely selfless way of life. What the Buddha provided to his audience was wise counsel in the form of guidelines for action. These wise guidelines were intended to assist a person in his or her interaction with other humans and animals. The initial selection for this chapter provides, moreover, an outline for proper ethical conduct with its discussion of correct thought, bodily conduct, verbal utterances, and mental behavior. This selection provides an excellent complement to the discussion of mindfulness in the previous chapter on meditation.

The second selection comes from the Abhidhamma body of Theravāda literature. *The Expositor* (*Aṭṭlasālinī*) is a text attributed to the monk Buddhaghoṣa, who lived during the fourth and fifth centuries C.E., and who wrote many commentaries on Buddhist texts. He is best remembered by his work *The Path of Purification* (*Visuddhimagga*). Buddhaghosa's name literally means "voice of the Buddha," which was given to him after he became a monk. He represents the orthodoxy of post-canonical Buddhism. *The Expositor* is Buddhaghosa's commentary on the *Dhammasangani*, which is the initial book of the *Abhidhamma Piṭaka*. *The Expositor* claims that Abhidhamma literature surpasses the Dhamma (teaching) of the suttas (texts) because it presents the definitive classification of the elements of existence instead of the generally haphazard classifications of the suttas. The Abhidhamma is also superior because it is presented from the perspective of absolute truth, whereas the suttas are based on preaching from the standpoint of conventional truth. The importance of the selection of *The Expositor* for this chapter is Buddhaghosa's discussion of the central role of intention in Buddhist ethical behavior.

Selection from the *Sevitabbāsevitabbasutta* (Discourse on What Is to Be Followed and What Is Not to Be Followed)

Thus have I heard: At one time the Lord was staying near Sāvatthī in the Jeta Grove in Anāthapindika's monastery. While he was there, the Lord addressed the monks, saying: "Monks." "Revered One," they replied. The Lord spoke thus: "I will teach you a discourse on Dhamma about what is to be followed and what is not to be followed. Listen to it and pay careful attention to what I say." "Yes, revered sir," these monks replied. The Lord said:

"Monks, I say that bodily conduct is of two kinds, one of which is to be followed and the other which is not to be followed; and there is this disparity in bodily conduct. And I, monks, say that verbal conduct is either one or the other. Mental conduct is of two kinds, one of which is to be followed and the other which is not to be followed; and there is this disparity in verbal conduct . . . mental conduct. And I, monks, say that the arising of thought is of two kinds, one of which is to be followed and the other which is not to be followed; and there is this disparity in the arising of thought. And I, monks, say that the acquisition of perception . . . the acquisition of views . . . the acquisition of individuality is of two kinds, one of which is to be followed and the other which is not to be followed;

and there is this disparity in the acquisition of perception . . . the acquisition of views . . . the acquisition of individuality."

When this was said, the venerable Sāriputta said to the Lord: "Revered sir, I understand this to be the complete meaning of what the Lord uttered briefly, without explaining the entire meaning: 'I, monks, say that bodily conduct is of two kinds, one of which is to be followed and the other which is not to be followed; and there is disparity in bodily conduct.' The Lord said this. In reference to what was it said? Revered sir, if a certain kind of bodily conduct is followed and unwholesome mental states increase, wholesome mental states decrease, this kind of bodily conduct is not to be followed. Revered sir, if a certain kind of bodily conduct is followed and unwholesome mental states decrease, wholesome mental states increase, this kind of bodily conduct is to be followed.

"And what kind of bodily conduct, revered sir, does a person follow that unwholesome mental states increase in him, and wholesome mental states decrease? This is an example, revered sir, that someone kills creatures, is cruel, bloody-handed, intend on injuring and violence, merciless to living creatures. He takes what is not given; he steals the property of others in the village or jungle. He commits misconduct with regard to sense pleasures; he has sexual intercourse with females protected by their mothers, protected by the fathers, . . . the parents, . . . brothers, . . . sisters, . . . relations, husbands, those who are protected by law, and even with those adorned with the garlands of betrothal. If such bodily conduct is followed, revered sir, unwholesome mental states increase, and wholesome states of mind decrease.

"And what kind of bodily conduct, revered sir, does a man follow that unwholesome mental states decrease in him, and wholesome mental states increase? As to this, revered sir, someone, abandoning the killing of creatures, abstains from killing creatures; the rod and weapon discarded, he lives gently, kindly, and compassionately to all living creatures. Abandoning stealing, he abstains from stealing; he does not steal any property of another in village or jungle that is not given to him. Abandoning misconduct with respect to sense pleasures, he abstains from misconduct with regard to sense pleasures; he does not have sexual intercourse with females who are protected by their mothers . . . nor even with those adorned with the garlands of betrothal. If this kind of bodily conduct is followed, revered sir, unwholesome mental states decrease, and wholesome states of mind increase. When the Lord said: 'I, monks, say that bodily conduct is of two kinds, one of which is to be followed and the other which is not to be followed; and there is this disparity in bodily conduct,' it was said in reference to this.

" 'I, monks, say that, verbal conduct is of two kinds, one of which is to be followed and the other which is not to be followed; and there is in this disparity in verbal conduct.' The Lord said this. In reference to what was it said? Revered sir, if a certain kind of verbal conduct is followed and unskilled states of mind grow much, skilled states of mind decrease, this kind of verbal conduct is not to be followed. Revered sir, if a certain kind of verbal conduct is followed and unwholesome states of mind decrease, wholesome states of mind increase; this kind of verbal conduct is to be followed.

"And what kind of verbal conduct, revered sir, does a man follow that unwholesome states of mind grow much in him, wholesome states of mind decrease? As to this, revered sir, someone lies; when he is summoned to court, a meeting, amid relations, to a guild, or a royal family and questioned as a witness, and is asked: 'Now, my good man, say what you know,' although he does not know, he says, 'I do know,' and although he knows, he says, 'I do not know'; although he has not seen, he says, 'I saw,' and although he has seen, he says, 'I did not see.' Thus his speech represents intentional lying either for his own sake, for that of another, for the sake of some material gain, or other. And he is slanderous; having heard something at one place, he makes it known elsewhere, dividing people; or having heard something elsewhere he makes it known among these people for dividing them. In this way he creates discord among those who were in harmony or foments future discord among those who disagree. Discord is his pleasure, his delight, his joy, and motive of his speech. He speaks harshly. He utters speech that is rough, hard, harmful, abusive, bordering on anger, and not conducive to concentration. And he is a gossip, he speaks at a wrong time, not in accordance with fact, speaks about what is useless, contrary to Dhamma and discipline. He utters speech that is worthless, unreasonable, immoderate, and unbeneficial. If this kind of verbal conduct is followed, revered sir, unwholesome mental states increase, and wholesome states of mind decrease.

"And what kind of verbal conduct, revered sir, does a person follow that unwholesome mental states decrease in him, wholesome states of mind increase? As to this, revered sir, someone, abandoning false speech is restrained from false speech. When he is summoned and questioned as a witness before a council, company, relatives, a guild, or a royal family, and is told: 'Now, my good man, tell what you know,' if he does not, know he says, 'I do not know,' and if he knows he says, 'I know'; if he has not seen, he says, 'I did not see,' and if he has seen, he says, 'I saw.' Thus his speech is not intentional lying either for his own sake or for that of another, or for the sake of some material gain. Abandoning malicious speech, he is restrained from malicious speech. Having heard something at one place, he is not one to repeat it elsewhere for causing division among those people; or having heard something elsewhere he is not one to repeat it among these people for causing division among them. In this way he is a reconciler of those who disagree and one who unites those who are friends. Concord is his pleasure, delight, joy, and the motive of his speech. Abandoning harsh speech, he abstains from harsh speech. Whatever speech is gentle, pleasing to the ear, affectionate, going to the heart, urbane, pleasant to the many, and agreeable to the many, this is the type of speech that he utters. Abandoning gossip, he abstains from gossip. He is one that speaks at a right time, factually, about the goal, about Dhamma, and about discipline. He utters speech that is valuable, reasonable, purposeful, and beneficial. If this kind of verbal conduct is followed, revered sir, unwholesome mental states decrease, wholesome mental states increase. When the Lord said: 'I, monks, say that verbal conduct is of two kinds, one of which is to be followed and the other which is not to be followed; and there is this disparity in verbal conduct,' it was said in reference to this.

" 'I, monks, say that mental conduct is of two kinds, one of which is to be followed and the other which is not to be followed; and there is this disparity in mental conduct.' The Lord said this. In reference to what was it said? Revered sir, if a certain kind of mental conduct is followed and unwholesome mental states increase, and wholesome mental states decrease in one who follows that which should not be followed.

"And what kind of arising of thought, revered sir, does a man follow that unwholesome mental states decrease in him, wholesome states of mind increase? As to this, someone is not covetous and does not live with his thought given over to covetousness; he is not malevolent . . . he is not harmful and does not live with his thought given over to harmfulness. If this kind of arising of thought is followed, revered sir, unwholesome states of mind decrease, and wholesome states of mind increase. When the Lord said: 'I, monks, say that the arising of thought is of two kinds, one of which is to be followed and the other which is not to he followed; and there is this disparity in the arising of thought,' it was said in reference to this.

"And what kind of mental conduct, revered sir, does a man follow that unwholesome mental states increase in him, and wholesome mental states decrease? As to this, someone is covetous and lives with his mental conduct subject to covetousness; he is malevolent and lives with his mental conduct subject to malevolence; he is harmful and lives with his mental conduct subject to harmfulness. If this kind of assumption of mental conduct is followed, revered sir, unwholesome mental states increase, wholesome mental states decrease.

"And what kind of mental conduct, revered sir, does a man follow that unwholesome mental states decrease in him, and wholesome mental states increase? As to this, revered sir, someone is not covetous and does not live with his mental conduct subject to covetousness; he is not malevolent . . . he is not harmful and does not live with his mental conduct subject to harmfulness. If this kind of mental conduct is followed, unwholesome mental states decrease, and wholesome mental states increase. When the Lord said: 'I, monks, say that, the mental conduct is of two kinds, one of which is to be followed and the other which is not to be followed; and there is this disparity in mental conduct,' it was said in reference to this.

" 'I, monks, say that the acquisition of views is of two kinds, one of which is to be followed and the other which is not to be followed; and there is this disparity in the acquisition of views.' The Lord said this. In reference to what was it said? Revered sir, if a certain kind of acquisition of views is followed and . . . unwholesome states of mind decrease, wholesome mental states increase, this kind of acquisition of views is to be followed.

Source: *Sevitabbāsevitabbasutta* [Discourse on What is to be Followed and What is not to be Followed] in the *Majjhima Nikāya* [Middle Length Sayings], volume 3, edited by Robert Chalmers (London: Pali Text Society, 1899; reprint London: Luzac, 1960), 46–52.

Selections from *The Expositor* (*Attasālini*)

Volition is an act leading to deed. But that (apperceptional) consciousness is not usually spoken of as mind-door. (That is to say) because of the arising of (bodily) movement it does not go under the name of mind-door. The non-restraint here is that of the moving body. When such apperception arises, resulting in the movement of the vocal door, pure and simple, without the body-door, then the contact co-existent with that consciousness is mind-contact.

Volition is an act giving rise to speech. But that (apperceptional) consciousness is not usually called mind-door. Because of the arising of the movement (of the vocal organs) it does not go under the name of mind-door. The non-restraint here is that of speech. But when such apperceptive consciousness arises, without the aid of physical limbs and vocal organs, as pure mind-door, then the contact co-existent with that consciousness is mind-contact.

Volition is a mental act; that consciousness is the door of mental act. The non-restraint here is that of mind.

The doors of non-restraint of the eye, of the ear, of the nose, of the tongue, of the sensitive part of the body, of the motor-body, of speech and of mind, by virtue of these eight non-restraints, should be understood as the eight doors of non-restraint.

The eight "restraints" are those of the eye, the ear, the nose, the tongue, the skin, the moving body, speech and mind. In the ultimate sense they are five principles, namely: virtue, mindfulness, knowledge, patience and energy. None of these arises in conscious processes up to the end of the determination-moment, but only in the moment of apperception. Though arisen in apperception restraint is referred to the doors. The arising of all these restraints should be understood in the same way as by the method described in the case of non-restraints: "Contact co-existent with visual cognition is eye-contact," etc. Thus by virtue of these eight restraints, the door of the restraint of the eye and so on should he understood as the eight doors of restraint.

The ten courses of immoral action are life-taking, theft, wrong conduct in sensual pleasure, falsehood, calumnious speech, harsh speech, frivolous talk, covetousness, ill-will, wrong views.

Of these, "life-taking" means taking life quickly or by violence. Slaughtering or killing of beings is meant. "Life" here (literally breathing thing), in common parlance, means a being; in its ultimate sense, living force. And the term "life-taking" is applied to the bodily and vocal doors of one who is conscious that a being is living, and who produces an effort to out off the living force in that being. Among animals devoid of virtues, it is a slight misdeed in the case of a small creature, and a great misdeed in that of a large one. Why? Owing to the greatness of effort, and owing to the great size of the object, even though the effort may be the same. Among men, etc., they being capable of virtue, it entails a small misdeed in the case of a being of small virtue, and a great misdeed in that of a being of great virtue. And it should be understood that when physical virtues are equal, the sin is smaller or greater according as the corruptions and efforts (of the criminal) are weaker or stronger. There are five constituent factors in the crime of murder:— a being, consciousness of there being a living creature, intention of killing, effort and consequent death. And the six means of carrying out the effort are:—one's own hands, instigation, missiles, permanent devices, art and potency. As it will be too lengthy to treat of them here in detail, we shall pass over them as well as other explanations. . . .

"Theft" means the "taking of what is not given," the taking of what is another's property, robbery, or the state of being a thief is meant. Here not given applies to property possessed by another. A property concerning which another has arrived at the state of doing whatever he likes, without incurring punishment or blame, is said to belong to another. The intention of stealing, producing the effort to take something with the consciousness that it belongs to another is termed "theft." And that entails a small sin if what belongs to another is mean, and a great sin if it be of excellence. And why? Owing to the excellence of the object. If they are of equal value, stealing objects which belong to those distinguished for virtue entails a greater crime than the theft of objects belonging to one inferior in virtue. There are five constituent factors (in theft):—another's property, awareness that it is so, the thieving mind, effort, and consequent removal—and six means;—taking with one's own hands, etc. One or other of these means may be carried out according to circumstances, in stealing by false measures and weights, by force, by concealment, by design or by forgery. This is an outlined account of theft. . . .

In the expression "wrong conduct in sensual pleasures," in "sensual pleasures" means "in matters of sexual intercourse"; "wrong conduct" means "base and truly blameworthy conduct." The characteristic of "wrong conduct in sensual pleasures" is the volition arising in the body-door, through the unlawful intention of trespassing upon a person to whom one has no right of going. Herein persons to whom men have no right to go are (a) ten classes of unmarried women:—a woman under the guardianship (1) of her mother, (2) of her father, (3) of her parents, (4) of her brother, (5) of her sister, (6) of her relations, (7) of her clan, (8) of her spiritual guide, (9) a woman under an engagement and (10) a woman undergoing punishment; and (b) ten classes of married women, namely: (1) one bought by wealth, (2) one who becomes a wife through her free-will, or (3) through love of property, or (4) of clothes, (5) one lawfully wedded by parents after the ceremony of dipping the hands of the couple in a bowl of water, (6) one who is taken from the poorer classes, (7) a slave-wife, (8) a servant-wife, (9) a wife captured in war and (10) a mistress kept for a time.

Of these a woman under an engagement and one under punishment together with (b) the latter ten:—these twelve it is not allowable for other men to approach. And the sin is smaller or greater according as the forbidden object is devoid of or endowed with virtues, such as the precepts. There are four constituent factors of this crime: the mind to enjoy the forbidden object, the effort to enjoy, devices to obtain, and possession. And only one means: personal experience.

"Lying" is applied to the effort of the body and speech, on the part of one who is deceitful, to destroy the good of others. The volition setting up the bodily and vocal effort to deceive, with the intention of cheating others, is termed "false speech." Another definition:—"lying" is applied to a thing which is not genuine or does not exist, and "speech" means the representation of that as real, true. The characteristic of "lying speech or falsehood" is the volition of one desirous of representing to others an untrue thing as true, which sets up a corresponding intimation. It is more or less an offence according as the welfare destroyed is greater or smaller. Or to put it in another way: It is a small offence in laymen if they tell an untruth:—"I have it not"—out of a desire not to give something belonging to themselves; and a great offence if they, as witnesses, perjure themselves in order to cause loss (to others). In recluses it is a small offence if, by way of an ironical joke, on getting but little oil or butter, they say:—"To-day, methinks, a river of oil flows in the village." It is, however, a great offence in those who say that they have seen something which they have not. There are four constituent factors of this [offence]: an untrue thing, intention to deceive, corresponding effort, the communication of the matter to others. There is only one means: personal action; and that should be understood as the act of deceiving others either by body, or by something connected with the body, or by speech. If by that act another knows that meaning, the volition producing that action is at that moment bound up with the act of lying. In the same way, as one deceives another by deed, by something connected therewith, or by speech, so a person who instigates another, "Say thus to him," or who lays a written leaf before another, or who records a permanent writing on walls, etc., to this effect, "This meaning should be understood thus," equally deceives others. Therefore it is reasonable to assume that instigation, transmission and permanent records are also involved in this form of immorality. But as the Commentaries have not admitted this, it should be adopted only after a critical examination.

"Slander" means calumnious speech which, by being said to another, reduces to nothing the love which that person, or the speaker bears at his own heart to a third person.

A word which makes one's self harsh, or causes another to be harsh, is in itself harsh, neither agreeable to the ear nor appealing to the heart. Such a word is termed "abuse."

"Frivolous talk" is speaking senseless, useless things. The volition which is at the root of all speech of this sort, and is named calumnious, etc., is here alone to be understood. The volition of one with a corrupt mind, producing the bodily and vocal effort to sow the seed of discord among others, or to endear oneself to others is termed the volition of calumnious speech. It is a smaller or greater offence, according as the virtue of the person whom he separates is smaller or greater. There are four constituent factors of this crime: (1) Other persons to be divided; (2) the purpose: "they will be separated," or the desire to endear oneself to another: "I shall become dear and intimate"; (3) the corresponding effort; (4) the communication. But when there is no rupture among others, the offence does not amount to a complete course; it does so only when there is a rupture.

By "harsh speech" is meant the entirely harsh volition, which produces a bodily and vocal effort, stabbing another as with a mortal wound. The following story is an illustration: It is related that a certain boy, without listening to his mother's word, went to a forest. The mother, being unable to prevent him, cursed him, saying, "May a wild she-buffalo chase thee!" And accordingly a she-buffalo appeared in the forest. The boy made an asseveration of truth, "May what my mother said happen not; what she thought in her mind, may that happen!" The buffalo stood as if there transfixed. Thus though her vocal effort was mortally wounding, yet her speech was not really harsh, because of her tender heart. For though parents sometimes say thus to their children: "May thieves cut you up into pieces!" yet they do not wish even a lotus leaf to fall on them. Teachers and spiritual guides sometimes say of their pupils: "What are we to do with these shameless, reckless lads? Turn them out!" and yet they wish that they may attain and accomplish. But as words are not harsh if the heart be tender, so are they not gentle, just because speech is soft. The words of one desirous of killing: "Let him sleep in comfort!" are not soft; because of the harshness of thought the words are harsh. Harsh speech is proportionate to the virtue of one concerning whom harsh words are spoken. The three constituent factors of this offence are: Another to be abused, angry thought, and the abuse.

Immoral volition producing the bodily and vocal effort to communicate useless things, is termed "frivolous talk." Its offence is great or small according as it is practiced repeatedly or not. The two constituent factors of this offence are: the inclination towards useless talk—like the stories of the fight of the Bhāratas and of the abduction of Sītā, etc.—and the narration of such themes. But the offence does not run through the full course of action when others do not accept the story; it does so only when they accept it.

"Covetousness" means coveting: a process of inclining towards another's property when confronted with it. It has the characteristic mark of thinking, 'Ah! would this were mine!' As offence it is small or great as in the case of theft. Its two constituent factors are: Another's property, and the bending over of oneself. Though greed for an object which is another's property has arisen, it does not receive the distinction of being a full course of action so long as one does not bend over to it saying, "Ah, would this were mine!"

That which destroys welfare and happiness is "ill-will." It has the characteristic mark of the mental fault of injury to others. The degree of offence is as in the case of harsh speech. Its two constituent factors are: another being, and the thought of doing harm. Mere anger with another being does not reach that distinctive stage of the course of action, so long as there is no destructive thought, such as: "Would he were out off and destroyed!"

"Wrong view" is that which sees wrongly by not taking the right view. It has the characteristic of perverted views, such as: "There is no [use in a] gift." And the offence is small or great as in the case of frivolous talk, or according as the wrong view is of a temporary or permanent character. Its two constituent factors are: perversion of the manner in which an object should be taken, and its manifestation according to the contrary view held of it. Here the distinctive stage of the course of action is reached by the views: (1) there is no *result* (in a moral act); (2) there are no *causes* (in happening); (3) there is no such thing as (moral) *action*, and not by other view.

As regards these ten courses of immoral action, we may come to decisions respecting them under five aspects, to wit: (1) as ultimate psychological factors, (2) as groups, (3) as objects, (4) as feelings and (5) as roots. (1) The first seven in order out of the courses of action are volitions only; the three beginning with covetousness are factors associated with volition. (2) The first seven and wrong view—those eight are courses of action, not roots. But covetousness and ill-will are both courses of action and roots. Covetousness as a root is the immoral root of greed, ill-will as a root is the immoral root of hate. (3) Life-taking has a conditioned thing for object, from its having the life-force as object. Theft has a living being or a thing for object. Wrong conduct has a conditioned thing for object by virtue of touch, or, as some say, a living being. Falsehood has either a living being or a conditioned thing for object. So has calumnious speech. Harsh speech has only a living being for object. Frivolous talk has either a living being or a conditioned thing for object by way of things seen, heard, felt and thought. So has covetousness. Ill-will has a living being for object, and wrong views have for object a conditioned thing in the three planes of existence. (4) Life-taking is associated with a painful feeling. For although kings on seeing a thief may say, laughing, "Go, kill him," the volition of decision is associated with pain only. Theft may be associated with the three kinds of feeling. He who on seeing another's property takes it with delight has a pleasurable feeling; if he steals it with fright, his feeling is painful; likewise if he does so while he reflects on the consequent fruits. If he takes it with indifference, the feeling is neutral. Wrong conduct is associated with two kinds of feeling, pleasurable and neutral; but in the thought of decision there is no neutral feeling. Falsehood has all three kinds of feeling as with theft; likewise calumnious speech. Harsh speech is associated with a painful feeling; frivolous talk has all three kinds of feeling. To illustrate:—When the story of the abduction of Sītā, or of the fight of the Bhāratas, etc., is recited, and (the hearers applaud him and throw up their turbans, etc., there is to the performer a delighted pleasurable feeling. When one who has thus rewarded him comes up later and says: "Tell us from the beginning," the narrator is displeased at the idea and thinks: "Shall I say something irrelevant and miscellaneous or not?" In such a case there is a painful feeling at the time of reciting; if he is indifferent during the recital, then there is a neutral feeling. Covetousness has two feelings, pleasurable and neutral; likewise wrong views. Ill-will has a painful feeling. (5) Life-taking has two roots by virtue of hate and delusion; theft has also two by virtue of hate and delusion or of greed and delusion; wrong conduct also has two by virtue of greed and delusion; likewise falsehood by virtue of either hate and delusion or greed and delusion; likewise calumnious speech and frivolous talk. Harsh speech by virtue of hate and delusion, and covetousness by virtue of delusion, have a single root; likewise ill-will. Wrong view has a double root by virtue of greed and delusion.

Here ends the Discourse on the Courses of Immoral Action.

Courses of Moral Action

The ten courses of moral action are:—abstinence from life-taking, etc., and disinterestedness, good-will and right views.

Of these, life-taking, etc., have been explained. "Abstinence" is that by which people abstain from life-taking, etc.; or that which itself abstains; or that which is the mere abstaining. In the passage where it says:—"That avoidance and abstinence from life-taking that there is, at that time, in one who abstains from taking life"—that abstinence which is associated with moral consciousness is threefold: (1) [in spite of] opportunity obtained, (2) because of observance, (3) eradication.

(1) When they who have not undertaken to observe any particular precept, but who, reflecting on their own birth, age, experience, etc, and saying, "It is not fit for us to do such a bad thing," do not transgress concerning an object actually met with, the abstinence is to be considered as "in spite of opportunity," like that of Cakkana, a lay-disciple in Ceylon. It is said that when he was young his mother

suffered from a disease and the doctor recommended fresh hare-flesh. Cakkana's brother then said to him, "Go, dear, roam the field," and sent him. He went there, and at that time a hare came to eat the tender crops. On seeing him it ran with speed, and was caught in the creepers, making the cry kiri! kiri! Cakkana went after the sound, caught, the hare and thought, "I shall make a medicine for mother." Again he thought, "It is not proper that for the sake of my mother's life I should take the life of another." He then freed the hare, saying, "Go, enjoy grass and water with other hares in the jungle," and when asked by the brother, "Well, dear, did you get a hare?" he told him what had happened, for that his brother scolded him. But he went to the mother's presence and stood averring a truth: "Since I was born, I declare that I have not intentionally taken the life of any creature." And straightway the mother recovered.

(2) The abstinence of those who have observed the precepts, both during and after the time-limit, without transgressing against the object even on pain of death, is to be considered as "by way of observance," like that of the lay-disciple dwelling in the mountain Uttaravaḍḍhamāna: It is said that, after taking the precepts in the presence of the Elder Piṅgalabuddharakkhita, who dwelt in the Ambariya monastery, he was ploughing his field. His ox got lost. While looking for it he ascended the Uttaravaḍḍhamāna mountain, where a great serpent seized him. He thought, "I will cut off its head with my sharp axe." Again he thought, "It is not proper that I, who have taken the precepts from my teacher of culture, should break them." And for the third time he thought, "I will sacrifice my life, but not the precepts," and threw away in the forest the sharp axe with its shaft from his shoulder. Immediately the boa-constrictor released him and went away.

(3) Abstinence "by way of eradication" should be understood as that associated with the Ariyan Path. When that Path has once arisen, not even the thought, "we will kill a creature," arises in Ariyans. Now, as with immoral states, so with those that are moral, there are five aspects under which decisions respecting them may be reached—namely, (1) as ultimate psychological factors, (2) as groups, (3) as objects, (4) as feeling and (5) as roots.

(1) Of the ten, the first seven are fit to be called volitions as well as abstinences; the last three are factors associated with volition.

(2) The first seven are courses of action and not roots; the last three are courses of action and roots. Disinterestedness, good-will and right view as roots become the moral roots: the opposites of greed, hate and delusion.

(3) These are the same as those of life-taking, etc. For abstention is from (the transgression against) the object be transgressed against. As the Ariyan Path with

nibbāna as its object abandons the corruptions, so these courses of action, having the faculty of life, etc., as their object, abandon the wickedness of life-taking and so forth.

(4) All are pleasurable feeling or neutral feeling, for with the attainment of good there is no painful feeling.

(5) The (first) seven are threefold, namely, disinterestedness, love, intelligence, in one abstaining with a consciousness associated with knowledge; twofold in one abstaining with a consciousness dissociated from knowledge. Disinterestedness is twofold in one abstaining with a consciousness associated with knowledge, and single when consciousness is dissociated from knowledge. Disinterestedness by itself is not its own root. Nor is good-will. Right view is twofold, as disinterestedness and as love. These are the ten courses of moral action.

Conclusions

To the foregoing discussion should be added a consideration of courses of action in connection with self-restraint, etc. Want of self-restraint arisen through the five doors of contact is an immoral mental act. That which has arisen through mind, the door of internal contact, is threefold in action. For when movement of the body-door is reached, it is an immoral act of body; when that of the vocal door is reached, it is an immoral act of speech. When movement of neither is reached, it is an immoral act of thought.

Want of self-restraint which has arisen through the five doors is also only an immoral act of body; that which has arisen through the unrestrained door of the moving body is only an immoral act of body; that which has arisen by the door of speech or by the door of mind is only an immoral act of speech or of thought respectively. The threefold misconduct of body is only an immoral act of body; the fourfold misconduct of speech is only an immoral act of speech; the threefold misconduct of mind is only an immoral act of thought.

Self-restraint, which has arisen through the five doors of (external) contact, is only a moral act of thought; if it has arisen through the door of mental contact, it is threefold in action, as in the case of non-restraint. Self-restraint arisen through the five doors is only a moral act of thought; if it has arisen by the door of the moving body, or through the door of speech, or through the door of mind, it is only a moral act of body, speech, or thought respectively.

Threefold good conduct of body is a moral act; fourfold good conduct of speech is a moral act of speech; threefold good conduct of mind is a moral act of thought.

An immoral act of body does not arise through the five doors of (external) contact, but through the door of mind-contact only; similarly with an immoral act of speech. But an immoral act of thought arises through the six doors of contact. If it results in movement in body and vocal doors, it is an immoral act of body and of speech; not attaining such movement, it is an immoral act of thought. As it does not arise through the contact-door, no immoral act of body takes place through the five unrestrained doors. But it arises through the unrestrained doors of the moving body and the moving vocal organ; it does not arise through the unrestrained door of mind. Nor does an immoral act of speech arise through the five doors when unrestrained; it arises through the door of the moving body when unrestrained and the moving vocal organ; it does not arise through the unrestrained door of mind.

An immoral act of thought arises even through eight unrestrained doors; and the same method holds in moral acts of body, etc., but with this difference:— Immoral acts of body and of speech do not arise through the unrestrained door of mind, but these are not so; without moving bodily limbs or vocal organs, they arise in the self-restrained door of the mind of one who is taking the precepts.

In such a case moral consciousness in the realm of sense arises through the threefold door of action, and not through the fire (external) sense-doors. The feeling, pleasurable, painful, or neutral, is conditioned by eye-contact. It does so by means of the six doors of contact, but not through the eight doors when unrestrained; it arises through the eight doors when restrained; it does not arise through the ten courses of immoral action; it arises through the ten courses of moral action. Therefore, whether this (first main type of moral) consciousness has arisen through the doors of threefold action, or through the six doors of contact, or through the eight restraint-doors, or the ten courses of moral action, it was said with reference to all classes of sensuous consciousness that "the sensuous moral consciousness that has arisen has either a visible or an audible object, etc., or an idea for its object."

Here ends the Discourse on "Doors."

Source: *The Expositor* (*Attasālinī*), volume 1, translated by Pe Maung Tin (London: Oxford University Press, 1920; reprint London: Luzac, 1958), 126–140.

9

Monastic Life and Regulations

Unlike the historical Jesus, the Buddha insisted on a monastic lifestyle and permanent organization, although the organization evolved slowly over a period of time. The Buddhist monastery was a voluntary association entered into freely by males and later by females. The monastery was united by a confession of faith embodied by the *Pāṭimokkha,* which summarized the rules of the order. It was by adhering to these rules that monks and nuns agreed to live and conduct their monastic life. These rules were chanted periodically by members, and the chanting functioned as a bond of monastic unity. When a member broke a rule it was necessary for that person to confess his or her transgression and to atone for it by various means, assuming that the violation was not serious enough to require immediate expulsion.

In addition to the bond that it created among members, the monastic rules also functioned to protect the purity of the order along with that of its individual monks and nuns. The rules also operated as a refuge from the sensual enticements of the world. Moreover, the rules provided a general structure and behavioral guideline for the monastic order. The various monastic rules can be understood as an attempt to guide and transform committed individuals rather than as an attempt to change society. Finally, the monastic rules were not divine commandments; they were, however, authoritative because they were based on the instructions of the Buddha.

From a historical perspective, the monastic rules grew over a period of time in response to new situations. Some of the selections in this chapter give the circumstances of a problem. After a problem arose for which there was no monastic rule, monks would approach the Buddha for his wise counsel and adjudication of the matter. This pattern worked well during the life of the Buddha, but after his death, surviving monks and nuns relied on Dhamma (teachings), another form of refuge.

The examples of monastic regulations selected for this chapter provide evidence that sexual matters were extremely important. A major reason for their importance was the Buddha's insistence on celibacy as the foundation of the order. Examples of issues like theft and killing are also included because of their central place in Buddhist ethics. Finally, violations with respect to false claims about spiritual attainments are included because theses rules attempted to protect the order from charlatans and deceivers.

Selections from the *Book of Discipline*

Examples of Sexual Regulations

Then these monks, having rebuked the venerable Sudinna in various ways, told this matter to the lord. And the lord for this reason, in this connection, having had the company of monks convened, questioned the venerable Sudinna, saying:

"Is it true, as is said, Sudinna, that you indulged in sexual intercourse with your former wife?"

"It is true, lord," he said.

The enlightened one, the lord, rebuked him, saying:

"It is not fit, foolish man, it is not becoming, it is not proper, it is unworthy of a recluse, it is not lawful, it ought not to be done. How is that you, foolish man, having gone forth under this Dhamma and discipline which are well taught, are not able for your lifetime to lead the Brahma-life which is complete and wholly purified? How can you strive, foolish man, while Dhamma is taught by me in various ways for the sake of passionlessness . . . foolish man, by me for the sake of passionlessness. Foolish man, is not Dhamma taught by me in various ways for the waning of passion . . . the destruction of pleasures of the senses . . . the allaying of the fever of the pleasures of the senses been declared? It were better for you, foolish man, that your male organ should enter the mouth of a terrible and poisonous snake, than that it should enter a woman. It were better for you, foolish man that your male organ should enter the mouth of a black snake, than that it should enter a woman. It were better for you foolish man, that your male organ should enter a charcoal pit burning, ablaze, afire, than that it should enter a woman. What is the cause for this? For *that* reason, foolish man, you would go to death, or to suffering like unto death, but not on that account would you pass at the breaking up of the body after death to the waste, the bad bourn, the abyss, hell. But for *this* reason, foolish man, at the breaking up of the body after death, you would pass to the waste, the bad bourn, the abyss, hell. Thus for this very deed, foolish man, you will enter upon what is not verily Dhamma, upon village Dhamma, upon a low Dhamma, upon wickedness, upon final ablution, upon secrecy, upon having obtained in couples. Foolish man, you are the first-doer of many wrong things. It is not, foolish man, for the benefit of unbelievers, nor for the increase in the number of believers, but, foolish man, it is to the detriment of both unbelievers and believers, and it causes wavering in some."

Then the lord, having rebuked the venerable Sudinna in various ways, and having spoken in dispraise of his difficulty in supporting and maintaining himself, of his arrogance, of his lack of contentment, of his clinging (to the obstructions) and of his indolence; and having spoken in various ways of the ease of supporting and maintaining oneself, of desiring little, of contentment, of expunging (evil), of punctiliousness, of what is gracious, of decreasing (the obstructions) and of the putting forth of energy, and having given suitable and befitting talk on Dhamma to the monks, he addressed the monks, saying:

"On account of this, monks, I will make known the course of training for monks, founded on ten reasons: for the excellence of the Order, for the comfort of the Order, for the restraint of evil-minded men, for the ease of well-behaved monks, for the restraint of the cankers belonging to the here and now, for the combating of the cankers belonging to other worlds, for the benefit of non-believers, for the increase in the number of believers, for establishing Dhamma indeed, for following the rules of restraint. Thus, monks, this course of training should be set forth:

Whatever monk should indulge in sexual intercourse is one who is defeated, he is no longer in communion."

And thus this course of training for the monks was set forth by the lord.

Now at that time a certain monk in the Great Wood at Vesālī, on account of his lust kept a female monkey. Then this monk, rising early and taking his bowl and robe, entered Vesālī for alms. Now at that time a large concourse of monks, who were engaged in touring for lodgings, came up to this monk's vihāra. The female monkey, seeing these monks coming from afar, went up to them and postured before them. Then these monks thought: "Undoubtedly this monk has committed fornication," and they hid themselves to one side. Then this monk, when he had gone about Vesālī for alms, returned with his almsfood, and eating half gave the other half to the female monkey. And there was some misbehavior. Then those monks said to that monk:

"Surely the course of training has been made known by the lord, your reverence? Why do you commit fornication, your reverence?"

"It is true, your reverences, that the course of training was made known by the lord, but it refers to the human woman and not to the female animal."

"But surely, your reverence, it refers just as much to that. It is not fit, your reverence, it is not suitable, it is not becoming, it is not worthy of a recluse, it is not lawful, it ought not to he done. How it is that you, your reverence, having gone forth under this Dhamma and discipline which are well taught, are not able to lead for your life-time the Brahma-life, complete and wholly purified? Has not, your reverence, Dhamma been taught in various ways by the lord for the sake of passionlessness and not for the sake of passion . . . and the allaying of the fever of the pleasures of the senses been declared? It is not, your reverence, for the benefit of non-believers . . . and it causes wavering in some."

Then these monks, having rebuked this monk in various ways, told this matter to the lord. And the lord for this reason and in this connection, having the company of monks convened, questioned this monk thus:

"Is it true, as is said, monk, that you committed fornication?"

"It is true, lord," he said.

Then the lord rebuked him, saying . . . It is not, foolish man, for the benefit of non-believers. . . . Monks, thus this course of training should be set forth:

Whatever monk should indulge in sexual intercourse even with an animal is one who is defeated, he is not in communion."

And thus this course of training for monks was made known by the lord.

Now at that time, a great company of monks, dwellers at Vesālī and sons of the Vajjins, ate as much as they liked, drank as much as they liked and bathed as much as they liked. Having eaten, drunk and bathed as much as they liked, not having paid attention to the training, but, not having disavowed it, they indulged in sexual intercourse not having declared their weakness. These, in the course of time being affected by misfortune to their relatives, being affected by misfortune to their wealth, being affected by the misfortune of disease, approaching the venerable Ānanda, spoke thus to him:

"Honored Ānanda, we are not abusers of the enlightened one, we are not abusers of Dhamma, we are not abusers of the Order. Honored Ānanda, we are self-abusers, not abusers of others. Indeed we are unlucky, we are of little merit, for we, having gone forth under this Dhamma and discipline which are well taught, are not able for our life-time to lead the Brahma-life, complete and wholly purified. Even now, honored Ānanda, if we might receive the pabbajjā, ordination in the presence of the lord, if we might receive the upasampadā ordination, then contemplating, we would dwell continuously intent upon states which are good, and upon making to become the states belonging to enlightenment. It were good, honored Ānanda, that you should explain this matter to the lord."

"Very well, your reverences," he said. And the venerable Ānanda having answered the dwellers in Vesālī, the sons of the Vajjins, went up to the lord. And, having come up to him, he told this matter to the lord.

"It is impossible, Ānanda, it cannot come to pass, that the tathāgata should abolish the teaching on defeat which has been made known for the disciples, because of the deeds of the Vajjins or the sons of the Vajjins."

Then the lord for this reason, in this connection, having given talk on Dhamma, addressed the monks thus:

"Monks, whatever monk should come, without having disavowed the training, without declaring his weakness, and indulge in sexual intercourse, he should not receive the upasampadā ordination. But, monks, if one comes, disavowing the training and declaring his weakness, yet indulging in sexual intercourse, he should receive the upasampadā ordination. And thus, monks, this course of training should be set forth:

Whatever monk, possessed of the training and mode of life for monks, but not disavowing the training and not declaring his weakness, should indulge in sexual intercourse, even with an animal, is one who is defeated, he is not in communion."

Whatever means: he who, on account of his relations, on account of his social standing, on account of his name, on account of his clan, on account of his morals, on account of his dwelling, on account of his field (of activity), an elder or a novice or one of middle standing:—this is called *whatever.*

Monk means: he is a monk because he is a beggar for alms, a monk because he submits to wandering for alms, a monk because he is one who wears the patchwork cloth, a monk by the designation (of others), a monk on account of his acknowledgment; a monk is called "Come, monk," a monk is endowed with going to the three refuges, a monk is auspicious, a monk is the essential, a monk is a learner, a monk is an adept, a monk means one, who is endowed with harmony for the Order, with the resolution at which the motion is put three times and then followed by the decision, with actions (in accordance with Dhamma and the discipline), with steadfastness, with the attributes of a man perfected. Whatever monk is endowed with harmony for the Order, with the resolution at which the motion is put three times, and then followed by the decision, with actions (in accordance with Dhamma and the discipline), with steadfastness and the attributes of a man perfected, this one is a monk as understood in this meaning. . . .

Three kinds of females: human women, non-human females, female animals. Three kinds of hermaphrodites: human hermaphrodites, non-human hermaphrodites, animal hermaphrodites. Three kinds of eunuchs: human eunuchs, non-human eunuchs, animal eunuchs. Three kinds of males: human males, non-human males, animal males. There is an offence involving defeat if he commits sexual intercourse with human women in three ways. Also with non-human women and with female animals. Also with human, non-human and animal hermaphrodites. There is an offence involving defeat for a human eunuch if he commits sexual intercourse in two ways. Also non-human and animal eunuchs. There is an offence involving defeat for human males, non-human males and male animals if they commit sexual intercourse in these two ways. . . .

Now at that time a certain monk, in the Gabled Hall in the Great Wood at Vesālī for his day-sojourn, was lying down having opened the door. All his limbs were stiff with pains. Now at that time a large company of women, bringing scents and garlands, came to the park looking at the vihāra. Then these women seeing that monk, sat down on him, and having taken their pleasure and saying: "Isn't he a bull of a man?" departed, piling up their scents and garlands. The monks, seeing the moisture, told this matter to the lord. He said, ". . . Monks, there is no offence for this monk. I allow you, monks, when you are in seclusion for meditation during the day, to meditate in seclusion, having closed the door."

Now at that time a certain monk of Bharukaccha, having dreamed that he committed sexual intercourse with his former wife, said: "I am not a (true) recluse, I will leave the Order," and going to Bharukaccha, and seeing the venerable Upāli on the road, he told him this matter. The venerable Upāli said: "There is no offence, your reverence, since it was in a dream."

Now at that time in Rājagaha there was a female lay-follower, called Supabbā, who believed in the enlightened one. She held this view: whatever (woman) gives sexual intercourse, gives the highest gift. Seeing a monk she spoke thus: "Come, honored sir, indulge in sexual intercourse."

"Not so, sister, it is not fitting," he said.

"Come, honored sir, (only) touch the region of the breasts, thus there will be no offence for you. . . . Come, honored sir, (only) touch the navel . . . the stomach . . . the waist . . . the throat . . . the ear . . . the coil of hair . . . the spaces between the fingers. . . . Come, honored sir, approaching (me only) with (your) hands, I will make you function, thus there will be no offence for you." The monk acted accordingly. On account of this he was remorseful. "Monk, there is no offence involving defeat; there is an offence entailing a formal meeting of the Order."

Now at that time at Sāvatthī was a female lay-disciple, called Saddhā, who believed in the enlightened one. She held this view: whatever (woman) gives sexual intercourse, gives the highest gift. Seeing a monk, she spoke thus: "Come, honored sir, indulge in sexual intercourse."

"Not so, sister, it is not fitting."

"Come, honored sir, touch the region of the breasts. . . . Come, honored sir, approaching (me only) with (your) hands, I will make you function, thus there will be no offence for you." The monk acted accordingly. On account of this he was remorseful. "Monk, there is no offence involving defeat, there is an offence entailing a formal meeting of the Order."

Examples of Theft

People became annoyed, vexed and angry, saying: "These recluses, sons of the Sakyans, are shameless, of bad conduct, liars. And they pretend to be followers of Dhamma, followers of tranquillity, followers of the Brahma-life, speakers of truth, those who are virtuous, of good conduct. There, is no recluseship among these, there is no brahmanhood among these; recluseship is lost among these, brahmanhood is lost among these. Where is recluseship among these? Where is brahmanhood among these? These have destroyed recluseship, these have destroyed brahmanhood. If these deceive the king, how much more then do other people?"

Monks heard these people who were annoyed, vexed and angry. Those who were modest, happy monks, conscientious, scrupulous, anxious for training, became annoyed, vexed, angry and said: "How can the venerable Dhaniya, the potter's son, take pieces of wood belonging to the king when they have not been given (to him)?" Then these monks told this matter to the lord. And the lord, on that occasion, in this connection, having the company of monks convened, questioned the venerable Dhaniya, the potter's son, saying:

"Is it true, as is said, Dhaniya, that you have taken pieces of wood belonging to the king when they were not given (to you)?"

"It is true, lord." . . .

Then the lord, blaming the venerable Dhaniya, the potter's son, in several ways for his difficulty in behaving himself . . ." Thus, monks, this course of training should be set forth:

"Whatever monk should take by means of theft what has not been given to him, in such manner of taking as kings, catching a thief in the act of stealing, would flog him or imprison him or banish him, saying: 'You are a robber, you are foolish, you are wrong, you are a thief,'—even so a monk, taking what is not given him, is also one who is defeated, he is not in communion." . . .

At one time, a certain monk, putting down his robe on a chair . . . his mat on a chair . . . putting down his bowl under the chair, entered the vihāra. A certain monk, saying: "Do not let the bowl be lost," put it aside. Having come out, he asked the monks: "Your reverences, who has stolen my bowl?" He said: "I have stolen it." He seized him . . . "your way of speaking."

At one time a certain nun, having spread out her robe on a fence, entered the vihāra. A certain nun, saying: "Do not let this robe be lost," put it aside. Having come out, she asked the nuns: "Ladies, who has stolen my robe?" She said: "I have stolen it." She seized her and said: "You are not a (true) woman recluse." On account of this she was remorseful. This nun told this matter to the nuns. The nuns told this matter to the monks. The monks told this matter to the lord. . . . "There is no offence, monks, because of her way of speaking."

At that time a certain monk seeing a cloak blown up during a whirlwind, took hold of it, saying: "I will give it to the owners." The owners reprimanded the monk, saying: "You are not a (true) recluse." On account of this he was remorseful. . . . "Of what were you thinking, monk?"

"I did not intend to steal it, lord," he said.

"Monk, there is no offence as you did not intend to steal."

At one time a certain monk intending to steal, laid hold of a turban which had been blown into the air during a whirlwind, "before the owners see." The owners reprimanded the monk, saying: "You are not a (true) recluse." Because of this he was remorseful. . . . "You, monk, have fallen into an offence involving defeat."

At one time a certain monk going to the cemetery took hold of rags taken from the dust-heap, which were on a body not (yet) decomposed. And the departed one was dwelling in this body. Then the departed one said to the monk: "Honored sir, do not take hold of my cloak." The monk, unheeding, went away. Then the body, arising, followed closely on the heels of the monk. Then the monk, entering the vihāra, closed the door. Then the body fell down at that very place. On account of this he was remorseful. . . . "Monk, there is no offence involving defeat. (But) a monk should not take rags from the dust-heap (which are) on a body not (yet) decomposed. Whoever should take them: this is an offence of wrong-doing."

Examples of Regulations about Killing

And some people were angry and said, ". . . these have departed from brahman-hood. These praised the beauty of death to the lay-follower; by these the lay-follower has been killed."

The monks heard these people who were annoyed, vexed and angry. Those who were modest monks were annoyed vexed, angry, and said: "How could the group of six monks praise the beauty of death to the lay-follower?" Then these monks told this matter to the lord. . . .

"Is it true, as is said, monks, that you praised the beauty of death to the lay-follower?" he said.

"It is true, lord," they said.

The enlightened one, the lord, rebuked them, saying: "Foolish men, it is not becoming, it is not seemly, it is not suitable, it is not worthy of a recluse, it is not right, it should not be done. Why did you, foolish men, praise the beauty of death to the lay-follower? Foolish men, this is not for the benefit of non-believers. . . . And thus, monks, this course of training should be set forth:

"Whatever monk should intentionally deprive a human being of life or should look about so as to be his knife-bringer, or should praise the beauty of death, or should incite (anyone) to death, saying, 'Hello there, my man, of what use to you is this evil, difficult life? Death is better for you than life,' or who should deliberately and purposefully in various ways praise the beauty of death or should incite (anyone) to death: he also is one who is defeated, he is not in communion." . . .

At one time a certain monk who was on his alms-round, receiving poisoned alms-food and bringing it back, on his return gave a first-taste to the monks. These died. He was remorseful. . . . "Of what were you thinking, monk?" he said.

"I did not know, lord," he said.

"There is no offence, monk, since you did not know," he said.

At one time a certain monk gave poison to a certain monk, intending to test it. This monk died. He was remorseful. . . . "Of what were you thinking, monk?" he said.

"I intended to test it, lord," he said.

"There is no offence involving defeat, monk; there is a grave offence," he said.

At one time the monks of Āḷavī were making a site for a vihāra. A certain monk being below, lifted up his head, and a stone badly held by a monk who was above, hit the monk who was below on the head, and that monk died. He was remorseful. . . . "There is no offence, monk, as it was unintentional," he said.

At one time the monks of Āḷavī were making a site for a vihāra. A certain monk being below, lifted up a stone. A monk who was above, intending to kill the one who was below, let loose the stone at his head. That monk died . . . that monk did not die. He was remorseful. . . . "There is no offence involving defeat, monk; there is a grave offence," he said.

At one time the monks of Āḷavī were erecting a wall for the vihāra. A certain monk, being below, lifted up a burnt brick, and the burnt brick being badly held by a monk who was above, fell on the head of the monk who was below. He died. He was remorseful. . . . "There is no offence, monk, since it was unintentional."

At one time the monks of Āḷavī were erecting a wall for the vihāra. A certain monk, being below, lifted up a burnt brick. A monk who was above, intending to cause the death of the monk who was below, let loose the burnt brick at his head. That monk died . . . that monk did not die. He was remorseful. . . . "There is no offence involving defeat, monk, but there is a grave offence." . . .

At one time a certain monk was ill. The monks anointed him with oil. This monk died. "There is a grave offence," he said.

At one time a certain monk was ill. The monks made him get up. This monk died. . . . "There is a grave offence," he said.

At one time a certain monk was ill. The monks made him lie down. This monk died. . . . "There is a grave offence," he said.

At one time a certain monk was ill. The monks gave him food . . . they gave him drink. This monk died. . . . "There is a grave offence," he said.

At one time a certain woman whose husband was living away from home became with child by a lover. She said to a monk who was dependent for alms on (her) family: "Look here, master, find me an abortive preparation."

"All right, sister," he said, and he gave her an abortive preparation. The child died. He was remorseful. . . . "You, monk, have fallen into an offence involving defeat," he said.

At one time a certain man had two wives: one was barren, and one was fertile. The barren woman said to the monk who was dependent for alms on (her) family: "If she should bring forth (a child), honored sir, she will become mistress of the whole establishment. Look here, master, find an abortive preparation for her."

"All right, sister," he said, and he gave her an abortive preparation. The child died, but the mother did not die. He was remorseful. ". . . defeat," he said.

At one time a certain man had two wives . . . he gave her an abortive preparation. The mother died, but the child did not die. He was remorseful. . . . "There is no offence involving defeat, monk, there is a grave offence," he said.

Examples of Claims about False Attainments

Now at that time a great company of monks, thinking they had seen what they had not seen, attained what they had not attained, found what they had not found, realized what they had not realized, spoke of profound knowledge with undue estimate of themselves. Their heart, not long afterwards, yielded to passion, their heart yielded to hatred, their heart yielded to confusion. On account of this they were remorseful and said:

"The course of training has been made known by the lord, and we thought to have seen what we did not see . . . and spoke with undue estimate of ourselves. What now if we have fallen into an offence involving defeat?" They told this matter to the venerable Ānanda. The venerable Ānanda told this matter to the lord. He said:

"Ānanda, these are monks who are aware of the seen in the unseen . . . and speak of profound knowledge through undue estimate of themselves; but this is negligible. And thus, monks, this course of training should be set forth:

"Whatever monk should boast, with reference to himself of a state of further-men, sufficient ariyan knowledge and insight, though not knowing it fully, and saying: 'This I know, this I see,' then if later on, he, being pressed or not being pressed, fallen, should desire to be purified, and should say: 'Your reverence, I said that I know what I do not know, see what I do not see, I spoke idly, falsely, vainly,' apart from the undue estimate of himself, he also is one who is defeated, he is not in communion."

Examples Concerning Issues about Robes and Money

At one time the enlightened one, the lord, was staying at Vesālī in the Gotamaka shrine. At that time three robes were allowed to monks by the lord. The group of six monks, thinking: "Three robes are allowed by the lord," entered a village in one set of robes, remained in the monastery in another set of three robes, went down to bathe in another set of three robes. Those who were modest monks looked down upon, criticised, spread it about, saying: "How can the group of six monks wear an extra robe?" Then these monks told this matter to the lord.

"Is it true, as is said, monks, that you wear an extra robe?"

"It is true, lord," they said.

The enlightened one, the lord, rebuked them, saying:

"How can you, foolish men, wear an extra robe? It is not, foolish men, for pleasing those who are not (yet) pleased. . . . And thus, monks, this rule of training should be set forth:

"Whatever monk should wear an extra robe, there is an offence of expiation involving forfeiture."

Thus this rule of training for monks came to be laid down by the lord.

At that time an extra robe accrued to the venerable Ānanda; and the venerable Ānanda was desirous of giving that robe to the venerable Sāriputta, but the venerable Sāriputta was staying at Sāketa. Then it occurred to the venerable Ānanda: "A rule of training laid down by the lord is that an extra robe should not be worn. And this extra robe has accrued to me, and I am desirous of giving this robe to the venerable Sāriputta, but the venerable Sāriputta is staying at Sāketa. Now what line of conduct should be followed by me?" Then the venerable Ānanda told this matter to the lord. He said: "But, Ānanda, how long before Sāriputta will come (here)?"

"Lord, on the ninth or tenth day," he said.

Then the lord on this occasion, in this connection, having given reasoned talk, addressed the monks, saying:

"Monks, I allow you to wear an extra robe for at most ten days. And thus, monks, this rule of training should be set forth:

When the robe-material is settled, when a monk's kaṭhina (privileges) have been removed, an extra robe may be worn for at most ten days. For him who exceeds that (period), there is an offence of expiation involving forfeiture." . . .

Monks heard that man who . . . spread it about. Those who were modest monks . . . spread it about, saying: "How ran the venerable Upananda, the son of the Sakyans, accept gold and silver?" Then these monks told this matter to the lord. He said:

"Is it true, as is said, that you, Upananda, accepted gold and silver?"

"It is true, lord."

The enlightened one, the lord, rebuked him, saying:

"How can you, foolish man, accept gold and silver? It is not, foolish man, for pleasing those who are not (yet) pleased. . . . And thus, monks, this rule of training should be set forth:

"Whatever monk should take gold and silver, or should get another to take it (for him), or should consent to its being kept in deposit (for him), there is an offence of expiation involving forfeiture."

Source: *The Book of Discipline* (*Vinaya-Piṭaka*), volumes 1 and 2, translated by I. B. Horner (London: Pali Text Society, 1938, 1940; reprint London: Luzac, 1970, 1969), 1:36–42, 48–61, 70, 72, 96–97, 125–126, 140–141, 144, 158–159; 2:1–5, 101–102.

10

The Feminine Thread
in Theravāda Buddhism

Although the historical Buddha acknowledged that women were just as religiously capable as men, secondary books on Buddhism have tended to neglect their role and contribution to the religion. This was due to dominance of the religious tradition by monks, which was reflected in the masculine viewpoint of its literature with the exception of the *Therīgāthā* (Verses of the Elder Nuns). Furthermore, there was a preponderance of male scholars working on Buddhism in the nineteenth and twentieth centuries in the West; they paid little attention to the role of women within the Buddhist tradition. Thus it was not until 1930 and the publication of I. B. Horner's book *Women in Primitive Buddhism* that much attention was given to the contribution of women in Buddhism. But it was not really until the 1970s that other female scholars led the way and focused on Buddhist women.

The initial selection of this chapter recounts the story of the origin of the order of nuns. The second body of selections is based on stories and verses composed by women about their lives and religious experiences. This work is the *Therīgāthā,* in which women rejoice about liberation, lament their former pain and attachment, and give thanks for their freedom from the constraints of gender stereotypes. This work fits into the *Khuddaka-nikāya,* a collection of numerous minor works, which is outside the four major Nikāya collections because of its perceived doubtful authenticity. The *Therīgāthā* contains seventy-three poems composed by seventy-one authors; they are arranged according to length into sixteen books. These poems are personal accounts of female experiences of spiritually free nuns who represented exceptions to traditional female social roles.

The final two selections come from a commentary on the so-called *Vimāna* stories from the women's (*Itthivimāna*) part. Vimānas are remote locations that can be within this world or beyond it. They are sometimes described as a paradise. The first selection relates the story of a woman giving water to thirsty monks. After her death, her meritorious deed leads to a positive rebirth into the realm of the thirty-three deities. The second narrative about the woman Rajjumālā relates the significance of her merit and rebirth. These stories reflect a popular folk quality. Such narratives were used to entertain and instruct ordinary people.

Selection from *The Book of the Discipline*

The venerable Ānanda saw the Gotamid, Pajāpatī the Great, standing outside the porch of the gateway, her feet swollen, her limbs covered with dust, with tearful face and crying; seeing her, he spoke thus to the Gotamid, Pajāpatī the Great:

"Why are you, Gotami, standing . . . and crying?"

"It is because, honored Ānanda, the Lord does not allow the going forth of women from home into homelessness in the *dhamma* and discipline proclaimed by the Truth-finder."

"Well now, Gotami, stay here a moment, until I have asked the Lord for the going forth of women from home into homelessness in the *dhamma* and discipline proclaimed by the Truth-finder."

Then the venerable Ānanda approached the Lord; having approached, having greeted the Lord, he sat down at a respectful distance. As he was sitting down at a respectful distance, the venerable Ānanda spoke thus to the Lord:

"Lord, this Gotamid, Pajāpatī the Great, is standing outside the porch of the gateway, her feet swollen, her limbs covered with dust, with tearful face and crying, and saying that the Lord does not allow the going forth of women from home into homelessness in the *dhamma* and discipline proclaimed by the Truth-finder. It were well, Lord, if women might obtain the going forth from home . . . by the Truth-finder."

"Be careful, Ānanda, of the going forth of women from home . . . by the Truth-finder." And a second time. . . . And a third time the venerable Ānanda spoke thus to the Lord: "It were well. Lord, if women might obtain the going forth . . . proclaimed by the Truth-finder."

"Be careful, Ānanda, of the going forth of women from home into homelessness in the Dhamma and discipline proclaimed by the Truth-finder. Then the venerable Ānanda, thinking:

"The Lord does not allow the going forth of women from home into homelessness in the *dhamma* and discipline proclaimed by the Truth-finder. Suppose now that I, by some other method, should ask the Lord for the going forth of women from home into homelessness in the *dhamma* and discipline proclaimed by the Truth-finder." Then the venerable Ānanda spoke thus to the Lord:

"Now, Lord, are women, having gone forth from home into homelessness in the *dhamma* and discipline proclaimed by the Truth-finder, able to realize the fruit of stream-attainment or the fruit of once-returning or the fruit of non-returning or perfection?

"Women, Ānanda, having gone forth . . . are able to realize . . . perfection."

"If, Lord, women, having gone forth . . . are able to realize . . . perfection—and, Lord, the Gotamid, Pajāpatī the Great, was of great service: she was the Lord's aunt, foster-mother, nurse, giver of milk, for when the Lord's mother passed away she suckled him—it were well. Lord, that women should obtain the going forth from home into homelessness in the *dhamma* and discipline proclaimed by the Truth-finder."

"If, Ānanda, the Gotamid, Pajāpatī the Great, accepts eight important rules, that may be ordination for her:

"A nun who has been ordained (even) for a century must greet respectfully, rise up from her seat, salute with joined palms, do proper homage to a monk ordained but that day. And this rule is to be honored, respected, revered, venerated, never to be transgressed during her life.

"A nun must not spend the rains in a residence where there is no monk. This rule too is to be honored . . . during her life.

"Every half month a nun should desire two things from the Order of monks: the asking (as to the date) of the Observance day, and the coming for the exhortation. This rule too is to be honored . . . during her life.

"After the rains a nun must 'invite' before both Orders in respect of three matters: what was seen, what was heard, what was suspected. This rule too is to be honored . . . during her life.

"A nun, offending against an important rule, must undergo *mānatta* (discipline) for half a month before both Orders. This rule too must be honored . . . during her life.

"When, as a probationer, she has trained in the six rules for two years, she should seek ordination from both Orders. This rule too is to be honored . . . during her life.

"A monk must not be abused or reviled in any way by a nun. This rule too is to be honored . . . during her life.

"From to-day admonition of monks by nuns is forbidden, admonition of nuns by monks is not forbidden. This rule too is to be honored, respected, revered, venerated, never to be transgressed during her life.

"If, Ānanda, the Gotamid, Pajāpatī the Great, accepts these eight important rules, that may be ordination for her."

Then the venerable Ānanda, having learnt the eight important rules from the Lord, approached the Gotamid, Pajāpatī the Great; having approached, he spoke thus to the Gotamid, Pajāpatī the Great:

"If you, Gotami, will accept eight important rules, that will be the ordination for you: a nun who has been ordained (even) for a century. . . . From to-day admonition of monks by nuns is forbidden . . . never to be transgressed during your life. If you, Gotami, will accept these eight important rules, that will be the ordination for you."

"Even, honored Ānanda, as a woman or a man when young, of tender years, and fond of ornaments, having washed (himself and his) head, having obtained a garland of lotus flowers or a garland of jasmine flowers or a garland of some sweet-scented creeper, having taken it with both hands, should place it on top of his head—even so do I, honored Ānanda, accept these eight important rules never to be transgressed during my life."

Then the venerable Ānanda approached the Lord: having approached, having greeted the Lord, he sat down at a respectful distance. As he was sitting down at a respectful distance, the venerable Ānanda spoke thus to the Lord: "Lord, the eight important rules were accepted by the Gotamid, Pajāpatī the Great."

"If, Ānanda, women had not obtained the going forth from home into homelessness in the *dhamma* and discipline proclaimed by the Truth-finder, the Brahma-faring. Ānanda, would have lasted long, true *dhamma* would have endured for a thousand years. But since, Ānanda, women have gone forth . . . in the *dhamma* and discipline proclaimed by the Truth-finder, now, Ānanda, the Brahma-faring will not last long, true *dhamma* will endure only for five hundred years.

"Even, Ānanda, as those households which have many women and few men easily fall a prey to robbers, to pot-thieves, even so, Ānanda in whatever *dhamma* and discipline women obtain the going forth from home into homelessness, that Brahma-faring will not last long.

"Even, Ānanda, as when the disease known as mildew attacks a whole field of rice that field of rice does not last long, even so, Ānanda, in whatever *dhamma* and discipline women obtain the going forth . . . that Brahma-faring will not last long.

"Even, Ānanda, as when the disease known as red rust attacks a whole field of sugar-cane, that field of sugar-cane does not last long, even so, Ānanda, in whatever *dhamma* and discipline . . . that Brahma-faring will not last long.

"Even, Ānanda, as a man, looking forward, may build a dyke to a great reservoir so that the water may not overflow, even so, Ānanda, were the eight important rules for nuns laid down by me, looking forward, not to be transgressed during their life."

Then the Gotamid, Pajāpatī the Great, approached the Lord; having approached, having greeted the Lord, she stood at a respectful distance. As she was standing at a respectful distance, the Gotamid, Pajāpatī the Great spoke thus to the Lord:

"Now, what line of conduct, Lord, should I follow in regard to these Sakyan women?" Then the Lord, gladdened, rejoiced, roused, delighted the Gotamid, Pajāpatī the Great, with talk on *dhamma*. Then the Gotamid, Pajāpatī the Great, gladdened . . . delighted by the Lord with talk on *dhamma*, having greeted the Lord, departed keeping her right side towards him. Then the Lord on this occasion, having given reasoned talk, addressed the monks, saying:

"I allow, monks, nuns to be ordained by monks."

Then these nuns spoke thus to the Gotamid, Pajāpatī the Great: "The lady is not ordained, neither are we ordained, for it was thus laid down by the Lord: nuns should be ordained by monks."

Then the Gotamid, Pajāpatī the Great approached the venerable Ānanda; having approached, having greeted the venerable Ānanda, she stood at a respectful distance. As she was standing at a respectful distance, the Gotamid, Pajāpatī the Great spoke thus to the venerable Ānanda: "Honored Ānanda, these nuns spoke to me thus: 'The lady is not ordained, neither are we ordained, for it was thus laid down by the Lord: nuns should be ordained by monks.'"

Then the venerable Ānanda approached the Lord; having approached, having greeted the Lord, he sat down at a respectful distance. As he was sitting down at a respectful distance, the venerable Ānanda spoke thus to the Lord: "Lord, the Gotamid, Pajāpatī the Great spoke thus: 'Honored Ānanda, these nuns spoke, to me thus . . . nuns should be ordained by monks.'"

"At the time, Ānanda, when the eight important rules were accepted by the Gotamid, Pajāpatī the Great, that was her ordination."

Then the Gotamid, Pajāpatī the Great approached the venerable Ānanda; having approached, having greeted the venerable Ānanda, she stood at a respectful distance. As she was standing at a respectful distance, the Gotamid, Pajāpatī the Great spoke thus to the venerable Ānanda: "I, honored Ānanda, am asking one boon from the Lord: It were well, Lord, if the Lord would allow greeting, standing up for, salutation and the proper duties between monks and nuns according to seniority."

Then the venerable Ānanda approached the Lord; having approached, having greeted the Lord, he sat down at a respectful distance. As he was sitting down at a respectful distance, the venerable Ānanda spoke thus to the Lord: "Lord, the Gotamid, Pajāpatī the Great spoke thus: 'I, honored Ānanda, am asking one boon . . . according to seniority.'"

"This is impossible, Ānanda, it cannot come to pass, that the Truth-finder should allow greeting, standing up for, salutation and the proper duties between monks and nuns according to seniority. Ānanda, these followers of other sects, although liable to poor guardianship, will not carry out greeting, standing up for, salutation and proper duties towards women, so how should the Truth-finder allow greeting . . . and proper duties towards women?" Then the Lord, on this occasion, having given reasoned talk, addressed the monks, saying:

"Monks, one should not carry out greeting, rising up for salutation and proper duties towards women. Whoever should carry out (one of these), there is an offence of wrong-doing."

Then the Gotamid, Pajāpatī the Great approached the Lord; having approached, having greeted the Lord, she stood at a respectful distance. As she was standing at a respectful distance, the Gotamid, Pajāpatī the Great spoke thus to the Lord: "Lord, those rules of training for nuns which are in common with those for monks, what line of conduct should we, Lord, follow in regard to these rules of training?"

"Those rules of training for nuns, Gotami, which are in common with those for monks, as the monks train themselves, so should you train yourselves in these rules of training."

"Those rules of training for nuns. Lord, which are not in common with those for monks, what line of conduct should we, Lord, follow in regard to these rules of training?"

"Those rules of training for nuns, Gotami, which are not in common with those for monks, train yourselves in the rules of training according as they are laid down."

Then the Gotamid, Pajāpatī the Great approached the Lord; having approached, having greeted the Lord, she stood at a respectful distance. As she was standing at a respectful distance, the Gotamid, Pajāpatī the Great spoke thus to the Lord: "Lord, it were well if the Lord would teach me *dhamma* in brief so that I, having heard the Lord's *dhamma*, might live alone, aloof, zealous, ardent, self-resolute."

"Whatever are the states, of which you, Gotami, may know: these states lead to passion, not to passionlessness, they lead to bondage, not to the absence of bondage, they lead to the piling up (of rebirth), not to the absence of piling up, they lead to wanting much, not to wanting little, they lead to discontent, not to contentment, they lead to sociability, not to solitude, they lead to indolence, not to the putting forth of energy, they lead to difficulty in supporting oneself, not to ease in supporting oneself—you should know definitely, Gotami: this is not *dhamma*, this is not discipline, this is not the Teacher's instruction. But whatever are the states of which you, Gotami, may know: these states lead to passionlessness, not to passion . . . (*the opposite of the preceding*) . . . they lead to ease in supporting oneself, not to difficulty in supporting oneself—you should know definitely, Gotami: this is *dhamma*, this is discipline, this is the Teacher's instruction."

Now at that time the Pātimokkha was not recited to nuns. They told this matter to the Lord. He said: "I allow you, monks, to recite the Pātimokkha to the nuns." Then it occurred to the nuns: "Now, by whom should the Pātimokkha be recited to nuns?" They told this matter to the Lord. He said: "I allow, monks, the Pātimokkha to be recited to nuns by monks."

Now at that time monks, having approached a nunnery, recited the Pātimokkha to nuns. People looked down upon, criticized, spread it about, saying: "These are their wives, these are their mistresses; now they will take their pleasure together." Monks heard these people who . . . spread it about. Then these monks told this matter to the Lord. He said:

"Monks, I the Pātimokkha should not be recited to nuns by monks. Whoever should reite it, there is an offence of wrong-doing. I allow, monks, the Pātimokkha to be recited to nuns by nuns."

The nuns did not know how to recite the Pātimokkha. They told this matter to the Lord. He said: "I allow you, monks, to explain to the nuns through monks, saving: 'The Pātimokkha should be recited thus.'"

Now at that time nuns did not confess offences. They told this matter to the Lord. He said: "Monks, an offence should not be not confessed by a nun. Whoever should not confess it, there is an offence of wrong-doing." The nuns did not know how to confess offences. They told this matter to the Lord. He said: "I allow you, monks, to explain to the nuns through monks, saying: 'An offence should be confessed thus.'"

Then it occurred to monks: "Now, by whom should nuns' offences be acknowledged?" They told this matter to the Lord. He said: "I allow you, monks to acknowledge nuns' offences through monks."

Now at that time nuns, having (each) seen a monk on a carriage-road and in a cul-de-sac and at cross-roads, having (each) laid down her bowl on the ground, having arranged her upper robe over one shoulder, having sat down on her haunches, having saluted with joined palms, confessed an offence. People . . . spread it about, saying: "These are their wives, these are their mistresses; having treated them contemptuously during the night now they are asking for forgiveness." They told this matter to the Lord. He said: "Monks, nuns' offences should not be acknowledged by monks. Whoever should acknowledge (one), there is an offence of wrong-doing. I allow, monks, nuns' offences to be acknowledged by nuns." The nuns did not know how to acknowledge offences. They told this matter to the Lord. He said: "I allow you, monks, to explain to the nuns through monks, saying: 'An offence should be acknowledged thus.'"

Now at that time (formal) acts were not carried out for nuns. They told this matter to the Lord. He said: "I allow, monks, a (formal) act to be carried out for nuns." Then it occurred to monks: "Now, by whom should (formal) acts for nuns be carried out?" They told this matter to the Lord. He said: "I allow, monks, (formal) acts for nuns to be carried out by monks."

Now at that time nuns on whose behalf (formal) acts had been carried out, having (each) seen a monk on a carriage-road and in a cul-de-sac and at cross-roads, having (each) laid down her bowl on the ground, having arranged her upper robe over one shoulder, having sat down on her haunches, having saluted with joined palms, asked forgiveness thinking, "Surely it should be done thus." As before people . . . spread it about, saying: "These are their wives, these are their mistresses; having treated them contemptuously during the night now they are asking for forgiveness." They told this matter to the Lord. He said: "Monks, a (formal) act on behalf of nuns should not be carried out by monks. Whoever should (so) carry one out, there is an offence of wrong-doing. I allow, monks, nuns to carry out (formal) acts on behalf of the nuns." Nuns did not know how (formal) acts should be carried out. They told this matter to the Lord. He said: "I allow you, monks, to explain to the nuns through monks, saying: 'A (formal) act should be carried out thus.'"

Now at that time nuns, in the midst of an Order, striving, quarrelling, falling into disputes, wounding one another with the weapons of the tongue, were not able to settle that legal question. They told this matter to the Lord. He said: "I allow you, monks, to settle nuns' legal questions by monks."

Now at that time monks were settling a legal question for nuns, but as that legal question was being investigated there were to be seen both nuns who were entitled to take part in a (formal) act and those who had committed an offence. The nuns spoke thus: "It were well, honored sirs, if the ladies themselves could carry out (formal) acts for nuns, if the ladies themselves could acknowledge an offence of nuns, but it was thus laid down by the Lord: 'Nuns' legal questions should be settled by monks.'" They told this matter to the Lord. He said:

"I allow you, monks, having cancelled the carrying out by monks of nuns' (formal) acts, to give it into the charge of nuns to carry out nuns' (formal) acts by nuns; having cancelled (the acknowledgment) by monks of nuns' offences, to give it into the charge of nuns to acknowledge nuns' offences by nuns."

Now at that time the nun who was the pupil of the nun Uppalavannā had followed after the Lord for seven years mastering discipline, but because she was of confused mindfulness, what she had learnt she forgot. That nun heard it said that the Lord wished to come to Sāvatthī. Then it occurred to that nun: "For seven years I have followed the Lord mastering discipline, but because I am of confused mindfulness what I have learnt is forgotten. Hard it is for a woman to follow after a teacher for as long as her life lasts. What line of conduct should be followed by me?" Then that nun told this matter to the nuns. The nuns told this matter to the monks. The monks told this matter to the Lord. He said: "I allow, monks, discipline to be taught to nuns by monks."

Source: *The Book of Discipline*, volume 5, *Cullavagga*, translated by I. B. Horner (London: Pali Text Society, 1975), 353–363.

Selections from the *Psalms of the Sisters*

Bhaddā of the Kapilas

Now she was born in the time of Padumuttara Buddha, in a clansman's house at Hansavatī. Come to years of discretion, she heard the Master preach, and saw him assign a Bhikkhunī the first rank among those who could recall previous lives.

Thereat she made her resolve, wishing that she, too, might acquire such a rank. Working merit all her life, she was reborn, when no Buddha had arisen, in a clansman's house at Benares, and in due course married.

Then one day a quarrel arose between her and her sister-in-law. And the latter having given food to a Silent Buddha, Bhaddā thought, 'She will win glory for this,' and taking the bowl from his hand, she filled it with mud instead of food. The people said, 'Foolish woman! What has the Silent Buddha done to offend you?' And she, ashamed of herself, took back the bowl, emptied and scrubbed it with scented powder, filled it with the four sweet foods, and sprinkled it on the top with ghee of the color of a lotus-calyx. Handing it back, shining, to the Silent Buddha, she registered a prayer: 'May I have a shining body like this bowl!'

After many fortunate rebirths, she was reborn, in the time of Kassapa Buddha, at Benares, as the daughter of the wealthy treasurer. But by the fruition of her previous karma her body was of evil odor, and she was repulsive to others. Much troubled thereby, she had her ornaments made into an ingot of gold, and placed it in the Buddha's shrine, doing reverence with her hands full of lotuses. Thereby her body, even in that birth, became fragrant and sweet. As a beloved wife she did good all her life, was reborn in heaven to celestial joys, and at length took birth as the daughter of the King of Benares. There she lived gloriously, ministering to Silent Buddhas. When they passed away she was greatly troubled, and left the world for ascetic practices. Dwelling in groves, she practiced Jhana, and was reborn in the Brahma heavens, and thence into the family of a brahmin of the Kosiya clan at Sāgala. Reared in great state, she was wedded to the young noble Pippali at the village of Mahā-tittha. When he renounced the world she handed over her great wealth to her kinsfolk that she too might go forth; and she dwelt five years in the Sophists' Grove, after which she was ordained by Great Pajāpatī, the Gotamid. Establishing insight, she soon won Arahantship.

And she became an expert in knowledge of her past lives, through the surplus force of her resolve (made in past ages), and was herein ranked first by the Master when, seated in the Jeta Grove among the company of Ariyans, he classified the Bhikkhunīs. . . .

Subhā (The Goldsmith's Daughter)

She, too, having made her resolve under former Buddhas, and heaping up good of age-enduring efficacy, so that she had progressively planted the root of good and accumulated the conditions of emancipation, was, in this Buddha-era, reborn at Rajagaha as the daughter of a certain goldsmith. From the beauty of her person she was called Subhā. Come to years of discretion, she went one day, while the Master was at Rājagaha, and belief in him had come to her, and did obeisance, seating herself on one side. The Master, seeing the maturity of her moral faculties, and in accordance with her wish, taught her the Norm enshrined in the Four Truths. She was thereby established in the fruition of Stream-entry, which is in countless ways adorned. Later she realized the disadvantages of domestic life, and entered the Order under the Great Pajāpatī the Gotamid, devoting herself to the higher Paths. From time to time her relations invited her to return to the world, urging its charms. To them thus come one day, she set forth the danger in house-life and in the world, preaching the Norm in the twenty-four verses below, and dismissed them cured of their desire. She then strove for insight, purifying her faculties, till at length she won Arahantship. As Arahant she spoke thus:

> A maiden I, all clad in white, once heard
> The Norm, and hearkened eager, earnestly,
> So in me rose discernment of the Truths.
> Thereat all worldly pleasures irked me sore,
> For I could see the perils that beset
> This reborn compound, 'personality,'
> And to renounce it was my sole desire.
> So I forsook my world—my kinsfolk all,
> My slaves, my hirelings, and my villages,
> And the rich fields and meadows spread around,
> Things fair and making for the joy of life?
> All these I left, and sought the Sisterhood,
> Turning my back upon no mean estate.
>
> Amiss were't now that I, who in full faith
> Renounced that world, who well discerned the Truth,
> Who, laying down what gold and silver bring,
> Cherish no worldly wishes whatsoe'er,
> Should, all undoing, come to you again!
> Silver and gold avail not to awake,
> Or soothe. Unmeet for consecrated lives,
> They are not Ariyan—not noble—wealth. . . .

Source: *Psalms of the Early Buddhists. 1. Psalms of the Sisters,* translated by C.A.F. Ryhs Davids (London: Pali Text Society, 1909; reprint London: Luzac, 1964), 47–49, 142–143.

Selections from the *Vimāna Stories*

Exposition of the Boat Vimāna

"Your boat with golden awnings." This is the Boat Vimana. How did it originate?

When the Lord was staying at Sāvatthi, as many as sixteen monks who had spent the residence of the rainy season dwelling in a certain village dwelling-place were, during the hottest part of the day, following the highway in the direction of Sāvatthi with the intention of seeing the Lord and of hearing Dhamma. And on the way there was a waterless wilderness where they, over-powered by the heat, tired, parched and not finding any water, went along nearby a certain village. There a certain woman was heading towards the well with a water-vessel with the aim of (fetching some) water. Now when those monks saw her they, overcome with thirst, headed in that direction thinking that if they were to go where that woman was going they would be able to get some water there, saw the well and stood near her. The woman drew water there from and when she was ready to turn back she saw those monks, realized that those worthy ones were thirsty and in need of water, gave rise to respect and thoughtfulness and invited them to (partake of) the water. They took out the water-strainer from the bag used for carrying the bowl, strained it and drank as much water as they needed, cooled down their hands and feet and then voiced their appreciation to that woman as regards her gift of water, thereafter going on their way. She established that meritorious deed in her heart; recollecting it time and again she later on died and came into being in the realm of the Thirty-three. Due to the majesty of her meritorious deed there arose for her a great vimāna embellished with a wish-granting tree. Surrounding that vimāna was a stream conveying water as stainless as a mass of gems and that was banked with pale-colored sandy mounds sprinkled with sand as though decorated with strings of pearls and silver. On both its shores and at the door to her vimāna-park there came into being a great lotus pond that was adorned with clusters of lotuses of (all) five colors together with a golden boat. She would roam about there experiencing heavenly excellence sporting and dallying in her boat. Then one day the venerable Mahāmoggallāna who was conducting a deva-tour saw that devadhītā sporting in her boat and, enquiring of the meritorious deed done by her, said:

1. "You stand, lady, having embarked into your boat with golden awnings; (then) you plunge into this lotus pond and pick a lotus with your hand.

2. Due to what is such complexion yours? Due to what is this accomplished for you here and that there should arise whatever pleasures your heart holds dear?

3. I ask you, devī of great majesty, what meritorious deed you did when you were human? Due to what are you of such shining majesty and your complexion radiates in all directions?"

Thereupon, this verse was spoken by those performing the rehearsal (of the Dhamma) to indicate the manner in which the devatā, questioned by the elder, answered:

4. That devatā, her heart delighted at being questioned by Moggallāna, explained the question as asked, of what deed this was the fruit.

This is the manner in which that devatā answered:

5. "When I was human, amongst men—in my former birth in the world of men— I saw some monks who were parched and tired; summoning up (energy) I gave them water to drink."

Exposition of Rajjumālā's Vimāna

"With surpassing complexion." This is Rajjumālā's Vimāna. How did it originate?

The Lord was staying at Sāvatthi, in Jeta's Grove. At that time the daughter of a certain brahmin in the village of Gaya who had been given (in marriage) to a brahmin's son in that same village and who had gone to her master's family, abided in that house wielding authority. Upon seeing the daughter of the servant-woman in that house, she could not endure her; and henceforward, from the time she (first) saw her, she would insult and abuse her, spluttering with anger, and slap her. Moreover when she became capable of duty after coming of age, she would even strike her with her knee, elbow and fist, after the manner of the malice to which she had in previous births (herself) been subjected.

It is said that during the time of the ten-powered Kassapa, the servant-girl had been her mistress, the other one the servant-girl, and that she constantly belabored her with clods of earth and sticks and so on and with her fists. She, having had enough of this, performed meritorious deeds of giving and so on in accordance with her ability and made the wish that she might in the future wield authority over her as her mistress. Then the servant-girl, fallen from there, ran on successively (until) in this Buddha-period she came into being in a brahmin family in the village of Gayā in the manner stated and (subsequently) went to her master's family. And the other became her servant-girl. She oppressed her because of the maliciousness to which she had thus tied her (in that former life); (and) in thus oppressing her she would, for no reason whatever, seize her by the hair and assail her mercilessly with her hands and feet. (Seeking to prevent this the servant-girl) went to the barber's shop, had him shave her (head) closely and then returned. Her mistress said, "What a rogue of a servant-girl you are! Do you think you can escape me merely by shaving (your head)?," tied a rope on her head and, seizing her with this, made her bend down and then beat her. And she would not allow her to remove the rope, whenceforth Rajjumālā became the name of that servant-girl.

Then one day the Teacher, who was surveying the world upon emerging, towards dawn, from the meditation of the great compassion, saw Rajjumālā's potential for the sotāpatti-fruit and that Brahmin woman's establishment in the Refuges and the Precepts; he entered the forest and seated himself at the foot of a tree, emanating the six-colored rays of a Buddha. Now Rajjumālā, being oppressed in that manner by her day in, day out, ostensibly having had enough of life thought, "What is there for me in this miserable life?," and, desiring to die, she took a pitcher, leaving the house as if going to the watering place, and in due course entered the jungle. She tied a rope on the branch of a certain tree not far from the tree at which the Lord was seated and made a noose; desiring to hang herself and looking, serene, inspiring serenity, having attained to the utmost in taming and calm and emanating the six-colored rays of a Buddha. Her heart being drawn through reverence for the Buddha when she saw him, she thought, "What if the Lord were to teach Dhamma even to those such as me, after hearing which I might be released from this miserable life here." Then the Lord surveying the way her mind was working, said "Rajjumālā." When she heard this she was entirely contacted by joy as if sprinkled with the Deathless; she approached the Lord, saluted him and then stood to one side. To her the Lord talked a progressive talk immediately followed by talk on the Four Truths. She became established in the sotāpatti-fruit.

The Teacher, reflecting that so much help to Rajjumālā had been proper and that she had now become inviolable to anyone, left the forest and seated himself at the foot of a certain tree not far from the village. Rajjumālā too, on account of her own inability to destroy herself and of her being endowed with forbearance, loving-kindness and kindness (generally), thought, "Let that brahmin woman kill me or oppress me or do what she will," and returned to the house with water in the pitcher. When he saw her the lord (of the household) who was stood at the door of the house asked, "Today, when you went to the watering-place, you were a long time before you came back; and the complexion of your face is extremely serene and you present yourself in a different manner—why is this?" She told him of the incident. When the brahmin heard these words of hers he became satisfied, went into the house, told his daughter-in-law that nothing further was to be done by her where Rajjumālā was concerned and then, his heart satisfied, went very quickly into the Teacher's presence, saluted him and, having respectfully extended a friendly greeting, invited the Teacher, conducted him to his house and waited upon him with the choicest foods both hard and soft; and when the Lord had finished his meal and removed his hand from the bowl he approached him and seated himself to one side. His daughter-in-law also approached him, saluted him and seated herself to one side; and when they heard of the incident the brahmin householders who were residents of the village of Gayā also approached the Lord, some greeting him and seating themselves to one side, others exchanging friendly greetings and then seating themselves to one side. The Teacher talked in detail of the deeds done in previous births by Rajjumālā and that brahmin woman and then taught Dhamma according with the company assembled there. When they heard this that brahmin woman and the people who had come together there became established in the Refuges and the Precepts. The Teacher rose from his seat and went straight back to Sāvatthi. The brahmin adopted Rajjumālā as his own daughter. His daughter-in-law took care of Rajjumālā with utterly pleasant affection as long as life lasted, looking upon her with loving eyes.

Later on Rajjumālā died and came into being amongst the Thirty-three. And a retinue of a thousand nymphs was hers. Her person adorned with heavenly decorations to the extent of sixty cartloads and surrounded by her retinue of a thousand nymphs she would, her heart jubilant, roam about in the Nandana Grove and so on experiencing great heavenly excellence. Then the venerable Mahāmoggallāna who had gone on a deva-tour saw her flashing forth with great heavenly majesty and with the great iddhi of a deva and questioned her about the deed done by her.

Source: *Elucidation of the Intrinsic Meaning So Named the Commentary on the Vimāna Stories*, translated by Peter Masefield (Oxford: Pali Text Society, 1989), 59–60, 318–321.

11

Theravāda
Hagiographic Literature

In contrast to the sacred biography of the Buddha (of which representative selections appear in chapter 2), hagiography is narrative about secondary religious figures, who may nevertheless be extremely important to the religious tradition. Hagiography depicts its subject as a figure who has realized an ideal religious paradigm, or it tells the story of a holy person who attains an ideal that is already recognized by that person's religious community.

When reading hagiography it is difficult to find a chronological account of a subject's life. What tend to be stressed are traditional virtues and the subject's religious achievements. This emphasis also tends to present an ideal portrait of the subject and neglects to mention the subject's personal weaknesses. The writers of hagiographical literature do not want to create any doubt about the sanctity of the subject by presenting a complete and objective portrait. Nonetheless, the writer wants to stress the subject's importance and to present a realistic setting in order to give credibility to the ideal portrait.

It is possible to see these features in the hagiography of the Buddhist monks Upagupta and Śāriputra. The selected narratives portray timeless Buddhist truths within their particular lives. If these two monks represent positive models for emulation, the narrative of the monk Devadatta symbolizes evil and deception. The narrative of Devadatta functions as a counterexample that an audience should avoid. The narrative of this personification of evil also serves to emphasize the compassion of the Buddha when the evil monk takes refuge with him. Although the selections in this chapter do not include later episodes associated with Deva-datta, the account of his death and torment in hell has soteriological importance in showing that enlightenment is possible for even a wicked individual. Overall, the three selected narratives represent an epic tradition of Theravāda Buddhism that gives readers a sacred history. In turn, this sacred history provides legitimization of the tradition and is itself informed by various aspects of the religious tradition that include its language, philosophy, worldview, ecclesiastical perspective, ritual prac-tice, and ethical virtues.

Selections from "The Story of Vāsavadattā"

Now in Mathurā, there was a courtesan named Vāsavadattā. One day, her servant girl happened to go to Upagupta to purchase some perfumes. And [when she had returned], Vāsavadattā said to her: "Dear girl, you must have robbed that mer-chant; you bring back so many perfumes!"

"Mistress," replied the girl, "Upagupta, the perfumer's son—an altogether handsome man of perfect cleverness and charm—does business honestly!" When Vasavadatta heard this, she developed an amorous longing for Upagupta, and she sent her servant girl to him announcing that she would come to him for she wished to pursue pleasure with him. But when the servant girl communicated this to Upagupta, he only replied that it was not yet time for her to see him.

Now Vāsavadattā['s price] was five hundred pieces of gold. It occurred to her that Upagupta was unable to pay this amount, so she sent her servant back again saying that she did not intend to receive even a penny from her lord; she only wanted to pursue pleasure with him. But when the servant girl communicated this to Upagupta, he again replied that it was not yet time for her to see him.

Some time later, the son of a certain guildmaster was staying with Vāsava-dattā, when a caravaneer, who had captured five hundred horses and brought them for sale from the North country, arrived in Mathurā. "Which courtesan," he wanted to know, "is the best of all?" He was told that it was Vāsavadattā. So, tak-ing five hundred pieces of gold and many presents, he set out for her house. [Hearing that he was coming], and moved by greed, Vāsavadattā [quickly] had the guildmaster's son beaten up and thrown out onto the dungheap; she then pur-sued her pleasure with the caravaneer.

The guildmaster's relatives, however, [found out about this]. They rescued the son from the dungheap, and reported the matter to the king. And the king ordered his men to go [and arrest] Vāsavadattā, to cut off her hands, feet, nose, and ears, and leave her on the cremation ground. They did so.

Now when Upagupta heard that Vāsavadattā had been abandoned on the cremation ground with her hands, feet, nose, and ears cut off, this thought occurred to him: "Previously she wished to see me for sensual reasons, but now her hands, feet, nose, and ears have been cut off; this is the time to see her." And he said:

> When her body was covered with excellent clothes
> and bedecked with variegated ornaments,
> then it was better for those who have turned away
> from rebirth, and are set on liberation,
> not to see her.
> But now that she has lost her pride,
> her passion and her joy,
> and has been wounded with sharp swords—
> this is the time to see her form
> in its true intrinsic nature.

Then, accompanied by a single servant carrying a parasol, he went to the cremation ground, tranquil, and observing the practices of a religious mendicant.

Now Vāsavadattā's servant girl, out of appreciation for her mistress's past virtues, had remained close to her, and was chasing away the crows and other carrion birds. [When she saw Upagupta coming] she said to Vāsavadattā:

"My lady, that Upagupta to whom you sent me again and again has arrived; surely, he must have come impelled by passion and desire."

When Vāsavadattā heard this, she said:

> How will he have any passion or desire
> when he sees me on the ground,
> red with blood, my lustre gone,
> afflicted by suffering?

And she told her servant to gather the hands, feet, nose, and ears that had been cut from her body, and to cover them with a piece of cloth. Upagupta then arrived and stood in front of Vāsavadattā. Seeing him standing there, Vāsavadattā said: "My lord, when my body was uninjured and well-disposed for sensual pleasure, I sent a servant girl to you again and again, but you only said: 'Sister, it is not yet time for you to see me.' Now my hands and feet and ears and nose have been cut off, and I sit in the mire of my own blood. Why have you come now?"

And she added:

When this body of mine was fit to be seen
soft like the womb of a lotus,
and bedecked with costly garments and jewels,
then I, the unfortunate one, did not meet you.
Why have you come here to see me now
that my body is unfit to be looked at,
plastered with mud and blood, causing fear,
having lost its wonder, joy, pleasure, and play?

Upagupta replied:

Sister, I have not come to you impelled by desire,
but have come to see the intrinsic nature
of desires and impurities.
When you were covered with clothes, ornaments,
and all the other variegated externals
conducive to passion,
those who looked at you
could not see you as you truly are,
even when they made the effort.
But now, free from outer trappings,
your form may be seen in its intrinsic nature.
Unlearned and wicked are those who take pleasure
in this gross living carcass.
Who would, how could, anyone feel attracted
to a body that is held together with skin,
encircled by blood, covered with hide,
plastered with lumps of flesh, and surrounded
on all sides by a thousand muscles and veins? . . .

Upon hearing this, Vāsavadattā became terrified of saṃsāra. Her heart was humbled by the recollection of the virtues of the Buddha, and she said:

All of this is just as the wise one says.
Since I have met you, may it please you
that I should hear the word of the Buddha.

Upagupta, therefore, preached to her a step-by-step discourse, and then exposed to her the Truths. And coming to an understanding of the inherent nature of

Vāsavadattā's body, he himself became disgusted with the realm of desire, and, from this clear understanding of the Truth that came with his own preaching of the Dharma, he attained the fruit of a non-returner and Vāsavadattā attained the fruit of entering the stream. . . .

Now, when Upagupta had finished instructing Vasavadatta with dharmic discourses, he departed. Soon thereafter, Vāsavadattā died and was reborn among the gods, and in Mathurā, the deities proclaimed: "Having heard the Dharma preached by Upagupta, Vāsavadattā perceived the Noble Truths. Now that she is dead, she has arrived in heaven." And when the residents of Mathurā heard this, they, as a group, paid homage to the body of Vāsavadattā.

Story of the Encounter between Upagupta and Māra

Soon thereafter, he was asked to preach at a Dharma meeting; and the word spread throughout Mathurā that, on that day, a Buddha without the marks named Upagupta would expose the Dharma. And hearing this, several hundred thousand persons set out.

The elder Upagupta then entered into meditation and examined the matter of how the assembly of the Tathāgata had customarily been seated. He perceived that that assembly sat down in the shape of a half-moon. Next, he contemplated the way the Tathāgata had preached the Dharma, and he perceived that the Buddha made an exposition of the Truth after giving a step-by-step discourse. Therefore, he too preached a step-by-step discourse, and then began to expose the Truth.

Just then, however, Māra caused a shower of strings of pearls to rain down on the assembly; and the minds of those who were about to be converted became agitated [by greed], and not one of them came to see the Truth. The elder Upagupta carefully considered the matter of who was causing this disturbance, and he perceived that it was Māra.

Then, on the second day, a very large number of men arrived in Mathurā, thinking "Upagupta preaches the Dharma and strings of pearls come down in a shower!" And again, on that day, just when Upagupta had finished the step-by-step discourse and was beginning to expose the Truth, Māra caused a shower of gold to rain down on the assembly; the minds of those who were about to he converted were agitated, and not one of them came to see the Truth. Once more, the elder Upagupta carefully considered the matter of who was causing this disturbance, and he perceived it was Māra being even more wicked.

Then, on the third day, an even larger number of men came out, thinking "Upagupta preaches the Dharma and showers of pearls or gold fall down!" And again, on that day, he had finished the step-by-step discourse and had just started to expose the Truths, when, not very far off, Māra began a theatrical performance; heavenly instruments were played and divine apsāras started to dance, and the once dispassionate crowd of men, seeing the divine forms and hearing the heavenly sounds, was drawn away by Māra.

Māra was so pleased that he had attracted Upagupta's assembly to himself, that he hung a garland around the elder's neck. Upagupta then focussed his mind [on the question] "Who is this?" And he perceived that it was Māra. Then he reflected: "This Māra causes a lot of disturbance to the Teaching of the Blessed One; why was he not converted by the Buddha?" And he realized: "He is to be converted by me; it was with reference to his conversion, and as a favor to all beings, that the Blessed One predicted that I should become a Buddha without the marks!"

Upagupta, therefore, focussed his mind [on the question] of whether or not the time for Māra's conversion had arrived and he perceived that it had come. He took, therefore, three carcasses—a dead snake, a dead dog, and a dead human being—and, by means of his magical powers, he transformed them into a garland of flowers and went up to Māra. When Māra saw him [and the flowers], he was delighted and thought that he had won over even Upagupta. He resumed, therefore his own bodily form, so that Upagupta could garland him personally. Then the elder crowned him with the snake carcass, and hung the dead dog around his neck, and the human corpse over his ears, and taking hold of them, he said:

> Just as you, sir, have bedecked me with a garland,
> which is inappropriate for a man who is a monk,
> so I have bound around you these carcasses,
> which are unfit for a man of desires.
> Show whatever powers you have,
> but today you have encountered a son of the Buddha
> Even when the water of the ocean surges up,
> its swollen waves blown by the wind,
> it still loses its force
> in the caverns of Mount Malaya.

Now Māra started to try to take off one of the carcasses; but, as he had entered into it personally, he was not able to remove it, just as an ant cannot lift up a great mountain.

Indignant, he rose up into the air and said:

If I myself am not able to remove

this dog's carcass from around my neck,

the other gods, whose power is greater

than mine, will release me! . . .

Māra went to Mahendra, to Rudra, to Upendra, to the Lord of Riches; to Yama, Varuṇa, Kubera, and Vasāva, and to the other gods as well, hut he did not achieve his purpose. Finally, he went to Brahmā. The latter said: "Pass me by, my child . . . ."

Māra said: "What then do you recommend? Whom shall I turn to now?"

Brahmā replied:

Go quickly and take refuge in Upagupta.

It was after encountering him that you fell

from the heights of your magical power,

fame, and happiness.

As they say, "One who has fallen on the ground

must support himself on the ground

in order to stand up again." . . .

Then Māra, the lord of the Realm of Desire, realized that, for him, Upagupta was the only way out [of his predicament]. Thus, he gave up all [his attempts to free himself], sought out he elder, fell at his feet, and said: "Reverend sir, you well know the hundreds of wicked things I did to the Blessed One at the Tree of Enlightenment and elsewhere:

When Gautama came to me

at a mansion in a Brahmin village,

I made him go without any food at all;

even so he did nothing unkind to me. . . .

Upagupta agreed to . . . [remove] the carcasses [from Māra's neck]; he then stood by, anxiously waiting for the sight of the form of the Tathāgata. Then Māra, after he had gone far into the forest and [magically] taken on the form of the Buddha, emerged again from that wood like an actor wearing a bright costume.

Source: John S. Strong, *The Legend of King Aśoka: A Study and Translation of the Aśokāvadāna* (Princeton: Princeton University Press, 1992), 179–184, 186–193. Translation by John S. Strong.

Selections from *The Book of the Discipline* (*Vinaya-Pitaka*)

Story of Śāriputra

At that time the wanderer Sañjaya was residing in Rājagaha together with a great company of wanderers, with two hundred and fifty wanderers. Now at that time Sāriputta and Moggallāna fared the Brahma-faring under the wanderer Sañjaya, and an agreement came to be formed by these: "Whoever attains the deathless first, let him announce it."

Then the venerable Assaji, having dressed in the morning, taking his bowl and robe, entered Rājagaha for almsfood. He was pleasing whether he was approaching or departing, whether he was looking in front or looking behind, whether he was drawing in or stretching out (his arm), his eyes were cast down, he was possessed of pleasant behavior. The wanderer Sāriputta saw the venerable Assaji walking for almsfood in Rājagaha—pleasing whether he was approaching . . . possessed of pleasant behavior—and seeing him, it occurred to him: "This is one of those monks who are indeed perfected ones in the world or who have entered on the way to perfection. What now if I, having approached this monk, should ask him: 'On account of whom are you, your reverence, gone forth, or who is your teacher, or whose *dhamma* do you profess?'"

Then it occurred to the wanderer Sāriputta: "But it is not the right time to question this monk, he has gone in among the houses, he is walking for almsfood. What now if I should follow close after this monk who has learnt a way for those who need it?" Then the venerable Assaji, having walked for almsfood in Rājagaha, taking his almsbowl, returned. Then the wanderer Sāriputta approached the venerable Assaji; having approached, he exchanged greetings with the venerable Assaji; having exchanged courteous and friendly greetings, he stood at a respectful distance. As he was standing at a respectful distance, the wanderer Sāriputta spoke thus to the venerable Assaji: "Your reverence, your faculties are quite pure, your complexion very bright, very clear. On account of whom, your reverence, have you gone forth, or who is your teacher, or whose *dhamma* do you profess?"

"There is, friend, a great recluse, a son of the Sakyans, gone forth from a Sakyan family. I have gone forth on account of this Lord and this Lord is my teacher and I profess this Lord's *dhamma*."

"But what is the doctrine of your reverence's teacher, what does he point out?"

"Now, I, friend, am new, not long gone forth, fresh to this Dhamma and discipline. I am not able to teach you *dhamma* in full, but I can tell you its purport briefly."

Then the wanderer Sāriputta spoke thus to the venerable Assaji: "So be it, your reverence, tell me little or tell me much, (but) in any case explain to me its purport; I want just its purport. Why should you make a great elaboration?"

Then the venerable Assaji uttered this terse expression of *dhamma* to the wanderer Sāriputta:

> "Those things which proceed from a cause, of these the Truth-finder has
>   told the cause,
> And that which is their stopping—the great recluse has such a doctrine."

When the wanderer Sāriputta had heard this terse expression of *dhamma*, there arose *dhamma*-vision, dustless, stainless, that "Whatever is of the nature to uprise all that is of the nature to stop." He said: 'If this is indeed *dhamma*, you have penetrated as far as the sorrowless path, unseen, neglected for many myriads of aeons."

Then the wanderer Sāriputta approached the wanderer Moggallāna. Then the wanderer Moggallāna saw the wanderer Sāriputta coming in the distance, and seeing the wanderer Sāriputta, he spoke thus: "Friend, your faculties are quite pure, your complexion very bright, very clear. Can it be that you, friend, have attained the deathless?"

"Yes, friend, I have attained the deathless." . . .

Then the wanderer Moggallāna spoke thus to the wanderer Sāriputta: "Let us go, friend, to the Lord, (for) this Lord is the teacher for us."

"Friend, these two hundred and fifty wanderers are staying here because of us, looking to us; do let us consult them so that they may do what they think (right)." Then Sāriputta and Moggallāna approached these wanderers; having approached, they spoke thus to these wanderers:

"We are going, friends, to the Lord, (for) this Lord is the teacher for us."

"We, venerable ones, are staying here because of you, looking to you. If the venerable ones will fare the Brahma-faring under the great recluse all of us will fare the Brahma-faring under the great recluse." . . .

Then Sāriputta and Moggallāna, taking those two hundred and fifty wanderers, approached the Bamboo Grove; but on that self-same spot hot blood issued from the mouth of Sañjaya the wanderer. The Lord saw Sāriputta and Moggallāna coming in the distance; seeing them, he addressed the monks saying:

"Monks, these two friends, Kolita and Upatissa, are coming. This pair of disciples will be my chief, my eminent pair." When, in the deep sphere of knowledge, they had attained the matchless freedom in which there is destruction of attachments, then the teacher explained about them in the Bamboo Grove: "These two friends, Kolita and Upatissa, are coming. This pair of disciples will be my chief, my eminent pair."

Story of the Evil Monk Devadatta

Then the Lord, having stayed at Anupiyā for as long as he found suiting, set out on almstour for Kosambī. Gradually, walking on tour, he arrived at Kosambī. The Lord stayed there at Kosambī in Ghosita's monastery. Then as Devadatta was meditating in private a reasoning arose in his mind thus: "Whom now could I please, so that because he is pleased with me, much gain and honor would accrue (to me)?" Then it occurred to Devadatta: "This Prince Ajātasattu is young and also has an auspicious future. What now if I were to make Prince Ajātasattu pleased, so that because he is pleased with me, much gain and honor would accrue (to me)?"

Then Devadatta, having packed away his lodging, taking his bowl and robe, set out for Rājagaha; in due course he arrived at Rājagaha. Then Devadatta, having thrown off his own form, having assumed the form of a young boy clad in a girdle of snakes, became manifest in Prince Ajātasattu's lap. Then Prince Ajātasattu was afraid, anxious, fearful, alarmed. Then Devadatta spoke thus to Prince Ajātasattu: "Are you, prince, afraid of me?"

"Yes, I am afraid. Who are you?"

"I am Devadatta."

"If you, honored sir, are really master Devadatta, please become manifest in your own form." Then Devadatta, having thrown off the young boy's form, stood, wearing his outer cloak and (other) robes and carrying his bowl, before Prince Ajātasattu. Then Prince Ajātasattu, greatly pleased with this wonder of psychic power on Devadatta's part, morning and evening went to wait on him with five hundred chariots, and five hundred offerings of rice cooked in milk were brought as a gift of food. Then there arose to Devadatta, overcome by gains, honors and fame, his mind obsessed by them, some such longing as this: "It is I who will lead the Order of monks." But at the very occurrence of this thought Devadatta declined in his psychic power.

Now at that time Kakudha the Koliyan, the venerable Moggallāna the Great's attendant, had just died and had arisen in a certain mind-made body, and such was the reinstatement. . . .

Now at that time the Lord was sitting down teaching *dhamma* surrounded by a large company, by a company which included the king. Then Devadatta, rising from his seat, having arranged his upper robe over one shoulder, having saluted the Lord with joined palms, spoke thus to the Lord: "Lord, the Lord is now old, worn, stricken in years, he has lived his span and is at the close of his life; Lord, let the Lord now be content to live devoted to abiding in ease here and now, let him hand over the Order of monks to me. It is I who will lead the Order of monks."

"Enough, Devadatta, please do not lead the Order of monks." And a second time . . . And a third time Devadatta spoke thus to the Lord: "Lord, the Lord is now old, worn, stricken in years . . . It is I who will lead the Order of monks."

"I, Devadatta, would not hand over the Order of monks even to Sāriputta and Moggallāna. How then could I to you, a wretched one to be vomited like spittle?"

Then Devadatta, thinking: "The Lord in an assembly which included a king disparaged me by (using) the term, 'one to be vomited like spittle,' while he extolled Sāriputta and Moggallāna," angry, displeased, having greeted the Lord, departed keeping his right side towards him.

And this was the first time that Devadatta felt malice towards the Lord.

Then the Lord addressed the monks, saying: "Well then, monks, let the Order carry out a (formal) act of information against Devadatta in Rājagaha to the effect that whereas Devadatta's nature was formerly of one kind, now it is of another kind; and that whatever Devadatta should do by gesture and by voice, in that neither the Awakened One nor *dhamma* nor the Order should be seen, but in that only Devadatta should be seen. And thus, monks, should it be carried out. . . .

Then Devadatta approached Prince Ajātasattu; having approached, he spoke thus to prince Ajātasattu: "Formerly, prince, people were long-lived, nowadays they are short-lived, and it is possible that you, while still a prince, might pass away. Well, now, do you, prince, having slain your father, become king? I, having slain the Lord, will become the Awakened One." And Prince Ajātasattu, thinking: "Now, master Devadatta is of great psychic power, of great majesty; master Devadatta must know (what is right)," having fastened a dagger against his thigh, at an early hour (although) afraid, anxious, fearful, alarmed, entered the (king's) private quarters forcibly. But the chief ministers in attendance in the private quarters saw Prince Ajātasattu . . . they laid hold of him. . . .

Then Devadatta approached Prince Ajātasattu; having approached, he spoke thus to Prince Ajātasattu:

"Your Majesty, command your men so that they deprive the recluse Gotama of life." Then Prince Ajātasattu commanded his men, saying: "My good men, do whatever master Devadatta says." Then Devadatta enjoined the men, saying: "Go along, friends, the recluse Gotama is staying at a certain place. Having deprived him of life, come back by a certain road," and he set two men on that road, saying: "Whatever man comes alone along this road, having deprived him of life, come back by this road," and having set four men on that road, saying: "Whatever couple of men come along by this road, having deprived them of life, come back by this road," and having set eight men on that road, saying: "Whatever four men come along by this road, . . . come back by this road," and having set sixteen men on that road, he said: "Whatever eight men come along by this road, having deprived them of life, come back."

Then that man who was alone, having grasped a sword and shield, having bound on a bow and quiver, approached the Lord; having approached, when he was quite near the Lord he stood still, his body quite rigid afraid, anxious, fearful, alarmed. The Lord saw that man standing still, his body quite rigid, afraid . . . alarmed and seeing him, he spoke thus to that man: "Come, friend, do not be afraid." Then that man, having put his sword and shield to one side, having laid down his bow and quiver, approached the Lord; having approached, having inclined his head to the Lord's feet, he spoke thus to the Lord:

"Lord, a transgression has overcome me, foolish, misguided, wrong that I was, in that I was coming here with my mind malignant, my mind on murder. Lord, may the Lord acknowledge for me the transgression as a transgression for the sake of restraint in the future." . . .

Then that one man approached Devadatta; having approached, he spoke thus to Devadatta: "Honored sir, I am not able to deprive that Lord of life, that Lord is of great psychic power, of great might."

"All right, friend, do not you deprive the recluse Gotama of life. I myself will deprive the recluse Gotama of life."

Now at that time the Lord was pacing up and down in the shade of Mount Vulture Peak. Then Devadatta, having climbed Mount Vulture Peak, hurled down a great stone, thinking: "With this I will deprive the recluse Gotama of life." But two mountain peaks, having met, crushed that stone, and (only) a fragment of it, having fallen down, drew blood on the Lord's foot. Then the Lord, having looked upwards, spoke thus to Devadatta: "You have produced great demerit, foolish man, in that you, with your mind malignant, your mind on murder, drew the Truth-finder's blood." Then the Lord addressed the monks, saying: "This, monks, is the first deed whose fruit comes with no delay accumulated by Devadatta since he, with his mind malignant, his mind on murder, drew the Truth-finder's blood." . . .

Now at that time there was a fierce elephant in Rājagaha, a man-slayer, called Nālāgiri. Then Devadatta, having entered Rājagaha, having gone to the elephant stable, spoke thus to the mahouts: "We, my good fellows, are relations of the king. We are competent to put in a high position one occupying a lowly position and to bring about an increase in food and wages. Well now, good fellows, when the recluse Gotama is coming along this carriage road, then, having let loose this elephant, Nālāgiri, bring him down this carriage road."

"Very well, honored sir," these mahouts answered Devadatta in assent.

Then the Lord, having dressed in the morning, taking his bowl and robe, entered Rājagaha for almsfood together with several monks. Then the Lord went along that carriage road. Then those mahouts saw the Lord coming along that carriage-road; seeing him, having let loose the elephant Nālāgiri, they brought him down that carriage-road. The elephant Nālāgiri saw the Lord coming from afar; seeing him, having lifted up his trunk, he rushed towards the Lord, his ears and tail erect. Those monks saw the elephant Nālāgiri coming in the distance; seeing him, they spoke thus to the Lord:

"Lord, this elephant Nālāgiri, coming along this carriage-road, is a fierce man-slayer; Lord, let the Lord turn back, let the well-farer turn back."

"Wait, monks, do not be afraid; this is impossible, monks, it cannot come to pass that anyone should deprive a Truth-finder of life by aggression; monks, Truth-finders attain nibbāna not because of an attack." . . .

Then the Lord suffused the elephant Nālāgiri with loving-kindness of mind. Then the elephant Nālāgiri, suffused by the Lord with loving-kindness of mind, having put down his trunk, approached the Lord; having approached, he stood in front of the Lord. Then the Lord, stroking the elephant Nālāgiri's forehead with his right hand, addressed the elephant Nālāgiri with verses. . . .

Then the elephant Nālāgiri, having taken the dust of the Lord's feet with his trunk, having scattered it over his head, moved back bowing while he gazed upon the Lord. Then the elephant Nālāgiri, having returned to the elephant stable, stood in his own place; and it was in this way that the elephant Nālāgiri became tamed.

Source: *The Book of the Discipline* (*Vinaya-Pitaka*), translated by I. B. Horner, volume 4, *Mahāvagga* (London: Routledge and Kegan Paul, 1951; reprint 1982), 52–55; and Volume 5, *Cullavagga* (London: Routledge and Kegan Paul, 1952; reprint 1963), 259–260, 264–269, 271–274.

PART II

Selections from the Mahāyāna Tradition

Introduction to Mahāyāna Buddhist Literature

After the death of the Buddha, monks gathered together at several councils to discuss problems that arose with respect to the nature of scriptures, monastic rules, and doctrine. These councils often resulted in schisms that eventually led to the creation of some eighteen different schools. From these many different schools, there eventually emerged a school called Mahāyāna (great vehicle) around 150 B.C.E. and 100 C.E. The Mahāyāna school did not develop from any single group or individual. It probably arose as a loose union of different groups that adhered to different texts. In fact, there is evidence of the existence of cult groups focused on specific texts. These various texts were believed to represent newly inspired visions that captured the authoritative teachings of the Buddha and incorporated the aspirations of the laity.

With its pluralistic origins in diverse groups adhering to different texts, Mahāyāna Buddhism was characterized by a wide variety of viewpoints. This diversity of religious perspectives resulted in the creation of new cosmological conceptions, a reinterpretation of the path to enlightenment, the new religious paradigmatic figure of the bodhisattva, new philosophical systems, and a new pantheon of divine beings. Its literature was often written in Prakrit or in the languages of Central Asia, such as Tocharian and Uighur. When the texts were studied at the University of Nālandā in northern India in the sixth century, many texts had been rewritten in Sanskrit, which was considered the language of higher learning and prestige in

Indian culture. Sanskrit was also the official language of the Gupta Dynasty, which originated around 320 C.E. This shift from Prakrit to Sanskrit was evident in many inscriptions from the pre-Gupta and Gupta monuments. After Buddhist texts evolved from an oral to a written tradition, it was possible for the literature to continue to develop as the Buddha-word (*Buddha-vacana*). When a text claimed to represent, for instance, the Buddha-word it could become accepted as part of the evolving literature. From its Prakrit and Sanskrit roots in India, Mahāyāna literature spread to other countries, where it was translated into such languages as Tibetan, Chinese, Korean, Japanese, and other languages of Asia.

The geographical spread of Buddhism functioned in many countries as a harbinger of civilization. Before the arrival of Buddhism, there was no system of writing, for instance, in many of these locations. China was, of course, an exception because it had a very ancient civilization; it was convinced that it was the center of the civilized world and that its society was the only genuinely civilized society in the world. In such a situation, Buddhism had to compete with various indigenous philosophical and religious systems as it carved a place for itself within Chinese culture.

As Mahāyāna spread eastward to China and adjacent countries, beginning around the first century B.C.E., its advance in China was hastened by the fall of the Han Dynasty in 220 C.E. From China, Buddhism spread to Campā (Vietnam) around the third century C.E., and it possibly reached Siam as early as the first century C.E. By 372 C.E., Buddhism was introduced into Korea, from which it spread to Japan around 552. By the sixth century, Buddhism was brought to Tibet after its king married Nepalese and Chinese princesses who practiced the religion.

Within China, Buddhism gradually integrated itself into the state apparatus, and monks recited religious texts for the welfare and protection of the state. In turn, the Chinese state built and financially supported national monasteries. After the fall of the Han Dynasty, ordinary people embraced Buddhism for spiritual comfort and social security during the Period of Disunity (220–589), a time of great instability. Although the state patronage of Buddhism continued during the Sui (589–618) and T'ang (618–907) dynasties and the religion continued to adapt to Chinese culture, it experienced periods of persecution in 574–577 and again in

845. During the T'ang Dynasty, Chinese Buddhist pilgrims traveled to India to collect texts in order to translate them into Chinese.

It is important to acknowledge that the Chinese pilgrims were unaware of the division of Buddhism into many sects in India. Thus they were also unaware to what extent the scriptures that they encountered, collected, and translated were sectarian writings. Potential Chinese readers were also unaware of the sectarian motivation of missionaries and the way they selected texts to translate. Chinese readers naively assumed that all translated texts were the word of the Buddha. If all the Buddha's teachings in these translated texts were true, there had to be some way to reconcile the often dramatic inconsistencies between them. Without denying the validity of what they called the Hīnayāna (lesser vehicle) tradition, Chinese thinkers taught that it represented a preparatory doctrine intended for an audience unprepared to understand a more sophisticated message that revealed the ultimate truth. Unlike the Theravāda (or Hīnayāna) tradition, with its ecclesiastical councils that canonized the body of scriptures, there was no similar process within Mahāyāna Buddhism. Schools within the latter tradition tended to prefer a single text or set of scriptures. It was not uncommon for Chinese Mahāyāna Buddhists to also arrange an entire canon by making a particular text the culmination of the Buddha's teaching.

Many of these newly translated texts stimulated the development of Chinese Buddhist schools. In general terms, Chinese schools of Buddhism manifested a tendency to be syncretistic, criticized opposing viewpoints as heretical, and created lineages of masters of a specific school in order to create for the school an authoritative tradition. The four major schools that will be covered in this reader are the Pure Land school, T'ien t'ai school, Hua-yen school, and Ch'an school. Even though certain Mahāyāna texts influenced particular schools of Chinese Buddhism, each of these individual schools also produced its own body of literature.

Among the first influential texts of the Pure Land tradition was *The Sūtra on the Meditation Which Brings Buddhas to Appear and Dwell in One's Presence* (*Pan-chou san-mei ching*), translated by Lokakṣema in 179 C.E. The text emphasized concentrating one's mind constantly on the Pure Land. If one does this for a week, the Pure Land will appear to one's vision. The technique stressed that the vision would occur in the present moment and that it was not necessary to die and be reborn there. The Pure Land was beyond all realms and beyond the cycle of rebirth. It was filled with light and described as pure. It was also purifying. It resembled a paradise or a realm of deities from an external perspective, whereas it was empty from an internal viewpoint.

The first master of the Chinese Pure Land lineage who can be identified was T'an-luan (476–542), who probably originated the practice of reciting and meditating on the name of Amitābha. With a distinction that was to be influential later in Japan, he differentiated between a self-powered person who practiced meditation and an other-powered person who relied on divine powers to be saved. The former practitioner tended to be egotistical and arrogant, he taught, whereas the other-powered person relied on the inherent power of the name of Amitābha in a nondualistic way to free himself or herself from sin and lead to rebirth in the Pure Land. This path of Buddhism was spread by Tao-ch'o (562–645), who stressed the difficulty of practicing the path during a period of the decline of Buddhism. These religious leaders helped to spread devotional Buddhism to ordinary people and provided them an opportunity to become more fully engaged in Buddhism without renouncing social obligations and connections.

In contrast to the relatively simple nature of the Pure Land movement, the two early major figures of the Hua-yen school, Chih-yen (602–668) and Fa-tsang (643–712), found their inspiration in the *Avataṃsaka Sūtra* (*Flower-ornament/Garland Sūtra*) and developed a notion of a self-creating, self-maintaining, and self-defining organism. Within this cosmos of identity and intercausality, everything was interdependent and empty, which Hua-yen thinkers grasped in a dynamic way. Due to the nature of this cosmos, it was possible to know all of reality by knowing a single phenomenon.

In contrast to the textual inspiration of the Hua-yen school, the T'ien t'ai school, which was established by Chih-i (538–597), found its inspiration in the *Lotus Sūtra*. From this it developed its three-truths doctrine, although ultimately truth was singular and nondual because everything was part of a single organic unity. By contemplating emptiness, conventional existence, and the middle, the human mind emptied itself of deluded thoughts, passion, and other obstacles to lucid understanding and insight into the non-dual nature of truth. This represented the instantaneous dawning of wisdom and destruction of ignorance. Although this Chinese school and the others represented periods of growth and creativity, there were other periods of persecution, stagnation, and decline.

The same kinds of historical vicissitudes can be found in different periods of Japanese Buddhism. After being imported from Korea in the mid-sixth century, Buddhism was accepted gradually by leading Japanese noble families, embraced next by the imperial court, and finally by much of the nation. Early in its Japanese history, Buddhists were involved in a struggle between three families that led to a civil war between the Soga (pro-Buddhism party) and the indigenous pro-Shinto (literally, way of the *kami* or gods) group of the Mononobe and Nakatomi families. The pro-Buddhist party won the war and assumed the imperial throne. The Soga reign lasted until it was overthrown in 645 by the Fujiwara clan, which established an absolute monarchy, centralized bureaucracy, land reform, and continued support of both Buddhism and Shinto.

Buddhism became a state religion in Japan in 728, when the Todaiji Temple was built by Emperor Shomu in the city of Nara, which served as the first permanent capital of Japan and gave the period (710–794) its historical identity. Several schools with Chinese roots were introduced into Japan during this time. Schools such as the Hosso (with a Yogācāra background), Kegon, Jojtsu, Sanron, Kusha, and Ritsu arrived during the seventh and eight centuries; they were based on one or more texts in Chinese translation. During the Nara period, Buddhism and Shinto reached an accommodation, but the period also witnessed priestly interference in politics, corruption, and moral decadence.

The Heian period (794–1185) was marked by the move of the capital to a city that was later to become known as modern Kyoto. Functioning as a figurehead for the Fujiwara family, the Emperor Kammu and his successors constituted the royalty. Gradually, a social and political gap developed between the royalty and the warrior class. The hierarchical structure of the society and lack of upward social mobility created a situation in which the priesthood became a major means of social mobility. Some of the upwardly mobile figures came from the two dominant Buddhist sects of this time: Shingon (True Word), founded by Kukai (773–836), and the Tendai founded by Saicho (767–822), in which the *Lotus Sūtra* represented the truth. Kukai attempted to harmonize Buddhism with the indigenous Chinese religions of Taoism and Confucianism by using an esoteric form of Buddhism that he discovered in the *Mahāvairocana Sūtra* (Text of the Great Radiant One). In order to achieve the goal of a unitive experience with the Great Sun Buddha (Vairocana), practitioners followed a path characterized by esoteric rituals and yogic meditation.

The Kamakura period (1185–1333) ushered into existence new Japanese Buddhist sects that competed with the predominant Tendai and Shingon. With the defeat of the Taira/Fujiwara clan during the Gempei War (1180–1185) by the Minamoto (Genji) clan, a strong feudal system developed, controlled by provincial landed barons (*daimyo*) by means of the strength of arms provided by samurai retainers and vassals. With the capital centered in Kamakura, Japanese culture flourished, and new religious sects such as Zen were introduced. The monk Eisai (1141–1215) founded the Rinzai school, whereas Dōgen Kigen (1200–1253) established the Sōtō school of Zen and late in his life composed the multivolume *Shōbōgenzō* based on his enlightenment experience. The Kamakura period also ushered into existence Japanese Pure Land movements established by Hōnen (1133–1212), his disciple Shinran (1173–1262), and the prophetic figure Nichiren (1222–1282). Providing an alternative to the individual and arduous effort necessary for spiritual success in Zen Buddhism, the devotional path of the Pure Land sects transformed Japanese Buddhism into a mass movement, and helped to send the formerly powerful Shingon and Tendai sects into decline because of lack of financial support. Zen and the devotional movements continued to thrive during the Muromachi period (1336–1573) and rise of the Ashikaga clan. But this era of disorder and conflict was replaced by the Tokugawa period (1600–1868) of peace, order, stability, and unity, centered at the city of Edo (modern Tokyo). This period was characterized by a cult of the emperor and a turn toward Confucianism, Neo-Confucianism, and Shinto. The ideals of social order and a strong moral code embodied within these traditions were also influential during the Meiji Restoration (1868–1912), which reestablished the power of the emperor and created a modern nation-state. During this period, Shinto combined with rising nationalism and eclipsed the influence of Buddhism. The social and emotional trauma associated with the defeat of Japan in World War II enabled new Buddhist religious movements to fill the cultural gap, such as Sōka Gakkai (Value Creation Society), which was inspired by the Nichiren sect and its reliance on the *Lotus Sūtra*.

Buddhism spread northward from India into Tibet in the seventh century C.E. Once introduced into Tibet, Buddhism spread from kings such as Songtsen Gampo (c. 618–650) and Trisong Detsen (c. 740–798) downward to common people. Trisong Detsen was responsible for inviting the first Tantric master, named Padmasambhava, to Tibet; he came to be viewed as a second Buddha. The reign of King Relbachen (815–836) marked a decline in the fortunes of Buddhism in Tibet. Buddhism was later persecuted by King Lang Darma (r. 838–842), who was eventually assassinated by a Buddhist monk. The subsequent collapse of the dynasty caused political chaos, regional fragmentation, and the demise of Tibet as a political power in central Asia. This period concluded the initial dissemination of Buddhism in Tibet.

The second dissemination had, however, more enduring consequences for Buddhism. The end of the tenth century marked a return to stability and a renewed interest in Buddhism. In the hope of revitalizing Buddhism in Tibet, aspiring monks were sent to India to study, and the monk Atiśa (982–1054) was invited to Tibet in 1042, which helped to spread Tantric practice as a method of enhancing the more rapid attainment of Buddhahood. Other gifted religious figures such as Marpa (1012–1096), the sorcerer Milarepa (1040–1123), and his disciple Gampopa (1079–1153) made significant contributions to the establishment of the religion. Tibetan Buddhism experienced a period of persecution at the hands of the Mongols during the thirteenth century, although this also proved to be a momentous time because the khan was converted to Buddhism and in turn appointed a monk regent of Tibet. This latter event ushered in the custom of monastic leaders becoming responsible for the social, political, and religious welfare of Tibetans. The fourteenth century marked a period of decline of Buddhism that was met by the reform efforts of Tsong Khapa (1357–1419), who created the Gelugpa (Order of Virtue) school and advocated Tantric methods. Aristocratic warlords persecuted Buddhist monasteries around the end of the sixteenth century until the Mongols were asked to destroy them. With the help of the Mongols, the fifth Dalai Lama was able to unite the country for the first time in its history. During the nineteenth century, Tibet became a British protectorate until it lost its independence in March of 1959, when the country was invaded by Communist Chinese, which motivated the fourteenth Dalai Lama to flee into exile in India.

In a general way, Tibetan Buddhism consists of an intertwining of Mādhyamika, Yogācāra, Tantra, and the indigenous folk religious tradition. Within the context of this reader, the chapter on Tibetan Buddhism stresses selected texts from Tantric sources, because this is a very significant tradition within Buddhism as a whole and Tibet in particular. The root meaning of the term *tantra* suggests weaving and thread, which for religious practice means a weaving together of apparent opposites such as *nirvāṇa* and *saṃsāra* (rebirth), male and female, wisdom (*prajñā*) and skillful means (*upāya*). In fact, these apparent opposites are really non-dual. The path of Tantra is also called Vajrayāna (diamond/thunderbolt vehicle) and Mantrayāna, due to the extensive usage of sacred formulas (*mantras*) that are continually recited in religious practice. The new Tantric literature represented a challenge to traditional Buddhist moral values and monastic practices. This literature was considered secret and was deliberately obscure and deceptive. It was intended only for the initiated, serious, and advanced aspirant. There was a tendency within Tantric literature to conceive of the microcosmic human body as the nexus of all truth about the macrocosmic universe. In addition, it was considered permissible to use sensual means to reach one's goal of liberation. In fact, the use of the senses and sexual passion can be construed as both dangerous and a more rapid way to attain liberation.

Overview of Mahāyāna Literature

Although the early Mahāyāna tradition created a new type of literature, this massive body of writings was still considered to be the teachings and words of the historical Buddha. This was because texts traced their origin to visionary experiences, vivid dreams, and meditative inspiration from one of several transcendent Buddhas or a Buddha residing in a Buddha realm or Pure Land. On the basis of such experiences, Mahāyāna advocates could insist that these new texts represented the word of the Buddha because the inspired discourses originated from him, even though he was no longer residing on the earth. These new texts accorded with the perfect wisdom of an enlightened being. A later tradition in Mahāyāna created the pious fiction that it represented the true and secret teachings of the Buddha. The rationale for this fiction was simple: These secret teachings represented a deeper and more profound level of the doctrine, and people needed more intellectually sophisticated preparation in order to understand them.

Taking into consideration the wide geographical spread of Mahāyāna Buddhism and the many languages in which its literature was preserved, we are considering a vast body of literature and numerous schools spread over many countries. Mahāyāna scriptures can be divided, for instance, into four major collections: *Prajñāpāramitā, Mahāratnakūta Sūtra, Buddhāyatamsaka,* and the *Mahāsamnipāta.* There is little historical evidence to help us understand the circumstances and contexts under which various individual works were composed or gathered together into these collections.

The style and tone of these texts are very different from those in the Pāli canon. In general terms, many of these texts are more sympathetic to ordinary laypeople; monastic adherents and laity are more devotional in their attitudes and practices; and the Buddha is depicted less as an historical figure and more like a supermundane being. It is possible to find, for instance, the Buddha described as a being of light that lectures to a prodigious multitude of listeners. The Mahāyāna texts present a vast, fantastic cosmology, a cosmos populated by celestial bodhisattvas and deities described in exaggerated terms. It is paradoxical that a more positive worldly attitude often exists alongside very abstract philosophical notions.

The earliest and most influential Mahāyāna body of literature was the *Prajñāpāramitā,* that is, Perfection (*pāramitā*) of Wisdom (*prajñā*). The Sanskrit term for perfection suggested two notions: what was derived from somewhere beyond this world and what was gone (*itā*) beyond this world or to the other side. In short, perfection implied transcendence. If the initial sermon given by the historical Buddha at the Deer Park in Benares after his enlightenment stood for the "first turning of the wheel of the Dharma (teaching)," the Perfection of Wisdom literature represented the "second turning of the wheel of the Dharma (teaching)" from the perspective of Mahāyāna adherents. This so-called wisdom literature inherited technical terminology from prior schools that it reinterpreted and presented as new insights into reality. For instance, the notion of emptiness (*śūnyatā*) involved becoming aware that all things were subject to causal conditions for their existence. Thus all things were devoid of any permanent "own-being" (*svabhāva*) because they owed their existence to something else within the cycle of causation and thus were considered empty.

The anonymous authors of the wisdom literature viewed meditation as the single path to realization, which resulted in a nondual, undifferentiated experience of emptiness. By focusing attention on one thing and meditating on it, its name and form disappeared, and it was no longer a representational object. What remained was reality, but this reality (emptiness) did not manifest itself in any form or representation because it was devoid of all designations, time, space, and limits. It was pure, quiescent, and alone. Among the other themes of the wisdom authors were the compassion, self-sacrificial action, and wisdom of the bodhisattva, who refused to enter final nirvāṇa until everyone was saved. Wisdom should not be understood as a moralizing wisdom about life. Within the context of these anonymous authors, wisdom indicated a direct insight into the true nature of experience and its elements. This insight represented the intuitive awareness of emptiness (*śūnyatā*).

A text called the *Ratnaguṇa-saṃcaya-gāthā* (The Accumulation of Precious Qualities) and another presenting the prose version of the *Aṣṭasāhasrika* (8,000 Line Sūtra) probably represented two of the earliest examples of Mahāyāna literature. These texts are dated around the second century B.C.E. Other works, titled according to the number of their lines, included such texts as the *Perfect Wisdom in 18,000 Lines, Perfect Wisdom in 25,000 Lines,* and *Perfect Wisdom in 100,000 Lines.* These texts were probably composed between 100 C.E. and 300 C.E. These texts give the impression of being disjointed, repetitive, and difficult to understand due to their diverse and subtle arguments and the philosophical perspectives of different authors. These long and difficult texts invited the creation of something shorter and easier to grasp intellectually.

Two outstanding examples of shorter texts of wisdom literature were the *Heart Sūtra* and the *Diamond Sūtra,* which were composed between 300 and 500 C.E. Both texts focused on the notion of emptiness (*śūnyatā*). Reality was broken down into conditioned and unconditioned elements of reality (*dharmas*). The reference to dharmas as existing things must be distinguished from the use of the term *Dharma,* which refers to Buddhist teachings. Everything within the world was conditioned by something else, whereas there were only two unconditioned facts of reality, namely, space and nirvāṇa (ultimate liberation). Due to their conditioned status, the vast majority of dharmas (elements of reality) were devoid of their own being. These texts strongly suggested that in order to become aware of the essential nature of dharmas it was necessary to gain an awareness of their emptiness and that no entities possessed a separate mode of existence.

In addition to the *Heart Sūtra* and the *Diamond Sūtra,* there were other shorter texts of the wisdom type. The *Perfection of Wisdom in 2,500 Lines* was composed before 500 C.E., whereas the *Perfection of Wisdom in 50 Lines* was probably composed in the sixth century C.E., and the *Perfection of Wisdom in 700 Lines* was composed between about 600 and 700 C.E. The *Abhisamayālankāra* (A Treatise Explaining the Perfection of Wisdom) attributed to Maitreya, a celestial bodhisattva, was an exegetical work and summary of the wisdom philosophy of emptiness. Following the format of these texts with their continual dialogue between the Buddha and various other human and supernatural figures, there was also the *Adhvarhaśatikā* (150 Verses) *Prajñāpāramitā* (Perfection of Wisdom). These texts were conceived as the word of the historical Buddha, and they were intended to promote salvation. The philosophy of emptiness embodied in these texts was believed to be verifiable by any diligent meditator. By 700 C.E., the creative energy of the wisdom literature gradually came to and end. The teachings of the wisdom literature were later compressed into very short magical spells with hidden meanings that were revealed to a selected few adherents. This development coincided with the spread of Tantric ideas, and it manifested its influence in the wisdom literature from 600 to 1200 C.E. Within the context of the historical development of Tantra, its practitioners used wisdom literature and notions as a source of wonder-working and ritual magic.

At a later stage of development, the wisdom literature was conceived as an independent spiritual power. This conception reflected a tendency to refer to Mahāyāna texts with the epithet *vaipulya* (extensively glorious). The Perfection of Wisdom found a place in the Mahāyāna pantheon alongside Buddhist bodhisattvas such as Maitreya (Kindly One), Mañjuśrī (Sweet Glory), Avalokiteśvara (the Lord who looks down), and the Buddha Amitābha. As with members of the pantheon, the Perfection of Wisdom now became an entity worthy of worship and reverence as either a member of the Mahāyāna pantheon or as a sacred text on earth. In fact, the Perfection of Wisdom became personified as the mother figure that gave birth to all Buddhas with her ability to give birth to the mind of awakening.

Mahāyāna Buddhists were originally organized around various particular texts, but it was not unusual to discover single texts being collected into an overarching anthology of sacred texts. An excellent example of such a collection of Buddhist texts is the *Mahāratnakūṭa* (Great Jewel Mountain) that consisted of forty-nine texts collected sometime after the fifth century C.E. Although the history of this collection of texts is obscure, we do know that the south Indian monk Bodhiruci edited these texts around the beginning of the eighth century in China. Prior to this date, the monk Dharmarakṣa translated the texts into Chinese during the third century. It is possible that the collection took shape in Central Asia before arriving in China. It appears to have been gathered from a smaller collection of texts in a haphazard way without a preconceived plan.

Another collection of texts was entitled the *Buddhāvataṃsaka* (Text of the Garland of Buddhas), which was redacted into a single text around 350 C.E. after circulating for centuries as various shorter and independent texts. The title is suggestive because it refers to a both discourse about the Buddha's garlands and a descriptive discourse about the garlands of an interconnected series of Buddhas. The Buddhist tradition recognizes the text as a visionary work and a summary of the most profound meaning of Buddhist thought. This recognition is suggested because the text represents an attempt to view the world from the perspective of perfect enlightenment. Two Chinese recensions consisting of thirty-four and thirty-nine chapters are also known. In addition, there is a reference to this composite work dating from the beginning of the fifth century C.E., along with refer-

ences to China and Kashgar in the text that suggest to scholars that it was originally compiled in Central Asia. The monk Buddhabhadra translated a version of
the text in sixty scrolls between 418 and 420 C.E., whereas Śikṣānanda translated
an eighty scroll version between 695 and 699 C.E. Two major components of
the text consist of the *Gaṇḍavyūha Sūtra* (Entry into the Absolute Text) and the
Daśabhūmika Sūtra (Ten Stages of the Bodhisattva's Career Text). The former text
relates the spiritual quest of the young man Sudhana and his encounter with
fifty-two teachers in his search for liberation, while the latter text gives the ten
stages of the path of the bodhisattva and suggests an earlier date of composition,
although both texts were probably compiled between 50 and 150 C.E. The overall
work of the *Buddhāvataṃsaka* reflects the influence of Yogācāra philosophy,
which is a path that stresses yogic techniques, meditation, and consciousness-only
as the ultimate reality.

The final major collection of Mahāyāna texts is the *Mahāsaṃnipāta Sūtra,*
with texts originally composed at various times between 200 and 300 C.E. The collection achieved its present form of seventeen texts at a later date. There is mini-
mal cohesion or rationale for the collection, which is only preserved in its entirety
in Chinese, whereas particular texts appear separately within the Tibetan canon.
The final collection probably reflects the Ephthalites' invasion of India in the sixth
century, because it embodies a negative conviction that the Buddha's religion
would only last for a thousand years. After this period, Buddhism would endure a
gradual decline until its total disappearance from the world. The historical decline
of Buddhism becomes an important theme in teachings of Pure Land Buddhism,
which emphasizes devotion and supernatural assistance in order to be reborn into
a state of paradise from which a person can achieve final liberation.

In addition to these major collections of Mahāyāna texts, there also circulated
independent texts such as the *Saddharma-puṇḍarīka* (Lotus Sūtra), *Vimalakīrti-
nirdeśa Sūtra* (Teachings of the Bodhisattva Unstained-Glory), *Laṅkāvatāra Sūtra*
(Text on the Descent into Lanka), *Sandhinirmocana Sūtra* (Text on Freeing the
Connections or Knots), and the *Avataṃsaka Sūtra* (Flower-ornament Text). The
Laṅkāvatāra Sūtra and *Sandhinirmocana Sūtra* influenced the Yogācāra school of
Mahāyāna Buddhism. The former text lacks the systematic nature of the latter.

Included within the contents of the *Sandhinirmorcana,* there are references to such important Yogācāra philosophical notions as the storehouse consciousness, the threefold unreality of phenomena, the three natures, and discussions of meditation. The *Lankāvatāra Sūtra* agrees with the *Sandhinirmocana Sūtra* about phenomena being products of minds, devoid of any independent reality. The *Lankāvatāra Sūtra* and the *Sandhinirmocana Sūtra* reached the apogee of their influence and popularity during the fifth century in China. The idealistic spirit of these texts can also be discovered in the *Avataṃsaka Sūtra,* where consciousness constitutes all phenomena; this leads to a conviction about the complete identity and interdependence of all existence. The text also taught that mutual identity and interdependence were two ways to express the emptiness of phenomena. Unlike other Mahāyāna texts in which the Buddha delivered a sermon to an assembly of people, the *Avataṃsaka Sūtra* represented a series of discourses given by various bodhisattvas describing their ecstatic states. The *Avataṃsaka Sūtra* became the foundational text of the Hua-yen school of Chinese Buddhism, founded by Tu-shun (557–640) and developed by Fa-tsang (643–712).

Exerting an influence similar to these types of texts, the *Vimalakīrtinirdeśa Sūtra* (Teachings of the Bodhisattva Unstained-Glory) which was composed around 100 C.E., functioned as a major influence upon the Mādhyamika school, which was founded by the monk Nāgārjuna (c. 150–250 C.E.), who developed a nondualistic philosophy and asserted that everything is empty, impermanent, contingent, and totally lacks any self-nature. This text also made an important contribution to the development of the notion of the lay bodhisattva. In other words, it was no longer necessary for a bodhisattva to be a monastic person and renounce society and the world, because it was now possible for an ordinary person living within the world to lead the life of a bodhisattva and help others. The message of the text was that the path of the bodhisattva was open to everyone.

The path of the bodhisattva and its ethical dimensions were examined by the eighth-century monk Śāntideva, who was a resident of the monastic university at Nālandā in his work entitled *Bodhicaryāvatāra* (Entering the Path of Enlightenment). According to a hagiographic narrative, other monks conspired to embarrass him because they thought that he was a lazy monk who did nothing but eat, sleep, and defecate. The monks asked him to give a learned recitation, to which he finally and reluctantly agreed. The conspiring monks created an extremely high chair on which he was instructed to sit in order to give his recitation. This was the physical aspect of their attempt to humiliate him. Due to his magical powers, Sāntideva lowered the seat, sat down, and asked whether they would like to hear something old or new. When the conspiring monks chose the latter, Sāntideva began to recite the *Bodhicaryāvatāra* from memory. At one point of the recitation, Sāntideva ascended into space and disappeared, although the monks could still hear his voice. Sāntideva was also famous for his work entitled *Śikṣāsamuccaya* (Compendium of Discipline), which was an anthology of Mahāyāna literture complied from various sources.

An early text, composed about the same time as the *Vimalakīrtinirdeśa* (c. 100 C.E.), the *Lotus Sūtra* was a composite work that became extremely popular. It inspired the development of the T'ien-tai school in China, which was imported to Japan; there it became known as the politically powerful and influential Tendai sect during the medieval period. The T'ien-t'ai (Celestial Platform) school was founded by Chih-i (538–597). It was also called the Lotus school because it asserted that the *Lotus Sūtra* represented the highest level of Buddhist teaching. The text was also central to later religious movements in Japan, such as the Nichiren sect of the thirteenth century and the Sōka Gakkai sect of the twentieth century. The *Lotus Sūtra* directed its appeal to a popular audience with a message of universal salvation and an endorsement of lay devotional practices such as relic worship, gaining merit, and the use of protective charms. These types of popular devotion were connected to the notion of skillful means (*upāya*), which included various means of conveying the message of Buddhism, such as using parables or performing miracles. The path of salvation in the *Lotus Sūtra* advocated faith and the importance of the true Dharma (teaching) that is embodied by the text. In short, the *Lotus Sūtra* represented the truth and the only means to salvation because other teachings were false or counterfeit. By adhering to the text, a person could expect the protection of the Buddha. Likewise, a person should keep, read, and recite the text, which brings earthly benefits that are social, personal, and ultimately liberating. Because Buddhas appeared on earth and eventually disappeared, the most enduring aspect of Buddhism was the teaching (Dharma). Since the *Lotus Sūtra* embodied the truth of the Buddha from the perspective of its believers, the text itself became an object of worship.

Overview of Major Mahāyāna Schools

In addition to these examples of independent texts, Mahāyāna Buddhism inspired an extensive philosophical literature that it is impossible to survey in this brief introduction. Because of the texts and figures included in this anthology, it is important to call attention to the Mādhyamika and Yogācāra schools of philosophy. This volume includes selections from the *Fundamentals of the Middle Way* by Nāgārjuna, who lived during the second century C.E., and who is given credit with establishing the Mādhyamika school, although it was the philosopher Candrakīrti who gave the school its name in the seventh century C.E. There are also selections by Vasubandhu, who was converted to the Yogācāra school by his brother Asanga. These two schools exerted a profound influence on later Buddhist schools in Tibet, China, Korea, and Japan.

Although Nāgārjuna's name is attached to numerous works, he is probably most famous for the authorship of *Fundamentals of the Middle Way*, a work written in response to the philosophy of the Sarvāstivāda Abhidharma school, which advocated the reality of dharmas (categories of existing entities). Nāgārjuna is given credit for developing the implications and systematizing the philosophy embodied within the *Prajñāpāramitā* (Perfection of Wisdom) literature into what he conceived to be a middle path between the two extremes of eternalism (is) and nihilism (is not). In the *Fundamentals of the Middle Way*, Nāgārjuna draws a distinction between two kinds of truth, which he identifies as conventional and ultimate. By using this distinction and his dialectic method, he develops the implications for a philosophy of emptiness that is intended to end all philosophical questions, answers, and positions.

The Yogācāra school, represented by the brothers Asanga and Vasubandhu, attempted to account for philosophical points neglected by the Mādhyamika school. The school also wanted to ground insight into emptiness in a critical understanding of consciousness and make its underlying structure explicit. The central position of this school is that only consciousness, which is identified with emptiness, truly exists. In addition, the school attempted to account for error, memory, subjectivity, suffering, and the nature of who or what experiences ultimate truth. The school is famous for its discussion of the nature of consciousness, identification of the storehouse consciousness, and its doctrine of the three bodies of the Buddha. The Yogācāra and Mādhyamika schools helped to shape the philosophy of Tibetan Buddhism.

The Tibetan tradition did a wonderful job of preserving older texts and composing new works. This is evident in its twofold canon of the *Kanjur* (Word) and *Tenjur* (Treatises). The *Tenjur* consists of works by individual thinkers, which are not considered the word of the Buddha although they embody the spirit of his teaching according to its authors. The *Kanjur* does represent the word of the Buddha, and consists of thirteen volumes of monastic rules, twenty-one volumes of wisdom teachings, forty-four volumes of various Mahāyāna sūtras (texts), and twenty-two volumes of Tantric texts. This voluminous body of literature also includes commentaries by various scholars.

Due to limitations of length, this anthology only includes selections from the great Tibetan reformer Tsong Khapa (1357–1419) and revitalizer of the Prāsangika Mādhyamika school of philosophy. Tsong Khapa intended to maintain ordinary reality and to also affirm something ultimate, while he also wanted to avoid any kind of reification that would lead to a kind of absolutism. He simultaneously repudiated nihilism. In his work as a religious reformer, Tsong Khapa allowed for the practice of Tantra at an advanced point in a person's quest for liberation.

The path of Tantra in Tibetan Buddhism is also called Vajrayāna, which means the diamond vehicle. The diamond is a Buddhist metaphor for that which is hard and indestructible. By extension, it represents that which is eternal or innate. Within the Buddhist context, it refers to the state of Buddhahood possessed by all beings and the ability of wisdom (*vajra*) to cut through anything, including illusion and false views. Buddhist Tantra can be traced to a variety of social groups within India that appropriated the designation Siddha (accomplished one) during the medieval period with their roots in the Hindu Śaiva religious movement. The

Siddhas attempted to gain power or authority by providing ethically dubious services to social leaders, which often took the form of prophecy, spirit possession, demonic control, love potions, generation of wealth, and magical or actual murder. The Buddhist Siddhas represented a new social type of disenfranchised people who attempted to establish regional centers of autonomous power on the fringes of the prevailing Hindu culture. The Siddhas introduced a pantheon of tribal and local goddesses, and ferocious, murderous, blood-drinking gods that was gradually adopted by Tibetan culture.

The literature that developed in Tibet from the Siddha-influenced tradition was believed to be revealed by deities, the Buddha—who is called Bhagavat (Lord)—or substitute figures such as Vajradhara (Diamond-holder). The texts were divided into four classes, although Tibetans debated which ones to include in each category. The first class was Kriyā, which was revealed for those who enjoy external ritual more than internal concentration. The Caryā class is for those who like external ritual and internal concentration equally, whereas the Yoga class is for those who enjoy inner concentration. The final class of Anuttara yoga texts are for those who only like inner concentration. The primary text of the Caryā class was the *Vairocanābhisambodhi-tantra* (Radiant Perfect Enlightenment Tantra), the *Tattvasamgraha* (Reality of Attractive Action) was a major example of the Yoga class. Some Tibetan schools stressed particular texts. The *Hevajra-tantra* served as a basic text for the Sakyapa sect before it turned to the *Kālacakra-tantra* (Wheel of Time Tantra) at a later date. Occasionally, Tibetan Tantric texts were classified according to the stages in the deities' courtship. Deities are depicted, for instance, laughing in the Kriyā class. Male and female deities gaze adoringly at each other in the Caryā class, whereas they hold hands in the Yoga class. The final Anuttara yoga classification imaged the deities in sexual union.

As is evident in the selections made for this anthology from two Tantric texts, there is a widespread use of sexual symbolism in which the germinal thought of awakening is identified with semen and dormant wisdom refers to a female waiting for insemination. The two important Mahāyāna notions of wisdom (*prajñā*) and skillful means (*upāya*) are reinterpreted and given explicit sexual connotations. The female is identified with wisdom, a mother figure, feminine yogi, and low-caste whore, whereas the male element is represented by skillful means, which can be used to visualize the female aspect as the consort of the male figure. The technique of visualization helps a couple mentally see the male and female deities in sexual embrace, and this provides a mental picture for them to copy in their own ritualized actions. The perfect union of wisdom and skillful means symbolizes the perfect union of nondual emptiness. Eating forbidden food like meat products, drinking liquor, and engaging in sexual techniques are practices intended to hasten release on the path to the goal of nonduality. In the highest and most esoteric group of Tantric literature called Anuttara yoga tantra, it is not unusual to find the Buddha preaching from the vagina (*bhaga*) of his consort, which symbolizes wisdom (*prajñā*).

The two Tantric texts chosen for inclusion in this anthology were very influential–the *Hevajra Tantra* and *Caṇḍamahāroṣaṇa Tantra* (Wrathful Caṇḍa Tantra). The former text can be dated to around the sixth century C.E., and the latter text probably belongs to the seventh century C.E. These texts and others like the *Mahāvairocana* (Great Illuminator) and the *Guhyasamāja* (Secret Union) are examples of the types of works studied at Nālandā University in northern India in the late seventh century, within the context of a thriving Tantric circle of scholars and masters who were members of the faculty. Their influence eventually extended to Tibet and aided the development of its schools.

As in Tibet and India, Mahāyāna Buddhism continued to develop in China into several major schools. This anthology focuses on four major Chinese schools: Hua-yen, T'ien t'ai, Pure Land, and Ch'an. These schools serve as excellent examples of Mahāyāna Buddhism as it underwent adaptation to Chinese culture. They were influenced by indigenous Chinese presuppositions, notions, and terms from Taoism that were used to translate or explain abstract Buddhist notions. The notion of causality is reinterpreted, for instance, in a more positive way that stresses the interdependence of things.

These types of development are evident in the Hua-yen school and the thought of Fa-tsang (643–712), who is credited by many scholars with establishing the school. Fa-tsang taught about the interdependent nature of all things. He also taught that things are different, just like fire and ice. This philosophical position is called identity in difference, because things are simultaneously the same and distinctive. Since things share an identical essence by virtue of being empty, this implies that one cause is identical with other causes and yet also different. A wheat seed is, for instance, the primary cause of a new plant, signifying that which is identical. Nonetheless, a grain of wheat needs soil, rain, and sun to grow into a healthy plant. Although each of these elements possesses a different nature, they are all necessary for the plant. The lesson is that intercausality is the result of supporting conditions and interpenetration. Thus the Hua-yen philosophy indicates that all things are coexistent, interwoven, interrelated, interpenetrating, mutually inclusive, and reflect each other.

The Hua-yen school views everything from the state of enlightenment in which a person sees the world as transparently illuminated by Vairocana Buddha. For this school, there is no difference between this world and that of enlightenment, with the exception of ignorant attachment to the notion of an enduring self, a mistaken belief that words and concepts are absolute, and a mistaken adherence to external forms as substantial. This position represents a unique Chinese contribution to Buddhism.

The T'ien t'ai school made another important contribution. Because a vast body of Buddhist literature confronted it, the T'ien t'ai school attempted to comprehend its vastness, numerous contradictions, and doctrinal differences by explaining these problems with its doctrine of the five periods of Buddha's life as a teacher and of the unfolding of Buddhist teachings. The Hua-yen school, based on the *Avataṃsaka* (Flower-ornament) text, represented the initial period. The Buddha preached this text after his enlightenment in a state of ecstatic bliss, a period that lasted three weeks. Because people were not ready for it, they could not comprehend it. The next period was marked by the A-han or Agama period, represented by Hīnayāna scriptures. This period lasted twelve years, during which the Buddha did not teach the full truth. Next, the Fang-teng or Vaipulya (Long Story) period lasted for eight years. During this time, the Buddha did not teach the Mahāyāna truths in their fullness, although he did teach about the superiority of the bodhisattva (literally, enlightened being) over the arhat (enlightened being). As suggested by the term Vaipulya, this period was "broad and equal" in the sense that the teaching was universal, on the one hand, and equal, on the other hand, because the texts taught the doctrine of the sameness (*samatā*) of the Buddha and human beings–they manifested the sameness of absolute and relative. This was called the period of the rebuke, because the Buddha rebuked the arhats. Next, the Tan-pan-jo or Mahāprajñāpāramitā (Great Perfection of Wisdom) period lasted twenty-two years. During this period, the Buddha began to discuss abstract metaphysical issues, and he taught the truth of emptiness so that disciples could overcome the mistakes of the Hīnayāna school. This period was concerned with indicating the absolute nonexistence of opposites such as saṃsāra (rebirth) and nirvāṇa or subject and object, which were merely figments of our imagination. This period was thus called "exploring and uniting all dharmas (existing entities)." Finally, there arrived the Fa-hua nieh-p'an or the *Lotus Sūtra* period. This period took place during the final eight years of the Buddha's life, when he stressed the absolute identity of opposites. At that time, all ways were united into one vehicle or path (*ekayāna*). The Buddha's mission to save all creatures marked this period.

These five periods were analogous to the story of the prodigal son that was adapted from the *Lotus Sūtra*. Due to poverty, a young man was forced to leave home to find a livelihood. During his absence, his father became very wealthy. When he returned home, the youth did not recognize his father, mistaking the old man for a prince. The father, however, recognized his son, while lamenting that he had no one with whom to share his fortune. The father sent messengers to retrieve his son, but the youth became frightened and fainted, because he feared being arrested. After reviving his son, the father did not reveal his identity–which was analogous to the first period when the Buddha explained his doctrine, although people could not understand it. Wondering what he had to do to rescue his son from his ignorance about his true identity, the father hired his son to work in his palace, so that he could be near him. Taking pity on his son, the father increased his wages and gave the youth whatever he desired. The older man instructed the unaware youth to treat him as his father–which was similar to the second period of the teaching. After the father began to call the boy "son," the young man began to feel more comfortable and at home. As he lost his fear, the young man acquired confidence, which represented the third period, in which a person possessed faith in the Mahāyāna teachings, but did not think that it was possible to attain enlightenment. After becoming ill and nearing death, the rich man beckoned his son to his side and gave him an inheritance. This represented the fourth period, when a person was not perfectly enlightened. The young man accepted the estate and wealth from his dying father, but he did not think that he owned it. The young man continued to reside in his straw hut. Finally, the dying father, who was aware of his impending demise, presented the young man to his relatives as his long-lost son. Now the son abandoned his straw hut and began to live in the palace. This represented the fifth period of teaching, during which a person fully grasped the deep meaning of Buddhahood. This period corresponded, of course, to the teachings of the T'ien t'ai school and the truth embodied within the *Lotus Sūtra*. Nonetheless, the T'ien t'ai school agrees with the Hua-yen school that delusion and enlightenment penetrate each other.

In addition to the Hua-yen and T'ien t'ai schools of Chinese Buddhism, another important development occurred with the founding of the Pure Land school. The selections in the Pure Land part of the anthology are intended to supplement the earlier selections from the shorter *Sukhāvatīvyūha Sūtra*. This text was translated by Kumārajiva in 402 C.E. The longer version of *Sukhāvatīvyūha Sūtra* was most likely composed in the northwestern region of India around 100 C.E. The term *sukhāvati* refers to possessing happiness, which functions as the antonym of suffering (*dukkha*). Another important text that only exists in a Chinese version is the *The Sūtra on the Visualization of the Buddha of Immeasurable Light* (*Kuan ching*), which was translated by Kalayaśas (424 C.E.) from a text composed in Central Asia. This text discusses nine grades of rebirth into the Pure Land. These nine grades can be divided into three classes: those skilled in meditation, unskilled meditators who are very ethical, and those who can only recite the name of Amitābha, the Buddha figure presiding over the Pure Land.

T'an-luan (476–542 C.E.) and Tao-ch'o (562–645 C.E.) are considered two of the most important representatives of the Pure Land School in China. T'an-luan was considered the first master of the Chinese Pure Land lineage, and his doctrine represented the fifth and final historical stage of the doctrine for this school. This final historical stage was preceded by an appearance of multiple Buddhas before the death of the historical Buddha, a belief in the existence of a single Buddha ruling the universe but existing simultaneously in other worlds, the emergence of Amitābha as the central figure in the Pure Land, and adoption of the practices of visualization and recitation. The fifth stage of Pure Land historical development emerged with the practices of reciting and meditating on the name of Amitābha introduced by T'an-luan. Tao-ch'o continued the spread of Pure Land Buddhism among common people by stressing the difficulty of practicing Buddhism during the current age of moral and intellectual decline. The path of Pure Land represented the best chance for salvation under the current degenerate era by means of reciting the name of Amitābha.

During the time that the Pure Land school gained adherents among the laity in China, another movement with an emphasis on meditation was simultaneously taking place in China. This movement became recognized as the Ch'an school, which traced its lineage back to the historical Buddha and more immediately to a south Indian figure named Bodhidharma in the sixth century C.E. The Ch'an tradition attributes six works to Bodhidharma. Among his works found among the Tun-huang manuscripts (named for an area in which they were discovered), there were *The Two Ways of Entrance* and *The Gate of Repose.* There was also the *Short Treatise on the Four Practices for Entering the Mahāyāna Way.*

The Platform Sutra of the Sixth Patriarch marked an important point in the development of Ch'an Buddhism and its literature. This text was composed after the death of its central figure, Hui-neng (638–713), but is more than a narrative about the life, teachings, and death of Hui-neng. It reflects a split between the northern and southern schools of Ch'an Buddhism in the seventh century C.E. over issues of the path of liberation and whether the experience of enlightenment should be termed gradual or sudden. The emphasis on the suddenness of enlightenment was led by the successor of Hui-neng, called Shen-hui (684–758), who launched an attack on the northern school, charging it with practicing and disseminating false teaching and practice. This attack on the northern school proved to be successful and helped to promote the Sixth Patriarch, although the northern school continued to be a religious force for several centuries.

The T'ang Dynasty (618–906) witnessed the emergence of a number of out-standing teachers, such as the dynamic Ma-tsu (709–788), who used shouting as a pedagogical tool; Chao-chou (778–897), who emphasized spontaneity; Pai-chang (729–814), who stressed the importance of work and monastic regulations in *The Pure Rule of Pai-chang;* Huang-po (d. c. 850), who used formalizing shouting as a teaching method; and Lin-chi (d. 866), who used physical beatings. It has been common practice to refer to this period as the golden age of Ch'an, but contem-porary historians have challenged this claim by showing that the Sung period (960–1279), which followed, represented both a transition in the structure of Chi-nese society and a cultural flowering of literature, art, and philosophy. The Sung Dynasty, therefore, was not a period of decline for Buddhism following an alleged golden age in the T'ang Dynasty. The Sung Dynasty was a period during which con-tending lineages of Buddhist schools continued to develop under the influence of the writings of Tsung-mi (780–841), who gave them a unified vision. Nonetheless, this anthology stresses the so-called golden age of Ch'an in China with selections about some of the great masters.

The Sung Dynasty marked a period when five major chronicles were compiled during a two-hundred-year time span. *The Five Records of the Lamp* was compiled by Wu-teng lu. The "lamp" was the authority that was passed from one generation to another on the basis of the enlightenment experience, which was traced back to the original experience of the historical Buddha. The second major chronicle was *The Chung-te Record of the Transmission of the Lamp,* gathered together by Tao-yüan and published in 1011, in which the Buddha's disciple Kāśyapa is the original transmitter of the mind of the Buddha. An industrious lay disciple compiled the *The T'ien-sheng Record of the Widely Extending Lamp;* a monk named Fo-kuo Wei-po compiled *The Chien-chung Ching-kuo Supplementary Record of the Lamp* and published it in 1103. The line of transmission ended with six Chinese patriarchs at the end of the T'ang around 906. A work published in 1183 by Hui-weng Wu-ming entitled *A Collection of Essential Material from the Ch'an Successive Records of the Lamp* makes available information on the seven prior Buddhas and their continu-ity with Indian and Chinese patriarchs. Finally, Lei-an Cheng-shou completed in 1204 *The Chia-t'ai Comprehensive Record of the Lamp,* which emphasizes the Sung period. In addition to these chronicles, there was also *The Collection of Four Houses* around the tenth century, which compiled the sayings, discourses, and stories of famous masters such as Ma-tsu, Pai-chang, Huang-po, and Lin-chi. During the eleventh to the twelfth centuries, the discourses of the influential master Lin-chi (born c. 810–815) appeared in the *Record of Lin-chi*. In a sense the appearance of this work stressed the dominance of his school in Chinese Ch'an Buddhism in succeeding centuries.

There was an historical continuity between developments of Buddhist schools in China and Japan, because the latter imported many from the former. Because of restrictions of length, it is impossible to cover all the Japanese Buddhist schools in this anthology, and so it focuses on Pure Land Buddhism and Zen Buddhism. There are selections of the seminal Pure Land figures Hōnen (1133–1212), founder of the Jōdo (Pure Land) School, and his disciple Shinran (1173–1262), founder of the Jōdo Shinshu (True Pure Land) sect. Finally, there are selections from the writings of Nichiren (1222–1282), who embraced the *Lotus Sūtra* as the embodiment of the truth. These teachers lived during the Kamakura period, a time of political violence and natural disasters associated with drought, storms, famine, epidemics, fires, and earthquakes. It was common for these types of misfortune to be used as proof that the end of time was approaching. At the very least, these events were taken as evidence of the degenerate nature of the period, when it was extremely difficult to practice religion and win salvation. It is important to keep this historical context in mind when reading the works of these three figures and the sense of urgency under which they composed their works.

If Pure Land Buddhism represented the easy path of the masses, Zen Buddhism was a difficult path for the few who possessed strong wills and determination. It emphasized the necessity of renouncing the world, monastic discipline, study, and meditation. The term "Zen" is a Japanese translation of the word Ch'an, which is the Chinese translation of the Sanskrit term for meditation (*dhyāna*). Although there were a number of Zen sects in Japanese history, the Rinzai and Sōtō sects were probably the two most influential. The former is represented by selections from the writings of the reformer Hakuin (c. 1685–1768), who emphasized the necessity for creating radical doubt by means of the *kōan* (enigmatic statements made by former masters). Dōgen (1200–1253) is the major representative of the Sōtō sect; his major work, the *Shōbōgenzō,* reflects his overall philosophy, understanding of method, and notion of Buddha-nature.

The anthology concludes with selections from the hagiographical literature from China, and Japan, and with material about women. Hagiographies are important because these various figures represent religious paradigms of Buddhism and function as resources for Buddhist folk culture within the context of both oral and written transmission of Buddhist ideals. These selections complement the hagiographical literature from the earlier Theravāda tradition. Similarly, the selections related to women are intended to complement the material from the Theravāda tradition.

12

Prajñāpāramitā Literature

The type of Mahāyāna literature exemplified in this chapter was originally composed around 100 B.C.E., and these early examples of the *Prajñāpāramitā* (Perfection of Wisdom) literature were texts titled according to the number of lines until some became very long, like the *Perfect Wisdom in 100,000 Lines.* Due to the repetitive nature of these texts, level of difficulty, and different arguments that tended to confound readers, Buddhists revised them into shorter, more manageable, and more comprehensible texts. The two selections for this chapter–from the *Heart Sūtra* and *Diamond Sūtra*–are excellent examples of these more concise writings. Both were composed between approximately 300 and 500 C.E., and proved to be both very influential and popular. Both texts discuss the philosophy of emptiness that was so important to various schools of Mahāyāna.

The *Heart Sūtra* is authoritative because it is based on a direct intuitive experience of emptiness, which the text attempts to explain by discussing conditioned and unconditioned elements of reality (*dharmas*). Every element of reality is conditioned with the exception of space and nirvāṇa. It is possible for a person to proceed from a mental act of differentiation of the elements and proceed to a second act of depersonalization and elimination of all references to the self; the final step is an act of evaluation that provides insight into the truth of the Buddhist position in contrast with a person's normal mode of knowing. Besides looking at the philosophical implications of emptiness, the text discusses the nature of its dialectic. Through a series of three stages, one realizes that emptiness is a transcendent and immanent reality, the essential mark of all things (*dharmas*), and finally one

realizes the complete emptiness of all elements. This dialectic concludes by denying the initial step. A person now realizes that all entities (*dharmas*) totally lack an
independent mode of existence.

The same philosophy of emptiness contained in the *Heart Sūtra* can also be
discovered in the *Diamond Sūtra*. The advantage of the *Diamond Sūtra* is that it
provides an outline of the bodhisattva's career. A reader should become aware of
its definition of the Tathāgata and its advice to those individuals that have not
reached perfection.

Selection from the *Heart Sūtra*

Homage to the Perfection of Wisdom! Thus have I heard. The Lord dwelled at
Rajagṛha, on the Vulture Peak, along with a large gathering of both monks and
bodhisattvas. At that time the Lord, after he had taught the discourse on Dharma
called "deep splendor," had entered into concentration seated alone. At that time
also the holy Lord Avalokiteśvara, the Bodhisattva, was meditating on the perfection of wisdom, he looked down from on high, and he saw the five aggregates, and
he grasped them as empty in their own being.

Thereupon the Venerable Śāriputra, influenced by the Buddha's absorption
in concentration, said to the holy Lord Avalokiteśvara, the Bodhisattva: "How
should the sons or daughters of good family train themselves if they want to practice the perfection of wisdom?"

The holy Lord Avalokiteśvara, the Bodhisattva, then said to the Venerable
Śāriputra: "If the sons or daughters of good family want to follow this profound
perfection of wisdom, they should thus consider:

"There are the five aggregates that constitute a person, and these he sees in
their own-being as empty. Here, O Śāriputra, form is emptiness and emptiness is
form; emptiness is not other than form, form is no different from emptiness;
whatever is form is emptiness, whatever is emptiness, that is form. The same
emptiness is evident in feelings, perceptions, impulses, and consciousness. Thus,
O Śāriputra, all dharmas are empty of own-being, are without marks; they are neither produced nor cease, neither defiled nor pure, neither deficient nor complete. Therefore then, O Śāriputra, where there is emptiness there is no form, no
feeling, no perception, no impulse, no consciousness; no eye, ear, nose, tongue,
body, or mind; no sound, no smell, no taste, no touch, no object of mind; no sight-

organ element; there is no ignorance, no extinction of ignorance; there is no old age and death, no extinction of old age and death; there are no Four Noble Truths; no suffering, no origination of suffering, no cessation of suffering, and no path leading to the end of suffering; there is no cognition, no attainment, and no non-attainment.

"Therefore then, O Śāriputra, due to a bodhisattva's indifference to any kind of personal attainment he lives as one who has relied solely on the perfection of wisdom. Without any objective support to his thought, he does not tremble, he has overcome confusion, and is sustained by nirvāṇa. All Buddhas in the three periods of time—through having relied on the perfection of wisdom—they reach full awakening and perfect enlightenment.

"Therefore, one should know the Perfection of Wisdom as the great mantra, the mantra of great knowledge, the invincible mantra, the unsurpassed mantra, conqueror of all suffering, in truth—for what could go wrong? In the Perfection of Wisdom has this mantra been uttered. It goes like this: gone, gone, gone beyond, gone altogether beyond, what and awakening, all hail! It is thus, O Śāriputra, that a bodhisattva should train himself in the path of the profound perfection of wisdom."

Thereupon, the Lord emerged from that meditative concentration, and he applauded the holy Lord Avalokiteśvara, the Bodhisattva: "Well said, well said, son of good family! Just so, son of good family, just so should one travel in the path of the deep perfection of wisdom. As you have explained it, so it is approved by all the tathāgatas."

Thus spoke the Lord. Enraptured the Venerable Śāriputra, the holy Lord Avalokiteśvara, the Bodhisattva, and those monks and those bodhisattvas, and the whole world with its gods, men, asuras, garudas, and gandharvas rejoiced in the Lord's teaching.

Source: *Hṛdaya Sūtra* (*Heart Sūtra of Perfect Wisdom*), edited by F. Max Müller (Oxford: Oxford University Press, 1884), pp. 25–28.

Selections from the *Diamond Sūtra*

1. Introduction

1. Thus have I heard. The Lord dwelt at Śravasti, in the Jeta Grove, in the garden of Anathapindada, together with a large gathering that consisted of 1,250 monks, and with many Bodhisattvas. Early in the morning the Lord dressed in his robes, carried his bowl, and entered the great city of Śravasti to beg for food.

When he had eaten and returned to the Jeta Grove, the Lord laid aside his bowl and robes, washed his feet, and sat down on the seat arranged for him, crossing his legs, holding his body upright, and mindfully fixing his attention in front of him. Then many monks approached the Lord's location, saluted his feet with their heads [that is, nodded], circumambulated him three times with their right side facing him, and sat down on one side.

2. At that time the Venerable Subhūti arrived in the midst of the assembly, and sat down. Then he rose from his seat, put his upper robe over one shoulder, kneeled on his right knee, pressed his folded hands toward the Lord, and said to the Lord: "It is wonderful, O Lord, it is exceedingly wonderful, O Well-Gone, how much the bodhisattvas have been helped by the Tathāgata, the Arhat, the Fully Enlightened One. It is wonderful, O Lord, how much the bodhisattvas have been favored by the Tathāgata, the Arhat, the Fully Enlightened One. How then, O Lord, should a son or daughter of good family, who has traveled on the bodhisattva-vehicle, stand, progress, and control his or her thoughts?"

After these remarks, the Lord said to the Venerable Subhūti: "Well said, well said, Subhūti! So it is, Subhūti, as you say! The Tathāgata, Subhūti, has helped the bodhisattvas, and he has favored them the most. Therefore, Subhūti, listen well, and attentively! I will teach you how those who have adopted the bodhisattva-vehicle should stand, progress, control their thoughts." "So be it, O Lord," replied the Venerable Subhūti, and he listened to the Lord.

2. The Bodhisattva's Career

3. The Lord said: "Here, Subhūti, someone who has chosen the vehicle of a bodhisattva should produce a thought in this manner: 'As many beings as there are in the universe of beings, comprehended under the term "beings"—hatched from an egg, born from a womb, moisture-born, or miraculously born; with or without form; with mental faculties, without mental faculties, and with neither perception nor nonperception—as far as any conceivable form of beings is conceived: all these I must lead to perfect nirvāṇa. And yet, although innumerable beings have thus been led to nirvāṇa, no being in reality has been led to nirvāṇa.' And why? If in a Bodhisattva the notion of a 'being' should take place, he could not be called an 'awakened being.' And why? He is not to be called an awakened being, if the notion of a self or of a being should arise, or the notion of a living soul or of a person."

4. "Moreover, Subhūti, a bodhisattva who gives a gift should neither be un-influenced by a thing, nor should he be influenced by anything. When he gives

gifts he should not be influenced by objects of sense, nor by sounds, smells, tastes, tangibles, or thoughts. For, Subhūti, the bodhisattva should give gifts in such a way that he is not influenced by these seductive phenomena. And why? Because the heap of merit of that awakened being who, uninfluenced, gives a gift is not easy to measure. What do you think, Subhūti—is the extent of space in the East easy to measure?" Subhūti replied: "No indeed, O Lord." The Lord asked: "In like manner, is it easy to measure the extent of space in the South, West, or North, downward, upward, in the intermediate directions, in all the ten directions?" Subhūti replied: "No indeed, O Lord." The Lord said: "Even so the attainment of that awakened being that, unsupported, gives a gift is not easy to measure. That is why, Subhūti, those who have joined the bodhisattva-vehicle should give gifts without being influenced by the notion of arbitrary concepts."

5. The Lord continued: "What do you think, Subhūti, can the Tathāgata be seen by the possession of his marks?" Subhūti replied: "No indeed, O Lord. And why? What has been taught by the Tathāgata as the possession of marks, that is truly a nonpossession of no-marks." The Lord said: "Wherever there is possession of marks, there is error, wherever there is nonpossession of no-marks there is no error. Hence the Tathāgata is characterized by no-marks as marks." . . .

3. The Scope of the Spiritual Life

9. The Lord asked: "What do you think, Subhūti, does it occur to the Stream-enterer, 'by me has the fruit of a Stream-enterer been attained?'" Subhūti replied: "No indeed, O Lord. And why? Because, O Lord, he has not attained any dharma. Therefore is he called a Stream-enterer. No sense object has been won, no sounds, smells, tastes, tangibles, or thoughts. That is why he is called a 'Stream-enterer.' If, O Lord, it would occur to a Stream-enterer, 'by me has a Stream-enterer's benefit been attained,' then that would be evidence by him of a conceptualizing about a self, grasping being, grasping a soul, grasping a person." The Lord asked: "What do you think, Subhūti, does it then occur to the Once-returner, 'by me has the benefit of an Once-returner been attained?'" Subhūti replied: "No indeed, O Lord. And why? Because there is not any dharma that has gained the status of an Once-returner. That is why he is called 'Once-returner.'" The Lord asked: "What do you think, Subhūti, does it then occur to the Never-returner 'by me has the fruit of a Never-returner been attained?'" Subhūti replied: "No indeed, O Lord. And why? Because there is not any dharma that has gained by the status of a Never-returner. Therefore is he called a 'Never-returner.'" The Lord asked: "What do you think, Subhūti, does it then occur to the Arhat (fully enlightened being),

'by me has Arhatship been attained?'" Subhūti replied: "No indeed, O Lord. And why? Because no dharma is called 'Arhat.' That is why he is called an 'Arhat.' If, O Lord, it would occur to an Arhat, 'by me has Arhatship been attained,' then that would be in him a grasping a self, grasping being, grasping a soul, grasping a person. And why? I am, O Lord, the one whom the Tathāgata, the Arhat, the Fully Enlightened One has pointed out as the foremost of those who dwell in Peace. I am, O Lord, an Arhat free from greed. And yet, O Lord, it does not occur to me, 'an Arhat am I and free from greed.' If, O Lord, it could occur to me that I have attained Arhatship, then the Tathāgata would not have declared of me that 'Subhūti, this son of good family, who is the foremost of those who dwell in peace, does not dwell anywhere; that is why he is called "a dweller in peace, a dweller in peace indeed."'" . . .

6. The Bodhisattvas

17a. Subhūti asked: "How, O Lord, should one committed to the bodhisattva-vehicle stand, progress, or control his thoughts?" The Lord replied: "Here, Subhūti, someone who has joined the bodhisattva-vehicle should produce the following thought: "'I must lead all beings to nirvāṇa, which leaves nothing behind; and yet, after beings have thus been led to nirvāṇa, it can be affirmed that no being has been led to nirvāṇa.' And why? If in a bodhisattva the notion of a 'being' should occur, he could not be called an awakened being. And likewise if the notion of a soul, or a person should arise in him. And why? He who has entered the bodhisattva-vehicle—he is not one of the dharmas." . . .

7. The Buddha

25. "What do you think, Subhūti, does it occur to a Tathāgata, 'by me have beings been set free'? This is not the way to understand it, Subhūti! And why? There is no being that the Tathāgata has set free. Again if there had been any being whom the Tathāgata had set free, then surely there would have been on the part of the Tathāgata a grasping after a self, a being, a soul, a person. 'Grasping of a self,' as a no-grasping, Subhūti, has that been taught by the Tathāgata. And yet the foolish common people have seized upon it. 'Foolish common people,' Subhūti, are really not people that have been taught by the Tathāgata. Therefore are they called 'foolish common people.'

26a. "What do you think, Subhūti, is the Tathāgata to be understood by means of his possession of marks?" Subhūti replied: "No indeed, O Lord!" The Lord said: "If, Subhūti, the Tathāgata could be recognized by his possession of marks, then also the universal monarch would be a Tathāgata. Therefore the Tathāgata is not to be seen by means of his possession of marks." Subhūti then said: "As I, O Lord, understand the Lord's teaching, the Tathāgata is not to be seen through his possession of marks." . . .

8. Advice to the Imperfect

30a. "And again, Subhūti, if a son or daughter of good family were to grind as many world systems as there are particles of dust in this great world system of 1,000 million worlds, as finely as they can be ground with incalculable vigor, and reduce them to something like an atomic size, what do you think, Subhūti, would that be an enormous collection of atomic sizes?" Subhūti replied: "So it is, O Lord, so it is, O Tathāgata, enormous would that collection of atomic sizes! And why? If, O Lord, there had been an enormous collection of atomic sizes, the Lord would not have called it an 'enormous collection of atomic sizes.' And why? What was taught by the Tathāgata as a 'collection of atomic sizes,'" is really a no-collection that was taught by the Tathāgata. Therefore is it called a 'collection of atomic sizes.'" . . .

31. "And what the Tathāgata taught as 'the world system of 1,000 million worlds,' that he has taught as a no-system. Therefore is it called 'the world system of 1,000 million worlds.' And why? If, O Lord, there had been a world system, that would have been a case of grasping on a material object, and what was taught as 'grasping on a material object' by the Tathāgata, just as a no-grasping was that taught by the Tathāgata. Therefore is it called 'grasping on a material object.'" The Lord added: "And also, Subhūti, that 'grasping on a material object' is a matter of linguistic convention, a verbal expression without factual content. It is neither a dharma nor a no-dharma. And yet the foolish common people have adopted it.

31a. "And why? Because whoever would say that the view of a self has been taught by the Tathāgata, the view of a being, the view of a living soul, the view of a person, would he, Subhūti, be speaking right?" Subhūti replied: "No indeed, O Lord, no indeed, O Tathāgata, he would not be speaking right. And why? That which has been taught by the Tathāgata as 'view of self,' as a no-view has that been taught by the Tathāgata? Therefore is it called 'view of self.'"

31b. The Lord said: "It is thus, Subhūti that someone who has set out in the bodhisattva-vehicle should know all dharmas, view them, and concentrate on them. And he should know, view, and concentrate on them in such a way that he does not create the perception of a dharma. And why? 'Perception of dharma,'

Subhūti, as no-perception—has this been taught by the Tathāgata? Therefore is it called 'perception of dharma.'

32a. "And finally, Subhūti, if a bodhisattva, a great being, filled the immeasurable and incalculable world-systems with the seven precious things, and gave them as a gift to the Tathāgatas, the Arhats, the fully Enlightened Ones—and if, on the other hand, a son or daughter of good family had taken from this Perfection of Wisdom, this discourse on Dharma, but one stanza of four lines, and were to bear it in mind, demonstrate, recite, and study it, and fully teach to others—on the strength of that this latter would beget a greater heap of merit, immeasurable and incalculable. And how would he illuminate it? So as not to reveal. Therefore is it said, 'he would illuminate.'"

Source: *Vajracchedikāprajñāpāramitā Sūtra* [Diamond Sūtra of the Perfection of Wisdom], edited by P. L. Vaidya, Buddhist Sanskrit Texts 17 (Darbhanga: The Mithila Institute, 1961).

13

Mahāratnakūta Sūtra

The *Mahāratnakūta Sūtra* (Great Jewel-Heap Sūtra) is a collection of forty-nine different Mahāyāna Buddhist texts that cover a wide range of topics, including monastic precepts, wisdom, compassion, illusion, skillful means, and emptiness. The collection of these texts appears to have been accomplished haphazardly, without a master plan. The literary style tends to be repetitious, and it offers a reader stereotyped formulas and excessive numbered lists of maxims. The repetitive nature of the different texts suggests the purposes behind reading a Buddhist text: a reader may grasp its meaning and gain religious insight and experience by repetition.

This chapter and the following one each contains a representative text from this collection of forty-nine texts. This chapter includes *The Elucidation of Consciousness,* whereas the next chapter includes selections from the *The True Lion's Roar of Queen Śrīmālā.* The former work was chosen because of its interesting discussion of consciousness. This text also served as a forerunner of the consciousness-only philosophy of the Yogācāra school. When the text refers to consciousness as a seed, it evokes similarities to the Yogācāra notion of the storehouse consciousness.

A reader will encounter a discussion of consciousness that describes it as without substance or form. It also compares consciousness to the wind. Moreover, it refers to the rebirth of consciousness and discusses karmic hindrances. Although consciousness is devoid of substance or form, it manifests itself through feelings and conceptions. The text also contains a discussion of memory and the body, which are also topics of importance to the Yogācāra school.

Selections from *The Elucidation of Consciousness*

Thus have I heard. Once the World-Honored One was dwelling in the bamboo grove of Elder Karaṇḍa, in the great city of Rājagṛha, together with twelve hundred fifty great monks who were all Arhats. These monks had ended their defilements and were no longer subject to afflictions. They had acquired ease and achieved liberation from passions and from ignorance. They perceived the past, the present, and the future without hindrance. These great dragons had, in accordance with the Buddha's teaching, done what they had set out to do and abandoned the great burden [of saṃsāra]. They had gained benefit for themselves. They had already freed themselves from the sufferings caused by existence in saṃsāra. By the power of right wisdom, they knew well sentient beings' propensities. These great Śrāvakas were led by Elder Śāriputra.

Also in the assembly were innumerable Bodhisattva-Mahāsattvas.

At that time, at the dwelling place of the World-Honored One, most of the monks felt tired and lethargic. They looked listless and could not deport themselves properly. Thereupon, the face of the World-Honored One beamed like an opened lotus flower. All the monks then became fully awake and straightened themselves up with dignity. They thought, "Now the Buddha, the World-Honored One, emits bright light from his face. What Dharma will he teach to benefit [sentient beings] greatly?"

At that time, Wise Protector, a youth, . . . joined his palms respectfully, bowed down with his head at the Buddha's feet, and said to him, "World-Honored One, you always take pity on all sentient beings and hold them in your embrace and protection. I wish to ask a few questions. May the World-Honored One grant me permission."

The Buddha said to Wise Protector, "Your request is granted. You may present your doubts and I will answer them with detailed explanations."

Wise Protector asked the Buddha, "World-Honored One, although sentient beings know that consciousness exists, they cannot understand it thoroughly if it is not explained clearly, just as no one knows that there is a treasure if it is locked up in a box. World-Honored One, what form does the consciousness assume? Why is it called consciousness? When sentient beings are dying, they frantically jerk their hands and feet, their eyes change color, they are constricted and cannot move freely, their sense-organs function no more, and their [four] elements disintegrate. After the consciousness leaves the body, where does it go? What is its self-nature? What form does it take on? How does it leave the old body to receive a new body? How can it leave one body here, and, taking all the sense-fields with it, be born again and again in various other bodies to undergo karmic results? World-Honored One, how can sentient beings produce sense organs again after their bodies decay and disintegrate? How can one be rewarded in future lives for meritorious deeds performed in this life? How can a future body enjoy the rewards of meritorious actions performed by the present body? How can the consciousness be nourished and grow in the body? How can the consciousness change and modify itself in accordance with the body?" . . .

The Buddha told Wise Protector, "The consciousness moves and turns, transmigrates and expires, and comes and goes like the wind. Wind has no color or shape and is invisible, yet it can [generate and] stir up things and cause them to take on different shapes. It may shake trees so violently that they break or split with a loud crack. It may touch sentient beings' bodies with cold or heat and make them feel pain or pleasure.

"The wind has no hands, no feet, no face, no eyes, and no shape; it is not black, white, yellow, or red. Wise Protector, the same is true of consciousness. Consciousness is without color, shape, or light, and cannot be manifested. It shows its various functions only when [proper] causes and conditions are met. The same is true of the elements of feeling, awareness, and dharmas. These elements, too, are devoid of color and shape and depend on [proper] causes and conditions to display their functions.

"Wise Protector, when a sentient being dies, the elements of feeling, awareness, and dharmas, together with consciousness, all leave the [old] body. Taking the elements of feeling, awareness, and dharmas with it, the consciousness is born again in a new body.

"As an illustration, when the wind passes over exquisite flowers, the flowers remain where they are, while their fragrance spreads far and wide. The substance of the wind does not take in a fragrance of the exquisite flowers. The substances of the fragrance, the wind, and the organ of touch have neither shape nor color, but the fragrance cannot spread far away without the power of the wind. Wise Protector, in the same way, after a sentient being dies, his consciousness will take birth again together with the elements of feeling, awareness, and dharmas. Accompanied by the elements of feeling, awareness, and dharmas, the consciousness is reincarnated through [the union of] its parents, who are the conditions of its rebirth. . . .

"Wise Protector, when a sentient being dies at the exhaustion of his karmic results [for that life], his consciousness is still bound by karmic hindrances. [At the moment of death,] the consciousness leaves the body and its elements to take birth in another body, just as the consciousness of an Arhat who has entered the dhyāna of ultimate quiescence disappears from his body. However, by the power of memory, the consciousness knows both the identity of the deceased and all he has done in life, which occur clearly to the dying person and press him mentally and physically.

"Wise Protector, what is the meaning of consciousness? Consciousness is the seed which can bring forth the sprout of various bodily forms as a result of karma. Perception, awareness, conception, and memory are all comprised in the consciousness, so that it can tell joy from pain, good from evil, and wholesome states from unwholesome ones. For this reason, it is called consciousness.

"You ask how the consciousness leaves the body and [takes birth] again to undergo other karmic results. Wise Protector, the consciousness moves into a body as a face appears in a mirror, or as the letters of a seal reveals themselves in the mud. When the sun rises, darkness disappears wherever the sunlight reaches. When the sun sets and there is no light, darkness reappears. Darkness has no form or substance, and is neither permanent nor impermanent; it is nowhere to be found. The same is true of consciousness: it is devoid of form and substance, yet it manifests itself by feelings and conceptions. The consciousness in the body is just like the substance of darkness; it cannot be seen or grasped. . . .

"Wise Protector, the consciousness, in its self-nature, pervades everywhere [in the body] but is not tainted by any part. Although it dwells in the six sense-organs, the six sense-objects, and the five aggregates which are defiled, it is not stained by any of them; it only functions through them.

"Wise Protector, a wooden puppet strung up somewhere can give a variety of performances, such as walking, prancing, jumping, throwing, playing, and dancing. What do you think? By whose power can the wooden puppet do so?"

Wise Protector said to the Buddha, "I am not intelligent enough to know the answer."

The Buddha told Wise Protector, "You should know that it is by the power of the puppeteer. The puppeteer is out of sight; only the operation of his intelligence can be seen. Similarly, the body does everything by the power of consciousness. Ṛṣis, gandharvas, dragons, gods, humans, asuras, and other beings in the various planes of existence all depend on the power of consciousness to act. The body is exactly like the wooden puppet. Consciousness is devoid of form and substance, but it upholds all in the dharmadhātu; it is fully endowed with the power of wisdom and can even know events of past lives. . . .

"Wise Protector, after leaving the body, the consciousness [takes birth again] with its good and evil karmas to undergo other karmic results. The wind becomes fragrant if it enters a grove of fragrant campaka flowers after coming out of a deep valley. However, if the wind passes through a stinking, dirty place where there are excrement and corpses, it catches an offensive smell. If the wind passes through a place which is permeated with both a fragrant odor and an offensive one, it carries good and bad odors at the same time, but the stronger of the two predominates. The wind is devoid of form or substance. Fragrance and stench, too, have no shape; however, the wind can carry both fragrance and stench far away. The consciousness takes good and evil karmas with it from one body to another to undergo different karmic results.

"Just as a person who is dreaming sees many images and events without knowing that he is lying asleep, so, when a blessed, virtuous person is dying and his consciousness departs, he is peaceful and unaware [of his death]; he passes away fearlessly as if he were dreaming.

"The consciousness does not leave from the throat or any other orifice. No one knows where it departs or how it goes out." . . .

"The consciousness transmigrates [into a new body] just as the sun sheds light, as a pearl shines, or as wood produces fire. [Transmigration] is also like the sowing of a seed. After a seed undergoes transformation in the soil, sprouts stems and leaves emerge. Then come flowers of various colors, such as white or red, manifesting a variety of powers and scents at maturity. . . .

"The power of memory is very strong in the dharmadhātu, so when the consciousness leaves a sentient being's body at his death, it combines with the power of memory to become the seed of his next life. Apart from consciousness, there is no dharmadhātu, and vice versa.

"The consciousness is reincarnated together with the prāṇa-element, and the elements of subtle memory, feeling, and dharmas."

Wise Protector asked the Buddha, "If so, why docs the World-Honored One say that consciousness is formless?"

The Buddha answered, "Wise Protector, form is of two kinds: one is internal; the other, external. Visual consciousness is internal, while the eye is external. Similarly, auditory consciousness is internal, while the ear is external; olfactory consciousness is internal, while the nose is external; gustatory consciousness is internal, while the tongue is external; tactile consciousness is internal, while the body is external.

"Wise Protector, suppose a man born blind sees a beautiful woman in a dream. Her hands, feet, and features are all extremely pretty, so in the dream the blind man becomes greatly delighted with her. When he wakes up, there is nothing to be seen. In the daytime, among the crowd, the blind man speaks of the pleasant event in his dream, saying, 'I saw a gorgeous woman in a magnificent garden, together with hundreds of thousands of people, all well-adorned and making merry. Her skin was lustrous, her shoulders plump, and her arms long and round like the trunk of an elephant. [Seeing these] in the dream, I was filled with joy, comfort, and admiration.'"

"Wise Protector, this man, blind from birth, has never seen anything in his life. How can he see those forms in the dream?"

Wise Protector said to the Buddha, "May you explain this to me!"

The Buddha told Wise Protector, "The forms seen in the dream are the internal objects of the eye. It is through the discrimination of intellect, not the physical eye, that the internal objects of the eye are seen. Because of the power of memory, the internal objects of the eye appear for a moment in the dream of the blind man. Also because of the power of memory, the blind man remembers them when he wakes up. Thus do the internal forms relate to the consciousness.

"Furthermore, Wise Protector, when a body dies, the consciousness leaves the body to be reincarnated. As an illustration, consider a seed: after being sown in the soil and supported by the four elements, it will gradually grow into sprouts, stems, branches, and leaves. In like manner, the consciousness leaves the dead body to be reincarnated under the control of four things—memory, feeling, wholesome dharmas, and unwholesome dharmas."

Wise Protector asked the Buddha, "World-Honored One, how do wholesome and unwholesome dharmas control the consciousness?"

The Buddha answered. "Wise Protector, as an illustration, a piece of precious crystal looks white or black according to whether it is put in a white or black place. Similarly, when the consciousness leaves the dead body to be reincarnated and undergo different karmic results, it will become virtuous or nonvirtuous according to whether it is controlled by wholesome or unwholesome dharmas."

Wise Protector further asked the Buddha, "In what way is the body connected with the consciousness?" . . .

[The Buddha said,] "Similarly, Wise Protector, the consciousness does not abide in any part of the body. It abides neither in the eye, nor in the ear, nose, tongue, nor body. The time when the consciousness gains slight awareness may be compared to the time when the seed sprouts; the time when the consciousness acquires feeling may he compared to the time when buds appear; and the time during which the consciousness has a body may be compared to the time during which the flower blossoms and the tree bears fruit.

"From consciousness the body arises, and consciousness covers all the body and its limbs. When we look for consciousness in the body, we cannot find it anywhere; yet without consciousness, the body cannot live. . . .

"Just as a silkworm makes a cocoon in which to wrap itself and then leaves the cocoon behind, so consciousness produces a body to envelop itself and then leaves that body to undergo other karmic results [in a new body].

"Because there is a seed, there are the color, fragrance, and flavor [of a plant]. [Similarly,] after the consciousness leaves the body, the sense-organs, sense objects, feeling, and the element of dharmas go wherever the consciousness goes. . . .

"When the consciousness leaves the body, it carries all the body's attributes with it. It assumes an [ethereal] form as its body; it has no body of flesh and bones. Because it has the senses, it has feelings and subtle memory and can tell good from evil. . . .

True Moon asked the Buddha, "World-Honored One, when a sentient being is on the point of death, how can the consciousness leave the body? How can it move into another body? How can it he aware of its own leaving the body?"

The Buddha replied to True Moon, "When a sentient being is rewarded with a body according to his karmas, the consciousness will maintain that body without interruption, like a stream. When the sentient being's life comes to an end and his body dies, the consciousness will leave his body to take birth again together with his karmas.

"As an illustration, consider a mixture of water and milk: when it is boiled over a fire, milk, water, and cream will all separate. Similarly, True Moon, when the life of a sentient being comes to an end, his body, consciousness, sense-organs, and sense-objects will all disperse because the power of karma is exhausted. The consciousness will then become the only reliance [of the ethereal mind-body complex] and will contact various objects, make up [all sorts of] notions about them, and be reincarnated, together with the good and evil karmas, to undergo other karmic results."

Source: "The Elucidation of Consciousness" in *A Treasury of Mahāyāna Sūtras: Selections from the Mahāranakūṭa Sūtra*, translated by the Buddhist Association of the United States and edited by Garmas C. C. Chang (University Park: Pennsylvania State University Press, 1983), 223–228, 230–231.

14

The True Lion's Roar
of Queen Śrīmālā

The anonymous author of the *Śrīmālā* probably composed this text in the Andhra region of southern India during the Īkṣvāku rule of the third century C.E. The author was probably from the Mahāsānghika school. This means that the text was composed soon after the appearance of the *Prajñāpāramitā Sūtras*. It is possible that the text was composed in part to honor eminent Buddhist women of south Indian Buddhism who were instrumental in promoting the religion. The name Śrīmālā means glorious garland, emphasizing the queen's innate beauty in comparison to other women, who must don flower garlands to beautifully adorn themselves. The queen given this name by her king and husband was allegedly a contemporary of the historical Buddha.

The initial translation of this text into Chinese was made by a native of central India, named Dharmakṣema, in the 420s. In the same area of India, Guṇabhadra (d. 468 C.E.) undertook the second Chinese translation in 436, whereas a third translation was made by Bodhiruci (672–727), a native of southern India, who contributed the Sanskrit version of the *Ratnakūṭa* collection that he translated between 706 and 713. The original Sanskrit text was not divided into chapters; it was a continuous text. There is, however, a structure that can be discovered which divides the text into two phases: cause and effect. The great vows and aspirations result, for instance, in entering the one vehicle and teaching the noble truths, Buddha body, and emptiness.

A reader should be aware that this document emphasizes the Buddhist path of the lay person as equal to that of the monk. Unlike the *Vimalakīrti Sūtra,* which exalts the path of the lay person, the *Śrīmālā* does not claim that one path is superior to the other. The text does reflect, however, an organization of lay bodhisattvas called the *bodhisattvagaṇa* (collective of enlightened beings). A reader will encounter discussions of the importance of vows, perfections of the bodhisattva, defilements, and Tathāgata-embryo. It is not insignificant that the Buddha prophesies enlightenment for the queen.

Selections from *The True Lion's Roar of Queen Śrīmālā*

Thus have I heard. Once the Buddha was dwelling in the garden of Anāthapindada, in the Jeta Grove, near Śrāvastī. At that time, King Prasenajit and Queen Mallikā of Kosala had just had an initial realization of the Dharma. They said to each other, "Our daughter, Śrīmālā, is kind, intelligent, learned, and wise. If she could see the Tathāgata, she would be quick to understand the profound Dharma and would have no doubt about it whatsoever. We should now send an eloquent messenger to her to arouse her sincere faith."

Immediately upon this decision, the king and queen wrote Queen Śrīmālā a letter extolling the true merits of the Tathāgata, and sent a messenger, Chandra, to deliver it to her at Ayodhyā. Queen Śrīmālā received the letter with reverence and joy. . . .

Then the World-Honored One spoke to Śrīmālā in verse:

"In your former lives I taught you
And revealed to you the path of enlightenment.
Now once again you meet me here;
We shall also meet in future lives."

After speaking this verse, the Buddha prophesied to the assembly that Queen Śrīmālā would attain supreme enlightenment, saying. "You now praise the superb merits of the Tathāgata. Because of this good root, you will be sovereign among gods and humans for incalculable kalpas. All your needs will be fulfilled. Wherever you are born, you will be able to meet me and praise me face to face, just as you do now. You will also make offerings to innumerable, countless other Buddhas, World-Honored Ones After twenty thousand incalculable kalpas, you, too, will become a Buddha, named Universal Light Tathāgata, the Worthy One, the perfectly Enlightened One. . . .

Then Queen Śrīmālā made three more great vows before the Buddha, saying, "I will benefit an infinite number of sentient beings through the power of these vows: first, I will, by my good roots, attain the wisdom of the true Dharma in all my lifetimes; second, after I have attained the true wisdom, wherever I may be born I will explain it untiringly to all sentient beings; third, in whatever form I may he born, I will not spare life or limb in embracing, protecting, and upholding the true Dharma."

When the World-Honored One heard these vows, he told Śrīmālā, "Just as all forms are contained in the realm of space, so all the Bodhisattva's vows, as numerous as the sands of the Ganges are contained in these vows. These three vows are truly vast."

Then Queen Śrīmālā said to the Buddha, "World-Honored One, through the eloquence vested in me by the Buddha's miraculous power. I would like to explain the great vow. Please grant me permission to speak."

The Buddha said. "Śrīmālā, speak as you wish."

Śrīmālā said. "The Bodhisattva's vows, as numerous as the sands of the Ganges, are all contained in one great vow This one great vow is called the embracing of the Tathāgata's True Dharma. This embracing of the true Dharma is truly great and vast."

The Buddha said, "Well said, Śrīmālā! You have practiced the Dharma for a long time; your wisdom and ingenuity are subtle and profound. Anyone who can understand your words must have planted many good roots in the long night. You speak of the embracing of the true Dharma; it is the teaching of the Buddhas of the past, present, and future. Now that I have attained supreme enlightenment, I, too, often teach the embracing of the true Dharma in various ways. The merits derived from praising the embracing of the true Dharma are limitless, just as the wisdom of the Tathāgata is limitless. Why? Because it is most meritorious and beneficial to embrace the true Dharma."

Queen Śrīmālā then said to the Buddha, "World-Honored One, by the Buddha's divine power, I wish to explain the broad meaning of the embracing of the true Dharma. . . .

"World-Honored One, the embracing of the true Dharma is no other than the pāramitās, and the pāramitās are no other than the embracing of the true Dharma. Why?

"For those sentient beings who can best be matured through giving, the good men and women who embrace the true Dharma practice charity, giving even their own lives and limbs. In this way, they bring those sentient beings to maturity in accordance with their inclinations, to establish them firmly in the true Dharma. This is called the pāramitā of giving.

"For those sentient beings who can best be matured by discipline, [those who embrace the true Dharma] guard their own six senses; purify their own verbal, bodily, and mental actions; and conduct themselves with dignity. In this way, they bring those sentient beings to maturity in accordance with their inclinations, to establish them firmly in the true Dharma. This is called the pāramitā of discipline.

"For those sentient beings who can best be matured by patience, those who embrace the true Dharma are free of ill will; intend only to benefit; and bear rebukes, scoldings, insults, outrage, slander, libel, annoyance, and harassment with the utmost patience, even without their faces changing color in the slightest. In this way, they bring those sentient beings to maturity in accordance with their inclinations, to establish them firmly in the true Dharma. This is called the pāramitā of patience.

"For those sentient beings who can best be matured by vigor, [those who embrace the true Dharma] do not have an indolent or negative mentality, but show great aspiration and supreme vigor, whether walking, standing, sitting, or lying down. In this way, they bring those sentient beings to maturity in accordance with their inclinations, to establish them firmly in the true Dharma. This is called the pāramitā of vigor.

"For those sentient beings who can best he matured by meditation, [those who embrace the true Dharma] are not distracted, and achieve right mindfulness and remembrance. In this way, they bring those sentient beings to maturity in accordance with their inclinations, to establish them firmly in the true Dharma. This is called the pāramitā of meditation.

"For those sentient beings who can best be matured by wisdom and who ask questions about the Dharma in order to benefit from it, [those who embrace the true Dharma] untiringly explain all doctrines, all sciences, and all techniques, until those sentient beings fully comprehend what is ultimate. In this way, they bring those sentient beings to maturity in accordance with their inclinations, to establish them firmly in the true Dharma. This is called the pāramitā of wisdom.

"Therefore, World-Honored One, the embracing of the true Dharma is not different from the pāramitās; the embracing of the true Dharma is the pāramitās."

The Queen Śrīmālā continued, "World-Honored One, through the eloquence vested in me by the Buddha's divine power, I wish to elaborate on the great meaning [of the embracing of the true Dharma]."

The Buddha said. "What is the great meaning?"

"World-Honored One, in referring to those who embrace the true Dharma, I do not mean that they constitute an entity that differs from the embracing of the true Dharma. The good men and women who embrace the true Dharma are the embracing of the true Dharma. Why?

"The good men and women who embrace the true Dharma give their bodies, lives, and possessions for the sake of the true Dharma. By giving their bodies, these people will realize that which transcends the limits of saṁsāra, will be free from old age and sickness, and will attain the Tathāgata's Dharma-body, which is indestructible, eternal, changeless, ultimately tranquil, and inconceivable. By giving their lives, they will realize that which transcends the limits of saṁsāra, will be forever released from death, will attain eternity, will acquire the inconceivable merits, and will securely abide in all the Buddha-Dharmas and miraculous powers. By giving their possessions, they will realize that which transcends the limits of saṁsāra, and will go far beyond the realm of sentient beings. They will attain inexhaustible, undiminishing, perfect accomplishments; will acquire inconceivable merits and magnificent attributes; and will he honored and served by other sentient beings."

"World-Honored one, the good men and women who give their bodies, lives, and possessions in order to embrace the true Dharma will receive the Tathāgata's prophecy [of their attainment of Buddhahood].

"World-Honored One, when the true Dharma is on the verge of extinction, the monks, nuns, laymen, and laywomen will gather in groups, form factions, and dispute with one another. At that time, the good men and women who, without crookedness or deceit, cherish and embrace the true Dharma will associate with the good faction"; those who associate with the good faction will definitely receive the Buddha's prophecy [of their attainment of enlightenment].

"World-Honored One, I see that to embrace the true Dharma has this tremendous power. The Tathāgata regards this [doctrine] as the eye [of the Dharma], the basis of the Dharma, the guide of the Dharma, and the understanding of the Dharma."

Then the World-Honored One ... exclaimed, ... "Śrīmālā, Mount Sumeru, the king of mountains, surpasses all other mountains in height, breadth, and beauty. In the same way, Śrīmālā, a novice in the Mahāyāna who, in order to benefit others, embraces the true Dharma without regard for his life or limb is superior to a person who has long been abiding in the Mahāyāna, but who is always concerned with his body and life, in spite of all his good roots.

"Therefore, Śrīmālā, you should reveal, demonstrate, and teach the embracing of the true Dharma to all sentient beings.

"Thus, Śrīmālā, to embrace the true Dharma yields great blessings, benefits, and karmic fruits. Śrīmālā, although for innumerable, incalculable kalpas I have praised the merits of embracing the true Dharma, I have not exhausted them. Therefore, to embrace the true Dharma brings about infinite merits."

The Buddha told Śrīmālā, "You should now explain further the embracing of the true Dharma, which I have taught, and which is cherished by all Buddhas alike."

Śrīmālā said, "Very well, World-Honored One. The embracing of the true Dharma is called the Mahāyāna. Why? Because the Mahāyāna gives birth to all Śrāvakas and Pratyekabuddhas, and all mundane and supramundane wholesome dharmas. Just as Lake Anavatapta is the source of the eight rivers, so the Mahāyāna produces all Śrāvakas and Pratyekabuddhas and all mundane and supramundane wholesome dharmas. . . .

The abiding of the true Dharma is taught for the sake of the Mahāyāna because the abiding of the Mahāyāna is the abiding of the true Dharma. The extinction of the true Dharma is taught for the sake of the Mahāyāna because the extinction of the Mahāyāna is the extinction of the true Dharma. As for the Prātimoksa and the Vinaya, these two Dharmas differ in name, but mean the same. Vinaya is instruction for the Mahāyāna. Why? It is for the sake of Buddhahood [which is the aim of the Mahāyāna,] that one leaves the household life and receives full monastic ordination. Therefore, the Vinaya, true renunciation of the household life, and full monastic ordination are all Mahāyāna disciplines. . . .

"There are two kinds of defilements: underlying defilements and active defilements. The underlying defilements are four in number. What are they? Attachment to a particular viewpoint, attachment to desire, attachment to form, and craving for existence World-Honored One, these four underlying defilements can produce all active defilements. The active defilements arise from moment to moment in concomitance with the mind. World-Honored One, the underlying defilement of ignorance never arises in concomitance with the mind from beginningless time.

"World-Honored One, the four underlying defilements are powerful; they can breed all the active defilements. Yet, in comparison with them, the underlying defilement of ignorance is so much more powerful that the difference is inexpressible either by figures or analogies. Thus, World-Honored One, the underlying defilement of ignorance is more powerful than the craving for existence. Just as the form, power, authority, and retinue of the demon king overshadow those of the gods of the Paranirmita-Vaśavartin Heaven, so the underlying defilement of ignorance overshadows the other four underlying defilements All other defilements, which are more numerous than the sands of the Ganges, depend on the underlying defilement of ignorance. It also causes the other four underlying defilements to endure. It can be eradicated only by the wisdom of the Tathāgata, not by the wisdom of the Śrāvakas or the Pratyekabuddhas This being the case, World-Honored One, the underlying defilement of ignorance is the most powerful of all.

"World-Honored One, with grasping as the condition and defiled karmas as the cause, the three realms are produced. Likewise, with the underlying defilement of ignorance as the condition and undefiled karmas as the cause, the mind-created bodies of Arhats, Pratyekabuddhas, and powerful Bodhisattvas are produced. These three kinds of mind-created bodies and the undefiled karmas all depend on the underlying defilement of ignorance, being conditioned as well as conditioning. Therefore, World-Honored One, the three kinds of mind-created bodies and undefiled karmas all have the underlying defilement of ignorance as their condition, just as the craving for existence [also depends on the underlying defilement of ignorance as its condition].

"World-Honored One, the underlying craving for existence functions differently from the underlying defilement of ignorance. The underlying defilement of ignorance is different from the other four underlying defilements, and for this reason it can he eradicated only by the Buddha. Why? Because, though the Arhats and Pratyekabuddhas have eradicated the four underlying defilements, they have not fully mastered the power of utter exhaustion of defilements. They have not realized that state. Why? World-Honored One, to say that their defilements have been exhausted is an exaggeration. Being clouded by the underlying defilement of ignorance, the Arhats, Pratyekabuddhas, and Bodhisattvas in their last [saṁsāric] existences do not know and perceive all dharmas. Because they do not know and perceive all dharmas, they have left uneradicated what should be eradicated, and left unfinished what should be finished. Because they have not eradicated and finished all that should be eradicated and finished, they have attained incomplete liberation, not complete liberation; incomplete purity, not complete purity; incomplete merits, not complete merits. World-Honored One, because they have only attained incomplete liberation, not thorough liberation, and only incomplete merits, not all merits, their knowledge of suffering is incomplete, their eradication of the cause of suffering is incomplete, their realization of the cessation of suffering is incomplete, and their following of the path is incomplete." . . .

Once the underlying defilement of ignorance is cut off, all these defilements will simultaneously be cut off. . . .

"One who realizes the One Vehicle attains supreme enlightenment. Supreme enlightenment is nirvāṇa. Nirvāṇa is the pure Dharma-body of the Tathāgata. To realize the Dharma-body is the One Vehicle. The Tathāgata is not different from the Dharma-body; the Tathāgata is the Dharma-body. The realization of the ultimate Dharma-body is the ultimate One Vehicle. . . .

"Why is the path of the One Vehicle taught? The Tathāgata, the Supreme One, is endowed with the four fearlessnesses and is able to make the true lion's roar. If the Tathāgatas, in accordance with sentient beings' needs, teach the two vehicles as skillful means [then the two vehicles they teach] are no other than the Great Vehicle, because in the highest truth there are no two vehicles. The two vehicles both merge into the One Vehicle, and the One Vehicle is the vehicle of supreme truth. . . .

"World-Honored One, the [real] noble truths are very profound, subtle, difficult to perceive, hard to understand, and not to be discriminated; they are beyond the realm of thought and speculation, and they transcend the credence of all the world. They are known only to Tathāgatas, Worthy Ones, Perfectly Enlightened Ones. Why? These truths explain the very profound Tathāgata-embryo. The Tathāgata-embryo belongs in the realm of the Buddha and is beyond the domain of the Śrāvakas and Pratyekahuddhas. Since the noble truths are explained on the basis of the Tathāgata-embryo, and since the Tathāgata-embryo is profound and subtle, the noble truths are also profound and subtle, difficult to perceive, hard to understand, and not to be discriminated; they are beyond the realm of thought and speculation, and transcend the credence of all the world. They can he known only by a Tathāgata, a Worthy One, a Perfectly Enlightened One.

"If one has no doubt about the Tathāgata-embryo, which [in ordinary beings] is wrapped in an incalculable number of defilements, he will also have no doubt about the Dharma-body of the Tathāgata, which is beyond all defilement.

"World-Honored One, if one can have true faith in the Tathāgata-embryo and the Buddha's Dharma-body—the inconceivable, esoteric realm of the Buddha—he will then be able to believe in and understand well the two meanings of the noble truths.

"What are the two meanings of the noble truths? They are the active and the nonactive. The active noble truths are the four noble truths in an incomplete sense. Why? When one has to rely on others for protection, he cannot completely know suffering, eradicate all causes of suffering, realize the complete cessation of suffering, or follow in its entirety the path leading to the cessation of suffering. Therefore, he cannot know conditioned things, unconditioned things, or nirvāṇa.

"World-Honored One, the nonactive noble truths refer to the four noble truths in the complete sense. Why? Because, when one can rely on himself for protection, he can completely know suffering, eradicate all causes of suffering realize the complete cessation of suffering, and follow in its entirety the path leading to the cessation of suffering. . . .

"World-Honored One, the Tathāgata-embryo is the Tathāgata's knowledge of emptiness. The Tathāgata-embryo has never been seen or realized by any Śrāvaka or Pratyekabuddha. It is perceived and witnessed only by the Buddhas.

"World-Honored One, the knowledge of emptiness of the Tathāgata-embryo is of two kinds. What are the two? The first is the knowledge that *the Tathāgata-embryo is empty:* that it is apart from all defilements and apart from knowledge which does not lead to liberation. The second is the knowledge that *the Tathāgata-embryo is not empty:* that it contains inconceivable Dharmas more numerous than the sands of the Ganges, which embody the Buddhas' wisdom of liberation. . . .

"World-Honored One, of the four noble truths, three truths are impermanent, and one truth is permanent. Why? The three noble truths (of suffering, the cause of suffering, and the path leading to the cessation of suffering) belong to the realm of conditioned dharmas. What is conditioned is impermanent, and what is impermanent is destructible. What is destructible is not true, not permanent, and not a refuge. Therefore, in the ultimate sense, the three noble truths are not true, not permanent, and not a refuge. . . .

"World-Honored One, if one sees saṃsāra as impermanent and nirvāṇa as permanent his view is neither nihilistic nor eternalistic, but is the right view. Why? When deluded people see that bodies, sense-organs, and that which thinks and feels all perish in this life, but do not understand the continuation of existence, then, being blind and without the eye of wisdom, they conceive a nihilistic view. When they see the continuity of the mind but fail to see the aspect of its momentary perishing, then being ignorant of the [true] state of consciousness, they conceive an eternalistic view.

"World-Honored One, the before-mentioned truth is beyond all discrimination and beyond inferior understanding. Because fools have delusive thoughts and cling to misconceived ideas, they believe either nihilism or eternalism. . . .

"World-Honored One, the cycle of birth and death [saṁsāra] is based on the Tathāgata-embryo. Because of the Tathāgata-embryo, the beginning [of saṁsāra] cannot be known. World-Honored One, if one says that because there is the Tathāgata-embryo there is saṁsāra, he speaks well.

"World-Honored One, the cycle of birth and death means the cessation of the sense faculties and the immediate arising of new sense faculties. World-Honored One, the two dharmas, birth and death, are the Tathāgata-embryo itself; they are called birth and death from the conventional viewpoint. World-Honored One, death means the cessation of sense faculties, and birth means the arising of sense faculties. The Tathāgata-embryo, however, neither arises nor ceases to be, neither emerges nor vanishes; it is beyond the realm of conditioned [dharmas].

"World-Honored One, the Tathāgata-embryo is permanent and indestructible. Therefore, World-Honored One, the Tathāgata-embryo is the base, the support, and the foundation of the wisdom of liberation. It is also the base, the support, and the foundation of all conditioned dharmas.

"World-Honored One, if there were no Tathāgata-embryo, there would be no abhorrence of suffering and no longing for nirvāṇa." Why? The seven dharmas— the six consciousnesses and their objects—are momentary and nonabiding. And therefore cannot retain the experience of suffering. Hence, they are unable to abhor suffering or aspire to nirvāṇa. The Tathāgata-embryo has no beginning, neither arises nor ceases, and can retain the experience of suffering. It is the cause of [sentient beings'] renunciation of suffering and aspiration for nirvāṇa.

"World-Honored One, the Tathāgata-embryo is not a self, a personal identity, a being, or a life. The Tathāgata-embryo is not in the domain of sentient beings who believe in a real self, whose thinking is confused, or who cling to the view of emptiness.

"World-Honored One, the Tathāgata-embryo is the store of the dharmadhātu, the store of the dharma-body, the store of the supramundane, and the store of intrinsic purity.

"This intrinsically pure Tathāgata-embryo, as I understand it, is always the inconceivable state of the Tathāgata even if contaminated by defilements, the adventitious dust. Why? World-Honored One, the mind, whether virtuous or non-virtuous, changes from moment to moment, and it cannot be contaminated by defilements, the adventitious dust. Why? Defilements are not in contact with the mind; the mind is not in contact with defilements. How can anything that is not in contact with the mind contaminate the mind? Yet, World-Honored One, because there are defilements there is a defiled mind. It is extremely difficult to know and understand contamination by defilements. Only the Buddha, the World-Honored One, who is the eye, the wisdom, the root of the Dharma, the guide, and the foundation of the true Dharma, can know and see it as it is."

Then the Buddha praised Queen Śrīmālā.

Source: "The True Lion's Roar of Queen Śrīmālā" in *A Treasury of Mahāyāna Sūtras: Selections from the Mahāranakūta Sūtra*, translated by the Buddhist Association of the United States, edited by Garmas C. C. Chang (University Park: Pennsylvania State University Press, 1983), 363–365, 367–381.

15

Pure Land Sūtra

Pure Land Buddhism represented a strong devotional spirit within Mahāyāna that appealed to ordinary people. In a sense, devotional Buddhism was not really something new, because it was possible to discover devotional types of religiosity during the lifetime of the Buddha. Pure Land Buddhism, which originated between around 100 B.C.E. and 100 C.E. in northwest India, however, was centered on the Buddha Amitābha (literally, Eternal Light), who was also called Amitāyus (literally, Eternal Life). This Buddha's light is unlimited, his audience is immeasurable, and likewise his longevity cannot be calculated. There is also a connection between Amitābha and the eternal nature of the three refuges of the Dharma, Saṅgha (Buddhist community), and Buddha.

Located in the western region of the universe there is a Pure Land (Sukhāvatī) in which Amitābha presides over gods and humans. This region of the universe is imagined as a massive *maṇḍala* (sacred diagram) devoid of evil and free of physical and mental suffering. The objective of a devotee is to be reborn in this land. This desirable rebirth is accomplished by hearing the name of Amitābha, which produces a desire to be reborn there and ultimately achieve enlightenment. In order to redirect oneself, a devotee is instructed to chant the name of Amitābha repeatedly. The sound of this Buddha's name redirects a devotee's mind toward meditation and the three refuges, and instigates the saving grace of Amitābha.

There are two versions—short and long—of the primary text of Pure Land Buddhism. This chapter contains the shorter version of the *Sukhāvatīvyūha Sūtra*

(Pure Land Sūtra), which stresses the necessity of faith and prayer for rebirth in the Pure Land, whereas the longer version of the text emphasizes the importance of meritorious deeds and devotion to Amitābha.

A reader should not confuse the Pure Land with nirvāṇa, although the former does share the blissful characteristic of the latter. With respect to the description of the Pure Land in the text, a reader will notice the emphasis on precious substances and the absence of organic matter. This is intended to stress the enduring nature of the land, eliminating any potential for decay. Other features of the land include bright colors, continuously blooming flowers, beautiful birds, and pleasant sights, sounds, and odors. The Pure Land is devoid of anything that might remind a person of death. In short, it is a paradise that can be used as a place from which to attain nirvāṇa.

Selection from *The Shorter Sukhāvatīvyūha Sūtra*

Preamble: The Setting and the Audience

This I have heard. At one time the Blessed One, the Buddha Shakyamuni, was staying near the city of Shravasti, in the cloistered garden that the generous Anathapindada gave to the Buddhist Order in Prince Jeta's grove.

He was staying there with a large gathering of monks numbering one thousand two hundred fifty. These monks were well known for their extraordinary powers. They were true elders, great disciples. They had all achieved the highest degree of sainthood, that of an arhat.

Among these arhats surrounding the Blessed One were the elder Shariputra and his close friend Maudgalyayana the Great. Kashyapa the Great was also among them, and Kapphina the Great, Katyayana the Great, and Kaushthila the Great. Also among these monks were Revata and Shuddhipanthaka, and the Buddha's half-brother Nanda, and his cousin and closest disciple, Ananda, as well as Rahula, the Buddha's son. Present there was also Gavampati, and Bharadvaja, Kalodayin, Vakkula, and Aniruddha. These and other, many more, great disciples accompanied the Buddha at that time.

And the Buddha was accompanied by many of those magnificent human beings well advanced on their way to full awakening, those who are called bodhisattvas or mahasattvas. For instance, the Bodhisattva Manjushri, the Prince of

Dharma, was present in that assembly—and so was the bodhisattva who is the Future Buddha of our age, the Bodhisattva Maitreya, who is called Invincible. And the bodhisattvas Gandhahastin, Nityodyukta, and Anikshiptadhura were there. These and other, many more, bodhisattvas or mahasattvas accompanied the Buddha at that time.

Also present were Shakra, known also as Indra, the King of the Gods, and Brahma, Lord of this, our world, known as the Saha World. These and other heavenly beings—many hundreds of thousands of millions—accompanied the Buddha at that time.

The Main Discourse: The Land of Bliss

Then, the Blessed One addressed the reverend Shariputra, saying: "To the west of us, Shariputra, a hundred thousand million buddha-fields from where we are, there is a world called the Land of Bliss. At this very moment, the tathagata, arhat, perfect and full buddha called Amitayus lives in that buddha-field; he abides and remains there, and even now continues to teach the Dharma in that field.

"Now, what do you think, Shariputra: Why is that world called the 'Land of Bliss?' Shariputra, physical and mental pain are unknown to the living beings that inhabit the world called the 'Land of Bliss'; on the contrary, they only experience conditions of boundless happiness. This is why that world is called the 'Land of Bliss.'

"Furthermore, Shariputra, the world known as the Land of Bliss is adorned and enclosed on every side by seven railings and seven rows of palm trees, all decked with nets of tinkling bells. It is made colorful and attractive by four precious substances, namely, gold, silver, emerald, and rock crystal.

"This is how that buddha-field is adorned, Shariputra, with such a panoply of the wondrous qualities of buddha-fields.

"Furthermore, Shariputra, in the world known as the Land of Bliss there are lotus ponds, all made of seven precious substances, namely, gold, silver, emerald, rock crystal, red pearl, sapphire, and mother of pearl as the seventh. These ponds are brimming with water that is cool, clear, sweet, light, soft, free from odor, free from disease, refreshing, and invigorating. In each of these ponds the bottom slopes gently along the shore, so that the water reaches the right depth in every bathing spot and a crow could drink from the edge of the pond. The bottom of each pond is covered with golden sand. And all around on each of the four sides of these lotus ponds four sets of stairways descend into the pools. These stairways are colorful, elegant, and made of four precious substances, namely, gold, silver, emerald, and rock crystal. And on every side of these lotus ponds grow gem trees, colorful and graceful, made from seven precious substances, namely, gold, silver, emerald, rock crystal, red pearl, sapphire, and mother of pearl as the seventh.

"And in those lotus ponds grow lotus flowers. Some are blue—intensely blue, or with a blue sheen, or with a tinge of blue. Some are yellow—intensely yellow, or with a yellow sheen, or with a tinge of yellow. Some are red—intensely red, or with a red sheen, or with a tinge of red. Some are white—intensely white, with a white sheen, or with a tinge of white. Some are multicolored—intensely multicolored, with a sheen of many colors, or with a tinge of many colors. And these lotus blossoms are as wide as chariot wheels.

"This is how that buddha-field is adorned, Shariputra, with such a panoply of the wondrous qualities of buddha-fields.

"Furthermore, Shariputra, in that buddha-field one hears heavenly musical instruments constantly being played. And the ground all around is golden in color, pleasant to look at. And in that buddha-field a shower of heavenly coral-tree blossoms pours down three times every day and three times every night. And the living beings who are born there travel before their forenoon meal to other worlds, where they worship a hundred thousand million buddhas, and then return to their own world, the Land of Bliss, in time for the afternoon nap, having showered a hundred thousand million flowers upon each one of those buddhas.

"This is how that buddha-field is adorned, Shariputra, with such a panoply of the wondrous qualities of buddha-fields.

"Furthermore, Shariputra, in that buddha-field wild geese curlews, and peacocks gather three times every night and three times every day to sing in chorus, each singing with a different voice. And as they sing, one hears that their voices proclaim Buddhist virtues, such as the five spiritual faculties, the five spiritual powers, and the seven elements of awakening. When human beings in that world hear these sounds, their thoughts turn to the Buddha, their thoughts turn to the Buddha's teaching, the Dharma, and their thoughts turn to the Buddha's Order, the Sangha.

"Now, Shariputra, what do you think? Are these birds born from other birds? You could not consider this possible. Why? Because even the names of the hells, the names of animal rebirths, and the name 'Realm of Yama, the King of Death' are unknown in that buddha-field—let alone actual birth in any of these forms. Rather, those flocks of birds gather there to sing with the voice of the Dharma only because they have been created magically by the Buddha who presides in that field, the Tathagata Amitayus.

"This is how that buddha-field is adorned, Shariputra, with such a panoply of the wondrous qualities of buddha-fields.

"Furthermore, Shariputra, when the rows of palm trees and nets of tinkling bells in that buddha-field sway in the wind, a sweet and enrapturing sound issues from them. This concert of sounds is, Shariputra, like a set of heavenly cymbals, with a hundred thousand million playing parts—when these cymbals are played by expert musicians, a sweet and enrapturing sound issues from them. In exactly the same way, a sweet and enrapturing sound proceeds from those rows of palm trees and those nets of tinkling bells when they sway in the wind. When human beings in that world hear this sound, they remember the Buddha and feel his presence in their whole body, they remember the Dharma and feel its presence in their whole body, and they remember the Sangha and feel its presence in their whole body.

"This is how that buddha-field is adorned, Shariputra, with such a panoply of the wondrous qualities of buddha-fields."

The Buddha Presiding over the Land of Bliss

"Now, what do you think, Shariputra? Why is that tathagata called Amitayus, or 'Measureless Life-span'? Now, Shariputra, the length of that tathagata's life and of the human beings in that buddha-field is immeasurable. This is why that tathagata is called Amitayus, 'Measureless Life-span.'

"And ten cosmic ages have passed, Shariputra, since this tathagata awoke to unsurpassable, perfect, and full awakening.

"What do you think, Shariputra? Why is this tathagata called Amitabha, or 'Measureless Light'? Now, Shariputra, the light of this tathagata spreads unimpeded over all buddha-fields. This is why this tathagata is called Amitabha, 'Measureless Light.'

The Inhabitants of the Land of Bliss

"And, Shariputra, this tathagata is surrounded by an immeasurable assembly of disciples, who are all pure arhats and whose number is impossible to count.

"This is how that buddha-field is adorned, Shariputra, with such a panoply of the wondrous qualities of buddha-fields."

"Furthermore, Shariputra, those sentient beings who are reborn in the buddha-field of the Tathagata Amitayus as pure bodhisattvas who will not fall back and will be separated from awakening by only one birth—the number of these bodhisattvas, Shariputra, is not easy to reckon. One can only approximate their numbers by saying that they are immeasurable and countless.

Exhortation

"Now, Shariputra, sentient beings should set their minds on rebirth in that buddha-field. Why? Because there they will meet persons like themselves, who practice the good. For, Shariputra, living beings are not reborn in that buddha-field of the Tathagata Amitayus as the result of an inferior root of merit.

"Shariputra, those sons or daughters of good families who will hear the name of the blessed Amitayus, the Tathagata, and then will bring it to mind, and will keep it in mind without distraction for one night, or two, or three, four, five, six, or seven nights—they will be met by the Tathagata at the moment of their death. When the moment of death approaches for one of these sons or daughters of good families, Amitayus the Tathagata, surrounded by an assembly of disciples and at the head of a host of bodhisattvas, will stand before this son or daughter, and this son or daughter will die with a mind that is free from distorted views. After they die, they will be reborn in the Land of Bliss, in the buddha-field of Amitayus the Tathagata."

"Therefore, Shariputra, as I understand well the meaning of this, I declare: 'Sons and daughters of a good family should direct their thoughts earnestly towards rebirth in that buddha-field.'"

Confirmation: All Buddhas Praise Their Fields

"Shariputra, in the same way that I now praise that buddha-field, the Land of Bliss, other buddhas, blessed ones, in the eastern regions of the universe, praise their fields—buddhas equal in number to the grains of sand in all the Ganges rivers in every world in the eastern regions of the universe. Led by the Tathagata Akshobhya, the Tathagata Merudhvaja, the Tathagata Mahameru, the Tathagata Meruprabhasa, and the Tathagata Manjudhvaja, each one of these buddhas covers his own buddha-field with his tongue and then reveals all that is in it. You should place your trust in this discourse on Dharma, called 'Embraced by All Buddhas,' which extols inconceivable wondrous qualities.

"In the same manner, other buddhas, blessed ones, in the southern regions of the universe, praise their fields—buddhas equal in number to the grains of sand in all the Ganges rivers in every world in the southern regions of the universe. Led by the Tathagata Candrasuryapradipa, the Tathagata Yashahprabha, the Tathagata Maharchiskandha, the Tathagata Merupradipa, and the Tathagata Anantavirya, each covers his own buddha-field with his tongue and then reveals all that is in it. You should place your trust in this discourse on the Dharma, called 'Embraced by All Buddhas' which extols inconceivable qualities.

"In the same manner, other buddhas, blessed ones, in the western regions of the universe, praise their fields—buddhas equal number the grains of sand in all the Ganges rivers in every world the western regions of the universe. Led by the Tathagata Amitayus, the Tathagata Amitaskandha, the Tathagata Amitadhvaja, Tathagata Mahaprabha, the Tathagata Maharatnaketu, and the Tathagata Shuddharashmiprabha, each covers his own buddha-field with his tongue and then reveals all that is in it. You should place your trust in this discourse on the Dharma, called 'Embraced by All Buddhas,' which extols inconceivable qualities.

In the same manner, other buddhas, blessed ones, in the northern regions of the universe, praise their fields—buddhas equal in number to the grains of sand in all the Ganges rivers in every world in the northern regions of the universe. Led by the Tathagata Maharuciskandha, the Tathagata Vaishvanaranirghosha, the Tathagata Dundubhisvaranirghosha, the Tathagata Dushpradharsha, the Tathagata Adityasambhava, the Tathagata Jaliniprabha, and the Tathagata Prabhakara, each covers his own buddha-field his tongue and then reveals all that is in it. You should place trust in this discourse on the Dharma, called 'Embraced by All Buddhas,' which extols inconceivable wondrous qualities.

"In the same manner, other buddhas, blessed ones, in the lower regions of the universe, praise their fields—buddhas equal in number to the grains of sand in all the Ganges rivers in every world in the lower regions of the universe. Led by the Tathagata named Shiksha, the Tathagata Yashas, the Tathagata Yashahprabhasa, the Tathagata Dharma, the Tathagata Dharmadhara, and the Tathagata Dharmadhvaja, each covers his own buddha-field with his tongue and then reveals all that is in it. You should place you trust in this discourse on the Dharma, called 'Embraced by All Buddhas,' which extols inconceivable wondrous qualities.

"In the same manner, other buddhas, blessed ones, in the higher regions of the universe, praise their fields—buddhas equal in number to the grains of sand in all the Ganges rivers in every world in the higher regions of the universe. Led by the Tathagata Brahmaghosha, the Tathagata Nakshatraraja, the Tathagata Indraketudhvajaraja, the Tathagata Gandhottama, the Tathagata Gandhaprabhasa, the Tathagata Maharciskandha the Tathagata Ratnakusumasampushpitagatra, the Tathagata Shalendraja, the Tathagata Ratnotpalashri, the Tathagata Sarvarthadarsha, and the Tathagata Sumerukalpa, each covers his own buddha-field with his tongue and then reveals all that is in it. You should place your trust in this discourse on the Dharma, called 'Embraced by All Buddhas,' which extols inconceivable wondrous qualities."

Trust, Commitment, Embracing

Exhortation by Shakyamuni

"Now what do you think about this, Shariputra, why is that discourse on Dharma called 'Embraced by All Buddhas'? Those sons or daughters of a good family who hear the name of this discourse on the Dharma and remember the names of these buddhas, blessed ones, will all be embraced by all these buddhas and will never retreat in their pursuit of unsurpassable, perfect, and full awakening. Therefore, Shariputra, believe in me, and believe in these buddhas, blessed ones; place your trust in us, and do not doubt us."

Benefits of the Vow

"Those sons or daughters of a good family, Shariputra, who have set their minds on rebirth in the buddha-field of Amitayus, the Blessed One, the Tathagata, or those who are now setting their minds, or will set their minds, on such rebirth, they will never retreat in their pursuit of unsurpassable, perfect, and full awakening; they have been reborn, are now being reborn, or will be reborn in that buddha-field. Therefore, Shariputra, sons or daughters of good families who have faith should actively direct their thoughts towards rebirth in that buddha-field."

Exhortation by All Buddhas: The Buddha's Task

"And, Shariputra, just as I at present here extol the inconceivable wondrous qualities of other buddhas, blessed ones, so in the same manner, Shariputra, all those other buddhas, blessed ones, extol these inconceivable wondrous qualities of mine, saying: 'A most difficult task has been accomplished by the Blessed One, Shakyamuni, the Sage of the Shakyas, the Monarch of the Shakyas. After he awakened to unsurpassable, perfect, and full awakening in this Saha World, he taught a Dharma that the whole world was reluctant to accept, at a time when the cosmic age was in a period of decay, when living beings were in a period of decay, when views and opinions corrupted human beings, when the length of human life had declined, when the afflictions vitiated human beings.'

"This was, even for me, Shariputra, a most difficult task, namely, that after I awakened to unsurpassable, perfect, and full awakening in this Saha World, I taught a Dharma that the whole world was reluctant to accept, at a time when living beings were in a period of decay, when views and opinions corrupted human beings, when the afflictions vitiated human beings, when the length of human life had declined, when the cosmic age was in a period of decay."

Coda

This was spoken by the Blessed One. The reverend Shariputra and the bodhi-sattvas, and the whole world as well—including its gods, humans, asuras, and heavenly gandharva musicians—felt enraptured, and they rejoiced at the words spoken by the Blessed One.

Source: "The Shorter Sukhāvatīvyūha Sūtra" in *The Land of Bliss: The Paradise of the Buddha of Measureless Light,* translated by Luis O. Gómez (Honolulu: University of Hawaii Press, 1996), 15–22.

16

Mahāyāna School of Thought:
Mādhyamika

The Mādhyamika school of Mahāyāna Buddhism was founded by a monk named Nāgārjuna (c. 150–250 C.E.), author of the *Fundamentals of the Middle Way.* This work and others were represented as secret teachings that originated with the historical Buddha. These teachings, it was explained, had been kept secret because people were not prepared to understand their subtle and difficult nature. They were finally revealed to humankind by Nāgārjuna in order to correct erroneous knowledge and lead people to enlightenment.

Nāgārjuna developed a vigorous logic and philosophical dialectic, which represented a middle way of thought that avoided the two extremes of eternalism and nihilism. Beyond the realm of language or concepts, this middle path was instead transcendental, which suggests being above and beyond the two extremes. It is this transcendental position and avoidance of the two extremes that a reader must keep in mind when reading the thought of Nāgārjuna. It is also important to keep in mind that his thought does not represent a particular philosophical position. He rather wants to bring an end to all philosophical speculation or theorizing, because no particular philosophical position is ultimate or limitless, not even his own position. This is the case because ultimate truth is not embodied in any specific philosophical position. Thus Nāgārjuna devotes considerable effort to deconstructing other philosophical positions and categories in order to undermine them and demonstrate their shortcomings.

Nāgārjuna accomplishes his philosophical goals by analyzing and deconstructing a postulated entity by showing that its substantial self-nature has been constructed and expressed in sets of related, binary terms (such as origination/ destruction, own being/other being, conditioned/unconditioned, or identity/ difference). Due to the binary, interrelated, and dependent concepts or categories, no term can claim to be a real entity with independent and substantial status. His method intends to reject and annul all speculative views, whatever their origin. This does not imply that Nāgārjuna's philosophy attempts to create a counter-postion that represents the reverse of that rejected. Nāgārjuna's method possesses more in common with a reductio ad absurdum.

When reading Nāgārjuna it is important to keep in mind that he writes from the perspective of an enlightened bodhisattva (enlightened being) who is attempting to bring his readers to liberation. This enlightened perspective is a nondualistic position, which is grounded in an intuitive experience devoid of content. This intuition is beyond the state of ordinary knowledge and reason because it represents the dissolution of the conceptual function of the human mind. Representing the dawn of freedom and release from the turmoil and ignorance of the world, this intuitive way of knowing is the direct seeing into emptiness, which is equivalent to realizing nirvāṇa.

The following selections demonstrate Nāgārjuna using his dialectic to show the lack of substantial nature of causation, self, time, and the Four Noble Truths. None of these items possesses self-nature because they are all caused by something else. Moreover, everything is empty, and that includes nirvāṇa. The intuitive realization of emptiness represents the nondualistic position of Nāgārjuna.

Selections from the *Fundamentals of the Middle Way*

An Analysis of Conditioning Causes (pratyaya)

1. Never are any existing things found to originate
   From themselves, from something else, from both, or from no cause.
2. There are only four conditioning causes:
   A primary cause, objects of sensations, immediately preceding condition, and the predominant influence. There is no fifth.
3. There is no self-existence (*svabhava*) of existing things in conditioning causes, etc.;

And if no self-existence exists, neither does other-existence (*parabhava*) exist.

4. The efficient cause (*kriyā*) does not exist possessing a conditioning cause,
   Nor does the efficient cause exist without possessing a conditioning cause.
   Conditioning causes are not without efficient causes,
   Nor are there [conditioning causes] which possess efficient causes.

5. Those things are called conditioning causes whereby something originates after having encountered them;
   If other conditions do not arise, why are they not nonconditions?

6. There can be a conditioning cause neither of a nonreal thing nor of a real thing.
   Of what non-real thing is there a conditioning cause? And if it is [already] real, what use is a cause?

7. If an element occurs which is neither real nor nonreal nor both real and non-real,
   How can there be a cause that is permissible in this situation?

8. An existent thing possesses no object;
   Since an element is devoid of any object of sensation, how is it possible to have an object of sensation?

9. When no elements have originated, cessation is not possible.
   Therefore, it is not reasonable to refer to an immediately preceding condition;
   If something has already ceased, what cause can it have?

10. Since existing things that have no self-existence are not real,
    It is not possible to assert the phrase: "This thing becomes when that becomes."

11. The effect does not reside in the individual or collective conditioning causes,
    How can that which does not reside in the conditioning cause result from conditions?

12. If a non-existent effect results from those conditioning causes,
    Why then does an effect not arise also from noncauses?

13. If effect consists in its conditioning causes, the causes do not consist of themselves.
    How can an effect whose essence is the conditioning causes not consisting of themselves derive from something that is without essence?

14. Therefore, that effect does not consist in those causes; and yet it is agreed that an effect does not consist of noncauses as their essence.

How can a conditioning cause or non-cause exist when an effect is not produced?

An Analysis of Fire and Fuel

1 If fire is identical to its fuel, then it is both producer and product.
And if fire is different from fuel, then fire exists without fuel.

2. It would be perpetually burning because it would exist without a cause, which is fuel.
Since another beginning would be meaningless; in this case [fire] is without its object [i.e. burning of fuel].

3. [Fire] would be without a cause, namely fuel, if it were independent of anything else;
In which case another beginning would be meaningless, and there is perpetual burning.

4. If it is maintained: Fuel is that which is burning,
By what is fuel burned, since fuel is only that being burned?

5. [Fire], when different and not obtained [through fuel], will *not obtain;*
Not burning, it will not burn later;

6. Without cessation, it will not be extinguished;
If there is no cessation, then it will persist with its own characteristics.

7. [The opponent claims:] If fire is different from fuel it could obtain the fuel
Just as a woman obtains a husband, and a man [obtains] a wife.

8. [Nāgārjuna answers:] Though fire is different from fuel, it could indeed obtain the fuel,
On the condition that both fire and fuel can be reciprocally differentiated [but this is impossible].

9. If the fire is dependent on the fuel, and if the fuel is dependent on the fire,
On what are fire and fuel established as dependent?

10. If fire is dependent on fuel, it would be the proof of the proved fire.
Thus, being fuel it will exist without fire.

11. When a thing is proved by being dependent on something else, then it proves the other by being dependent.
If that which is required for dependence must be proved, then what is dependent on what?

12. If that thing is proved by being dependent, how can that which has not been proved be dependent?
However, if it is proved that it is dependent, that dependence is not possible.

13. Fire does not exist dependent upon fuel; and fire does not exist independent
    of fuel.
    Fuel does not exist independent of fire; and fuel does not exist independent
    of fire.
14. Fire does not come from something else; and fire does not exist in fuel.
    The remaining [analysis] in regard to fuel is described by the examination
    of moved, not moved, and gone.
15. Fire is not identical to fuel, but fire does not originate in anything other than
    fuel.
    Fire does not have fuel as its nature; also, the fuel is not in fire, and vice
    versa.
16. By the discussion of fire and fuel, the syllogism of the individual self and the
    aggregates, Is all together explained, as well as the other analogies.
17. Those who specify the nature of the individual self and of existing things as
    radically different—
    Those people I do not regard as ones who understand the sense of the
    doctrine.

An Analysis of a Self-existent Thing (svabhāva)

1. The production of a self-existent thing by a conditioning cause is not
   possible,
   If being produced through dependence on a cause, a self-existent thing
   would be fabricated.
2. How, indeed, will a self-existent thing become fabricated?
   A self-existent thing [by definition] is not produced and is independent of
   anything else.
3. If there is an absence of a self-existent thing, how will an other-existent thing
   (parabhāva) come into being?
   Certainly the self-existence of an other-existent thing is called difference.
4. Further, how can a thing [exist] without either self-existence or other-
   existence?
   If either self-existence or other-existence exists, then an existing thing,
   indeed, would be established.
5. If there is no proof of an existent thing, then a nonexistent thing cannot be
   proved,
   Since people call the other-existence of an existent thing a nonentity.
6. Those who perceive self-existence and other-existence, and an existent thing
   and a nonexistent thing,

Do not perceive the true nature of the Buddha's teaching.

7. In "The Discourse of Kātyāyana" both "it is" and "it is not" are opposed

By the Victorious One, who has ascertained the meaning of "existent" and "nonexistent."

8. If there would be an existent thing by its own nature, there could not be nonexistence.

Certainly an existent thing different from its own nature would never be tenable.

9. [An opponent asks:] If there is no basic self-nature, of what could become other?

[Nāgārjuna answers:] If there is basic self-nature, of what will there be other?

10. "It is" is a notion of eternity. "It is not" is a nihilistic view.

Therefore, one who is wise does not have recourse to "being" or "nonbeing."

11. That which exists by its own nature is eternal since "it does not exit."

If it is maintained: "That which existed before does not exist now," there follows the error of nihilism.

An Analysis of Action (karma) *and Its Product* (phala)

[An opponent presents the traditional causal theory of action:]

1. The self-disciplined, helping others,

And compassion is the Dharma; that is the seed for the fruit in this and future lives.

2. The most perceptive sage [Buddha] has said that there is action (*karma*) as volition and as a result of having willed.

The varieties of acts of these actions has been explained in many ways.

3. Thus, that action which is called "volition": that is considered [by tradition] as mental desire,

But that action which is a result of having willed: that is considered [by tradition] as physical or verbal.

4. Sound, action, and all that which does not rest which is considered as unknown,

Also the other unknown that is considered to be at rest;

5. That which is pure as a result of pleasure, that which is impure as a result of pleasure, And volition: these seven basic elements are considered as the modes of action.

[Another opponent argues by the imagery of a process:]

6. If an action endures to the time of its ripening, that action would be eternal.
   If [an action] ceased, what will it produce?

7. There is fruit (*phala*) when a process, a sprout, and so on, starts from a seed;
   But without a seed that [process] does not come to be.

8. Inasmuch as the process is dependent on a seed and the fruit is produced
   from the process,
   The seed precedes the fruit; it neither comes to an end nor is eternal.

9. There is a product (*phala*) when an intention starts from a thought;
   But without a thought that does not proceed.

10. Inasmuch as the intention is dependent on a thought and the product (*phala*)
    is produced from the intention,
    The product, presupposing the thought, neither comes to an end nor is
    eternal.

11. The ten pure paths of action are the method for realizing the Dharma.
    And the five qualities of desired objects [that is, desire to know the form,
    sound, odor, taste, and touch of existence] are fruits (*phala*) of the Dharma
    both now and after death.

[A third opponent argues for an imperishable element:]

12. There would be many great errors if that explanation [were accepted].
    Therefore, that explanation is not possible.

13. In rebuttal I will explain the interpretation, which can be made to fit [the
    facts]:
    That which is followed by the Buddha, the self-sufficient enlightened ones
    (*pratyekabuddhas*) and the disciples [of Buddha].

14. As the imperishable, it is like an obligation, so an action (karma) is like the
    execution of duty.
    The imperishable is of four kinds within the realm of action and indetermi-
    nate in its essential nature.

15. [An imperishable force] is not destroyed qua destruction; rather it is
    destroyed according to meditation.
    Therefore, the fruit of actions originates by the imperishable force.

16. If [the imperishable force] were that which is destroyed by [usual] destruction
    or by transference of action,
    Errors like the destruction of action would logically result.

17. At the moment of transition that [imperishable force]

Of all identical and different actions belonging to the same element, only one arises.

18. That [imperishable force] is the Dharma, having arisen by one action after another in visible existence;
And it remains [constant] even in the development of all separating action.

19. That [imperishable force] is destroyed by death and by avoiding the product.
There the difference is characterized as impure and pure.

20. Emptiness, no annihilation, existence-in-flux, permanence,
And the imperishable reality of action: such was the teaching taught by the Buddha.

[Nāgārjuna refutes the above arguments:]

21. Why does the action not originate? Because it is without self-existence.
Since it does not originate, it does not perish.

22. If an action did exist as a self-existent thing, without a doubt, it would be eternal.
An action would be uncreated because there is no eternal thing which is produced.

23. If the action were uncreated, then there could be the fear of attaining something from something uncreated;
Then the opposite to a saintly discipline would arise.

24. Then, undoubtedly, all daily actions would be contradicted.
And even the distinction between virtue and evil is not possible.

25. Then an act whose development had taken place would develop again,
If an act, because it persists, exists through its own nature.

26. An action is that whose self (ātma) is desire, and the desires do not really exist.
If these desires do not really exist, how would the action really exist?

27. Action and desire are declared to be the conditioning causes of the body.
If action and desire are empty, what need one say about bodies?

[An opponent tries to establish an identifiable entity by saying:]

28. The man obstructed by ignorance, and confused by craving
Is one who seeks enjoyment. He is not different from the one who acts, nor identical to it.

[Nāgārjuna answers:]

29. Since action does not originate from a condition nor fails to arise from causeless conditions,
There is no one acting.

30. If there is no action, how could there be one who acts and the product of action?

And if there is no product, how can there be an experiencer?

31. Just as a teacher, by his magical power, created a magical illusion,

And this magical illusion formed again another magical illusion.

32. Just as an agent is himself being formed magically; and the act performed by him Is like a magical illusion being magically created by another magical illusion.

33. Desires, actions, bodies, agents, and products

Are like a city of heavenly beings, resembling a mirage, a dream.

An Analysis of the Individual Self (atma)

1. If the individual self (*ātma*) were the aggregates, then it would partake of origination and destruction.

If it were different from the aggregates, then it would be without the characteristics of the aggregates.

2. If the self does not exist, how then will there be something which is mine? There is lack of possessiveness and no ego on account of the cessation of self and that which is mine.

3. He who is without possessiveness and who has no ego—He, also, does not exist.

Whoever sees "he who is without possessiveness" or "he who has no ego" does not perceive.

4. When "I" and "mine" are extinguished, then also there is not an outer nor an inner.

The acquisition of karma is stopped; on account of that destruction, rebirth ceases.

5. On account of the destruction of the pains of action there is release; for pains of action exist for him who constructs them.

These pains result from mental fabrication; but this mental fabrication comes to a stop by emptiness.

6. There is the teaching of "individual self" (*ātma*), and the teaching of "non-self" (*anātma*); But neither "individual self" nor "non-self" whatever has been taught by the Buddhas.

7. When the domain of thought is nonexistent, that which can be stated is nonexistent.

The natures of those things which are unoriginated and not terminated, like nirvāṇa, represent the Truth.

8. Everything is "actual" or "not actual," or both "actual and not actual," or "neither actual nor not actual": This is the teaching of the Buddha.

9. Not caused by something else, peaceful, not fabricated by discursive thought, Indeterminate, unidfferentiated: that are the characteristics of reality.

10. Whatever exists, being dependent on something else, is certainly not identical to that thing,
    Nor is a thing different from that; therefore, it is neither destroyed nor permanent.

11. The immortal essence of the teaching of the Buddhas, the lords of the world, is
    Without identity or distinction; it is not destroyed nor is it eternal.

12. When fully developed enlightened beings do not arise and the disciples of the Buddha disappear,
    Then, independently, the knowledge of the self-produced enlightened ones
    Will arise without a teacher.

An Analysis of Time (kāla)

1. If the present and future exist presupposing the past,
   The present and future will exist in the past.

2. If the present and future did not exist there in the past,
   How could the present and future exist assuming that past?

3. Without presupposing the past, the other two moments cannot be proved to exist.
   Therefore neither present nor future time exists.

4. In this way the remaining two [times] can be inverted.
   Thus one would regard "highest," "lowest," and "middle," and so on, and oneness and difference.

5. A nonstatic time cannot be grasped; and a nonstatic time which can be grasped does not exist.
   How, then, can one grasp time if it is not known?

6. Since time is dependent on a thing, how can time [exist] without a thing?
   There is not any thing which exists; how, then, how can time exist?

An Analysis of the Four Noble Truths

[An opponent claims:]

1. If everything is empty, there is no origination nor destruction.
   Then you must incorrectly conclude that there is nonexistence of the Four Noble Truths.

2. If the Four Noble Truths do not exist, the saving knowledge, the elimination [of illusion],

   The becoming [enlightened], and the realization of the goal are totally impossible.

3. If there is nonexistence, then also the Four Noble Truths do not exist.

   In the nonexistence of fruit there is no attainers of the fruits or faithful.

4. When the community [of Buddhists] does not exist, then those eight kinds of persons do not exist.

   Because there is no existence of the Four Noble Truths, the true Dharma does not exist.

5. And if there are no Dharma and community, how will the Buddha exist?

   If you conceive of emptiness in this way, certainly you deny the three jewels [that is, the Buddha, the Dharma, and the monastic community].

6. You deny the real existence of fruits, of right and wrong, Dharma itself.

   And all the practical behavior of the world as being empty.

[Nāgārjuna replies:]

7. We reply that you do not comprehend the point of emptiness;

   You eliminate both the significance of emptiness itself and its purpose harming yourself.

8. The teaching of the Buddha about the Dharma is grounded in two truths:

   A truth of world convention and an ultimate truth.

9. Those who do not know the distinction between the two kinds of truth

   Do not understand the profound truth in the teaching of the Buddha.

10. The highest sense [of the truth] is not taught apart from conventional truth,

    And without having understood the highest sense one cannot achieve liberation.

11. By misperceiving emptiness, an unintelligent person is utterly destroyed.

    It is like a snake wrongly grasped or [magical] knowledge incorrectly applied.

12. Therefore, the mind of the Buddha was despaired of teaching the Dharma,

    Having thought about the incomprehensibility of the Dharma by the stupid.

13. Time and again you have presented refutations that are not relevant to emptiness,

    But those refutations do not apply to my grasp of emptiness.

14. When emptiness is lucid, then everything in existence is lucid.

    If emptiness is not lucid, then all existence is not lucid.

15. When you project you own faults on us,

    You are like a person who, having mounted his horse, forgot the horse!

16. If you recognize genuine existence on account of the self-existence of things,

    Then this perception is without causes and conditions.

17. You deny effects, causes, the producer, instrument, and the producing action,

    And the origination, destruction, and fruit.

18. Whatever is originating dependently we call emptiness;

    This apprehension, being a dependent designation, represents understanding of the middle way.

19. Since there is no particular thing whatever originating independently,

    No particular thing whatever exists which is not empty.

20. If all existence is not empty, there is neither origination nor cessation.

    You must wrongly conclude then that the Four Noble Truths do not exist.

21. Having originated without being conditioned, how will suffering come into existence?

    It is said that suffering is not eternal; therefore, certainly it does not exist by its own nature (*svabhāva*).

22. How can that which is existing by its own nature originate again?

    For him who denies emptiness there is no arising.

23. There is no destruction of suffering if it exists by its own nature.

    By trying to establish self-existence, you deny cessation.

24. If the path is self-existent, then there is no way of bringing it into existence;

    If that path is brought into existence, then self-existence, which you claim, does not exist.

25. When suffering, origination, and cessation do not exist,

    What kind of path will obtain the cessation of suffering?

26. If there is no complete knowledge as to self-existence, how [can there be] any understanding of it?

    Indeed, is it not true that self-existence is that which endures?

27. As in the case of complete knowledge, neither destruction, realization, origination,

    Or the four holy truths would be impossible for you.

28. If you accept self-existence, and a fruit is not known by its self-existence,

    How can it be known at all?

29. Without existence of fruits, there are no attainments nor obtaining [the fruits]; When the spiritual community does not exist, then those eight kinds of persons do not exist.

30. Because there is nonexistence of the four holy truths, it follows that the real
    Dharma does not exist.

    And if there is no Dharma and community, how could the Buddha exist?

31. For you, either the one who is enlightened (Buddha) comes into being in-
    dependent of enlightenment,

    Or enlightenment comes into being independent of the one who is
    enlightened.

32. For you, a person who is a non-Buddha by his own nature (*svabhāva*) but
    strives for enlightenment,

    Will not attain the enlightenment though practicing the path to it.

33. Neither the right Dharma nor wrong actions will be done anywhere.

    What is produced which is nonempty? That with self-existence is not
    produced.

34. For you, there is a result without [the distinction] of right or wrong actions,

    Since, for you, the product caused by Dharma or non-Dharma does not
    exist.

35. If, for you, the product is caused by right or wrong actions,

    How can that product, being originated by right or wrong actions, be
    nonempty?

36. You deny all ordinary and customary activities

    When you deny emptiness [in the sense of] dependent co-origination.

37. If you reject emptiness, there would be action that is unactivated.

    There would be nothing begun, and an agent without action.

38. According to the notion of self-existence, the world is free from different
    conditions;

    Then it will exist as static, undestroyed and immutable.

39. If nonemptiness does not exist, then something is attained which is not
    attained;

    There is cessation of suffering and actions, and all evil is destroyed.

40. He who perceives dependent co-origination

    Also understands suffering, origination, and cessation as well as the path of
    liberation.

An Analysis of Nirvāṇa

1. [An opponent says:]

   If everything is empty, there is no origination nor cessation.

   Then whose nirvāṇa through elimination [of suffering] and destruction [of
   illusion] would be affirmed?

2. [Nāgārjuna replies:]

   If all existence is nonempty, there is no origination nor cessation. Then whose nirvāṇa through elimination [of suffering] and cessation [of illusion] would be postulated?

3. Nirvāṇa has been said to be neither eliminated nor attained, neither annihilated nor eternal,

   Neither disappeared nor originated.

4. Nirvāṇa is not an existing thing, for then it would be characterized by old age and death.

   There is no existent entity that would not become old and be without death.

5. And if nirvāṇa is an existing thing, nirvāṇa would be constructed,

   Since no existing thing has been found to be a nonconstructed product.

6. But if nirvāṇa is an existing thing, how could [nirvāṇa] exist nondependently?

   A nondependent existent does not exist.

7. If nirvāṇa is not an existing thing, would nirvāṇa become a nonexisting thing?

   Wherever there is no existing thing, neither is there a nonexisting thing.

8. But if nirvāṇa is a nonexisting thing, how could [nirvāṇa] exist nondependently?

   Certainly nirvāṇa is not a nonexisting thing which exists without dependence.

9. That which comes and goes is dependent and conditioned,

   This [state], when not dependent or not conditioned, is understod to be nirvāṇa.

10. The teacher has taught that becoming and nonbecoming are destroyed;

    Therefore, it entails that: nirvāṇa is neither an existent thing nor a nonexisting thing.

11. If nirvāṇa were both an existent and a nonexistent thing,

    Final release (mokṣa) would be [both] an existent and a nonexistent thing.

12. If nirvāṇa were both an existent and a nonexistent thing,

    There would be no nondependent nirvāṇa, since both depend on conditions.

13. How can nirvāṇa exist as both existent and nonexistent,

    For nirvāṇa is uncompounded, while both an existent thing and a nonexistent thing are compounded.

14. How can nirvāṇa exist as both an existent and a nonexistent thing?

There is no existence of both in the same place, as in the case of both darkness and light.

15. The assertion: "Nirvāṇa is neither an existent thing nor a nonexistent thing"
Would be proved if [the assertion]: "It is an existent thing and a nonexistent thing" were proved.

16. If nirvāṇa is neither an existent thing nor a nonexistent thing,
Then, who can really arrive at [the assertion]: "neither an existent thing nor a nonexistent thing?"

17. By passing into nirvāṇa, Glorious One is said to exist after his death,
Or does not exist, or both or neither.

18. Also, it is not expressed if the Glorious One exists while remaining [in the world],
Or does not exist, or both or neither.

19. There is no difference whatever between cyclic existence (saṃsāra) and nirvāṇa; And there is nothing whatever that distinguishes nirvāṇa from cyclic existence.

20. The extreme limit of nirvāṇa is also the extreme the limit of cyclic existence;
There is not the slightest bit of difference between them.

21. Views about whether that which is beyond death is limited by a beginning or an end or some other alternative
Depend on a nirvāṇa limited by a beginning and an end.

22. Since all dharmas are empty, what is finite? What is infinite?
What is both finite and infinite? What is neither finite or infinite?

23. Is there anything which is this or something else, which is permanent or impermanent,
Which is both permanent and impermanent, or which is neither?

24. The cessation of objectification is a welcome cessation of illusion;
No Dharma anywhere has been taught by the Buddha about anything, at any
Time, in any place, or to any person.

Source: Nāgārjuna, *Mādhyamakaśātra of Nāgārjuna with the Commentary of Prasannapadā of Candrakīrti*, edited by P. L. Vaidya (Darbhanga: Mithila Instiute, 1960).

17

Mahāyāna School of Thought:
Yogācāra

The Mahāyāna Buddhist tradition bestows credit for establishing the Yogācāra school on the brothers named Asanga and Vasubandhu (c. fourth or fifth century C.E.). The school is also called Vijñānavāda (literally meaning holders of the doctrine of consciousness) because consciousness is equated with the highest reality. The school is committed to the practice of yoga in order to eradicate the two root problems of life, which are identified with ignorance and craving. The school traces craving to the existence of desirable objects and to human ignorance that objectifies images in the mind. Thus, it is important for humans to realize that their minds are the origin of all objectifications. If the origin of the problem of ignorance is located within consciousness, the way to overcome ignorance is also discovered in the mind.

Vasubandhu argues that the apparent objective world is produced by consciousness-only, because the world and its objects are nothing more than products of one's consciousness. Thus the only entity that truly exists is consciousness, which the school equates with emptiness. If all that exists is consciousness, there is an identity of consciousness and object, which represents a nondualistic position. This implies that when consciousness sees a thing as it truly is in fact, it is consciousness seeing itself, which is an enlightened insight. To intuitively realize that everything is consciousness suggests that a person's thinking is devoid of conceptualizing and objectifying types of thinking. This insight represents the culmination of wisdom for this school.

When reading the selections from Vasubandhu it is important to be aware that he is writing from his conviction that the only thing that exists is consciousness-only. The work selected for this collection begins by mentioning the "storehouse consciousness," which is the location for the private and universal seeds deposited on consciousness. It helps to explain why humans have similar notions and different experiences. Vasubandhu continues by discussing obstructions to enlightenment, the path to the goal, perfections of the bodhisattva to be developed, and stages of enlightenment. This essay is an effective and brief summary of the path of the bodhisattva from the perspective of the Yogācāra school.

Selections from the *Thirty Verses* (*Trimśika-kārikā*) by Vasubandhu

1. The metaphors of "self" and "events" which develop in so many different ways take place in the transformation of consciousness: and this transformation is of three kinds:

2. Maturation, that called "always reflecting," and the perception of sense-objects.
   Among these, "maturation" is that called "the store-consciousness" which has all the seeds.

3. Its appropriations, states, and perceptions are not fully conscious, yet it is always endowed with contacts, mental attentions, feelings, cognitions, and volitions.

4. Its feelings are equaniminous: it is unobstructed and indeterminate
   The same for its contacts, etc. It develops like the currents in a stream.

5. Its de-volvement takes place in a saintly state: Dependent on it there develops a consciousness called "manas," having it as its object-of-consciousness, and having the nature of always reflecting;

6. It is always conjoined with four afflictions, obstructed-but-indeterminate, known as view of self, confusion of self, pride of self, and love of self.

7. And wherever it arises, so do contact and the others. But it doesn't exist in a saintly state,
   or in the attainment of cessation, or even in a supermundane path.

8. This is the second transformation. The third is the apprehension of sense-objects of six kinds; it is either beneficial,
   or unbeneficial, or both.

9. It is always connected with [motivating dispositions], and sometimes with factors that arise specifically,

   with beneficial events associated with citta, afflictions, and secondary afflictions: its feelings are of three kinds.

10. The first are contact, etc.; those arising specifically are

    zest, confidence, memory, concentration, and insight.

11. The beneficial are faith, inner shame, dread of blame,

    the three starting with lack of greed, vigor, tranquility, carefulness, and non-harming;

    the afflictions are attachment, aversion, and confusion,

12. pride, views, and doubts. The secondary afflication are anger, malice, hypocrisy, maliciousness, envy, selfishness, deceitfulness,

13. guile, mischievous exuberance, desire to harm, lack of shame,

    lack of dread of blame, mental fogginess, excitedness, lack of faith, sloth, carelessness, loss of minfulness,

14. distractedness, lack of recognition, regret, and torpor,

    initial mental application, and subsequent discursive thought: the last two pairs are of two kinds.

15. In the root-consciousness, the arising of the other five takes place according to conditions,

    either all together or not, just like waves in water.

16. The co-arising of a mental consciousness takes place always except in a non-cognitional state,

    or in the two attainments, or in torpor, or fainting, or in a state without citta.

17. This transformation of consciousness is a discrimination, and

    as it is discriminated, it does not exist, and so everything is perception-only.

18. Consciousness is only all the seeds, and transformation takes place in such and such a way,

    according to a reciprocal influence, by which such and such a type of discrimination may arise.

19. The residual impressions of actions, along with the residual impression of a "dual" apprehension,

    cause another maturation (of seeds) to occur,

    where the former maturation has been exhausted.

20. Whatever range of events is discriminated by whatever discrimination

    is just the constructed own-being, and it isn't really to be found.—

21. The interdependent own-being, on the other hand, is the discrimination which arises from conditions,

and the fulfilled is its state of being separated always from the former.

22. So it is to be spoken of as neither exactly different nor non-different from the interdependent,

just like impermanence, etc., for when one isn't seen, the other is.

23. The absence of own-being in all events has been taught with a view towards the three different kinds of absence or own-being in the three different kinds of own-being.

24. The first is without own-being through its character itself, but the second because of its non-independence, and the third is absence of own-being.

25. It is ultimate truth of all events, and so it is "Suchness," too,

since it is just so all the time, and it's just perception-only.

26. As long as consciousness is not situated within perception-only,

the residues of a "dual" apprehension will not come to an end.

27. And so even with the consciousness: "All this is perception only,"

because this also involves an apprehension,

For whatever makes something stop in front of it isn't situated in "this-only."

28. When consciousness does not apprehend any object-of-consciousness, it's situated in "consciousness-only,"

for with the non-being of an object apprehended, there is no apprehension of it.

29. It is without citta, without apprehension, and it is supermundane knowledge;

It is revolution at the basis, the ending of two kinds of susceptibility to harm.

30. It is the inconceivable, beneficial, constant Ground, not liable to affliction, bliss, and the liberation-body called the Dharma-body of the sage.

Selections from the
Commentary on the Separation of the Middle Extremes

The Obstructions

Concerning obstructions, the author says:

"The pervading and the limited ones,
the excessive and the equal,
accepting and abandoning,
are called obstructions of the two."

In this passage, "the pervading" is the obstructions consisting simply of afflictions, and the obstructions of the knowable, because both are obstructions to those of the Bodhisattva-lineage. "The limited" is the obstruction to the Śrāvaka-lineages, which is affliction only (i.e., the sole goal of the Śrāvakas, that is the followers of the "Hīnayāna," is the eradication of their own afflictions). The "excessive" is the obstruction in those who act with attachment (hostility or confusion). The "equal" is that in those who make everything alike. The obstruction of accepting or abandoning Saṃsāra is an obstruction to those of the Bodhisattva-lineage, because of being an obstruction to Nirvāṇa without a basis. Thus, the obstructions of those of the Bodhisattva-lineage, those of the Śrāvaka-vehicle, and those of others, have been made known.

> "The characteristics of the obstructions that are simply
> affliction are nine-fold, being the fetters."

The nine fetters are the obstructions that are simply afflictions. To what are they obstructions?

> "to excitement and to equanimity,
> and to the seeing of reality."

The fetter of complacency is an obstruction to excitement, and the fetter of aversion is an obstruction to equanimity. (Because of the former, there is no passion, compassion, or energy); because of the latter, one cannot stay calm in face of the disagreeable or hostile. The rest of the fetters are obstructions to the seeing of reality. How does this occur?

> "Leading towards the view of self,
> obstructing insights regarding this and 'external objects,'
> regarding the cessation of suffering, the Path, the Gems,
> others' attainments, and regarding the knowledge of
> being satisfied with little."

The fetters become specific obstructions. The fetter of pride becomes an obstacle leading to the view of self. This is because this view has not been cast off through proper practice in a time of clear understanding, working against the pride of thinking that "I exist" in what is internal or external. The fetter of ignorance is an obstacle to knowledge about external objects and also involves the view of a self. This is because it is a lack of knowledge concerning the appropriating aggregates. The fetter of holding fast to views is an obstruction to the knowledge of the truth of the cessation of suffering. This is because such holding fast goes against the possibility of the cessation of suffering, because of the various anxieties caused by the view of a self in the body, and views regarding the permanence or impermanence of the elements constituting personality. The fetter of adherence to mere rules and rituals is an obstruction to the knowledge of the truth of the Path, because of its adherence to the view that the highest clarity lies elsewhere than it really does. The fetter of doubt is an obstruction to the knowledge of the Three Gems (Buddha, Dharma, Saṅgha), because it involves a lack of faith in the good qualities of these three. The fetter of envy is an obstruction to satisfaction in others' attainment, because one wishes to see only others' flaws. The fetter of selfishness leads to a lack of knowledge of satisfaction with little, because of one's obsession with possession.

"Further obstructions stand in the way of welfare, etc. in ten ways."

There are further obstructions that stand in the way of welfare, etc. in ten ways. What are these obstructions, and what is meant here by "welfare, etc."?

"The lack of means to rouse "oneself" from inactivity,
the lack of complete use of "one's" sense-fields,
careless activity, non-arising of the beneficial,
lack of mental attention to what lies around you,
unfulfillment of the necessary preparation (to live in the Great Vehicle),
separation from "one's" spiritual lineage, and separation from good
    friends,
wearying distress and agitation of citta,
lack of opportunity to practice the Great Vehicle,
being forced to live with stupid or depraved people,
susceptibility to harm, lack of control, and lack of maturation of insight
    because of the three,
susceptibility to harm by nature, sloth, and carelessness,
attachment to being, and longing for enjoyment,
muddle-headedness,
lack of confidence, lack of faith,
deliberation according to words,
lack of reverence for the Good Dharma,
respect for gain,
lack of compassion,

casting away what one has heard,

being ill-versed in what's been heard,

and lack of engagement in meditation."

These are the obstructions to welfare, etc. And what is welfare, etc.?

"Welfare, enlightenment, the full taking up of Saṃsāra, insight,

lack of confusion, lack of obstructions,

ability to evolve, fearlessness,

lack of selfishness and potency."

So that it can be known how many obstructions can arise to which of these factors: welfare, etc. he says,

"By threes, the obstructions of the knowable arise for these."

To each of these beneficial factors, three obstructions can arise. To welfare, arise the lack of means to rouse "oneself" from inactivity, the lack of complete use of "one's" sense-fields, and careless activity. To enlightenment, arise the non-arising of good caittas, lack of mental attention to what lies around you, and the unfulfillment of the necessary preparation. To the full taking up of Saṃsāra, which is the arising of the enlightenment-citta, arise separation from "one's" spiritual lineage, separation from good friends, and wearying distress and agitation of citta. To insight, which is the state of a Bodhisattva, arise the lack of opportunity to practice the Great Vehicle, and being forced to live with either stupid or depraved people. In this passage, "stupid people" are fools, and "depraved people" are frustrated, harmed people. To lack of confusion, arise susceptibility to harm through reversals, lack of potency because of the three kinds of obstructions: afflictions, etc. and lack of maturation in insight which matures confidence. As obstructions to the abandonment of obstructions, arise natural susceptibility to harm, sloth, and carelessness. To the ability to evolve, arise attachment to (rigid) being, longing for enjoyment, and muddle-headedness, through which citta evolves otherwise than towards supreme perfect enlightenment. To fearlessness, arise lack of confidence in the "personality," lack of trust in Dharma, and deliberations according to words. To lack of selfishness, arise lack of reverence for the Dharma, respect for the acquisition and worship of gain, and lack of compassion for sentient beings. To potency, arise three, because of which one can't attain (psychic) power, which are casting away what has been heard (regarding Dharma), because it brings about actions leading to the rejection of Dharma, being ill-versed in what's been heard, and lack of engagement in meditation.

Because these obstructions become ten kinds of causes in relation to welfare; etc. these ten kinds of causes are to be made known now, because of their bearing upon them. There is a cause as one thing's being the direct condition for the arising of another, such as when the eye gives rise to a visual consciousness. There is a cause as one thing's maintaining another's existence, such as the four foods maintaining sentient beings. (The four "foods" are: morsel-food maintaining the organism itself, contact giving stimuli to the living being, *manas* and volition motivating its activity, and consciousness.) There is a cause as one thing's sustaining another, in the sense of providing a support, as the inhabited world does for the world of sentient beings. There is a cause as one thing's manifesting another, as the action of looking does the visible. There is a cause as one thing's transforming another, as fire does that which is being cooked. There is a cause as one thing's disjoining another—such is the relation of a cutting instrument to that which is being cut. There is a cause as one thing's evolving another step by step, such as the action of a goldsmith, who works bracelets out of masses of gold. There is a cause as one thing's giving rise to the idea of another, such as the perception of smoke, etc. giving rise to the idea of fire, etc. There is a cause as one thing's causing us to form the idea of another, as a justification does for a thesis. There is a cause as one thing's leading to the attainment of the other, as the Path leads to Nirvāṇa, etc.

Thus, an obstruction to the arising of alleviation is an obstruction to welfare, because of its causing it to arise. An obstruction to its maintenance is an obstruction to enlightenment (i.e., the enlightenment-citta), because of its resulting in an absence of anger and frustration. An obstruction to sustaining it is an obstruction to the full taking up of Saṁsāra, because this becomes the support for the enlightenment-citta. An obstruction to manifesting it to others is an obstruction to insightedness, because of its making it clear to others. An obstruction to its transformation is an obstruction to lack of confusion, because of its folding away all confusions obstructing alleviation. An obstruction to its disjunction is an obstruction to the lack of obstruction, because it causes separation from obstructions. An obstruction to its evolving gradually is an obstruction to citta's ability to evolve towards enlightenment. An obstruction to giving rise to the idea (of the Great Vehicle) is an obstruction to fearlessness, because this idea does not arise where there is any fear. An obstruction to causing the idea to arise in others is an obstruction to lack of selfishness, because it is the lack of selfishness in the

Dharma that causes the idea (of the Great Vehicle) to arise in others. An obstruction to its attainment is an obstruction to potency, because it has the characteristic of the attainment of powers.

> Causes of ten kinds: for arising, maintaining, sustaining, manifesting,
>   transforming, disjoining, evolving,
> causing the idea to arise, causing the idea to be formed in others,
> and attaining: for these the eye, foods, the earth,
> a lamp, a fire, are examples,
> and a cutting instrument, an artisan's skill, smoke, justifications, and the
>   Path.

It is through the desire to obtain enlightenment that the roots of the beneficial are at first caused to arise. Then, through the power of the roots of the beneficial, enlightenment (the enlightenment-citta) can be attained. The enlightenment-citta is the basis for the arising of the roots of the beneficial. The Bodhisattva is the support of the enlightenment-citta. Again, with these roots of the beneficial attained through the enlightenment-citta which has been made to arise, reversals will be abandoned by the Bodhisattva, and a complete absence of reversals will be caused to arise. Thus, freed from reversals in the Path of Seeing, all obstructions are abandoned in the Path of Cultivation. Again, the three roots of the beneficial, once obstructions have been gotten rid of, will become evolved to supreme complete enlightenment. Then, through the exercise of the power of this transformation, one will not be afraid of the various kinds of teachings in the deep extensive Dharma. Thus, through not being alarmed, seeing the various qualities in the events of the teachings, one can explain these events in detail to others. Thereafter, the Bodhisattva, having thus attained the exercise of these powers through these various qualities, quickly attains supreme complete enlightenment, and attains also potency in all events. This is the gradual sequence of welfare, etc.

> "Furthermore, there are other obstructions;
> to the allies, pāramitās, and stages."

First of all, to the allies of enlightenment:

> Lack of skill as regards the meditational object,
> sloth, two defects in meditational concentration,
> lack of planting, weakness,
> being flawed by views and susceptibility to harm.

Lack of skill as regards the meditational object is an obstruction to the application of mindfulness. Sloth is an obstruction to the right exertions. Two defects in meditational concentration are a lack of completion of meditation due to a deficiency in either zest, vigor, citta, or exploration, and a lack of completion of meditation due to a deficiency in the secondary motivational dispositions necessary for efforts in meditating. These (lack of completions of meditation) are obstructions to the bases of psychic power. To the faculties, non-planting of the factors conducive to liberation is an obstruction. To the powers, weakness of these same faculties due to the interference of adverse factors is an obstruction. To the limbs of enlightenment, the flaw of views is an obstruction due to their working against the Path of Seeing. To the limbs of the Path, the flaw of susceptibility to harm is an obstruction, because of its working against the Path of Cultivation.

Obstructions to the pāramitās:

"Obstructions to having, happy states,

to not forsaking sentient beings,

to casting off and growth of flaws and virtues, to descent."

"to liberating, to inexhaustibility, to continuance in welfare,

to making certain, to enjoyment and maturation of Dharma."

Here it is explained which result of which among the ten pāramitās is liable to damage by which obstruction. In this connection, an obstruction to having is an obstruction to (the effect of) the pāramitā of giving. An obstruction to a happy state is an obstruction to (the effect of) the pāramitā of good conduct towards others. An obstruction to the non-abandonment of sentient beings is an obstruction to (the effect of) the pāramitā of forbearance. An obstruction to the casting off of flaws and the growth of virtues is an obstruction to (the effect of) the pāramitā of vigor. An obstruction into descent into what is to be mastered is an obstruction to (the effect of) the pāramitā of meditation. An obstruction to the act of liberating ("self" and "others") is an obstruction to (the effect of) the pāramitā of insight. An obstruction to the inexhaustibility of giving, etc. is an obstruction to (the effect of) the pāramitā of skill in means, because of their inexhaustibility through the enlightenment-transformation. An obstruction to a beneficial uninterrupted continuance in all kinds of being again is an obstruction to (the effect of) the pāramitā of resolve, because it is through the power of the Bodhisattva's resolve that one takes on births which are favorable to this continuance in Saṃsāra. An obstruction to making the beneficial unfailing is an obstruction to (the effect of) the pāramitā of power, because it is through the two powers of contemplation and cultivation that adverse factors are overpowered. An obstruction to the enjoyment and maturation of Dharma in both "oneself" and "others" is an obstruction to (the effect of) the pāramitā of knowledge, because of one's not truly understanding the meaning of what one has heard.

And to the stages, there may be obstructions, in this order:

"In regard to the all-encompassing aim,
to the higher aim,
to the yet higher aim which flows from that,
to the aim of non-grasping,
to a lack of division in the series,
to the aim of neither affliction or alleviation,
to the aim of a lack of diversity,
to the aim that there is neither "inferior" nor "superior,"
and to the four-fold basis of potency,
there is this ignorance in the Ground of Events,
a ten-fold non-afflicted obstructing,
by way of factors adverse to the Stages,
but the antidotes to them *are* the Stages!"

An unafflicted ignorance which arises successively in the ten-fold Ground of Events in relation to its all-encompassing, and other, aims, is an obstruction to the stages of enlightenment, because it is an adverse factor to them. That is, on the first, all-encompassing stage, it counter-acts the all-encompassing aim by which one understands the sameness of "self" and "others." On the second stage, it counter-acts a further aim (of the Great Vehicle), by which one decides that one should do practices (*yoga*) for the sake of bringing about a clearing of all aspects. (in a total rooting-out of afflicting characteristics). On the third stage, it counter-acts a further aim which flows from that, by which one is able, after having realized the ultimate nature of what has been heard which flows from the Ground of Events, to hurl oneself into a fire-pit which has the extent of the whole Tri-Chiliocosm. On the fourth stage, it counter-acts the aim of non-grasping, for here even the craving for Dharma is abandoned. On the fifth stage, it counter-acts the aim of a lack of division in the citta-series, with its ten samenesses of citta and intention in total clearing (i.e. with the sameness of cittas and intentions in all ten stages). On the sixth stage, it counter-acts the aim where there is neither affliction nor alleviation, because of its counter-acting the realization that there is no event which is being afflicted or alleviated in dependent origination. On the seventh stage, it counter-acts the aim of that lack of true diversity, for here there is a lack of dealing with any diversity of mental signs in the events spoken of in the sūtras, etc. On the eighth stage, it counter-acts the aim that there is neither "inferior" or "superior," because of the lack of observing any "lesser" or "greater" in any event of affliction and alleviation, because there is the forbearance (through realizing) the non-arising of "events." There is a four-fold potency: potency in absence of discriminations, potency in the total clearing of the Bud-dha-field, potency in knowledge, and potency in action. One penetrates the state for the basis of the first and second potencies in the Ground of Events on the eighth stage, one completely attains the state of a basis for potency in knowledge on the ninth stage, with the attainment of the particular knowledges, and the state of the basis for potency in action on the tenth stage, which is the state of being able to do actions for the sake of sentient beings through various transfor-mations at will.

Again, in brief:

"Those which are called the obstructions which are afflictions,
and the obstructions of the knowable,
are all obstructions,
and liberation is sought through their extinction."

Through extinction of these obstructions of two kinds, liberation from all ob-structions is sought.

The compact meaning of the obstructions: the great obstruction, which is the same as "the pervading"; the narrow obstruction, which is the same as "the lim-ited"; the obstruction through courses of action, which is the same as "the exces-sive"; the obstruction to attainment, which is the same as "the equal"; the obstruction to special attainment, which is the same as "accepting or abandon-ing"; the obstruction to right application, which are the nine-fold obstructions which are afflictions; the obstruction to the cause, which is the same as an obstruction to welfare, etc. because of its position as a ten-fold cause of obstruc-tion; obstruction to entering into reality, which is the same as an obstruction to the allies of enlightenment; obstruction to supremacy in welfare, which is the same as obstructions to the pāramitās; an obstruction to special states, which is the same as an obstruction to the Stages. In brief, these obstructions may be com-prised together as two-fold: afflictions and obstructions of the knowable.

Source: Vasubandhu, "Thirty Verses (Trimśika-kārikā)" and "Commentary on the Separation of the Middle from Extremes (Madhyānta-vibhāga-bhāṣya)" in the *Seven Works of Vasubandhu: The Buddhist Psychological Doctor*, edited and translated by Stefan Anacker (Delhi: Motilal Banarsi-dass, 1983), 186–189, 222–231.

18

Tibetan Buddhist Tradition

Tibetan Buddhism weaves together Mādhyamika philosophy, Yogācāra thought, indigenous culture, and Tantric elements. Since selections of Mādhymika and Yogācāra philosophy are already included in this anthology, this chapter stresses two influential Tantric texts and the contribution of a major Tibetan thinker who provides an important place for Tantra in his philosophy. Tantra is a path to liberation that combines opposites (such as male and female) and permits forbidden practices such as certain foods and illicit sexual behavior. Tantric thinkers believe that forbidden practices and things speed the attainment of one's goal to liberation. Due to the illicit, powerful, and dangerous nature of its practice, Tantric teachings are secret and esoteric. The two selected Tantric texts are sexually explicit and are intended for advanced practitioners of the path. The uses of sexual techniques to achieve liberation are considered very dangerous and have the potential of leading to disastrous consequences for who practice them incorrectly. For this reason, these techniques are traditionally kept secret from novices and dilettantes.

These esoteric texts are called yoginī-tantras and mahāyoga-tantras. The latter designation is collectively changed to anuttara-yoga (unexcelled yoga). Selections from two major yoginī-tantras are included in this chapter, the *Caṇḍamahāroṣaṇa Tantra* and the *Hevajra-tantra*. Scholars date the former to the seventh century, and the latter text in its present form probably dates to the end of the sixth century. There are parts of the *Hevajra-tantra* that include a discussion of mantras (sacred formulas/sounds) that embody a power in their sound. A reader should be forewarned that these mantras are not intended to make sense, nor can they be translated into something intelligible. Also worth mentioning is the exalted position of the female partner who attains the status of a goddess. It will be seen that bodily fluids normally considered polluting are transformed into sacred substances, and forbidden and illicit behavior is transformed, to become holy. These aspects are typical Tantric examples of utilizing forbidden elements or practices and regarding them as positive and transforming, with the ability to hasten advancement on the path to the goal of liberation.

The third selection in this chapter is from a major work of the great Tibetan reformer, eminent scholar, and founder of the Geluk school named Tsong Khapa (1357–1419). Entitled *The Great Treatise on the Stages of the Path to Enlightenment*, this text was inspired by a work of the renowned Bengali master Atiśa (982–1054). Tsong Khapa labored to produce a work that would synthesize various aspect of Buddhist thought, which he accomplished at age forty-five (1402). He believed that Tantra is necessary to become a fully enlightened person, but that it is absolutely necessary for a person to study texts for the purpose of the preliminary development of wisdom and compassion. For the Tibetan reformer, the relationship of Tantra to the text (*sūtra*) is comparable to that between method and wisdom.

The final selection is from arguably the most well-known Tibetan Buddhist text, the *Tibetan Book of the Dead*, or *Bar do thos grol*. *Bardo* means literally "between two." This text functions as a mortuary text that is intended to be read aloud to a person dying or someone already dead. It provides instructions to delay death, or to ensure that a deceased person can find his or her way to the other world. The text also describes the process of death and rebirth in terms of three intermediate states. The instant of death is the shortest. At this moment, the deceased is conscious of a clear light. By realizing this light as reality, the deceased is immediately liberated from rebirth. If one does not successfully make this realization, the bardo (intermediate state) begins. When death causes the disintegration of a person this reveals reality as a diagram of fifty-eight wrathful deities and another diagram of forty-two peaceful deities. If one is again unable to recognize reality, a third bardo of ordinary existence begins. During this period, one is reborn into any of six realms, which include hell. Redacted during the fourteenth century, the text represents a process of accommodation between foreign and indigenous cultural elements that become fused with each other.

Selections from *The Hevajra Tantra*

The Performance

a. (1) Now we shall further tell of the practice so excellent and supreme, the cause of perfection by means of which one gains the finality of this perfection in Hevajra.

(2–3) The yogin must wear the sacred ear-rings, and the circlet on his head; on his wrists the bracelets, and the girdle round his waist, rings around his ankles, bangles round his arms; he wears the bone-necklace (4) and for his dress a tiger-skin, and his food must be the five ambrosias. He who practices the yoga of Heruka should frequent the five classes.

(5) These five classes that are associated together, he conceives of as one, for by him no distinction is made as between one class or many.

(6) Meditation is good if performed at night beneath a lonely tree or in a cemetery, or in the mother's house, or in some unfrequented spot.

(7) When some heat has been developed, if one wishes to perform this practice and to gain perfection, then upon this course one should proceed.

(8–9) Take a girl of the Vajra-family, fair-featured and large-eyed and endowed with youth and beauty, who has been consecrated by oneself and is possessed of a compassionate disposition, and with her the practice should be performed. In the absence of one from the Vajra-family, it should be performed with a girl from the family of one's special divinity, or (if this fails) from some other. Take her then who is now consecrated with the depositing of the seed of enlightenment.

(10) If in joy songs are sung, then let them be the excellent Vajra-songs, and if one dances when joy has arisen, let it be done with release as its object. Then the yogin, self-collected, performs the dance in the place of Hevajra.

(11) Akṣobhya is symbolized by the circlet, Amitābha by the ear-rings, Ratneśa by the necklace, and Vairocana (by the rings) upon the wrists.

(12) Amogha is symbolized by the girdle, Wisdom by the khaṭvāṅga and Means by the drum, while the yogin represents the Wrathful One himself.

(13) Song symbolizes *mantra*, dance symbolizes meditation, and so singing and dancing the yogin always acts. (14) He should always eat herbs and drink water, then old age and death will not harm him and he will always be protected.

(15) Now he, whose nature is HŪM (viz. Hevajra), should arrange his piled-up hair as a crest and for the performance of the yoga he should wear the skull-tiara, representing the five buddhas. (16) Making pieces of skull five inches long, he should secure them to the crest. He should wear the two-stranded cord of hair, that symbolizes Wisdom and Means, the ashes and the sacred thread of hair; (17) the sound of the drum is his invocation, and the khaṭvāṇga of Wisdom is his meditation. It is this that is intoned and meditated in the practice of Vajra and Skull.

b. (18) He should abandon desire and folly, fear and anger, and any sense of shame. He should forgo sleep and uproot the notion of a self, and then the practice may be performed, there is no doubt. (19) Only when he has made an offering of his own body, should he commence the practice. Nor should he make this gift with the consideration of who is worthy and who is not. (20–21) Enjoying food and drink he should take it as it comes, making no distinction between that which is liked or disliked, eatable or uneatable, drinkable or undrinkable. Nor should he ever wonder whether a thing is suitable or unsuitable. (22) Even when he has attained to *siddhi* and is resplendent in his perfect knowledge, a disciple respectfully greets his master, if he wishes to avoid the *Avīci* Hell.

(23) Free from learning and ceremony and any cause of shame, the yogin wanders, filled with great compassion in his possession of a nature that is common to all beings. (24) He has passed beyond oblations, renunciation, and austerities, and is freed from *mantra* and meditation.

Released from all the conventions of meditation, the yogin performs the practice.

(25) Whatever demon should appear before him, even though it be the peer of Indra, he would have no fear, for he wanders like a lion.

(26) For the good of all beings, his drink is always compassion, for the yogin who delights in the drink of yoga, becomes drunk with no other drink.

Consecrations and Oblations

For Propitiation it is white, for the Bestowing of Prosperity it is yellow, (9) for Slaying black, and for Subduing red.

Conjuring forth is as for Subduing, and causing Hatred is as for Slaying.

(10) As for the actual oblations, for Propitiation one uses sesame oil, for Bestowing Prosperity curds, for Slaying, causing Hatred and other harmful rites one uses thorns, and a blue lotus for Subduing and Conjuring forth.

(11) The mantra for invoking Fire:

OM Agni of mighty energy, fulfiller of all desires, who in compassion serves all beings, be thou present here.

(12) The invocation of the Earth-Goddess:

> Thou Goddess, honoured by Hevajra's wrath,
>
> Mother of the Earth, and bearer of many kinds of gems,
>
> Thou art witness here, for I, so and so, would lay out the *maṇḍala*.

(13) The *mantra* for gratifying Fire:

Go thou, O Consumer of the Offering, to prosper the affairs of yourself and of others. At the right time you will approach.

Grant me complete success.

(14) Mantra *of the offerings:* OM JAḤ HŪM VAM HĀḤ KHAM RAM

Mantra *of the water for the feet:* OM NĪ RĪ HŪM KHAḤ

Mantra *of the food-offering:* OM DHVAM DHVAM DHVAM

The Certainty of Success

a. (1) Vajragarbha said: "But how should beings reach perfection by means of their chosen divinity, when they find themselves amidst all the elements of existence as extensive as space, (lost) like a goad in the ocean?"

(2) The Lord replied: "One who desires perfection should keep his inner self in union with Nairātmyā or Śrī Heruka, and not even for a moment should his thought be deflected elsewhere. (3) For one who is persevering for the first time, that place is considered propitious, where single-minded and self-collected a yogin may gain success. (4) At night in his own house, confident of gaining perfection, the wise man should meditate upon the Yoginī or upon Śrī Heruka in his manifested form. (5) (Moreover at all times) whether washing the feet or eating, rinsing the mouth or chewing betel-nut, rubbing the hands with sandal-wood, or girding the hips with the loin-cloth, (6) going-out, making conversation, walking, standing, in wrath, in laughter, the wise man should honor the Lady, strong in his vows, he should meditate upon the Yoginī. (7) Seekers of perfection with perfection as their goal strive never for one moment to have their thought deflected elsewhere with the mind defiled by ignorance. (8) O Vajragarbha, I call meditation the destroyer of evil. Try one fortnight with zeal, making perfection your goal, (9) abandoning all discursive thought, your

mind set on the form of the divinity. Try it one day, meditating uninterrupt-edly. (10) There are no other means in the *saṃsāra* for gaining the end of your-self and others, for a spell, once acquired, brings about immediate realization.

b. (11) By fears and passions and sorrows, by griefs and torments and such calami-ties by passion, wrath, and delusion, the yogin is not disturbed. (12) Thus understanding the ripening of the fruit of good and evil acts, how should yogins stay one moment in the Raurava Hell?

(13) Perpetrators of the five great evil acts and those who delight in taking life, also those of wretched birth, and fools who are wicked in their conduct, (14) and ugly brutes with distorted limbs, these gain perfection by the right use of thought. So certainly will he succeed who practices the ten virtues, is devoted to his master with his senses well controlled, (15) and is free from pride and wrath.

c. Keeping continuously to the practice, perfected in the *siddhi* and self-collected, (16) for one month one should privately continue, while one awaits the acquiring of a *mudrā*. The yogin then receives instructions. He is instructed by the *yoginīs:* (17) 'Take such and such a Mudrā, O Vajradhṛk, and serve the cause of living-beings.' Taking this girl, who has wide-open eyes and is of age and endowed with youth and beauty, (18) he should consecrate her with the seed of enlightenment. Beginning with the ten rules of virtuous conduct, he should expound to her the *Dharma*, (19) how the mind is fixed on the divine form, on the meaning of symbolic forms and concerning one-pointedness of mind, and in month she will be fit, of that there is no doubt. (20) And so the girl is there, now freed from all false notions, and received as though she were a boon. Or else he should produce a Mudrā by conjuring her forth by his own power (21) from amongst the gods or titans or men, or the *yakṣas* or *kinnaras.* Then taking her, one should perform the practice with the realization of one's own composure. (22) For this practice, which is called terrifying in appear-ance, is not taught for the sake of enjoyment, but for the examination of one's own thought, whether the mind is steady or waving."

d. (23) Vajragarbha said: "By one who is joined in union with Nairātmyā how can any distinction be made in the meaning of *mudrā*? And with this Mudrā and that Mudrā, with two Mudrās in fact, how should the perfection of the Great Mudrā come about?"

(24) The Lord replied: "Relinquishing her form as a woman, she would assume that of her Lord. Gone are her breasts, and his *vajra* is manifest with a bell on each side, where the *lotus* had been.

(25) The rest of the form of the mighty and blissful Heruka (26) easily assumes the masculine condition of the man who is in union with Heruka, and from this the perfection of the Great Symbol would come about for the yogin of such manifest power. (27) This identity of Wisdom and Means remains unharmed by the twofold process of origination and dissolution, for Means is the origination and Wisdom the dissolution and end of existence. (28) So in truth there is neither destruction nor origination. Having dissolved away, it has come to its end, and since there can now be no dissolution, neither is there destruction. (29) The yogin conceives of the diversity of existence as the Process of Emanation, and realizing the dream-like nature of this diversity, he renders it undiversified by means of its diversity. (30) Like a dream, like a mirage, like the "intermediate state," so the *maṇḍala* appears from continuous application to the practice. (31) The great bliss, such as one knows it in the consecrations of the Great Symbol, of that the *maṇḍala* is the full and efficacious expression, for nowhere else does it have its origin. (32) This bliss is black and yellow, red and white, dark green, dark blue, all things moving and unmoving.

(33) This bliss is Wisdom, this bliss is Means, and likewise it is their union. It is existence, it is non-existence, and it is Vajrasattva."

(34) Vajragarbha said: "This state of unity achieved in the Process of Realization is deemed as Excellent Bliss, as Great Bliss, so what is the use of the Process of Emanation except for conceiving it as Realization?"

(35) The Lord replied: "Oho, Great Bodhisattva, by dint of faith it is destroyed, they say.

e. Without bodily form how should there be bliss? Of bliss one could not speak The world is pervaded by bliss, which pervades and is itself pervaded. (36) Just as the perfume of a flower depends upon the flower, and without the flower becomes impossible, likewise without form and so on, bliss would not be perceived. (37) I am existence, I am not existence, I am the Enlightened One for I am enlightened concerning what things are. But me they do not know, those fools, afflicted by indolence. (38) I dwell in Sukhāvatī in bliss with the Vajra-yoginī, in that place which is symbolized by the syllable E, in that casket of buddha-gems.

(39) I am the teacher, and I am the doctrine, I am the disciple endowed with good qualities. I am the goal, and I am the trainer. I am the world and worldly things. (40) My nature is that of Innate Joy and I come end of the Joy that is Perfect and at the beginning of the Joy of Cessation.

So be assured, my son, it is like a lamp in darkness.

(41) I am the Master with the thirty-two marks, the Lord with the eighty characteristics and I dwell in bliss in Sukhāvatī and my name is *śukra*. (42) Without this there would be no bliss, and without bliss this would not be. Since they are ineffective one without the other, bliss is found in union with the divinity.

(43) So the Enlightened One is neither existence nor non-existence; he has a form with arms and faces and yet in highest bliss is formless.

(44) So the whole world is the Innate, for the Innate is its essence. Its essence too is *nirvāṇa* when the mind is in a purified state.

(45) The divine form consists of just something born, for it is a repository of arms and face and colors, and moreover arises by the normal influence of past actions.

f. (46) With the very poison, a little of which would kill any other being, a man who understands poison would dispel another poison. (47) Just as a man who suffers with flatulence is given beans to eat, so that wind may overcome wind in the way of a homeopathic cure, so existence is purified by existence in the countering of discursive thought by its own kind.

(48) Just as water entered in the ear is drawn out again by water, so also the notion of existing things is purified by appearances. (49) Just as those who have been burned by fire must suffer again by fire, so those who have been burned by the fire of passion must suffer the fire of passion. (50) Those things by which men of evil conduct are bound, others turn into means and gain thereby release from the bonds of existence. (51) By passion the world is bound, by passion too it is released, but by the heretical buddhists this practice of reversals is not known.

g. (52) In the one essential unity a fivefold aspect subsists expressed in the set of five elements, and the Joy Supreme which is essentially one becomes five through their distinctions.

(53) From the contact that comes of the union of vajra and lotus, there arises the effect of hardness. The nature of hardness is delusion, and Vairocana is deemed to be delusion.

(54) The *bodhicitta* is a flow and this flow is deemed as water. The nature of water is wrath and this wrath is Akṣobhya.

(55) From the rubbing together of two things fire always arises. From heat arises passion and this passion is Amitābha.

(56) The *bodhicitta* in the lotus has the nature of air. From air arises envy, and envy is Amoghasiddhi.

(57) The blood is bliss and passion and the nature of bliss is space. From space arises malignity and malignity is Ratnasambhava.

(58) Thought is one but consists in this fivefold form. This develops into the five families, and then there develop many thousands. (59) So this is the single self-existent, it is the great bliss, perfect and eternal, but it becomes five by the fivefold distinction of thought as passion and the other four. (60) As numerous as the sands of ten River Ganges are the companies of the *tathāgatas* in these single families. In these companies there are numerous clans, and in these clans yet hundreds of clans. (61) These many thousands of clans become many millions of clans, and in these clans there are still innumerable clans. Yet they all arise from the one clan of perfect joy."

The Basis of All Tantras

(1) Then the Adamantine Lord spoke to the *yoginīs* of the Means, which are the basis of all *tantras,* of the Union, of consecrations and of secret language, of the different Joys and Moments, of feasting and the rest.

a. (2) "Now the union of all buddhas consists in the sound EVAM. This sound EVAM, the great bliss itself, is known from the process of consecration."

(3) Then the *yoginīs* said to the Lord Vajrasattva: "Is the sound EVAM then called the union of the *dākinīs*? May the Lord, the Teacher, the Master of the World please expound the matter as it is."

(4) The Lord replied: "The sacred syllable E, adorned at its centre by the syllable VAM, is the abode of all delights, the casket of buddha-gems. (5) It is there that the four Joys arise, distinguished by the Moments, and from knowledge of these Moments the knowledge of Bliss is consummated in that sound EVAM. (6) So yogins know that the sound EVAM is attainable through the four Moments: *Variety, Development, Consummation,* and *Blank.* (7) It is called *Variety,* because it involves different things, the embrace, the kiss and so forth. *Development* is the reverse of this, for it is the experiencing of blissful knowledge. (8) *Consummation* is defined as the reflection that this bliss has been experienced by oneself. *Blank* is quite other than these three, and knows neither passion nor the absence of passion. (9) The first Joy is found in *Variety,* Perfect Joy in *Development,* the Joy of Cessation in *Consummation* and the Joy of the Innate in *Blank.*

(10) These four Joys are to be experienced in due order in accordance with the list of the four consecrations, that of the Master, that of the Secret, that of the Prajñā and the Fourth. (11) The first is represented by a smile, the second by a

gaze, the third in an embrace, and the fourth in union. (12) This fourfold set of consecrations is for the purpose of perfecting living-beings. The word consecration or sprinkling is used because one is sprinkled or cleansed.

b. (13) The *Prajñā* of sixteen years he clasps within his arms, and from the union of the *vajra* and bell the Master's consecration comes about. (14) She is fair-featured, wide-eyed, and endowed with youth and beauty. Then with thumb and fourth finger he drops the *bindu* in the pupil's mouth. (15) In that very act the flavour of sameness should be placed within the pupil's range. Then having honoured and worshipped the *Prajñā*, he should consign her to the pupil, (16) saying: 'O Great Being, take thou the Mudrā who will bring you bliss,' and knowing his pupil to be worthy, free of envy and wrath, (17) he then further commands him: 'Be ye one, O Vajradhṛk.'

Now I shall tell you of the pupil's part and how he begs for consecration, (18) how he pronounces words of praise and worship when he beholds his master with the *mudrā*.

'O great tranquil Lord, intent on the *vajra*-practice,
(19) Thou perfecter of the Symbol, that hast thine origin in the oneness of the indestructible *vajra*,
As you now do for yourself, may you also do for me.
(20) I am sunk in the thick mud of the *saṃsāra*. Save me who am without a helper.'

(21) Then with pleasing food and drink, with wine and meat of good quality, with incense, oblations, and garlands, with bells and banners and ointments, with all these he should honor his lord.

(22) When the pupil has now reached the moment of Perfect Joy which is free from all notions of diversity, the master should say: "O Great Being, hold thou to the great bliss. (23) Until the time of enlightenment, O Vajradhṛk, serve thou the cause of beings.' Thus should speak the Adamantine Lord as he sees his pupil overwhelmed in compassion.

c. (24) This is the great knowledge that exists in all phenomenal forms, dual by nature and yet free of duality, the Lord whose essence is both existence and non-existence. (25) He abides pervading all things, moving or motionless, for he manifests himself in these illusive forms. But by means of the *maṇḍala* and so on, he goes with certainty to his eternal condition."

d. (26) Then Vajragarbha, begging all the *yoginīs* to have patience, addressed the Lord: "May the *maṇḍala* be called a stronghold, which is the essence of all buddhas? Tell me Lord, just how things are, for doubt assails me."

(27) The Lord replied: "The *maṇḍala* is the very essence, we say; it is *bodhicitta* and the great bliss itself. This it takes to itself, and so in this sense *maṇḍala* is said to be *malana*, 'the act of taking.' (28) *Cakra* is an assembly (of divinities) which purifies the spheres of sense and so on, and thus it is as void as space. By the union of *vajra* and lotus its bliss is experienced."

e. (29) Vajragarbha said: "What usage and observance should one follow?" The Lord replied:

> "You should slay living-beings.
>> You should speak lying words.
>> You should take what is not given.
>> You should frequent others' wives."

(30) Now to practice singleness of thought is the taking of life, for the thought is the life. To vow to save all men is interpreted as lying-speech. That which is not given is the bliss of woman, and she is your own Nairātmyā who is the wife of all others."

f. 31) Then all the *yoginīs* addressed the Lord: "What are the spheres and faculties of sense? What are the bases of consciousness and how many are the component groups of personality? What are the spheres of consciousness and what is their true nature?"

(32) The Lord replied: "There are six spheres of sense: form, sound, smell, taste, touch, and thought. (33) Likewise there are six faculties of sense: the eye, the ear, the nose, the tongue, the body, and the mind. (34) From spheres and faculties together we then have the twelve bases of consciousness. The five *skandhas* are bodily form, feeling, impulses, power of perception and consciousness. (35) The eighteen spheres of consciousness are the six faculties and six spheres of sense together with the six kinds of consciousness belonging to each pair. (36) Their nature is that of the essentially non-arisen and is neither true nor false, for all is like the reflection of the moon in water. O yoginīs, understand it as you will.

(37) For just as fire suddenly arises from the two fire-sticks and the action of a man's hand, and cannot be located in either of the sticks nor in the hand's action, and although sought everywhere, is not to be found anywhere, and is therefore neither a true thing nor a false thing, even thus, O *yoginīs*, should you conceive of all the elements."

g. (38) Then all the *vajra-ḍākinīs* with Nairātmyā to the fore, took up the five ambrosias and the ingredients of the sacrament, and honouring the Lord Vajrasattva, they drank the *vajra*-elixir of immortality.

(39) At that the Lord was greatly pleased and told them of effective power. "Good, good O *vajra-ḍākinīs*, that truth which I keep secret and is honored by all buddhas, of that I now tell you, for I am compelled thereto by the power of your *vajra*-praise, so listen if you will."

(40) Then all the goddesses became very zealous, and touching the ground with one knee, they stretched forth their hands in worship to where the Lord stood, and listened to that which he said.

h. (41) The Lord said: "Food and drink must be just as it comes. One should not avoid things, wondering whether they are suitable or unsuitable. One should not perform special ablutions or purifications, nor avoid the affairs of the town. (42) The wise man does not mutter *mantras,* nor devote himself to meditation; he does not abandon sleep, nor restrain his senses. (43) He should eat all meat and associate with all manner of men. He keeps the company of all women, his mind quite free of trepidation. (44) He should have no love for friend, nor hatred for any enemy. Those gods he should not honor, which are made of wood and stone and clay. For the yogin should always be consubstantiated with the form of his own divinity. (45) Men of all castes he may touch as readily as his own body, *ḍombas, caṇḍālas, carmāras, haḍḍikas* and the rest, brahmans and *kṣatriyas, vaiśyas,* and *śūdras.* (46–48) Nor is there anything he may not consume, for his mind conceives no distinctions. (49) His loin-cloth is many-colored and he adorns himself with clay-markings of different colors. Finding a flower in a cemetery he should bind it in his hair." . . .

c. (48) Then the Goddess asks about the *maṇḍala,* (49) and the Master of Mighty Knowledge, blissful and self-collected, draws it there himself. (50) There is one circle, surrounded by flames of different hues, with four doors and four portals, adorned with *vajra*-threads and the series of five colors. (51) He draws then the eight vessels, all done with powder made from the five kinds of gem or from rice and so on, or else from cemetery bricks or the charcoal from the funeral pyre. (52) In the center he draws a lotus with its pericarp and eight petals. At the center of this he draws a skull, white and in three sections. (53) Then on the north-east petal he draws a lion, on the south-east a monk, on the south-west a wheel and on the north-west a *vajra,* (54) on the eastern a knife, on the southern a drum, on the western a tortoise, and on the northern a serpent. (55) These are the eight symbols of the goddesses in accordance with their different categories. In the center he draws a white skull, signed with a crossed-*vajra,* (56) and (to the east) he places the sacred Vessel of Victory with branches in it and enwrapped with cloth, the five gems inside and filled with *śālija.* (57) But why say more? The *maṇḍala*-ritual should be performed as it is given in the Tattvasaṃgraha.

(58) Into the *maṇḍala* one should cause to enter the eight blissful Spells, twelve or sixteen years of age, and adorned with necklaces and bangles. (59) They are called wife, sister, daughter, niece, maternal uncle's wife, maternal aunt, mother-in-law, and paternal aunt. (60) These the yogin should honor with deep embraces and kisses. Then he should drink camphor and sprinkle the *maṇḍala* with it. (61) He should cause them to drink it and he should quickly gain *siddhi.* Wine is drunk and meat and herbs are eaten. (62) Next he removes their garments and kisses them again and again. They honour him in return and sing and dance to their best, (63) and they play there together in the union of *vajra* and lotus.

Then at the second stage he should cause the pupil to enter, (64) and having covered his eyes with a cloth, he should afterwards display to him the *maṇḍala.* Consecration is given there in that lonely place at night. (65) The consecrations are as ordained, distinguished as that of the Master and so on. Good pupils should first pronounce words of praise and worship. (66) Then he initiates him in the truth itself, which is experienced at the beginning of the Joy of Cessation, and at the end of the Joy Perfect. That which is concealed in all the *tantras,* is here finally made manifest."

d. (67) Then the Goddess asked: "What is that moment like? May the Great Lord please tell me." (68) The Lord replied: "There there is no beginning, no end, no middle; there is neither *saṃsāra* nor *nirvāṇa.* It is the great and perfect bliss, where there is neither self nor other. (69) The thumb of one's own right hand and the fourth finger of the other hand, with these the yogin should press the two waves at the *sambhogacakra* (the throat), (70) and from this what happens, you ask. Then there arises knowledge blissful like that of union with a maiden or like the dream of a fool. This is the end of the Joy Perfect and the beginning of the Joy of Cessation, Void and non-Void, the state of Heruka."

Source: *The Hevajra Tantra: A Critical Study* by D. L. Snellgrove (London: Oxford University Press, 1959), 63–66, 89–98, 113–114. Translation by D. L. Snellgrove.

Selections from *The Caṇḍamahāroṣaṇa Tantra*

This tantra is not to be disclosed to one who has not seen its maṇḍala,
  nor should this king of tantras be shown to one who has entered another
    maṇḍala.

This tantra should be taught to one who has devoutly entered the maṇḍala
of Caṇḍamahāroṣaṇa, and whose highest striving is toward faith in
    Caṇḍamahāroṣaṇa.

One should show this tantra to him who is kind, and devoted to his teacher, a
follower of the Mantrayāna, and always devoted to the Master
    Caṇḍamahāroṣaṇa.

However, if some yogi, knowing that, deceived by greed, teaches this best
of tantras to one who has not seen the maṇḍala of Caṇḍamahāroṣaṇa,

He will suffer great afflictions, soiled with stools and urine, and
within six months, his will be the pain of death. . . .

Then, in his presence, he should confess his evil deeds, and rejoice
in all his merit. He should repeat the Triple Refuge, begging and praying.

He should give himself and bring his merit to fruition. Then,
having made resolve, he should apply his mind to Enlightenment.

Then, having paid him homage, he should dissolve Caṇḍamahāroṣaṇa again
    into the rays of light.
Then, uttering the following mantra, he should concentrate on the Void.
"Oṁ, my essence is the Void—the Vajra of Knowledge!"

He should think with great effort that the Hūṁ-syllable is burned to ashes by
    the rays of light;
then should he think of it as burning like camphor, and then he should not
    even imagine any rays of light.

Then, having meditated that everything is like sky and only momentary, he
should meditate that his own body is pellucid, like pure crystal.

Beginning as above, he should subsequently meditate, in front of him, the
    four syllables yaṁ, raṁ, vaṁ, laṁ,
out of which he should meditate that wind, fire, water, and earth are created.

Then, concentrating on the syllable bhruṁ, he should imagine a celestial
palace, with four corners, four doors, and adorned with eight pillars.

He should concentrate that in the middle of that is a Universal Lotus with
    eight petals, emerging from the seed-syllable, pāṁ.

The moon comes out from the syllable, aṁ.

The sun is produced from the syllable raṁ, and above that there is again the
    production of the syllable hūṁ.
One should think that Akṣobhya, embraced by Māmakī, emerges from that.

The chief of yogis should then enter through the aperture in the top of
    Akṣobhya's head.
And by the yoga called the Course of a Shooting Star, intent on the Bhaga of
    Māmakī, he should then fall on the inside of her Bhaga in the form of
    white juice.

Then he should issue forth from her Bhaga in the completed form of
    Caṇḍamahāroṣaṇa.
And after killing his father, Akṣobhya, with a sword, then he should eat him.

He should consider that Māmakī also partakes of the meal. Then, indeed,
    having seized Māmakī,
he should make love to his mother, and he should think that he is embraced
    by her in the form of Anger Vajrī.

In his right fist he holds a sword, and in his left he holds a noose.
Threatening with the forefinger and pressing the lower lip with the teeth, he
    kicks with his right foot, crushing the Four Demons.

With his left knee placed on the ground, squint-eyed, and with a dreadful
    face,
he threatens the earth, with his left knee placed in front.

Having a blue crown adorned with Akṣobhya, and a jewelled head ornament,
he is a youth with five knots of hair, decorated with all ornaments.

He has the form of a sixteen-year-old, with two red, far-reaching eyes.
He should meditate with resolute mind: "I am the Perfected One,
    Caṇḍamahāroṣaṇa."

Then, by the Yoga of Mixing, he should create White Immoveable in the East;
he should create Delusion Vajrī in the Southeast, with the luminosity of the
    autumn moon.

In the South, he should create Yellow Immoveable; and, in the Southwest,
    Calumny Vajrī.

He should create Red Immoveable in the West and Lust Vajrī, in red, in the Northwest.

And in the North, he should create Green Immoveable; and in the Northeast, he should create Envy Vajrī, in green.
Then he should invite the coming forth of Wisdom. . . .

The yogi of green color should meditate on Green Immoveable.
The woman of black color should meditate on Calumny Vajrī.

The woman of red color should meditate on Lust Vajrī.
The woman of green color should meditate on Envy Vajrī.

Every man is Vajrayogi and every woman is Vajrayoginī. By the distinction of color, black, etc., all this should be determined.

Or by difference in action the
distinction is made into five parts.

Black means killing and anger; white means rest and thinking; yellow means restraining and nourishing;
red means subjugation and summoning; and green is said to mean exorcizing.

Or also the distinction is made by caste: Black is the lowly musician; white is priest; and yellow is said to be the sweeper.
Red is the dancer, and thus also is green the washerman.

The black practitioner should make love to a black girl with large eyes.
The white one to a white girl, the yellow one to a yellow girl, the red indeed to a red girl, and the green man to a green girl.

Or, whatever girl he has taken, and whomever among the five Immoveables he is meditating upon, he should make love with fixed mind, secretly.

These young ladies give good Success with only a fortnight of practice.
The white of them becomes a vajra, all of which he should taste with the tongue.

He should drink urine as he likes, placing his mouth on the Bhaga, and placing it on the anal lotus he should eat feces as he likes.

There should not be even a slight disgust, otherwise Success would be ruined. This diet is the best, eaten by all Buddhas.

Thus ends the fourth chapter, concerning the god, in the Caṇḍamahāroṣaṇa
Tantra, called the Sole Hero. . . .

Then the Lord said:

> The yogi who is situated in the yoga of the Stage of Completion should be
>   devoted only to yoga.
> He should meditate day and night on my form with one-pointed mind.
>
> He should ardently consider his own wife to have your form, until,
> with great and firm practice, it accordingly becomes perfectly clear.
>
> Mother, daughter, sister, niece, and any other female relative, as well as a
>   female musician, Bràhman,
> sweeper, dancer, washerwoman, and prostitute; holy woman, yoginī, and
>   ascetic as well—
>
> Or whatever other he may receive with a woman's figure: these he
> should serve in the proper way without making any distinction.
>
> But if he makes a distinction, Caṇḍamahāroṣaṇa will be provoked
> and slay the practitioner. And he will throw him into the Avīci Hell and
>   threaten him with a sword and noose.
>
> Nor will he obtain Success in this world or the next. Therefore,
> this must be kept very secret and not be made visible.
>
> Like the mantra of the Ḍākinī, the practice of Caṇḍamahāroṣaṇa should be
>   secret.
> And this has been explained by me, the Buddha, for the sake of those who
>   cherish the esoteric.
>
> In a pleasing place where there are no disturbances, in secret,
> he should take a woman who has desire.
>
> "I am Buddha, and the Perfected One, Immoveable, she is cherished
>   Prajñāpāramitā,"
> thus the wise person should meditate with fixed thought, each one having his
>   respective [divine] form.
>
> And having made a lonely hermitage, and with whatever he has for food and
>   property,

he should meditate ardently—the two coupled with each other.

He should bring the woman into his presence and seat her before him.
Each should gaze steadily at the other, with mutual desire.

Then, concentrating on the enjoyable view, each should remain with
    one-pointed mind.
Just then she should utter the following speech which arouses pleasure:

"You are my son and my husband; you are my brother and father.
I am your mother, wife, sister, and niece.

For seven generations you have been my slave, my lowly servant.
I bought you with cowrie shells; I am called your mistress."

He should fall at her feet ardently with his palms pressed together.
Then he should utter this speech arousing the highest pleasure:

"You are my mother's father's wife, and you are my niece. You
are my sister's son's wife; you are my sister and aunt.

I am your slave in all ways, keenly active in devotion to you.
O Mother, look upon me with kindness, casting a loving glance."

Then she, in the man's embrace, should kiss him again and again.
She places the Three Syllables on his head, and in his mouth sweet saliva.

She should have him suck the Lotus, and show him rolling eyes. Placing
lipstick on his mouth, she should press his heart with her breast.

In front of him, looking him in the face, she should pinch him on the chest.
She should speak to him in this way: "Eat my Vairocana!

Drink the water of Akṣobhya! O Son, be a slave as well as a father!
I am your formal wife as well as your royal mother.

Constantly take refuge at my feet, my dear. You were raised
by me, hence your invaluable nature.

Be gracious, O my dear, give me the pleasure of the vajra!
Look at my three-petalled Lotus, decorated in the middle with stamen.

Oh, it is the field of Pleasureful Heaven adorned with the Red Buddha.
Peace beyond all imagination, giving pleasure to the lustful.

Alight on my reclining form; my mind trembles with desire.
Place my two feet on your shoulder, and look me up and down.

Then make the throbbing Vajra enter the opening in the center of the Lotus.
Give a thousand strokes, one hundred thousand, ten million, one hundred
 million, in my three-petalled lotus, bound round with flesh.

Insert your Vajra and offer your mind with pleasure. O Air, Air! My Lotus is the
 quintessence, the very highest,
and aroused by the top of the Vajra, it is as red as the Banduka flower."

Concentrating on her speech, he should become motionless, with one-pointed
 mind.
Without moving, he should meditate on the pleasure arising from that, with a
 fixed mind.

Then he should answer her: "Wait a moment, my dear, that I may consider,
for just a moment, your womanly form.

Woman alone is the birth giver, the giver of true pleasure to the Three
 Worlds, the kind one.
Those chattering fools engaged in evil action, who now disparage her out of
 hostility, will, by their action,
remain constantly tortured for three eons in the fathomless Raudra Hell,
 wailing as their bodies burn in many fires.

On the contrary, one should say that women's merit encompasses all living
 beings.
Whether it be kindness or protectiveness it must be in the mind of women.

Friend or stranger, she nourishes him with food. The woman who is
like that is none other than Vajrayoginī.

Be it her look, touch, or rub—when far away,
the mere remembrance produces pleasure at that instant.

Woman, as object of the five senses, is endowed with a divine form.
Men, who take her as a wife, enjoy pleasure.

Therefore, O you who are faultless, adorned with all good qualities,
O Purity, Purity, Great Purity, favor me, O Reverend Mother!"

Then, look at her fixedly, he should press his lip with his teeth.
Making a gasping sound, the yogi should make her naked.

He should perform the "Pleasure-Evoking" position, and the "Swing-Rocking"
   position,
the "Knee-Holding" position, as well as the position "Thigh-Rubbing," the
   "Foot-Moving" position,
and the "Ground-Pressing" position, the "Equal Summit" (?) position, and the
   position known as "Variegated,"
the "Honeycomb" position, "Mounted on the Machine," and "One Leg Up," as
   well as the "Tortoise" position, and also "In Every Way Auspicious."

Then, in the middle of a bed, with the woman assuming the squatting seat,
he should have her clasp her arms firmly together on his shoulders.

His own two arms should be joined, emerging from the middle of her girth,
and with the Vajra inserted in the Lotus, that is called the "Pleasure-Evoking"
   position.

With the two arms of both of them joined to each other like braids of hair, the
   two should rock slowly. This is called "Swing-Rocking."
Embracing, with her two knees against his heart, and with the hands in the
   same position as in the "Swing-Rocking," this is called "Knee-Holding."

He should place the soles of her feet on the base of his thighs,
and with the hands in the same position as in the "Pleasure-Evoking," this is
   called "Thigh-Rubbing."

With the soles of her feet on the navel, heart, and the two flanks also,
and with the hands placed according to "Swing-Rocking," this position is
   "Foot-Moving."

With her buttocks placed on the ground, hollow-chested, with the hands
   placed in the same position
as in the "Pleasure-Evoking," this position is called "Ground-Pressing."

Placing her in the Squatting seat, he should have her stretch out her two legs.
This position is called "Equal Summit" (?), and he should make [the legs (?)] of
   each one stretch out.

With her two legs bent, with his heart against her back, he should join on the
   left, on the right, and in front,

rubbing her, beginning with her hands. This position is known as "Variegated."

Again taking the "Pleasure-Evoking" position, he should have her fall on her back.
Then he should insert the Vajra into the Lotus with the right hand, and catching the crooks of his elbows behind the knees, he should join her;
and with each other's arms like braids of hair, this is known as the "Honeycomb."

With her two legs placed firmly on his shoulders, this position is, indeed, "Mounted on the Machine,"
and should be performed with passionate entrance (?).

With her right leg on his shoulder and left on the base of his thigh,
this position is "One Leg Up," which is true pleasure, destructive of misery.

He should have her place the two soles of her feet together in the middle of his chest.
He should press the knee with his two arms, and this is called the "Tortoise" position.

He should place the soles of her feet on the eye, ear, and head.
This position is "In Every Way Auspicious," and grants the pleasure of all desires.

Up to the "Variegated" he should do all the following various things.
He should press firmly with the chest, united with Caṇḍamahāroṣaṇa.

He should kiss her mouth as much as he likes, again and again.
Looking at her face lying down, saying whatever words he likes, he should suck her tongue, and drink the saliva of the mouth.

He should eat the lipstick and waste of the teeth, meditating that it is pleasureful.
And he should pinch the tongue gently with the teeth, and also the lips.

With the tongue he should clean the holes of the nose and the corners of the eyes.
And he should eat all the waste produced from between the teeth.

He should kiss the forehead, eye, neck, ear, side, armpit, hand, and breast;
and pinch them, with the exception of the woman's two eyes.

He should rub the nipple with the hand, suck, then bite. Having the woman
lie on her back,

he should kiss her lovely belly, remembering again and again, "Here was I
formerly situated."

He should touch the Lotus with the hand, saying, "Lovely, O Air!"
He should kiss and pinch, looking there drawing down with the hand.

Smelling the odor, he should clean with the tongue that hole of the woman.
He should then say this kind of speech: "As I have entered through this, so too
have I emerged numerous times."

This path, which is straight as the nose, if practiced without Knowledge,
would be the path to the six states of rebirth.
But when practiced with Knowledge it would be the Success of
Caṇḍamahāroṣaṇa.

Then, converting it entirely to pleasure, he should eat the white and red of
the Lotus,
while looking at her face again and again.

And, after pinching her thigh, he should rub her feet like a slave.
He should place the Three Syllables on her forehead, and a light blow of the
fist on her heart.

Then the yogi should perform concentratedly those positions, after the
"Variegated" position.
He should pay attention to that with desire, having his mind solely on
pleasure.

Optionally he may secrete or not secrete, having his mind solely on pleasure.
If he does, he should lick the Lotus, on his knees.

And he should eat with his tongue, the white and red of the Lotus.
And he should inhale it through a pipe in the nose, to increase his power.

After washing the Lotus with the tongue, he should have Wisdom stand up
and he should kiss her. And, after hugging her, he should eat meat and fish.

He should drink milk or wine, in order to increase his desire.
After his fatigue has decreased, he should desire with pleasure, etc.

And, in the foregoing manner, the couple should begin again with each other.
By this repeated practice, Great Pleasure is attained, and in this very lifetime
the practitioner gains the title of Caṇḍamahāroṣaṇa.

I have disclosed this practice
for the sake of giving Success to the lustful.

Placing easily the right shank above the left shank, this is called "Sattva"
posture of sitting,
which gives the pleasure of all desires.

Placing easily the left shank above the right shank, this is called the "Lotus"
posture,
which gives the pleasure of all desires.

Assuming the "Lotus" posture, he should easily place the right shank
above the left shank. This is called the "Vajra" posture.

Placing the soles of the feet on the ground, while the legs should lie together
over all their length,
this is known as the "Squatting" seat, which gives all desires.

Placing the soles of the feet on the ground, with the legs bent and making an
oblique angle between them,
this is known as the "Half-moon" seat, which gives the pleasure of desire.

With the knees oblique and on the ground, and with the buttocks on the
center of the ankle,
this is the "Bow" seat, which gives the pleasure of divine desire.

"Sattva," "Lotus," and "Vajra" are considered postures,
and "Squatting," "Half-moon," and "Bow" are called seats.

He should have the woman sit in the "Half-moon" seat, and immediately
fall down and lick the Lotus, grasping the auspicious Three Syllables.

Again, having her assume the "Bow" seat, he should have his face fall
in the middle of her anus. He should also stroke her anus with his nose.

He should concentrate that the Pleasure produced by that is from the joining
with Caṇḍamahāroṣaṇa.
Then the yogi should be liberated, with all predilections abandoned.

Making his mind devoid of aversion, he should make love to his mother.

By following Lust, merit is obtained; from aversion demerit accrues.

There is no greater evil than aversion, no greater merit than pleasure.

Then he should concentrate upon the pleasure arising from desire.

Then the Lady joyfully paid homage to the Lord, and praising him said this:

O Lord, is this means of Success for human beings only, or is it for others, also?

The Lord said:

Those beings situated in all directions

who are devoted to this. Gods, demons,

men, and Nāgās, too, succeed as practitioners.

Then, when they heard that, the gods, Maheśvara, etc., taking the goddesses Gaurī, Lakṣmī, Śacī, Ratī, etc., began to meditate. Then, at that instant, all of them, just at that very moment obtained the title of Caṇḍamahāroṣaṇa and roamed the earth. There, Maheśvara succeeded, by the name of Vajraśaṅkara; Vāsudeva as Vajranārāyaṇa; Devendra as Vajrapāṇi; and Kāmadeva as Vajrānaṅga. In the same way as these principal ones, godlings succeeded equal in number to the sands of the Ganges River. Although involved with the desirous objects of the five senses, they act for the benefit of all beings.

Source: *The Caṇḍamahāroṣaṇa Tantra,* edited and translated by Christopher S. George (New Haven: American Oriental Society, 1974), 46, 58–60, 63–64, 66–77.

Selections from Tsong Khapa

Uniting Insight and Serenity

(c) A summary of the key points for sustaining insight and serenity

As I have explained, when you have found the view of what has definitive meaning, you will have determined that the self and that which belongs to the self do not intrinsically exist in the basis in relation to which the conceptions of "I" and "mine" arise. And just as when you initially made this determination, you continue to use extensive analysis with discriminating wisdom to bring the force of certainty to bear upon that conclusion. You alternate between stabilizing meditation—which stays with that conclusion without scattering—and analysis with discriminating wisdom. At that time, if stability decreases due to excessive analytical meditation, do more stabilizing meditation and restore stability. As stability increases under the influence of extensive stabilizing meditation, if you lose interest in analysis and thus fail to analyze, then your ascertainment of reality will not become firm and powerful. In the absence of a firm and powerful ascertainment of reality, you will not do even the slightest damage to the countervailing superimpositions which conceive of the existence of the two selves. Therefore, cultivate a balance of serenity and insight by doing extensive analytical meditation. Kamalaśila's third *Stages of Meditation* says:

> When, through cultivating insight, wisdom becomes extremely strong, serenity decreases. Therefore, like a flame placed in the wind, the mind wavers so that it does not see reality very clearly. For that reason, you should then cultivate serenity. Also, when serenity becomes very strong, you will not see reality very clearly, like a person who is asleep. Therefore, you should then cultivate wisdom.

Understand that the way to prepare for a session, the way to conclude a session, and the way to conduct yourself between sessions are just as I explained them in the section on persons of small capacity. In the section on serenity, I explained how to identify laxity and excitement, how to use mindfulness and vigilance to eliminate them, and how to relax your efforts after you have attained an equanimity which operates naturally, without being unbalanced by laxity or excitement. Realize that all of this is the same when meditating on selflessness.

Ratnākaraśānti's *Instructions for the Perfection of Wisdom* says that sustaining serenity with respect to the object of meditation produces pliancy, and that the analytical meditation of insight into that object also produces pliancy. After you have established those two separately, you then unite them. According to this text, it is not required that you do analysis and stabilization within one continuous session. Hence, Ratnākaraśānti explains that it is acceptable to do them in separate sessions. Here the important point is that by eradicating the cognitive process in which ignorance reifies things, you produce a powerful certainty about emptiness—the absence of intrinsic existence, the opposite of this reification— and that you must then meditate on emptiness. If you fail to refute the conceptions of self and the cognitive processes of ignorance, and you put emptiness off to one comer, then your meditation will do nothing to hinder the two conceptions of self. Earlier teachers often said, "It is like sending an effigy to the western door to ward off a demon at the eastern door." It is evident that this is quite true.

The things that I have said here are only a rough explanation. To understand the fine points of what is advantageous and disadvantageous when meditating, you must rely on wise teachers, and you have to use your own meditative experience. Therefore, I will not elaborate.

Regarding these meditations, I have taken the earlier instructions on the stages of the path as a foundation and then enlarged upon them. One of those early instructions, Bo-do-wa's (Po-to-ba) *Little Digest of Instructions* (*Be'u bum*), says:

Some say that you determine the absence of intrinsic existence
Using reason during study and reflection,
But meditate strictly without conceptual thought at the time of
   meditation.
If this were so, then this would be an emptiness disconnected from that
   of study and reflection.
And, because of being meditated upon in a separate way it would not be
   a remedy
Therefore, even at the time of meditation
Analytically discriminate by using whatever you are accustomed to—
Such as the lack of being single or plural, or dependent-arising—
And then stabilize your mind without even the slightest discursive
   thought.
If you meditate in that way, it will remedy the afflictions.
For those who wish to follow the Sole Deity [Atisha]
And for those who wish to practice the system of the perfections,
This is the way to cultivate wisdom.
By first becoming accustomed to the selflessness of the person,
You can then proceed in this way.

Also, Atisha [in his *Introduction to the Two Truths* (*Satya-dvayāvatāra*)] said:

Who understood emptiness?
Candrakīrti, the disciple of Nāgārguna—
Who was prophesied by the Tathāgata
And who saw the true reality.
One will learn the true reality
From instructions which derive from him.

This teaching is like what Atisha says in his *Madhyamaka Instructions* (*Madhya-makopadeśa*); he says that you alternate between analytical mediation and meditation which stabilizes on the conclusions of such analysis. There is no difference between this and the system of the master Kamalaśīla. As explained before, the intended meanings of Candrakīrti's *Commentary on the "Middle Way,"* Bhāva-viveka's *Heart of the Middle Way,* and the writings of master Śātideva are also the same. This is also explained many times in the teachings of Maitreya and in the texts of the noble Asaṅga, and it is clearly explained in the *Instructions for the Perfection of Wisdom* by the scholar Ratnākaraśānti, who considers Asaṅga's system to be accurate. Therefore, it is evident that the texts and instructions deriving from Nāgārjuna and Asaṅga agree about the way to sustain insight.

(d) The measure of achieving insight through meditation

When you meditate using discriminating wisdom to analyze in this way, you have an approximation of insight until you develop such pliancy as I explained above; once you develop pliancy, it is genuine insight. The nature of pliancy and the way to produce it are as I explained them above. Pliancy is also induced by a previously attained and continuing serenity, so insight is not simply a matter of having pliancy. What is it? Insight is when the power of analytical meditation itself is able to induce pliancy. In this regard, insight observing the diversity and insight observing the real nature are alike. . . . This means that in meditation on the diversity of conventional phenomena, serenity, insight, and the way they are united are comparable to what is done in meditation on the real nature. When analysis itself can induce pliancy, it can also induce one-pointed focus. Therefore, the advantage of having already attained serenity is that the analytical meditation of discrimination can itself induce this one-pointed focus. So for those who have well-established serenity, even analytical meditation helps serenity. Thus, do not think, "If I carry out the analytical meditation of discrimination, my stability will diminish."

Your meditation will constitute an insight that combines stabilizing meditation and analytical meditation on the real nature only when you meet the standard of having found an authentic, accurate understanding of the philosophical view of either of the two selflessnesses and after having focused and meditated upon this. This is what distinguishes genuine insight; it cannot be distinguished by any other means.

What kinds of things do *not* distinguish it? Meditation on any object may stop the coarse perception of the dualistic appearance of object and subject, leaving your mind like a stainless sky; your mind may be endowed with qualities of knowledge, clarity, and limpidity. Like a flame undisturbed by wind, the mind may remain steady for a long time; external and internal objects may appear to your mind like rainbows or wispy smoke, and may continue to appear that way for a long time. When you focus attention on any object that appears before the mental consciousness, it may not be able to stand even the slightest attention, and then your serenity is restored. At first, coarse external objects such as forms and sounds do appear, but as you grow accustomed to this meditative state, eventually it seems that understandings and experiences of the sort which you formerly possessed have been expelled; when you focus your mind on them, they disappear without bearing the slightest attention. Such experiences occur, but cannot be considered cases of finding the view which knows the reality beyond the two extremes; nor can these hazy, indistinct appearances be at all considered as "illusion-like" in the Madhyamaka sense. This is because many such things appear when you sustain stability for a long time, even when your mind is not directed toward the view. As I explained before, the sense of "illusion-like" requires that an appearance be based on two factors: (1) the certainty of a reasoning consciousness which has concluded that phenomena lack essence, and (2) conventional valid cognition's undeniable establishment of appearances.

Things such as forms may appear to your mind under a sheer and diaphanous aspect, like a rainbow; this is simply the combination of the absence of any tangible object and a glimmering appearance which occurs despite the absence of anything tangible. Thus, since this sort of ascertainment lacks even the slightest certainty about the absence of intrinsic existence, it is not right to consider this an illusion-like appearance, because to do so is to call the tangible "intrinsic existence," treating two objects of negation—intrinsic existence and the tangible—as though they were the same. Otherwise, if you did claim that the Madhyamaka sense of illusion and falsity is something of this sort, then when a rainbow and wispy smoke are taken as the substrata, the idea that they intrinsically exist would never occur, because according to your approach the very ascertainment of the substrata would be an ascertainment that they appear but lack intrinsic existence. Also, when the tangible is itself taken as the substratum, this approach would not lead to the ascertainment that the tangible lacks intrinsic existence, because according to your approach the ascertainment of the substratum is a conception of intrinsic existence. Therefore, when form and such appear in that way, this is not what it means to appear like an illusion, because there is not even the slightest refutation of the object of the misconception which thinks that this sheer and diaphanous appearance is the mode of being, or ontological status, of those objects. As I explained, illusion-like appearance refers to what appears to someone who has previously found, and who has not forgotten, the authentic view.

The stages of the path tradition deriving from Geshe Gön-ba-wa (dGe-bshes dGon-pa-ba) describes how to generate that understanding of emptiness as follows: First, you meditate on the selflessness of the person. You then meditate on the meaning of the selflessness of objects, bringing mindfulness and vigilance to bear. In a long session, failure to use mindfulness will cause you to fluctuate between laxity and excitement, and thus there will be little benefit. Therefore, doing four sessions in each of the four periods—morning, evening, dusk, and dawn—you meditate in sixteen sessions per day. When you think that the object is becoming clear or that you are having some experience, you should stop. When you meditate in this way, and then, supposing that you have not been meditating long, check the time and see that the night or day have been foreshortened, this means that the mind has linked to its object. If you check the time supposing that you have been meditating a very long time and see that no time has passed, this means that your mind is not linked to its object. When the mind is linked to its object, afflictions diminish in your mind, and you wonder whether you will ever need to sleep again.

When you are successful in each session of the day and night, your concentration will develop four characteristics: (1) non-discursiveness—when you are in equipoise, you will not feel the movement of inhalation and exhalation, and your breath and thought will become very subtle; (2) brightness—it will be just like the brightness of the sky at noontime in autumn; (3) limpidity—it will be like the clarity you see when you pour water into a clear metal cup and put it in the sun; and (4) subtlety—watching from within the condition that has the former three characteristics, you see what happens to a fraction of a split hair-tip. This approximates the creation of nonconceptual wisdom. As compared to actual nonconceptual wisdom, its nature is conceptual; it is therefore said to be mistaken. This explains what is stated in Maitreya's *Separation of the Middle from the Extremes*, "The approximation is mistaken." According to what is said in the *Separation of the Middle from the Extremes*, even the most auspicious meditation on emptiness by an ordinary being is an approximation and must be considered mistaken.

When you meditate on the meaning of the accurate view as explained above, then even though the other characteristics have not arisen, this is meditation on the meaning of selflessness. If you do not meditate on the meaning of the view, accurately determined, then even if the four characteristics arise, it cannot be considered meditation on the definitive meaning. Therefore, whether something is a meditation on the meaning of the real nature is determined as I explained above. The way that things appear as illusions after meditation on that real nature should be understood in accordance with what I explained above.

(iii) How to unite serenity and insight

As I explained in the sections on the standards for achieving serenity and insight, if you do not achieve them, then there will not be anything to unite. Therefore, in order to unite them, you must definitely attain the two. Also, from the time that you first attain insight, you will have that union. So it is said that the way to attain that union is to perform analytical meditation based upon earlier serenity, sequentially developing the four attentions—such as tight focus—here at the time of insight. Thus, when you have developed the fourth attention [spontaneous focus] as explained above, this constitutes union. Also, at the end of analytical meditation, you practice and sustain stabilizing meditation; it is union when the serenity thus attained becomes stabilizing meditation of this kind. Thus, Asaṅga's *Śrāvaka Levels* says:

> How do you combine and balance serenity and insight? And why is it called a path of union? It is said that it is reached through the nine mental states. Based on having attained the ninth, equipoise, and having fully achieved concentration, you apply yourself to the higher wisdom—the differentiation of phenomena. At that time, you naturally and effortlessly enter the path of differentiating phenomena. Because the path of serenity is unencumbered by striving, insight is pure, clean, comes after serenity, and is fully suffused with delight. Therefore, your serenity and insight combine and are balanced; this is called the path of the union of serenity and insight.

Kamalaśila's third *Stages of Meditation* says:

> Through being isolated from laxity and excitement, your mind becomes balanced and operates naturally. When this makes your mind extremely clear about reality, you achieve equanimity by easing your effort. Understand that you have then achieved the path of the union of serenity and insight.

Why is this called "union"? Prior to attaining it, the analytical meditation of discrimination cannot by itself bring about the stability of non-discursiveness. Therefore, you must work at cultivating analytical meditation and stabilizing meditation separately. Upon attaining both, the activity of the analytical meditation of discrimination can itself bring about serenity. Therefore, it is called union.

Also, analysis at this point is insight. The stability at the end of analysis is a special serenity observing emptiness. Ratnākaraśānti's *Instructions for the Perfection of Wisdom* says:

> Thereafter, the mind observes that discursive image. When that mind experiences both serenity and insight in a continuous and uninterrupted stream of attention, then this is called the path of union (*zung 'brel*) of serenity and insight. Serenity and insight are a pair (*zung*); connection (*'brel ba*) means possessing each other; they operate bound to each other.

"Uninterrupted" means that after you finish the analytical meditation itself, you do not have to stabilize your mind in a non-discursive state, but your analytical meditation itself brings about non-discursiveness. "Experiences both" means that you experience both serenity which observes a non-discursive image and insight which observes a discursive image. They are not simultaneous, but you experience them within a continuous process, without interruption of your meditative attention.

Question: Is it not contradictory to explain that, after previously achieving serenity, you use the analytical meditation of discrimination to establish stability?

Reply: If, prior to achieving serenity, you repeatedly alternate between analysis and post-analytical stabilization, then it will be impossible to achieve serenity. Doing such meditation after reaching serenity indicates that you are achieving an enhanced serenity. Therefore, there is no contradiction.

Moreover, there is one special case to consider: The analytical meditation immediately preceding the achievement of insight can induce one-pointed focus. I did explain above that it is impossible to establish serenity if, prior to achieving insight, you repeatedly alternate between analysis and post-analytical stabilization, and I explained that after you reach serenity, analytical meditation cannot induce non-discursiveness. I made these explanations in terms of the situation prior to the attaining of insight, leaving aside the exceptional case of analysis at the inception of insight. In brief, prior to achieving serenity, it is impossible to reach serenity by doing stabilizing meditation in alternation, stabilizing your mind at the conclusion of analysis. Once serenity is established, but prior to achieving insight, analytical meditation cannot itself induce a solid, one-pointed stability. Therefore, reaching solid stability through analysis—extensive analysis by discriminating wisdom—comes about when insight is achieved; thus the union of insight and serenity is also posited at that point.

So do not mistake the union of serenity and insight for a composite in which wisdom can analytically discriminate the meaning of selflessness from within an essentially unchanging non-discursive state of solid stability, like a small fish moving beneath still water without disturbing it.

Know how to unite serenity and insight according to what appears in the original texts. Do not put confidence in explanations derived from anything else. From the viewpoint of these Indian texts, it would seem that I must distinguish the many features of how you sustain serenity and insight in meditation. But I am wary of being long-winded, so I will write no more.

Summary and Conclusion

Now I will give a brief summation of the general meaning of the path. At the outset, the root of the path derives from your reliance upon a teacher, so consider this seriously. Then, once you have developed an uncontrived desire to take advantage of your leisure, this desire will spur you to practice continually. Therefore, in order to develop this, meditate on the topics connected with leisure and opportunity. Unless you then stop the various sentiments which seek the aims of this life, you will not diligently seek the aims of future lives. So work at meditating on how the body you have is impermanent in the sense that it will not last for long, and on how after death you will wander in the miserable realms. At that time, by creating a genuine awareness which is mindful of the frights of the miserable realms, build certainty from the depths of your heart about the qualities of the three refuges. Be constant in the common vow of going for refuge and train in its precepts. Then, from a range of perspectives develop faith, in the sense of conviction, in karma and its effects—this being the great foundation of all positive qualities. Make this faith firm. Strive to cultivate the ten virtues and to turn away from the ten nonvirtues, and always stay within the path of the four powers.

When you have thus trained well in the teachings associated with a person of small capacity and have made this practice firm, you should contemplate often the general and specific faults of cyclic existence, and in general turn your mind away from cyclic existence as much as you can. Then, having identified the nature of karma and the afflictions—the causes from which cyclic existence arises—create an authentic desire to eliminate them. Develop broad certainty about the path that liberates you from cyclic existence, i.e., the three trainings, and particularly make effort at whichever of the vows of individual liberation you have taken.

When you have thus trained well in the teachings associated with a person of medium capacity and have made this practice farm, consider the fact that just as you yourself have fallen into the ocean of cyclic existence, so have all beings, your mothers. Train in the spirit of enlightenment which is rooted in love and compassion and strive to develop this as much as you can. Without it, the practices of the six perfections and the two stages are like stories built on a house with no foundation. When you develop a little experience of this spirit of enlightenment, confirm it with the rite. By making effort in this training, make the aspiration as solid as you can. Then study the great waves of the bodhisattva deeds, learning the boundaries of what to discard and what to adopt, and make a strong wish to train in those bodhisattva deeds. After you have developed these attitudes, take the vow of the engaged spirit of enlightenment through its rite. Train in the six perfections that mature your own mind and the four ways of gathering disciples which mature the minds of others. In particular, risk your life in making a great effort to avoid the root infractions. Strive not to be tainted by the small and intermediate contaminants and faults, and even if you are tainted, work to repair it. Then, because you must train specifically in the final two perfections, knowledgeable in the way to sustain meditative stabilization and then achieve concentration. As much as you can, develop the view of the two selflessnesses, a purity free from permanence and annihilation. After you have found the view and stabilized your the mind upon it, understand the proper way to sustain the view in meditation, and then do so. Such stabilization and wisdom are called serenity and insight, but they are not something separate from the last two perfections. Therefore, after you have taken the bodhisattva vows, they come about in the context of the training in its precepts.

You have reached a critical point when, while meditating on the lower levels, you increasingly wish to attain the higher levels, and when studying the higher levels, your wish to practice the lower levels becomes stronger and stronger. Some say to expend your energy only to stabilize your mind and to understand the view, ignoring all earlier topics, but this makes it very difficult to get the vital points. Therefore, you must develop certainty about the whole course of the path. When you meditate on these topics, train your understanding and then go back to balance your mind. So if it seems that your faith in the teacher who instructs you on the path is decreasing, since this will cut the root of everything good that has come together, work on the methods for relying on the teacher. Similarly, if your joy in your practice loses strength, make meditation on the topics connected with leisure and opportunity your primary focus; if your attachment to this life increases, make meditation on impermanence and the faults of the miserable realms your primary focus. If you seem to be lazy about the proscriptions you have accepted, consider that your certainty about karmic cause and effect is meager and make meditation on karma and its effects your primary focus. If your sense of disenchantment with all of cyclic existence decreases, your desire to seek liberation will become just words. Therefore, contemplate the faults of cyclic existence. If your intention to benefit living beings in whatever you do is not strong, then you will sever the root of the Mahāyāna. Therefore, frequently cultivate the aspirational spirit of enlightenment together with its causes. Once you have taken the vows of a conqueror's child and are training in the practices, if the bondage of the reifying conception of signs seems strong, use reasoning consciousnesses to destroy all objects which are apprehended by the mind which conceives of signs, and train your mind in the space-like and illusion-like emptiness. If your mind is enslaved to distraction and does not remain on a virtuous object, you should primarily sustain one-pointed stability, as former teachers have said. From these illustrations, you should understand the cases I have not explained. In brief, without being partial, you have to be able to use the whole spectrum of virtues.

Among the stages of the path of a person of great capacity, I have explained how one who trains in the bodhisattva path practices insight, which is wisdom.

How to train specifically in the Vajrayāna

After you have trained in this way in the paths common to both sūtra and mantra, you must undoubtedly enter the mantra path because it is very much more precious than any other practice and it quickly brings the two collections to completion. If you are to enter it, then as Atisha's *Lamp for the Path to Enlightenment* says, you must first please the guru—even to a greater extent than explained earlier—with deeds such as respect and service and with practice that is in accordance with the guru's words. And you must do this for a guru who meets at least the minimum qualifications of a teacher explained there.

Then, at the outset, your mind should be matured through the ripening initiation as explained in a source tantra. You should then listen to the pledges and vows to be taken, understand them, and maintain them. If you are stricken by root infractions, you may make these commitments again. However, this greatly delays the development of the good qualities of the path in your mind. Make a fierce effort not to be tainted by those root infractions. Strive not to be tainted by the gross infractions, but in the event that you are tainted, use the methods for restoring your vows. Since these are the basis of the practice of the path, without them you will become like a dilapidated house whose foundation has collapsed. *The Root Tantra of Mañjuśrī* (*Mañjuśrī-mūla-tantra*) says, "The Master of the Sages does not say that faulty ethical discipline achieves the tantric path," meaning that those with faulty ethical discipline have none of the great, intermediate, or low attainments. And it says in the highest yoga tantra texts that those who do not maintain their vows, those who have inferior initiation, and those who do not understand reality do not achieve anything despite their practice. Therefore someone who talks about practicing the path without maintaining the pledges and vows has completely strayed from the tantric path.

In order to cultivate the mantra path someone who keeps the pledges and vows should at the outset meditate on the stage of generation, the complete divine wheel as explained from a source tantra. The unique object to be eliminated on the tantric path is the conception of ordinariness which regards the aggregates, constituents, and sensory sources as common. It is the stage of generation itself that eliminates this and transforms the abodes, bodies, and resources so that they appear as special. The conquerors and their children continually bless the person who clears away the conception of ordinariness in this way; such a person easily brings to completion the limitless collections of merit, thereby becoming a suitable vessel for the stage of completion.

This person should then meditate on what appears in the source tantras on the stage of completion. Neither the tantras nor the scholars who explain their intended meanings hold that you should discard the first stage and merely classify it within the latter stage, training only in individual portions of the path. Therefore, you must bear in mind the vital points of the two stages of the complete corpus of the path of highest yoga tantra.

Considering only the terms, I have described a mere fraction of what is involved in entering into the mantra path. Therefore, understand this in detail by using works on the stages of the mantra path. If you train in this way, you will train in the entirely complete corpus of the path, which includes all the vital points of sūtra and mantra. As a result, your attainment of leisure in this lifetime will have been worthwhile, and you will be able to extend the Conqueror's precious teaching within both your own and others' minds.

Source: Tsong-kha-pa, *The Great Treatise on the Stages of the Path to Enlightenment*, volume 3, translated by the Lamrim Chenmo Translation Committee (Ithaca: Snow Lion, 2002), 351–363.

Selections from *The Tibetan Book of the Dead*

The Mild Deity Reality Between

Hey, noble one! Listen unwavering with intense concentration! There are six kinds of between: the natural life between, the dream between, the contemplation between, the death-point between, the reality between, and the emergent existence between.

Hey, noble one, three betweens will dawn for you; the death-point between, the reality between, and the existence between will dawn. Until yesterday, in the death-point between, the reality clear light dawned. But you did not recognize it, so you had to wander here. Now the reality between and the existence between will dawn for you. As I describe them, you must recognize them without fail.

Hey, noble one! Now you have arrived at what is called "death." You are going from this world to the beyond. You are not alone; it happens to everyone. You must not indulge in attachment and insistence on this life. Thought you are attached and you insist, you have no power to stay, you will not avoid wandering in the life cycle. Do not lust! Do not cling! Be mindful of the Three Jewels!

Hey, noble child! Whatever terrifying visions of the reality between may dawn upon you, you should not forget the following words. You must proceed remembering in your mind the meaning of these words. Therein lies the key of recognition.

Hey! Now when the reality between dawns upon me,
I will let go of the hallucinations of instinctive terror,
Enter the recognition of all objects as my mind's own visions,
And understand this as the pattern of perception in the between;
Come to this moment, arrived at this most critical cessation,
I will not fear my own visions of deities mild and fierce!

You should proceed clearly saying this verse aloud and remembering its meaning. Do not forget this, as it is the key to recognizing whatever terrifying visions dawn as certainly being your own perceptions.

Hey, noble one! At this time when your mind and body are parting ways, pure reality manifests in subtle, dazzling visions, vividly experienced, naturally frightening and worrisome, shimmering like a mirage on the plains in autumn. Do not fear them. Do not be terrified! Do not panic! You have what is called an "instinctual mental body," not a material, flesh and blood body. Thus whatever sounds, lights, and rays may come at you, they cannot hurt you. You cannot die. It is enough just for you to recognize them as your own perceptions. Understand that this is the between.

Hey, noble one! If you don't recognize them as your own perceptions in this way—whatever other meditations and achievements you may have experienced in the human world, if you did not meet this particular instruction—the lights will frighten you, the sounds will panic you, the rays will terrify you. If you don't know the key of this instruction, you will not recognize the sounds, lights, and rays, and you will wander in the life cycle.

The First Day

Hey, noble one! Having fainted for four and a half days, you are now proceeding. You have woken up with the worry, "What is happening to me?" recognize that you are in the between! Now, since the life cycle is in suspension, all things dawn as lights and deities. All space dawns full of azure light. Now, from the central Buddha-land, All-pervading Drop, the Lord Vairochana appears before you, white bodied, sitting on a lion throne, holding in his hand an eight-spoked wheel, united with his consort Akasha Dhatvishvari. The natural purity of the consciousness aggregate, the blue light of the Reality Perfection wisdom, a clear and vivid color blue, frighteningly intense, shines piercingly from the heart center of this Vairochana couple, dazzling your eyes unbearably. Simultaneously the soft white light of the gods shines upon you and penetrates you in parallel with the bright blue light. At that time, influenced by negative evolution, you panic and are terrified of that bright blue light of Reality Perfection wisdom and you flee from it. And you feel a liking for the soft white light of the gods, and you approach it. But you must not panic at that blue light, the clear, piercing, brilliant, frightening supreme wisdom clear light! Do not fear it! It is the light ray of the Transcendent Lord, the Reality Perfection wisdom. Feel attracted to it with faith and reverence! Make it the answer to your prayer, thnking. "It is the light ray of the compassion of Lord Vairochana—I must take refuge in it!" It is the way Lord Vairochana comes to escort you through the straits of the between. It is the light ray of the compassion of Vairochana. Don't be enticed by the soft white light of the gods. Don't be attached to it! Don't long for it! If you cling to it, you will wander into the realm of the gods, and you will continue to cycle through the six realms of driven existence. It is an obstacle to cessation, the path of freedom. So don't look upon it, but be devoted to the brilliant penetrating blue light, aim your intense willpower toward Vairochana, and repeat after me the following prayer:

> When I roam the life cycle driven by strong delusion,
> May the Lord Vairochana lead me on the path
> Of the clear light of reality-perfection wisdom!
> May his Consort Buddha Dhatvishvari back me on the way,
> Deliver me from the dangerous straits of the between,
> And carry me to perfect Buddhahood!

Thus praying with fierce devotion, you dissolve in rainbow light into the heart of the Vairochana couple, whence you will enter the central pure land Ghanavyuha, Dense Array, and become a Buddha by way of the Body of Perfect Beatitude!

The Second Day

Hey, noble one! Listen without wavering! On this second day, the white light that is the purity of the element water dawns before you. At this time, from the blue eastern pure land of Abhirati, Intense Delight, the blue Lord Vajrasattva Akshobhya arises before you seated on an elephant, carrying a five-pronged vajra scepter, in union with his consort Buddhalochana, attended by the male Bodhisattvas Kshitigarbha and Maitreya and the female Bodhisattvas Lasya and Pushpa—a group of six Archetype Deities. The white light of the Mirror wisdom, purity of the form aggregate, white and piercing, bright and clear, shines from the heart of the Vajrasattva couple before you, penetrating, unbearable to your eyes. At the same time the soft smoky light of the hells shines before you in parallel with the wisdom light. At that time, under the influence of hate you panic, terrified by that brilliant white light, and you flee from it. You feel a liking for that soft smoky light of the hells and you approach it. But now you must fearlessly recognize that brilliant white, piercing, dazzling clear light as wisdom. Be gladdened by it with faith and reverence! Pray, and increase your love for it, thinking, "It is the light of the compassion of Lord Vajrasattva! I take refuge in it!" It is Lord Vajrasattva's shining upon you to escort you through the terrors of the between. It is the tractor-beam of the light of the compassion of Vajrasattva—have faith in it! Don't be enticed by that soft smoky light of hell! Hey! That is the path of destruction from the sins you have accumulated by your strong hatred! If you cling to it, you will fall into the hells; you will be stuck in the mire of unbearable ordeals of suffering, without any escape. It is an obstacle to the path of liberation. Don't look upon it, and abandon all hate! Don't cling to it! Don't long for it! Have faith in that dazzlingly bright white light! Aim your intense willpower toward lord Vajrasattva and make the following prayer:

> Alas! When I roam the life cycle driven by strong hate,
> May the Lord Vajrasattva lead me on the path
> Of the clear light of the mirror wisdom!
> May his Consort Buddhalochana back me on the way,
> Deliver me from the dangerous straits of the between,
> And carry me to perfect Buddhahood!

By praying in this way with intense faith, you will dissolve into rainbow light in the heart of Lord Vajrasattva, and you will go to his eastern pure land Abhirati and attain Buddhahood in the Boby of Perfect Beatitude. . . .

The Eighth Day

Hey, noble one! Listen without wavering! The peaceful between already dawned, but you did not recognize the light. So now you still must wander here. Now on this eighth day, the Heruka Fierce Deity host will arise. Do not waver! Recognize them! Hey, noble one! The great, glorious Buddha Heruka appears, wine maroon in color, with three faces, six arms, and four legs stretched out, his front face maroon, his right face white, his left face red, his entire body blazing with light rays. His eyes glare, fiercely terrifying, his eyebrows flash like lightning, his fangs gleam like new copper. He roars with laughter, "A la la," and "Ha, ha, ha," and he makes loud hissing noises like "shu-uu." His bright orange hair blazes upward, adorned with skull crown and sun and moon discs. His body is adorned with black snakes and a freshly severed head garland. His first right hand holds a wheel, the middle an ax, and the third a sword; his first left hand holds a bell, the middle a plowshare, and the third a skull bowl. His Consort Budddha Krodhishvari enfolds his body, her right arms embracing his neck, her left hand offering him sips of blood from her skull bowl. She clucks her tongue menacingly and roars just like thunder. Both are ablaze with wisdom flames, shooting out from their blazing vajra hairs. They stand in the warrior's posture on a throne supported by garudas. Thus they arise manifestly before you, having emerged from within your own brain! Do not fear them! Do not be terrified! Do not hate them! Recognize them as an image of your own awareness! He is your own Archetype Deity, so do not panic! In fact, they are really Lord Vairochana Father and Mother, so do not be afraid! The very moment you recognize them, you will be liberated.

The Ninth Day

Hey, noble one! Listen without wavering! Now on the ninth day the Lord Vajra Heruka of the Vajra-clan will arise before you, emerging from within your brain. He is dark blue, with three faces, six arms, and four legs stretched out. His front face is dark blue, his right face white, his left face red. His first right hand holds a vajra, the middle a skull bowl, and the third an ax; his first left hand holds a bell, the middle a skull bowl, and the third a plowshare. His Consort Buddha Vajra Krodhishvari enfolds his body, her right arm embracing his neck, her left hand offering him sips of blood from her skull bowl. Thus they arise manifestly before you, having emerged from within your own brain! Do not fear them! Do not be terrified! Do not hate them! Recognize them as an image of your own awareness! They are your own Archetype Deity, so do not panic! In fact, they are really Lord Vajrasattva Father and Mother, so have faith in them! The very moment you recognize them, you will be liberated! . . .

Encountering the Lord of Death

Hey, noble one! You named So-and-so, listen to me! This suffering of yours comes from your own evolutionary acts; there is no one else to blame. It is your own evolution, so pray strongly to the Three Jewels. They can protect you. It you don't pray to them, don't know how to meditate on the Great Seal, and don't meditate on an Archetype Deity, then your native angel will count out a white stone for each virtue you accumulated, and your native demon will count out a black stone for every sin.

Then you will be very worried, angry, and terrified. Trembling, you will lie, saying, "I committed no sins!" But then Yama, the Judge of the Dead, will say, "I will look into the mirror of evolution!" When he looks into the mirror of evolution, all your sins and virtues willclearly and distinctly appear therein. Your lies will not help. Yama will tie a rope around your neck and lead you away. He will cut off your head, rip out your heart, pull out your guts, lick your brains, drink your blood, eat your flesh, and gnaw your bones. But since you cannot die, even though your body is cut to pieces, you revive again. Being cut up again and again, you will suffer immense pain.

So when the white stones are being counted, don't be afraid, don't panic, do not lie! Don't fear Yama! Your body is mental, so even if it is killed and cut up, you cannot die. In fact, your form is the void itself, so you have nothing to fear. The Yama-deities are your own hallucinations and themselves are forms of the void. Your own instinctual mental body is void. Voidness cannot harm voidness. Signlessness cannot harm signlessness. You should recognize that there is nothing other than your own hallucination. There is no external, substantially existent Yama, angel, demon, or bull-headed ogre, and so on. You must recognize all this as the between!

Source: *The Tibetan Book of the Dead,* translated by Robert A. F. Thurman (New York: Bantam Books, 1994), 131–136, 15–154, 174–175.

19

Chinese Buddhist Tradition

Rather than include selections of literature that would duplicate material already covered by the previous chapters on the Mādhyamika and Yogācāra schools, this chapter on the Chinese Buddhist tradition will concentrate on schools that are unique to China. These schools are the Hua-yen, T'ien t'ai, Pure Land, and Ch'an. Fa-tsang (643–712) represents the Hua-yen school in this chapter with his discussion of the golden lion, which functions as a metaphor for his philosophy. The T'ien-t'ai is represented by a work of Chih-i (538–597). The Pure Land school represents devotional Buddhism in the Chinese tradition with selections from T'an-luan (476–542) and Tao-ch'o (562–645). This school appealed to ordinary people and became a mass movement. Explaining in part its broad appeal, the writings of this school are much less philosophically abstract than those of some of the other schools. Finally, Ch'an Buddhism is represented by writings from Hui-neng, the so-called Sixth Patriarch, and selections from the recorded sayings of the Ch'an master Lin-chi.

Fa-tsang is considered the third patriarch of the Hua-yen school, although many scholars give him credit for establishing the school. His famous "Essay on the Golden Lion" is an attempt to explain the relationship between the noumenon (*li*) and the phenomenal world of things (*shih*). In his essay, the gold of the lion symbolizes the noumenon, whereas the physical figure of the lion symbolizes phenomena. The principle of the noumenon is innately clear, pure, all-perfect, brilliant, and the primary cause of the lion, whereas the phenomenal is the exact opposite of the noumenon. The golden lion is an attempt to explain the inter-dependent and interpenetrative nature of things within the context of emptiness. Fa-tsang argues that the identity of things reflects their static nature, whereas their interpenetration indicates their dynamic nature. It is emptiness or the nonsub-stantial nature of things that makes interpenetration possible. Everything is identi-cal because of shared emptiness. Things are, however, also different, much as fire is distinguished from ice. When reading Fa-tsang's essay it is important to recall that his philosophical position represents identity in difference. This means that things share an identical essence because they are empty. But it also implies that a particular cause, for instance, is identical with other causes and yet are also dif-ferent. In summary, the Hua-yen school wants to affirm that all things are coexis-tent, interwoven, interrelated, interpenetrating, mutually inclusive, and reflect each other.

In sharp contrast to the Hua-yen school, the T'ien-t'ai school received inspi-ration from the *Lotus Sūtra,* and it discusses the doctrine of emptiness from within the context of its notion of the threefold truth. A reader will encounter examples of Chih-i quoting from the *Lotus Sūtra* in order to support his position, because he believes that this text embodies the truth. The threefold truth for Chih-i begins with emptiness, conventional truth, and a third, middle, truth that suggests that things are both empty and existent. This signifies the intersection of the particular and universal at the same instant. The second truth implies that things are tem-porary because they are involved in a constant state of flux, whereas the middle truth rises above the other two truths. When referring to emptiness, it is impor-tant to remember that it includes the subjective notions that we have a tendency to superimpose upon things and their emptiness. Chih-i's position on his three-truths doctrine indicates that truth is both singular and nondual because every-thing is part of one organic unity. Therefore, it is possible to affirm accurately that the Buddha can be discovered in a single grain of sand because the whole and its parts are identical, due their common emptiness.

In contrast to the abstract nature of the T'ien-t'ai and Hua-yen schools, a dif-ferent and more down-to-earth spirit can be discerned in the works of the Pure Land school. This school addresses the issues of salvation and what a peson needs to do during life in order to secure a place in the paradisical realm of the Pure Land. The essay by T'an-luan provides a good example of his emphasis on the importance of reciting and meditating on the name of Amitābha, which is precisely the type of action that an other-powered person should perform, in contrast to a self-powered person. By relying on Amitābha and reciting his name, an other-powered person is freed from sin and gains rebirth in the Pure Land. It is important for a reader to keep in mind that the Pure Land perspective of T'an-luan is grounded on a nondualistic position, because a person relies only on Amitābha. The selection from the writings of Tao-ch'o are a good example of his direct response to various forms of criticism leveled against the Pure Land school.

Critics of the Pure Land school included members of the Ch'an school. The selections from Ch'an literature include excerpts from the historically important the *Platform Sūtra of the Sixth Patriarch* and sayings of Lin-chi. Both of these works were composed and or compiled long after the events depicted in the texts.

The earliest version of The *Platform Sūtra of the Sixth Patriarch* dates from about 780 C.E. The text incorporates notions of the Oxhead school, which originated in the latter half of the eighth century among monks renowned for their literary ability and tendency to define themselves independently from either the Northern or Southern schools of Ch'an, and their effective use of the narrative style. By the time that the text appeared, it represented an account of alleged events that occurred a century before its date of appearance. The text recognizes Hui-neng as the Sixth Patriarch and promotes the Southern school at the expense of the so-called Northern school, which favored the *Lankāvatāra Sūtra* over the *Diamond Sūtra,* the Southern school's preferred text. This promotion of the Sixth Patriarch was carried out by the monk Shen-hui (684–758), an inspiring orator, vigorous debater, and monastic recruiter, against Shen-xiu and his disciples. The text should be understood as a fictive historical allegory.

The central figure of the text is Hui-neng (638–713), who evolved from humble origins to be spiritually awakened by a person reciting the *Diamond Sūtra.* When he approached the Fifth Patriarch for instruction, Hui-neng was asked how he could expect to attain Buddhahood when he was a mere barbarian. Undeterred by these harsh words, Hui-neng replied that there was no difference between a barbarian and a civilized person in the Buddha-nature. Thereafter, he was employed as an acolyte to do menial tasks within the monastery. As the narrative makes clear, Hui-neng's illiteracy did not imply that he was short of wisdom. A reader should anticipate the dispute and distinction, according to Shen-hui, of the path of gradual awakening of the Northern school and the sudden enlightenment of the Southern school, represented as superior.

The final selections of Ch'an literature are derived from the collected sayings of Lin-chi I-hsuan (d. 866–867 C.E.), whose name is derived from a small temple called "Overlooking the ford." Lin-chi is famous for his strict and harsh teaching method, which included beating students and shouting at them. It is obvious that he did not believe that a teacher should teach or explain anything. A teacher should rather force students to experience truth for themselves. This pedagogical conviction is consistent with his focus on wordless teaching. There is also an emphasis on naturalness, which included the elements of no concern and no seeking. A reader will discover an egalitarian spirit in Lin-chi's philosophy which implies that no person should hold rank or title over another person. If a reader places this attitude into its historical or cultural context of China, Lin-chi's position appears radical, because the genuine person is free of all fetters. Such a person exists concretely in the present moment. Instead of a static and hierarchical conception of human nature, Lin-chi's true human is lively, dynamic, attuned to nature, dependent on nothing, ordinary, simple, and direct, although such a person is grounded in transcendence. It is this concrete person that reveals the Buddha-nature.

HUA-YEN SCHOOL

Selections from the *Treatise on the Golden Lion*
by Fa-tsang (643–712)

1. Clarifying the Fact that Things Arise through Causation

It means that gold has no nature of its own. As a result of the conditioning of the skillful craftsman, the character of the lion consequently arises. This arising is purely due to causes. Therefore it is called arising through causation.

2. Distinguishing Matter and Emptiness

It means that the character of the lion is unreal; there is only real gold. The lion is not existent, but the substance of the gold is not nonexistent. Therefore they are [separately] called matter and Emptiness. Furthermore, Emptiness has no character of its own; it shows itself by means of matter. This does not obstruct its illusory existence. Therefore they are [separately] called matter and Emptiness.

3. Simply Stating the Three Natures

The lion exists because of our feelings. This is called [the nature] arising from vast imagination. The lion seems to exist. This is called [the nature of] dependence on others (gold and craftsman) [for production]. The nature of the gold does not change. This is therefore called [the nature of] Perfect Reality.

4. Showing the Nonexistence of Characters

It means that as the gold takes in the lion in its totality, apart from the gold there is no character of the lion to be found. Therefore it is called the nonexistence of characters.

5. Explaining Non-coming-into-existence

It means that at the moment when we see the lion come into existence, it is only gold that comes into existence. There is nothing apart from the gold. Although the lion comes into existence and goes out of existence, the substance of the gold at bottom neither increases nor decreases. Therefore we say that [dharmas] do not come into existence [nor go out of existence].

6. Discussing the Five Doctrines

(1) Although the lion is a dharma produced through causation, and comes into and goes out of existence every moment, there is really no character of the lion to be found. This is called the Small Vehicle (Hinayāna) Doctrine of Ordinary Disciples [that is, the Hinayāna schools].

(2) These dharmas produced through causation are each without self-nature. It is absolutely Emptiness. This is called the Initial Doctrine of the Great Vehicle (Mahāyāna) [that is, the Three-Treatise and Conscious-Only schools].

(3) Although there is absolutely only Emptiness, this does not prevent the illusory dharmas from being clearly what they are. The two characters of coming into existence through causation and dependent existence coexist. This is called the Final Doctrine of the Great Vehicle [that is, the T'ien-t'ai School].

(4) These two characters eliminate each other and both perish, and [conse-quently] neither [the products of] our feelings nor false existence remain. Neither of them has any more power, and both Emptiness and existence per-ish. Names and descriptions will be completely discarded and the mind will be at rest and have no more attachment. This is called the Great Vehicle's Doctrine of Sudden Enlightenment [that is, the Zen School].

(5) When the feelings have been eliminated and true substance revealed, all becomes an undifferentiated mass. Great function then arises in abundance, and whenever it does, there is surely Perfect Reality. All phenomena are in great profusion, and are interfused but not mixed (losing their own identity). The all is the one, for both are similar in being nonexistent in nature. And the one is the all, for [the relation between] cause and effect is perfectly clear. As the power [of the one] and the function [of the many] embraces each other, their expansion and contraction are free and at ease. This is called the Rounded (inclusive) Doctrine of the One [all-inclusive] Vehicle. [The Hua-yen School.]

7. Mastering the Ten Mysteries [Gates]

(1) The gold and the lion exist simultaneously, all-perfect and complete in their possession. This is called the gate of simultaneous completion and mutual correspondence.

(2) If the eye of the lion completely takes in the lion, then the all (the whole lion) is purely the eye (the one). If the ear completely takes in the lion, then the all is purely the ear. If all the sense organs simultaneously take in [the lion] and all are complete in their possession, then each of them is at the same time mixed (involving others) and pure (being itself), thus constituting the per-fect storehouse. This is called the gate of full possession of the attributes of purity and mixture by the various storehouses.

(3) The gold and the lion are mutually compatible in their formation, the one and the many not obstructing each other. In this situation the principle (the one or the gold) and facts (the many or the lion) are each different, but whether the one or the many, each remains in its own position. This is called the gate of mutual compatibility and difference between the one and the many.

(4) Since the various organs and each and every hair of the lion completely take in the lion by means of the gold, each and every one of them penetrates the whole. The eye of the lion is its ear, its ear is its nose, its nose is its tongue, and its tongue is its body. They each exist freely and easily, one not hinder-

ing or obstructing the other. This is called the gate of mutual identification of all dharmas existing freely and easily.

(5) If we look at the lion [as lion], there is only the lion and no gold. This means that the lion is manifest while the gold is hidden. If we look at the gold, there is only the gold and no lion. This means that the gold is manifest while the lion is hidden. If we look at them both, then both are manifest and both hidden. Being hidden, they are secret, and being manifest, they are evident. This is called the gate of the completion of the secret, the hidden, and the manifest.

(6) The gold and the lion may be hidden or manifest, one or many, definitely pure or definitely mixed, powerful or powerless, the one or the other. The principal and the companion mutually shine. Principle and fact appear together and are completely compatible with each other. They do not obstruct each other's peaceful existence, and thus the subtle and the minute are accomplished. This is called the gate of the compatibility and peaceful existence of the subtle and the minute.

(7) In each of the lion's eyes, ears, limbs, joints, and in each and every hair, there is the golden lion. All the lions embraced by all the single hairs simultaneously and instantaneously enter a single hair. Thus in each and every hair there are an infinite number of lions, and in addition all the single hairs, together with their infinite number of lions, in turn enter into a single hair. In this way the geometric progression is infinite, like the jewels of Celestial Lord Indra's net. This is called the gate of the realm of Indra's net.

(8) The lion is spoken of in order to show the meaning of ignorance while its golden substance is spoken of in order to make sufficiently clear the true nature. And principle and fact are discussed together as a description of the storehouse consciousness so that correct understanding may be created. This is called the gate of relying on facts in order to explain dharmas and create understanding.

(9) The lion is a dharma produced from causes, coming into existence and going out of existence at every moment. Each of these instants is divided into three periods, that is, past, present, and future, and each of these periods contains past, present, and future. Altogether there are three times three units, thus forming nine ages, and these, grouped together, become the total gate [to truth]. Although there are nine ages, each separate from the other, yet, since they are formed because of one another, they are harmoniously merged and mutually penetrated without obstacle and together constitute one instant of

time. This is called the gate of different formation of separate dharmas in ten
ages (the nine ages separately and all of them together).

(10) The gold and the lion may be hidden or manifest, and may be one or many.
Neither has self-nature. They are [always] turning and transforming in accordance with the mind. Whether spoken of as fact or principle, there is the way
(the mind) by which they are formed and exist. This is called the gate of the
excellent completion through the turning and transformation of the mind
only.

8. Putting together the Six Characters

The lion represents the character of universality. The five sense organs, being various and different, represent the character of specialty. The fact that they all arise
from one single cause represents the character of similarity. The fact that its eyes,
ears, and so forth do not exceed their bounds represents the character of difference. Since the combination of the various organs becomes the lion, this is the
character of integration. And as each of the several organs remains in its own
position, this is the character of disintegration.

9. Achieving Perfect Wisdom (bodhi)

"Bodhi" means in Chinese the Way or enlightenment. It means that when we look
at the lion, we see right away that all dharmas produced through causes, even
before disintegration, are from the very beginning quiescent and extinct. By being
free from attachment or renunciation one will flow right along this way into the
sea of perfect knowledge. Therefore it is called the Way. One understands right
away that from time immemorial all afflictions resulting from passions originally
have no reality. This is called enlightenment. The ultimate possession of the wisdom that knows all is called the achievement of perfect wisdom.

10. Entering Nirvāna

When we look at the lion and the gold, the two characters both perish and afflictions resulting from passions will no longer be produced. Although beauty and
ugliness are displayed before the eye, the mind is as calm as the sea. Erroneous
thoughts all cease, and there are no compulsions. One gets out of bondage and is
free from hindrances, and forever cuts off the source of suffering. This is called
entry into Nirvāna.

Source: "Treatise on the Golden Lion" by Fa-tsang in *Source Book of Chinese Philosophy,* translated
by Wing-tsit Chan (Princeton: Princeton University Press, 1963), 409–413.

T'IEN T'AI SCHOOL

Selections from the *Threefold Truth* by Chih-i (538–597)

[A correct understanding of] the resultant essence [of Buddhahood] has three meanings. First, the essence [of true reality] pervades all places. This is called "vast in essence." Second, [the Buddha] has already attained Buddhahood for an eternity. This is called "eminence in stages." Third, from the beginning [the Buddha] has manifested himself in the past, present and future in order to benefit sentient beings. This is called "long in function."

[*The Lotus Sūtra*] differs from other Sūtras with regard to these six meanings of the causes and result [of Buddhahood], and is therefore "subtle."

In the Sūtras of the Milk [Teachings], some parts of [its teaching on] the causes and result [of Buddhahood] are vast, eminent, and long; but some parts of [its teaching on] the causes and result [of Buddhahood] are narrow, inferior, and short. Therefore it is partially crude and partially subtle.

In the Sūtras of the Cream [Teachings] there is only one type of [teaching concerning] the causes and result [of Buddhahood]: the narrow, inferior, and short. It is only crude and not subtle.

In the Sūtras of the Curd [Teachings], there are three types of [teaching concerning] the causes and result [of Buddhahood] which are narrow, inferior, and short; there is one type of [teaching concerning] the causes and result [of Buddhahood] which is vast, eminent, and long. Therefore it is crude in three ways and subtle in one.

In the Sūtras of the Butter [Teachings] there are two types of [teaching concerning] the causes and result [of Buddhahood] which are narrow, inferior, and short, and one type of [teaching concerning] the causes and result [of Buddhahood] which is vast, eminent, and long. Therefore it is crude in two ways and subtle in one.

The Sūtras of the Ghee [Teachings] has one type of [teaching concerning] the causes and result [of Buddhahood] which is vast, eminent, and long. It is only subtle and lacking in crudity. Also, [the teachings concerning] the subtle causes and subtle result [of Buddhahood] in the Sūtra of the Ghee [Teachings] and [the teachings concerning] the subtle causes and subtle result [of Buddhahood] in the other Sūtras is not different. Therefore they are all called "subtle."

Next I will interpret [the meaning of subtle] from the viewpoint of contemplating the mind. [First,] if one contemplates one's own mind as not including the minds of sentient beings and the Buddha, this is a narrow [interpretation of] essence. [If the mind is contemplated as] including [the minds of sentient beings and the Buddha], this is a vast [interpretation of] essence. [Second,] if [one contemplates] one's own mind as not equal to the mind of the Buddha, this is an inferior [interpretation of the] stage [of one's attainment]. If [contemplated as] equal to the mind of the Buddha, this is an eminent [interpretation of the] stage [of one's attainment]. [Third,] if [one contemplates] one's own mind and the mind of sentient beings and the Buddha as not "simultaneously empty of substantive Being yet having conventional existence," this is a short [interpretation of] function. To affirm the simultaneous emptiness and conventional existence [of reality] is a long [interpretation of] function.

Also, [to teach that] one dharma-realm penetrates all ten dharma-realms and the levels of the six identities is [an interpretation] vast in essence, eminent in stages, and long in function. With regard to the ten dharma-realms, this is manifested as the Oneness of Reality. Next, with regard to the Five Flavors, this is summarized as the Oneness of Teaching. Next, with regard to contemplating the mind, this is summarized as the Oneness of Practice. Next, with regard to the six identities, this is summarized as the Oneness of Persons. This ends the brief summary of the meaning of "subtle."

As for the detailed explanation, first [I will discuss] "dharma"and then "subtle."

Fa: *Dharma*

Master [Hi-ssu] of Mt. Nan-yüeh suggests three types [of dharmas], i.e., sentient beings, the Buddha, and mind.

As the *Lotus Sūtra* says, the Buddha manifests himself in the world] in order to lead sentient beings to expose, point out, realize, and enter [an understanding of] the Buddha's knowledge and insight. If sentient beings [inherently] lack the Buddha's knowledge and insight, how can it be exposed through discussion? It should be known that the Buddha's knowledge and insight dwells [inherently] within sentient beings.

The [*Lotus*] *Sūtra* also [refers to the seeing] merely with "eyes engendered by one's parents." This refers to physical eyes. That which can see through the "inner and outer mounts Meru . . ." is called the "Divine Eye." That which has penetrating insight which sees through all visible forms without being defiled by attachment is called the "Eye of Wisdom." That which perceives visible forms without error is the "Dharma Eye." In this way, even though one has not yet attained the state of no outflow [of passions], nevertheless one's sight organ is [inherently] pure. For one eyesight to include all of these eyesights is called the Buddha Eye. This text in the *Lotus Sūtra* clarifies that the dharma of sentient beings is subtle [because they inherently have the Buddha's knowledge and insight].

The *Mahāparinirvāṇa Sūtra* says, "To study Mahāyāna means that [or, "for one who studies Mahāyāna"], although one has physical eyes, they are called "Buddha Eyes." The other five sense organs such as the ear and nose are also like this. The *Aṅgulimālika Sūtra* says, "The so-called sight organ, when it is the Tathāgata's, is eternally endowed with non-decreasing and cultivates perfectly clear insight," and the same is true for the other sense organs including the mind. . . .

The subtlety of the dharma of the Buddha means, as the *Lotus Sūtra* says, "Cease, cease, do not try to explain. My dharma is subtle and difficult to conceptualize." The dharma of the Buddha does not go beyond the conventional and the real. [The *Lotus Sūtra* says,] "This dharma is exceedingly profound, subtle, difficult to see and difficult to perfect," and "Of all types of sentient beings, none are able to know the Buddha." This is the subtle real wisdom. . . .

The subtlety of the dharma of mind is, as it is written in the chapter on "The Practice of Peace" [in the *Lotus Sūtra*], "to cultivate and collect one's thoughts . . . while contemplating all dharmas . . . without moving nor retreating.". . . This is called the subtlety of the dharma of mind.

Now I will make further extensive distinctions concerning these three dharmas. If one were to extensively discuss the dharma of sentient beings, one should discuss completely all causes and results and all dharmas [i.e., all of the ten dharma realms]. If one were to extensively discuss the dharma of the Buddha, this would be limited to [a discussion of] the result [of Buddhahood and the tenth Buddha realm.] If one were to discuss extensively the dharma of mind, this would be limited to [a discussion of] the causes [of Buddhahood, i.e., the nine dharma realms from hell to bodhisattva].

[The discussion of] the dharma of sentient beings consists of two parts. First I will list the number of dharmas, and then explain the marks of the dharmas.

"Number" refers to where the Sūtras and *śāstras* clarify that all of reality is contained in one [or more] dharmas. For example, [the *Ta chih lu lun* describes] mind as: "In the triple world there is no other dharma; only that created by the single mind." Or, it is explained that two dharmas contain all of reality; i.e., name and visible form [*nāmarūpa*]. These texts teach that in the entire universe there is only name and visible form. Others explain that three dharmas embrace all reality; i.e., life, consciousness, and warmth. Such numerical listings continue up to one hundred thousand.

Thus *Lotus Sūtra* utilizes [the number of] ten dharmas to embrace all of reality [*sarvadharma*]; i.e., all dharmas are of suchlike appearance, suchlike nature, suchlike essence suchlike power, suchlike function, suchlike causes, suchlike conditions, suchlike results, suchlike retributions, and suchlike beginning and end ultimately the same. . . .

Chih-i says that, depending on the meaning, there are three way of reading these phrases. The first is [to emphasize their suchness]: "the suchness of this their appearance, the suchness of this their nature . . . the suchness of this their retribution." Second is [to emphasize their characteristics]: "suchlike appearance, suchlike nature . . . suchlike retribution." Third is [to emphasize their thusness]: "their appearance is like this, their nature is like this . . . their retribution is like this."

First, if all are referred to in their "suchness," this "suchness" is non-differentiated and is identical to the meaning of emptiness. Second, if one speaks of suchlike appearance, suchlike nature, and so forth, one goes beyond the empty nature and characteristic [of dharmas], constructs names and words, and makes differentiations. This is the meaning of the "conventional." Third, if one speaks of "their appearance is like this," and so forth, this refers to the real aspect of the middle path, which is the meaning of the middle.

Distinctions are made in order to facilitate understanding; therefore [the threefold truth of] emptiness, conventional existence, and the middle is clarified. If one understands the meaning and tries to put it into words, the result is [expressed as] "the identity of emptiness with conventional existence and the middle." If one clarifies emptiness with regard to suchness, [one should say that] the emptiness of one [dharma] is the emptiness of all. If one clarifies appearances [and so forth] by going beyond suchness, [one should say that] one conventional existence is the conventional existence of all. Following this, if one discusses the middle, [one should say that] the middleness of one [dharma] is the middleness of all. It is not one, two, or three, yet it is one, two, and three. The true aspects of reality are neither horizontal nor vertical.

Only a Buddha can completely understand this reality. All reality is included within these ten dharmas. If one were to discuss this according to the convenience of the meaning, the meaning can be discriminated into three parts. If one were to read further, the verses say. "The suchlike great results and retributions, and the various meanings of natures and appearances . . ." and so forth.

Next, in classifying the tentative and real, Fa-yün classified the first five suchlikes as the tentative which belongs to common ignorant people. The next four suchlikes were classified as the real which belong to sages. The last suchlike is a general one which brings together the tentative and the real. This verse [from Chapter Four of the *Lotus Sūtra*] is quoted as proof: "the suchlike great results and retributions." Because they are "great," therefore one can know the real. Because of "various meanings of nature and appearance" one can know the tentative.

I think that this [interpretation by Fa-yün] is mistaken. There are three meanings to the word "great": large, many, and superior. If one accepts "large" to be the meaning of the real, then one should also accept the meanings of "many" and "superior." But is not the fact of having various names [which is the defining characteristic of conventional existence] the meaning of "many"? If one says that the tentative belongs to ordinary ignorant people, does that mean that ordinary people lack [participation in] the real? If the real belongs to the sages, then does that mean that sages lack [participation in] tentative existence? If one examines this position, one can see that it is unreliable.

Also, the northern Master[s] say that the first five are the tentative and the later five are the real. This [interpretation is based on] human emotions.

Now I will clarify [the correct meaning of] the tentative and the real. The ten suchnesses [are interpreted] in relation to the ten dharma realms, i.e., the six destinies [of hell to people] and the four noble ways [of śrāvaka, pratyekabuddha, bodhisattva, and Buddha]. They are all called "dharma realms" for three reasons. First, all ten are based on the *dharmadhātu,* for there is no dharma outside the *dharmadhātu.* Therefore all of them taken together are referred to as the ten dharma realms. Second, these ten various dharma realms are classified distinctly and thus are not the same. Their causes and results are distinct and there are differences between ordinary ignorant men and sages. Therefore with this in mind they are called [distinct] realms. Third, these ten [dharma realms] are all identical with the *dharmadhātu* and include all of reality.

All of reality is included in hell and does not transcend this destiny. Verily essence is identical to the principle [of reality], and since it does not depend on anything it is called the *dharmadhātu.* The same is true for all destinies up to and including the Buddha realm. The ten dharma realms are [all] based on the *dharmadhātu;* that which is based depends on the basis. [From this perspective] one understands the realm of emptiness. [The perspective of] each realm of the ten realms being distinct is the realm of conventional existence. To say that all ten realms are the *dharmadhātu* is the realm of the middle.

I have made these distinctions to facilitate understanding, but to understand it correctly and put it into words [one must say that] "emptiness is identical to conventional existence and the middle." There is [ultimately] neither one nor two nor three, as discussed above.

Each one of these ten dharma realms contains the ten suchlike [characteristics]. The ten dharma realms [therefore] contain one hundred suchlike [characteristics]. Also, one dharma realm contains the [other] nine dharma realms, therefore there are one hundred dharma realms and one thousand suchlike [characteristics]. All together there are five categories [of dharma realms]: evil, good, the two vehicle [of Śrāvaka and pratyekabuddha], bodhisattvas, Buddhas. These are classified into two categories: the first four are tentative dharmas, and the last one is the real dharma.

A detailed discussion [would reveal that] each [dharma realm] contains both the tentative and the real, but these are dichotomized only as a practical expedient. However, [the reality which is conventionally dichotomized into] the tentative and the real is beyond conceptual understanding and is the object [which can be understood only by] the double [tentative and real] wisdom of the Buddhas of past, present, and future.

If one takes this [inconceivable reality] as an object, what dharma is not included in it? If this objective realm arouses wisdom, what wisdom is there which is not aroused?

Therefore it is written, "All dharmas [sarvadharma]." "All dharmas" means that the objective realm which is to be understood is vast. "Only Buddhas can completely exhaust . . ." shows that the wisdom which understands [this objective realm] is deep, reaching the limits and exhausting the depths. . . .

In this way there are many and various examples, but they are all names for [the one reality of] the ten suchnesses and the conventional and real dharma. The Tathāgata penetrates deeply to reach the ends of the ten dharmas and exhausts the limits of the ten dharma [realms]. He clearly knows the potential, level of growth, maturity, and possibility for salvation of [all] sentient beings. This he knows according to their true state, and he is not mistaken. Aṅgulimāla was an evil person, but when he matured his true [good] aspects, he attained deliverance. Though monks who have attained the state of the fourth *dhyana* are good people, they will not sustain their deliverance if the evil aspect of their nature matures.

It should be known that the dharmas of sentient beings are beyond conceptual understanding. They are real yet tentative; tentative yet real. Their real and tentative aspects are mutually non-obstructing. It is not possible to perceive [the true reality of] sentient beings with the eyes of a bull or sheep. It is not possible to measure [the true reality of] sentient beings with the mind of an ignorant man. Wisdom like that of the Buddha is able to measure it. Why is this so? Because the dharma of sentient beings is subtle.

Source: "Threefold Truth" in *Foundations of T'ien-T'ai Philosophy: The Flowering of the Two Truths Theory in Chinese Buddhism,* translated by Paul L. Swanson (Berkeley: Asian Humanities Press, 1989), 176–184.

CHINESE PURE LAND SCHOOL

Selections from *Commentary to Vasubandhu's Essay on Rebirth* by T'an-Luan (476–542)

The reason that the [Amita] Buddha brings forth the pure merit of these adornments of his sphere is that He sees the phenomena of the three worlds as false, ceaselessly changing in a cycle, and without end, going round like a cankerworm, imprisoned like a silkworm in its own cocoon. Alas for the sentient beings, bound to these three worlds, perverse and impure! He wishes to put the beings in a place that is not false, not ceaselessly changing in a cycle, not without end, that they may find a great, pure place supremely happy. For this reason He brings forth the pure merit of these adornments. What is meant by "perfection?" The meaning is that this purity is incorruptible, that it is incontaminable. It is not like the phenomena of the three worlds, which are both contaminable and corruptible.

"Behold" means "observe." "Yon" means "that happy land." "The phenomena of yon sphere" means "the pure character of that happy sphere." . . . "It surpasses the paths of the three worlds." "Path" means "passageway." By such-and-such a cause one obtains such-and-such an effect. With such-and-such an effect one requites such-and-such a cause. Through the passageway of the cause one reaches the effect. Through the passageway of the effect one requites the cause. Hence "paths" . . . . These three worlds, in sum, are the dark house in which the common man, subject to life and death, drifts and goes in a cycle. Though pain and pleasure may differ slightly, though long and short may vary for a time, if one looks at these common men in their totality, there is none without defilement. Holding one another up, leaning on one another, they go in a cycle without end. . . . Now as cause, now as effect, vanity and falsehood succeed each to the other. But happiness is born of the bodhisattva's merciful right view, it is founded on the original vow of the Thus-Come-One's divine power. Those born of womb, eggs, and moisture, as a result of them rise above themselves; the long rope with which karma binds is, by them, forever cut. . . . "It surpasses the Three Worlds,"—truly these are words near to the understanding.

It is completely like the atmosphere,
Extensive and great and without limit.

These two verses refer to the perfection of the merit of the quantity of the adornments of this sphere. The reason that the Buddha brings forth this merit of the quantity of these adornments is that He sees the three worlds as narrow and small, in ruins and with gaping holes and bumps. Their shrines and temples are cramped, or their lands and fields are restricting. The road of ambition is short, or the mountains and rivers are insurmountable. Or else countries are divided by boundaries. Such are the various impediments there. For this reason the bodhisattva raised the prayer concerning the merit of the quantity of adornments: "I pray that my land may be like the atmosphere, extensive and great without limits." "Like the atmosphere" means that, though those who come to be reborn therein may be numerous, yet they shall be as if they were nought. "Extensive and great without limits" completes the above meaning of being like the atmosphere. Why like the atmosphere? Because it is extensive and great without limits. "Perfection" means that, though the beings of the ten directions that go to be reborn there, whether those already reborn, those now being reborn, or those going to be reborn are incalculable and unlimited, basically the place shall ever be like the atmosphere, extensive and great and without limits, never at any time full. Therefore he says, "It is completely like the atmosphere, extensive and without great limit."

Question: Vasubandhu . . . says: "All together with the sentient beings shall go to be reborn in the Happy Land." To which "beings" does this refer?

Answer: If we examine the *Scripture of the Buddha of Limitless Life,* preached at Rājagriha city, we see that the Buddha announced to Ānanda: "The Buddhas, the Thus-Come-Ones of the ten directions, as numerous as the sands of the Ganges, shall all together praise the incalculable awesome divinity and merit of the Buddha of Limitless Life. Then all of the beings that are, if, hearing his name, they shall with a believing heart rejoice for but a single moment of consciousness and with minds intent on being reborn in His land, shall be immediately enabled to go there and be reborn and stay there without return. There shall be excepted only those who commit the Five Violations and malign the True Law." From this we see that even the commonest of men may go thither to be reborn. . . .

Question: The Scripture of the Buddha of Limitless Life says: "Those who pray to go thither to be reborn can all go thither to be reborn. Only those who commit the Five Violations and malign the True Law are excepted." *The Scripture of the Con-*

templation of the Buddha of Limitless Life says: "They who perpetrate the Five Violations and the Ten Evils, indeed, they who do all manner of evil, may also go
thither to be reborn." How are these two scriptures to be reconciled?

Answer: The one scripture specifies two kinds of grave sin. One is the Five Violations, the other is the maligning of the True Law. By virtue of both of these two
kinds of grave sin one is unable to go thither to be reborn. The other scripture
merely speaks of perpetrating the sins of the Ten Evils and the Five Violations, but
says nothing of maligning the True Law. Since one does not malign the True Law,
therefore one is able to be reborn there.

Question: Even if a man is completely guilty of the Five Violations, as long as
he does not malign the True Law, the scripture allows that he can be reborn there.
On the other hand, if there is a man who merely maligns the True Law but is not
guilty of the sins of the Five Violations, if he prays to go thither to be reborn, can
he be reborn there or not?

Answer: If he merely maligns the True Law, though he might have no other
sins, he most certainly cannot be reborn there. Why do I say this? The scriptures
say: "Those guilty of the Five Violations descend into the midst of the Hell of
Uninterrupted Suffering and there suffer fully one cosmic period of grave punishment. Those who malign the True Law descend into the midst of the Hell of
Uninterrupted Suffering, and, when this period is exhausted, turn about and go
into the midst of another Hell of Uninterrupted Suffering. In this way they go
through hundreds and thousands of such hells." The Buddha records no time at
which they are able to leave, because the sin of maligning the True Law is
extremely grave. Also, the "True Law" is the Law of Buddha. Once these foolish
men have given expression to such calumny, how can they possibly pray for
rebirth in Buddha's Land? Even if they were to pray for rebirth there out of a sole
desire for the comforts and pleasures of that Land, it would still be like seeking
waterless ice or smokeless fire. How could there be any way of obtaining it?

But there are some who call upon His name and bear it in mind, but whose
ignorance persists and whose wishes remain unfulfilled. Why? Because they do not
practice truly, nor in keeping with His name and its meaning. What is meant by
"not practicing truly, nor in keeping with His name and its meaning?" The meaning is ignorance of the fact that the Thus-Come-One is the Body of True Character, the Body that acts for the sake of the beings. Also, "not in keeping" is of three
kinds. First is impure faith, since it seems to exist and yet seems not to exist. Second is the lack of unity of faith, since it is not firm. Third is the discontinuity of
faith, since it is interrupted by other thoughts.

How does one give rise to a prayerful heart? One always prays, with the whole heart single-mindedly thinking of being ultimately reborn in the Happy Land, because one wishes truly to practice *samatha* [concentration]. . . .

Śamatha is rendered *chih* [stop] in three senses. First, one thinks single mindedly of Amita Buddha and prays for rebirth in His Land. This Buddha's name and that Land's name can stop all evil. Second, that Happy Land exceeds the paths of the three worlds. If a man is born in that Land, he automatically puts an end to the evils of body, mouth, and mind. Third, Amita Buddha's power of enlightenment and persistent tenacity can naturally arrest the mind that seeks after lower stages of the Vehicle. These three kinds of *chih* arise from Buddha's real merit. Therefore it is said that "one wishes truly to practice *samatha* [concentration].

How does one observe? With wisdom one observes. With right mindfulness one observes Him, because one wishes truly to practice *vipaśyanā* [insight]. . . .

Vipaśyanā is translated *kuan* [insight] in two senses. First, while yet in this world, one conceives a thought and views the merit of the above-mentioned three kinds of adornments. This merit is real, hence the practitioner also gains real merit. "Real merit" is the ability to be reborn with certainty in that Land. Second, once one has achieved rebirth in that Pure Land one immediately sees Amita Buddha. The pure-hearted bodhisattvsva who has not yet fully perceived is now able to perceive fully the Law Body that is above differences and, together with the pure-hearted bodhisattvas and the bodhisattvas of the uppermost station, to attain fully to the same quiescent equality. Therefore it is said that "one wishes truly to practice *vipaśyanā*."

How does one apply [one's own merit] to and not reject all suffering beings? By ever making the vow to put such application first, in order to obtain a perfect heart of great compassion.

"Application" has two aspects. The first is the going aspect, the second is the returning aspect. What is the "going aspect?" One takes one's own merit and diverts it to all the beings, praying that all together may go to be reborn in Amita Buddha's Happy Land. What is the "returning aspect?" When one has already been reborn in that Land and attained to the perfection of concentration and insight, and the power of saving others through convenient means, one returns and enters the withered forest of life and death, and teaches all beings to turn together to the Path of the Buddha.

Source: "Commentary to Vasubandhu's Essay on Rebirth" in *Sources of Chinese Tradition*, edited by Wm. Theodore deBary et al. (New York: Columbia University Press, 1966), 376–380.

Selections from *Compendium on the Happy Land*
by Tao-ch'o (562–645)

The refutation of the misunderstanding of the characterlessness of the Great Vehicle consists of two parts. First is a summary statement of origination, the purpose of which is to enable scholars of later generations to understand right and wrong clearly, to depart from the crooked and face toward the straight. Second is a clarification of right, with reference to the attachments, and consequent refutation. . . .

Question: There are some persons who say that the Great Vehicle is characterless, that it takes no thought of "that" or "this." If one vows to be reborn in the Pure Land, then one is clinging to a characteristic, which ever increases one's impurities and fetters. Why should one seek after this?

Answer: If one reckons thus, it must be said not to be so. Why? The preaching of the Law by all the Buddhas must be accompanied by two conditions. Firstly, it must depend upon the true principles of the dharma-nature. Secondly, it must harmonize with the Twofold Truth. Some people claim that the Greater Vehicle, being free of any false conceptions, is based only on the Dharma-Nature, but they malign the Great Vehicle by saying that there is no condition on which to seek it. This does not harmonize with the Twofold Truth. One who views it in this way falls into the trap of the Emptiness which annihilates. . . .

Question: According to the holy doctrine of the Great Vehicle, if the bodhisattva evinces toward the beings a loving view or great compassion, he should immediately resist it. Now the bodhisattva encourages all beings to be reborn in the Pure Land. Is this not a combining with love, a grasping at character? Or does he escape defiling attachments [in spite of this]?

Answer: The efficacy of the dharmas practiced by the bodhisattva is of two kinds. Which are they? One is perception of the understanding of Emptiness and Perfect Wisdom. The second is full possession of great compassion. In the case of the former, by virtue of his practice of the understanding of Emptiness and Perfect Wisdom, though he may enter into the cycles of life and death of the six stages of existence, he is not fettered by their grime or contamination. In the case of the latter, by virtue of his compassionate mindfulness of the beings, he does not dwell in Nirvāna. The bodhisattva, though he dwells in the midst of the Twofold Truth, is ever able subtly to reject existence and nonexistence to strike the mean in his acceptances and rejections and not to run counter to the principles of the Great Way.

Refutation of the notion that there are no dharmas outside of the Mind consists of two parts. First is the refutation of the feelings that reckon thus; second is an interpretation in questions and answers.

Question: There are some who say: "The realm of purity which one contemplates is restricted to the inner mind. The Pure Land is all-pervasive; the mind, if pure, is identical with it. Outside of the Mind, there are no dharmas. What need is there to enter the West[ern Paradise]?"

Answer: Only the Pure Land of the dharma-nature dwells in principle in empty all-pervasion and is in substance unrestricted. This is the birth of no-birth, into which the superior gentlemen may enter. . . . There are the middle and lower classes [of bodhisattvas], who are not yet able to overcome the world of characters, and who must rely on the circumstance of faith in the Buddha to seek rebirth in the Pure Land. Though they reach that Land, they still dwell in a Land of characters. It is also said "If one envelops conditions and follows the origin, this is what is meant by 'no dharmas outside the Mind.' But if one distinguishes the Twofold Truth to clarify the doctrine, then the Pure Land does not conflict with the existence of dharmas outside the Mind." Now let us interpret through question and answer.

Question: A while ago, when you said that the "birth of no-birth" is something into which only superior gentlemen can enter, while the middle and inferior ones cannot, were you merely creating this interpretation by fitting the doctrine to the man, or is there also proof of this in the Sacred Doctrine?

Answer: According to the *Treatise of the Perfection of Wisdom:* "The bodhisattvas who have newly aroused their minds [to the ultimate goal of Buddhahood] are by receptivity and understanding soft and weak. Though one may say that they have aroused their minds, most of them vow to be reborn in the Pure Land. For what reason is this so? They are like a child which, if not close to the loving care of its father and mother, may descend into a pit, or fall into a well, or suffer calamity at the hands of fire or snake and the like, or may be deprived of milk and die, but which must rely on the care and nurture of its father and mother in order to grow and be able to carry on the heritage of the family. So also is the bodhisattva. If he can arouse his bodhi-mind, pray much for rebirth in the Pure Land, approach the Buddhas, and advance the dharma-body, only then can he properly carry on the household heritage of the bodhisattva and in all ten directions ferry the beings over. For the sake of this benefit, most of them vow for rebirth in the Pure Land."

Fourth is the refutation of the notion that one should vow to be reborn in this filthy land, not in that Pure Land.

Question: There are some who say that one vows to be reborn in this filthy land in order to convert the beings by one's teaching, and that one does not vow to go to the Pure Land to be reborn. How is this?

Answer: Of such persons also there is a certain group. Why? If the body resides in [an estate from which there is] no backsliding, or beyond, in order to convert the sundry evil beings it may dwell in contamination without becoming contaminated or encounter evil without being transformed, just as the swan and the duck may enter the water but the water cannot wet them. Such persons as these can dwell in filth and extricate the beings from their suffering. But if the person is in truth an ordinary man, I only fear that his own conduct is not yet established, and that if he encounters suffering he will immediately change. He who wishes to save him will perish together with him. For example, if one forces a chicken into the water, how can one not get wet?

Fifth is the refutation of the proposition that those who are reborn in the Pure Land mostly take pleasure in clinging to enjoyment.

Question: There are some who say: "Within the Pure Land there are only enjoyable things. Much pleasure in clinging to enjoyment hinders and destroys the practice of the Way. Why should one vow to go thither and be reborn?"

Answer: Since it is called "Pure Land," it means that there are no impurities in it. If one speaks of "clinging to enjoyment," this refers to lust and the afflictions. If so, why call it pure?

Question: The scriptures of the Great Vehicle say that the way of karma is like a scale, the heavier side showing its influence first. How can beings who throughout their lives until this day, whether for a hundred years or for ten, have practiced all evils, how can they, when they approach their end, meet a benevolent person and after ten uninterrupted moments of thought [of the Buddha, etc.] be enabled to go thither to be reborn? If this is so, how can one believe what is said about the heavier side showing its influence first?

Answer: You say that the evil karma of one lifetime is heavy, while you suppose the good of ten moments of thought in the life of an inferior man to be light. Let us now compare their relative lightness and heaviness on the basis of principle precisely to make dear that what matters lies in the mind, in the conditions and one's determination, and not in the distance or length of time involved. In what sense is it in the mind? By that we mean that when such a man commits a sin the sin is born from a vain and perverse mind, while these ten moments of thought are born from hearing the dharma of real character from a benevolent man who by resorting to expedient means comforts him. In the one case it is reality, and in the other it is vanity. How can they be equated? Why do we say this? Suppose a room has been dark for a thousand years. If light enters it for but a moment, it will be clear and bright. How could one say that the darkness, having been in the room for a thousand years, cannot be eliminated? . . . This is what is meant by "in the mind." Secondly, in, what sense do we mean "in conditions"? We mean that when that man commits sin, his sin is born from false notions, from among beings who suffer the retribution of the afflictions. But now these ten moments of thought are born out of a mind of supreme faith, out of the name of Amita the Thus-Come-One, a true and pure name of infinite merits. It is as if a man were to be struck by a poisoned arrow, which pierced his sinews and broke his bone, and were immediately to have the arrow removed and the poison cleared away by the mere act of hearing the sound of a drum advertising a remedy. How could one say that, though the arrow was deep and the poison dangerous, he was not able, as soon as he heard the sound of the drum, to pull out the arrow and clear away the poison? This is what is meant by "in conditions." Thirdly, in what sense do we mean "one's determination"? When that man commits sin, the sin is born from a mind that fears consequences and has interruptions, while these ten moments of thought arise from a mind that has neither consequences nor interruptions. This is what is meant by "determination."

Question: If I wish now to practice diligently the concentration of the mindfulness of the Buddha, I do not know what the character and form of this mindfulness look like.

Answer: Suppose a man in an empty and distant place encounters a bandit who, drawing his sword, comes forcefully and directly to kill him. This man runs straight on, looking ahead to cross a river. But before reaching the river he would have the following thoughts: "When I reach the river bank, shall I take off my clothes and cross or wear them and float? To take them off and cross I fear there may not be time. If I wear them and float, then I fear that my life will not be saved." At such a time he has only the single thought of a means to cross the river, and no other thoughts would be mingled with it. So also is the practitioner. When he is contemplating Amita Buddha, he is like the man contemplating the crossing. The thought is continuous, no others being mingled with it. He may contemplate the Buddha's Dharma-Body, or he may contemplate the Buddha's supernatural might, or he may contemplate the Buddha's wisdom, or he may contemplate the Buddha's hair-mark, or he may contemplate the goodness of the Buddha's character, or he may contemplate the Buddha's original vow. In the same way he may recite the name of the Buddha. If one is able to concentrate on it wholeheartedly, continuously and without interruption, one will certainly be reborn in the Buddha's presence.

Question: The Scripture of the Buddha of Limitless Life says: "If the beings of the ten directions shall with intense belief and desire for as much as ten moments wish to be reborn in my Land, and if then they should not be reborn there, may I never attain enlightenment." Now there are men in the world who hear this holy teaching and who in their present life never arouse their minds to it, but wait until the end approaches and then wish to practice such contemplation. What do you say of such cases?

Answer: Such cases are not true. Why? The scriptures say: "Ten continuous moments may seem not to be difficult. However, the minds of ordinary men are like a zephyr, their consciousness is more capricious than a monkey's. It runs through the six objects of sensual perception without rest." Everyone should arouse his faith and first conquer his own thoughts, so that through the accumulated practice it will become his nature and the roots of goodness become firm. As the Buddha proclaimed to the great king, if men accumulate good conduct, at death they will have no evil thoughts, just as, when a tree is first bent in a certain direction, when it falls it will follow that bent. Once the sword and the wind arrive, and a hundred woes concentrate upon the body, if the practice is not there to begin with, how can contemplation be consummated? Everyone should form a bond with three or five comrades to enlighten one another. When life's end faces them, they should enlighten one another, recite Amita Buddha's name to one another, and pray for rebirth in Paradise in such a way that voice succeeds upon voice until the ten moments of thought are completed. It is as, when a wax seal has been impressed in clay, after the wax has been destroyed, the imprint remains. When this life is cut off, one is reborn immediately in the Comfortable and Pleasant Land. At the time one enters completely into the cluster of right contemplation. What more is there to worry about? Everyone should weigh this great blessing. Why should one not conquer one's own thoughts ahead of time?

Source: "Compendium on the Happy Land" in *Sources of Chinese Tradition*, edited by Wm. Theodore deBary et al. (New York: Columbia University Press, 1966), 381–386.

CH'AN SCHOOL

Selections from *The Platform Sutra of the Sixth Patriarch*

2. The Master Hui-neng said: "Good friends, your minds and concentrate on the Dharma of the Great Perfection of Wisdom."

The Master stopped speaking and quieted his own mind. Then after a good while he said: "Good friends, listen quietly. My father was originally an official at Fan-yang. He was [later] dismissed from his post and banished as a commoner to Hsin-chou in Ling-nan. While I was still a child, my father died and my old mother and I, a solitary child, moved to Nan-hai. We suffered extreme poverty and here I sold firewood in the market place. By chance a certain man bought some firewood and then took me with him to the lodging house for officials. He took the firewood and left. Having received my money and turning towards the front gate, I happened to see another man who was reciting the Diamond Sutra. Upon hearing it my mind became clear and I was awakened.

"I asked him: 'Where do you come from that you have brought this sutra with you?'

"He answered: 'I have made obeisance to the Fifth Patriarch, Hung-jen, at the East Mountain, Feng-mu shan, in Huang-mei hsien in Ch'i-chou. At present there are over a thousand disciples there. While I was there I heard the Master encourage the monks and lay followers, saying that if they recited just the one volume, the Diamond Sutra, they could see into their own natures and with direct apprehension become Buddhas.'

"Hearing what he said, I realized that I was predestined to have heard him. Then I took leave of my mother and went to Feng-mu shan in Huang-mei and made obeisance to the Fifth Patriarch, the priest Hung-jen.

3. "The priest Hung-jen asked me: 'Where are you from that you come to this mountain to make obeisance to me? Just what is it that you are looking for from me?'

"I replied: 'I am from Ling-nan, a commoner from Hsin-chou. I have come this long distance only to make obeisance to you. I am seeking no particular thing, but only the Buddhadharma.'

"The Master then reproved me, saying: 'If you're from Ling-nan then you're a barbarian; How can you become a Buddha?'

"I replied: 'Although people from the south and people from the north differ, there is no north and south in Buddha nature. Although my barbarian's body and your body are not the same, what difference is there in our Buddha nature?'

"The Master wished to continue his discussion with me; however, seeing that there were other people nearby, he said no more. Then he sent me to work with the assembly. Later a lay disciple had me go to the threshing room where I spent over eight months treading the pestle.

4. "Unexpectedly one day the Fifth Patriarch called his disciples to come, and when they had assembled, he said: 'Let me preach to you. For people in this world birth and death are vital matters. You disciples make offerings all day long and seek only the field of blessings, but you do not seek to escape from the bitter sea of birth and death. Your own self-nature obscures the gateway to blessings; how can you be saved? All of you return to your rooms and look into yourselves. Men of wisdom will of themselves grasp the original nature of their prajñā intuition. Each of you write a verse and bring it to me. I will read your verses, and if there is one who is awakened to the cardinal meaning, I will give him the robe and the Dharma and make him the Sixth Patriarch. Hurry, hurry!'

5. "The disciples received his instructions and returned, each to his own room. They talked it over among themselves, saying: 'There's no point in our purifying our minds and making efforts to compose a verse to present to the priest. Shen-hsiu, the head monk, is our teacher. After he obtains the Dharma we can rely on him, so let's not compose verses.' They all then gave up trying and did not have the courage to present a verse.

"At that time there was a three-sectioned corridor in front of the Master's hall. On the walls were to be painted pictures of stories from the Laṅkāvatāra Sutra, together with a picture in commemoration of the Fifth Patriarch transmitting the robe and Dharma, in order to disseminate them to later generations and preserve a record of them. The artist, Lu Chen, had examined the walls and was to start work the next day.

6. "The head monk Shen-hsiu thought: 'The others won't present mind-verses because I am their teacher. If I don't offer a mind-verse, how can the Fifth Patriarch estimate the degree of understanding within my mind? If I offer my mind to the Fifth Patriarch with the intention of gaining the Dharma, it is justifiable; however, if I am seeking the patriarchship, then it cannot be justified. Then it would be like a common man usurping the saintly position. But if I don't offer my mind then I cannot learn the Dharma.' For a long time he thought about it and was very much perplexed.

"At midnight, without letting anyone see him, he went to write his mind-verse on the central section of the south corridor wall, hoping to gain the Dharma. 'If the Fifth Patriarch sees my verse and says that it . . . and there is a weighty obstacle in my past karma, then I cannot gain the Dharma and shall have to give up. The honorable Patriarch's intention is difficult to fathom.'

"Then the head monk Shen-hsiu, at midnight, holding a candle, wrote a verse on the central section of the south corridor, without anyone else knowing about it. The verse read:

> The body is the Bodhi tree,
> The mind is like a clear mirror.
> At all times we must strive to polish it,
> And must not let the dust collect.

7. "After he had finished writing this verse, the head monk Shen-hsiu returned to his room and lay down. No one had seen him.

"At dawn the Fifth Patriarch called the painter Lu to draw illustrations from the Lankāvatāra Sutra on the south corridor wall. The Fifth Patriarch suddenly saw this verse and, having read it, said to the painter Lu: 'I will give you thirty thousand cash. You have come a long distance to do this arduous work, but I have decided not to have the pictures painted after all. It is said in the Diamond Sutra: "All forms everywhere are unreal and false." It would be best to leave this verse here and to have the deluded ones recite it. If they practice in accordance with it they will not fall into the three evil ways. Those who practice by it will gain great benefit.'

"The Master then called all his disciples to come, and burned incense before the verse. The disciples came in to see and all were filled with admiration.

"The Fifth Patriarch said: 'You should all recite this verse so that you will be able to see into your own natures. With this practice you will not fall into the three evil ways.'

"The disciples all recited it, and feeling great admiration, cried out: 'How excellent!'

"The Fifth Patriarch then called the head monk Shen-hsiu inside the hall and asked: 'Did you write this verse or not? If you wrote it you are qualified to attain my Dharma.'

"The head monk Shen-hsiu said: 'I am ashamed to say that I actually did write the verse, but I do not dare to seek the patriarchship. I beg you to be so compassionate as to tell me whether I have even a small amount of wisdom and discernment of the cardinal meaning or not.'

"The Fifth Patriarch said: 'This verse you wrote shows that you still have not reached true understanding. You have merely arrived at the front of the gate but have yet to be able to enter it. If common people practice according to your verse they will not fall. But in seeking the ultimate enlightenment (*bodhi*) one will not succeed with such an understanding. You must enter the gate and see your own original nature. Go and think about it for a day or two and then make another verse and present it to me. If you have been able to enter the gate and see your own original nature, then I will give you the robe and the Dharma.' The head monk Shen-hsiu left, but after several days he was still unable to write a verse.

8. "One day an acolyte passed by the threshing room reciting this verse. As soon as I heard it I knew that the person who had written it had yet to know his own nature and to discern the cardinal meaning. I asked the boy: 'What's the name of the verse you were reciting just now?"

"The boy answered me, saying: 'Don't you know? The Master said that birth and death are vital matters, and he told his disciples each to write a verse if they wanted to inherit the robe and the Dharma, and to bring it for him to see. He who was awakened to the cardinal meaning would be given the robe and the Dharma and be made the Sixth Patriarch. There is a head monk by the name of Shen-hsiu who happened to write a verse on formlessness on the walls of the south corridor. The Fifth Patriarch had all his disciples recite the verse, [saying] that those who awakened to it would see into their own self-natures, and that those who practiced according to it would attain emancipation.'

"I said: 'I've been treading the pestle for more than eight months, but haven't been to the hall yet. I beg you to take me to the south corridor so that I can see this verse and make obeisance to it. I also want to recite it so that I can establish causation for my next birth and be born in a Buddha-land.'

"The boy took me to the south corridor and I made obeisance before the verse. Because I was uneducated I asked someone to read it to me. As soon as I had heard it I understood the cardinal meaning. I made a verse and asked someone who was able to write to put it on the wall of the west corridor, so that I might offer my own original mind. If you do not know the original mind, studying the Dharma is to no avail. If you know the mind and see its true nature, you then awaken to the cardinal meaning. My verse said:

> Bodhi originally has no tree,
> The mirror also has no stand.
> Buddha nature is always clean and pure;
> Where is there room for dust?

"Another verse said:

The mind is the Bodhi tree,
The body is the mirror stand.
The mirror is originally clean and pure;
Where can it be stained by dust?

"The followers in the temple were all amazed when they heard my verse. Then I returned to the threshing room. The Fifth Patriarch realized that I had a splendid understanding of the cardinal meaning. Being afraid lest the assembly know this, he said to them: 'This is still not complete understanding.'

9. "At midnight the Fifth Patriarch called me into the hall and expounded the Diamond Sutra to me. Hearing it but once, I was immediately awakened, and that night I received the Dharma. None of the others knew anything about it. Then he transmitted to me the Dharma of Sudden Enlightenment and the robe, saying: 'I make you the Sixth Patriarch. The robe is the proof and is to be handed down from generation to generation. My Dharma must be transmitted from mind to mind. You must make people awaken, to themselves.'

"The Fifth Patriarch told me: 'From ancient times the transmission of the Dharma has been as tenuous as a dangling thread. If you stay here there are people who will harm you. You must leave at once.'

10. "I set out at midnight with the robe and the Dharma. The Fifth Patriarch saw me off as far as Chiu-chiang Station. I was instantly enlightened. The Fifth Patriarch instructed me: 'Leave, work hard, take the Dharma with you to the south. For three years do not spread the teaching or else calamity will befall the Dharma. Later work to convert people; you must guide deluded persons well. If you are able to awaken another's mind, he will be no different from me.' After completing my leave-taking I set out for the south.

11. "After about two months I reached Ta-yü ling. Unknown to me, several hundred men were following behind, wishing to try to kill me and to steal my robe and Dharma. By the time I had gone halfway up the mountain they had all turned back. But there was one monk of the family name of Chen, whose personal name was Hui-ming. Formerly he had been a general of the third rank and he was by nature and conduct coarse and violent. Reaching the top of the mountain, he caught up with me and threatened me. I handed over the dharma-robe, but he was not willing to take it.

"[He said]: 'I have come this long distance just to seek the Dharma I have no need for the robe.' Then, on top of the mountain, I transmitted the Dharma to Hui-ming, who when he heard it, was at once enlightened. I then ordered him to return to the north and to convert people there.

12. "I was predestined to come to live here and to preach to you officials, monks, and laymen. My teaching been handed down from the sages of the past; it is not my own personal knowledge. If you wish to hear the teachings of the sages of the past, each of you must quiet his mind and hear me to the end. Please cast aside your own delusions; then you will be no different from the sages of the past." (What follows below is the Dharma).

The Master Hui-neng called, saying: "Good friends, enlightenment (*bodhi*) and intuitive wisdom (*prajñā*) are from the outset possessed by men of this world themselves. It is just because the mind is deluded that men cannot attain awakening to themselves. They must seek a good teacher to show them how to see into their own natures. Good friends, if you meet awakening, [Buddha]-wisdom will be achieved.

13. "Good friends, my teaching of the Dharma takes meditation (*ting*) and wisdom (*hui*) as its basis. Never under any circumstances say mistakenly that meditation and wisdom are different; they are a unity, not two things. Meditation itself is the substance of wisdom, wisdom itself is the function of meditation. At the very moment when there is wisdom, then meditation exists in wisdom; at the very moment when there is meditation, then wisdom exists in meditation. Good friends, this means that meditation and wisdom are alike. Students, be careful not to say that meditation gives rise to wisdom, or that wisdom gives rise to meditation, or that meditation and wisdom are different from each other. To hold this view implies that things have duality—if good is spoken while the mind is not good, meditation and wisdom will not be alike. If mind and speech are both good, then the internal and the external are the same and notation and wisdom are alike. The practice of self-awakening does not lie in verbal arguments. If you argue which comes first, meditation or wisdom, you are deluded people You won't be able to settle the argument and instead will cling to objective things, and will never escape from the states of phenomena.

14. "The *samādhi* of oneness is straightforward mind at all times, walking, staying, sitting, and lying. The *Ching-ming ching* says: 'Straightforward mind is the

place of practice; straightforward mind is the Pure Land.' Do not with a dishonest mind speak of the straightforwardness of the Dharma. If while speaking of the *samādhi* of oneness, you fail to practice straightforward mind, you will not be disciples of the Buddha. Only practicing straightforward mind, and in all things having no attachments whatsoever, is called the *samādhi* of oneness. The deluded man clings to the characteristics of things, adheres to the *samādhi* of oneness, [thinks] that straightforward mind is sitting without moving and casting aside delusions without letting things arise in the mind. This he considers to be the *samādhi* of oneness. This kind of practice is the same as insentiency and the cause of an obstruction to the Tao. Tao must be something that circulates freely; why should he impede it? If the mind does not abide in things the Tao circulates freely; if the mind abides in things, it becomes entangled. If sitting in meditation without moving is good, why did Vimalakīrti scold Śāriputra for sitting in meditation in the forest?

"Good friends, some people teach men to sit viewing the mind and viewing purity, not moving and not activating the mind, and to this they devote their efforts. Deluded people do not realize that this is wrong, cling to this doctrine, and become confused. There are many such people. Those who instruct in this way are, from the outset, greatly mistaken.

15. "Good friends, how then are meditation and wisdom alike? They are like the lamp and the light it gives forth. If there is a lamp there is light; if there is no lamp there is no light. The lamp is the substance of light; the light is the function of the lamp. Thus, although they have two names, in substance they are not two. Meditation and wisdom are also like this.

16. "Good friends, in the Dharma there is no sudden or gradual, but among people some are keen and others dull. The deluded recommend the gradual method, the enlightened practice the sudden teaching. To understand the original mind of yourself is to see into your own original nature. Once enlightened, there is from the outset no distinction between these two methods; those who are not enlightened will for long kalpas be caught in the cycle of transmigration.

17. "Good friends, in this teaching of mine, from ancient times up to the present, all have set up no-thought as the main doctrine, non-form as the substance, and non-abiding as the basis. Non-form is to be separated from form even when associated with form. No-thought is not to think even when involved in thought. Non-abiding is the original nature of man.

"Successive thoughts do not stop; prior thoughts, present thoughts, and future thoughts follow one after the other without cessation. If one instant of thought is cut off, the Dharma body separates from the physical body, and in the midst of successive thoughts there will be no place for attachment to anything. If one instant of thought clings, then successive thoughts cling; this is known as being fettered. If in all things successive thoughts do not cling, then you are unfettered. Therefore, non-abidings is made the basis.

"Good friends, being outwardly separated from all forms, this is non-form. When you are separated from form, the substance of your nature is pure. Therefore, non-form is made the substance.

"To be unstained in all environments is called no-thought. If on the basis of your own thoughts you separate from environment, then, in regard to things, thoughts are not produced. If you stop thinking of the myriad things, and cast aside all thoughts, as soon as one instant of thought is cut off, you will be reborn in another realm. Students, take care! Don't rest in objective things and the subjective mind. [If you do so] it will be bad enough that you yourself are in error, yet how much worse that you encourage others in their mistakes. The deluded man, however, does not himself see and slanders the teachings of the sutras. Therefore, no-thought is established as a doctrine. Because man in his delusion has thoughts in relation to his environment, heterodox ideas stemming from these thoughts arise, and passions and false views are produced from them. Therefore this teaching has established no-thought as a doctrine.

"Men of the world, separate yourselves from views; do not activate thoughts. If there were no thinking, then no-thought would have no place, to exist. 'No' is the 'no' of what? 'Thought' means 'thinking' of what? 'No' is the separation from the dualism that produces the passions. 'Thought' means thinking of the original nature of True Reality. True Reality is the substance of thoughts; thoughts are the function of True Reality. If you give rise to thoughts from your self-nature, then, although you see, hear, perceive, and know, you are not stained by the manifold environments, and are always free. The Vimalakīrti Sutra says: 'Externally, while distinguishing well all the forms of the various dharmas, internally he stands firm within the First Principle.'

18. "Good friends, in this teaching from the outset sitting in meditation does not concern the mind nor does it concern purity; we do not talk of steadfastness. If someone speaks of 'viewing the mind,' [then I would say] that the 'mind' is of itself delusion, and as delusions are just like fantasies, there is nothing to be seen.

If someone speaks of 'viewing purity,' [then I would say] that man's nature is of itself pure, but because of false thoughts True Reality is obscured. If you exclude delusions then the original nature reveals its purity. If you activate your mind to view purity without realizing that your own nature is originally pure, delusions of purity will be produced. Since this delusion has no place to exist, then you know that whatever you see is nothing but delusion. Purity has no form, but, nonetheless, some people try to postulate the form of purity and consider this to be Ch'an practice." . . .

26. "What is *prajñā*? *Prajñā* is wisdom (*chih-hui*). When at all times successive thoughts contain no ignorance, and you always practice wisdom, this is known as the practice of *prajñā*. If but one instant of thought contains ignorance, then *prajñā* is cut off; but if one instant of thought contains wisdom, then *prajñā* is produced. Within the mind there is always ignorance. [People] themselves say: 'I practice *prajñā*,' but it has neither shape nor form. This, then, is the nature of wisdom.

"What is *po-lo-mi-to* (*pāramitā*)? This is the Indian Sanskrit pronunciation and means 'other-shore-reached.' When its meaning is understood you are apart from birth and destruction. When you are attached to environment, birth and destruction arise. Take waves rising on the water—they are something that occurs on 'this' shore. Being apart from environment and putting an end to birth and destruction is like going along with the flow of the water. Thus it is called 'reaching the other shore,' in other words, *pāramitā*. The deluded person recites it; the wise man practices with the mind. If you have delusion [in your mind] when you recite it, the very existence of this delusion is not a true existence. If in successive thoughts you practice it, this is called true existence. Those who awaken to this Dharma have awakened to the Dharma of *prajñā* and are practicing the *prajñā* practice. If you do not practice it you are an ordinary person; if you practice for one instant of thought, your Dharma body will be the same as the Buddha's. Good friends, the very passions are themselves enlightenment (*bodhi*). When past thoughts are deluded, this is the common man; when future thoughts are awakened to, this is Buddha.

"Good friends, the *Mahāprajñāpāramitā* is the most honored, the supreme, the foremost. It does not stay, it does not leave, nor does it come, and all the Buddhas of the three worlds issue from it. With great wisdom it leads to the other shore and destroys the passions and the troubles of the five skandhas. Since it is the most honored, the supreme, the foremost, if you praise the supreme Dharma and practice according to it, you will certainly become Buddha. Not leaving, not staying, not going or coming, with the identity of wisdom and meditation, and unstained in all things, the various Buddhas of the three worlds issue forth from it, and change the three poisons into discipline, meditation, and wisdom.

27. "Good friends, this teaching of mine [derives] from the eighty-four thousand wisdoms. Why is this so? Because there are eighty-four thousand passions in this world. If the passions are done away with, *prajñā* is always there, and is not apart from your own nature. If you awaken to this Dharma you will have no thoughts, no recollections, no attachments. Do not depart from deceptions and errors; for they of themselves are the nature of True Reality. When all things are illumined by wisdom and there is neither grasping nor throwing away, then you can see into your own nature and gain the Buddha Way.

28. "Good friends, it you wish to enter the most profound Dharma realm of the *prajñā samādhi*, you must straightforwardly practice the *prajñāpāramitā*. With only the one volume of the Diamond Sutra you may see into your own natures and enter into the *prajñā samādhi*. You will surely understand that the merit of such a person is without bounds. In the sutras it is clearly praised and there is no need for me to elaborate. It is the Dharma of the Supreme Way that is expounded for men of great wisdom and high capacities. Should a man of small capability for knowledge hear this Dharma, faith would not be produced in his mind. Why is this so? Should a great dragon deluge the earth (Jambūdvīpa) with a great rain, [then cities, towns, and villages would all be washed away] like floating grass and leaves. But should this great rain fall in the great ocean, its waters would neither increase nor lessen.

"Should a person of the Mahāyāna hear the Diamond Sutra, his mind will open and he will gain awakening. Therefore we can say that in the original nature itself the wisdom of *prajñā* exists, and that by using this wisdom yourself and illuminating with it, there is no need to depend on written words. It is as though the rain waters did not come from heaven, but from the beginning the dragon king draws up the water from the rivers and seas and covers all beings, trees and grasses, things sentient and nonsentient, with its wetness. All these waters flow together and enter into the great sea, and the sea gathers them together and combines them into one. So it is with the *prajñā* wisdom of the original natures of sentient beings.

29. "When people of shallow capacity hear the Sudden Doctrine being preached they are like the naturally shallow-rooted plants on this earth, which, after a deluge of rain, are all beaten down and cannot continue their growth. People of shallow capacity are like such plants. Although these people have *prajñā* wisdom and are not different from men of great knowledge, why is it that even though they hear the Dharma they are not awakened? It is because the obstructions of their heterodox views are heavy and the passions deep-rooted. It is like the times when great clouds cover the sun; unless the wind blows the sun will not appear. There is no large and small in *prajñā* wisdom. Because all sentient beings have of themselves deluded minds, they seek the Buddha by external practice, and are unable to awaken to their own natures. But even these people of shallow capacity, if they hear the Sudden Doctrine, and do not place their trust in external practices, but only in their own minds always raise correct views in regard to their own original natures; even these sentient beings, filled with passions and troubles, will at once gain awakening. It is like the great sea which gathers all the flowing streams, and merges together the small waters and the large waters into one. This is seeing into your own nature. [Such a person] does not abide either inside or outside; he is free to come or go. Readily he casts aside the mind that clings [to things], and there is no obstruction to his passage. If in the mind this practice is carried out, then [your own nature] is no different from the *prajñā-pāramitā.*

If you know your original mind, this then is deliverance. Once you have attained deliverance this then is the *prajñā samādhi.* If you have awakened to the *prajñā samādhi,* this then is no-thought. What is no-thought? The Dharma of no-thought means: even though you see all things, you do not attach to them, but, always keeping your own nature pure, cause the six thieves exit through the six gates. Even though you are in the midst of the six dusts, you do not stand apart from them, yet are not stained by them, and are free to come and go. This is the *prajñā samādhi,* and being free and having achieved release is known as the practice of no-thought. If you do not think of the myriad things, but always cause your thoughts to be cut off, you will be bound in the Dharma. This is known as a biased view. If you awaken to the Dharma of no-thought, you will penetrate into all things thoroughly, and will see the realm of the Buddha. If you awaken to the sudden doctrine of no-thought, you will have reached the status of the Buddha." . . .

48. The Master passed away on the third day of the eighth month of the second year of Hsien-t'ien (=August 28, 713). On the eighth day of the seventh month

he called his disciples together and bade them farewell. In the first year of Hsien-t'ien the Master had constructed a pagoda at the Kuo-en Temple in Hsin-chou, and now in the seventh month of the second year of Hsien-t'ien he was taking his leave.

The Master said: "Come close. In the eighth month I intend to leave this world. If any of you have doubts, ask about them quickly, and I shall resolve them for you. I must bring your delusions to an end and make it possible for you to gain peace. After I have gone there will be no one to teach you."

Fa-hai and the other monks heard him to the end and wept tears of sorrow. Only Shen-hui was not impressed, nor did he weep. The Sixth Patriarch said: "Shen-hui, you are a young monk, yet you have attained the [status of awakening] in which good and not good are identical, and you are not moved by judgments of praise and blame. You others have not yet understood: what have you been practicing at this temple these several years? You're crying now, but who is there who's really worried that I don't know the place to which I'm going? If I didn't know where I was going then I wouldn't be leaving you. You're crying just because you don't know where I'm going. If you knew where I was going you wouldn't be crying. The nature itself is without birth and without destruction, without going and without coming." . . .

54. On the day the Master died a strange fragrance, which did not fade for several days, filled the temple. Mountains crumbled, the earth trembled, and the forest trees turned white. The sun and moon ceased to shine and the wind and clouds lost their colors.

He died on the third day of the eighth month, and in the eleventh month his sacred coffin was received and interred on Mount Ts'ao ch'i. From within his resting place a bright light appeared and rose straight toward the heavens, and two days passed before it finally dispersed. The prefect of Shao-chou, Wei Ch'ü, erected a memorial stone, and to this day offerings have been made before it. . . .

Source: *The Platform Sutra of the Sixth Patriarch,* translated by Philip B. Yampolsky (New York: Columbia University Press, 1967), 126–140, 174, 153, 182.

Selections from the Ch'an Teachings of Master Lin-chi

The Master one day had occasion to go to the Ho-pei prefectural office. Constant Attendant Wang, head of the prefecture, requested the Master to step up to the lecture seat.

At that time Ma-yü came forward and asked, "Of the eyes of the thousand-armed thousand-eyed bodhisattva of great compassion, which is the true eye?"

The Master said, "Of the eyes of the thousand-armed thousand-eyed bodhisattva of great compassion, which is the true eye? Answer me! Answer me!"

Ma-yü dragged the Master down from the lecture seat and sat in it himself.

The Master went up close to him and said, "How are you?"

Ma-yü was about to say something when the Master dragged him down from the seat and sat in it himself.

Ma-yü thereupon walked out of the gathering, and the Master stepped down from the lecture seat.

The Master ascended the hall and said, "Here in this lump of red flesh there is a True Man with no rank. Constantly he goes in and out the gates of your face. If there are any of you who don't know this for a fact, then look! Look!"

At that time there was a monk who came forward and asked, "What is he like—the True Man with no rank?"

The Master got down from his chair, seized hold of the monk and said, "Speak! Speak!"

The monk was about to say something, whereupon the Master let go of him, shoved him away, and said, "True Man with no rank—what a shitty ass-wiper!"

The Master then returned to his quarters.

The Master ascended the hall. A monk came forward and made a deep bow. The Master gave a shout.

The monk said, "Old Reverend, it would be well if you didn't try to spy on people!"

The Master said, "Then tell me, where have you gotten to?"

The monk immediately gave a shout.

Another monk asked, "What is the basic meaning of Buddhism?"

The Master gave a shout.

The monk bowed low.

The Master said, "Do you think that was a shout of approval?"

The monk said, "The countryside thieves have been thoroughly trounced!"

The Master said, "What was their fault?"

The monk said, "A second offense is not permitted!"

The Master gave a shout.

The same day the head monks of the two parts of the meditation hall caught sight of each other and simultaneously gave a shout.

A monk asked the Master, "In this case, was there any guest and any host, or wasn't there?"

The Master said, "Guest and host are perfectly obvious!" Then the Master said, "All of you—if you want to understand what I have just said about guest and host, go ask the two head monks of the meditation hall."

With that he stepped down from the lecture seat.

The Master ascended the hall. A monk asked, "What is the basic meaning of Buddhism?"

The Master held his fly whisk straight up.

The monk gave a shout.

The Master struck him.

Another monk asked, "What is the basic meaning of Buddhism?"

Again the Master held his fly whisk straight up.

The monk gave a shout.

The Master also gave a shout.

The monk was about to say something, whereupon the Master hit him.

The Master said, "All of you—if it's for the sake of the Dharma, don't hesitate to sacrifice your bodies or give up your lives! Twenty years ago, when I was at Huang-po's place, I asked three times what was clearly and obviously the real point of Buddhism, and three times he was good enough to hit me with his stick. It was as though he had brushed me with a sprig of mugwort. Thinking of it now, I wish I could get hit once more like that. Is there anyone who can give me such a blow?"

At that time a monk stepped forward from the group and said, "I'll give you one!"

The Master picked up his stick and handed it to the monk. The monk was about to take it, whereupon the Master struck him. . . .

The Master instructed the group, saying: "Followers of the Way, what is important is to approach things with a true and proper understanding. Walk wherever you please in the world but don't let yourselves be muddled or misled by that bunch of goblin spirits. The man of value is the one who has nothing to do. Don't try to do something special, just act ordinary. You look outside yourselves, going off on side roads hunting for something, trying to get your hands on something. That's a mistake. You keep trying to look for the Buddha, but *Buddha* is just a name, a word.

"Do you know what it is that everyone is rushing around looking for? All the buddhas and patriarchs of the three existences of past, present, and future and in all the ten directions make their appearance in this world just so they can seek the Dharma. And you followers of the Way who have come to study, you are here now just so you can seek the Dharma. Once you get the Dharma, that will settle things, but until you do, you will go on as before being reborn again and again in the five paths.

"What is this thing called Dharma? Dharma is the Dharma, or Truth, of the mind. The Dharma of the mind has no fixed form; it penetrates all the ten directions. It is in operation right before our eyes. But because people don't have enough faith, they cling to words, cling to phrases. They try to find the Dharma of the buddhas by looking in written words, but they're as far away from it as heaven is from earth.

"Followers of the Way, when I preach the Dharma, what Dharma do I preach? I preach the Dharma of the mind. So it can enter into the common mortal or the sage, the pure or the filthy, the sacred or the secular. But you who are sacred or secular, common mortals or sages, can't start fixing names or labels to all the others who are sacred or secular, common mortals or sages. And those sacred or secular, common mortals or sages can't fix a name or label to a person like this. Followers of the Way, get hold of this thing and use it, but don't fix a label to it. This is what I call the Dark Meaning.

"My preaching of the Dharma is different from that of other people in the world. Even if Manjushri and Samantabhadra were to appear here before my eyes, each manifesting his bodily form and asking about the Dharma, they would no sooner have said, 'We wish to question the Master,' than I'd have seen right through them.

"I sit calmly in my seat, and when followers of the Way come for an interview, I see through them all. How do I do this? Because my way of looking at them is different. I don't worry whether on the outside they are common mortals or sages, or get bogged down in the kind of basic nature they have inside. I just see all the way through them and never make an error."

The Master instructed the group, saying: "Followers of the Way, the Dharma of the buddhas calls for no special undertakings. Just act ordinary, without trying to do anything particular. Move your bowels, piss, get dressed, eat your rice, and if you get tired, then lie down. Fools may laugh at me, but wise men will know what I mean.

"A man of old said, 'People who try to do something about what is outside themselves are nothing but blockheads.' If, wherever you are, you take the role of host, then whatever spot you stand in will be a true one. Then whatever circumstances surround you, they can never pull you awry. Even if you're faced with bad karma left over from the past, or the five crimes that bring on the hell of incessant suffering, these will of themselves become the great sea of emancipation.

"Students these days haven't the slightest comprehension of the Dharma. They're like sheep poking with their noses—whatever they happen on they immediately put in their mouths. They can't tell a gentleman from a lackey, can't tell a host from a guest. People like that come to the Way with twisted minds, rushing in wherever they see a crowd. They don't deserve to be called true men who have left the household. All they are in fact is true householders, men of secular life.

"Someone who has left household life must know how to act ordinary and have a true and proper understanding, must know how to tell buddhas from deevils, to tell true from sham to tell common mortals from sages. If they can tell these apart, you can call them true men who have left the household. But if they can't tell a buddha from a devil, then all they've done is leave one household to enter another. You might describe them as living beings who are creating karma. But you could never call them true men who have left the household.

"Suppose there were a substance made of buddhas and devils blended without distinction into a single body, like water and milk mixed together. The hamsa goose could drink out just the milk. But followers of the Way, if they have really keen eyes, will thrust aside buddhas and devils alike. While you love sages and loath common mortals, you're still bobbing up and down in the sea of birth and death."

Someone asked, "What is the Buddha devil?"

The Master said, "If you have doubts in your mind for an instant, that's the Buddha devil. But if you can understand that the ten thousand phenomena were never born, that the mind is like a conjurer's trick, then not one speck of dust, not one phenomenon will exist. Everywhere will be clean and pure, and this will be Buddha. Buddha and devil just refer to two states, one stained, one pure.

"As I see it, there's no Buddha, no living beings, no long ago, no now. If you want to get it, you've already got it—it's not something that requires time. There's no religious practice, no enlightenment, no getting anything, no missing out on anything. At no time is there any other Dharma than this. If anyone claims there is a Dharma superior to this, I say it must be a dream, a phantom. All I have to say to you is simply this.

"Followers of the Way, this lone brightness before my eyes now, this person plainly listening to me—this person is unimpeded at any point but penetrates the ten directions, free to do as he pleases in the threefold world. No matter what environment he may encounter, with its peculiarities and differences, he cannot be swayed or pulled awry. In the space of an instant he makes his way into the Dharma-realm. If he meets a buddha he preaches to the buddha, if he meets a patriarch he preaches to the patriarch, if he meets an arhat he preaches to the arhat, if he meets a hungry ghost he preaches to the hungry ghost. He goes everywhere, wandering through many lands, teaching and converting living beings, yet never becomes separated from his single thought. Every place for him is clean and pure, his light pierces the ten directions, the ten thousand phenomena are a single thusness.

"Followers of the Way, the really first-rate fellow knows right now that from the first there's never been anything that needed doing. It's because you don't have enough faith that you rush around moment by moment looking for something. You throw away your head and then hunt for a head, and you can't seem to stop yourselves. You're like the bodhisattva of perfect and immediate enlightenment who manifests his body in the Dharma-realm but who, in the midst of the Pure Land, still hates the state of common mortal and prays to become a sage. People like that have yet to forget about making choices. Their minds are still occupied with thoughts of purity or impurity.

"But the Ch'an school doesn't see things that way. What counts is this present moment—there's nothing that requires a lot of time. Everything I am saying to you is for the moment only, medicine to cure the disease. Ultimately it has no true reality. If you can see things in this way, you will be true men who have left the household, free to spend ten thousand in gold each day.

"Followers of the Way, don't let just any old teacher put his stamp of approval on your face, don't say 'I understand Ch'an! I understand the Way!' spouting off like a waterfall. All that sort of thing is karma leading to hell. If you're a person who honestly wants to learn the Way, don't go looking for the world's mistakes, but set about as fast as you can looking for a true and proper understanding. If you can acquire a true and proper understanding, one that's clear and complete, then you can start thinking of calling it quits."

Someone asked, "What do you mean by a true and proper understanding?"

The Master said, "You enter all sorts of states of the common mortal or the sage, of the stained or the pure. You enter the lands of the various buddhas, you enter the halls of Maitreya, you enter the Dharma-realm of Vairochana, and everywhere all these lands are manifest, coming into being, continuing, declining, and passing into emptiness. The Buddha appears in the world, turns the wheel of the great Law, and then enters nirvana, but you cannot see any semblance of his coming and going. If you look for his birth and death, in the end you can never find it. You enter the Dharma-realm of no-birth, wandering everywhere through various lands, you enter the world of the Lotus Treasury and you see fully that all phenomena are empty of characteristics, that none have any true reality.

"You listening to the Dharma, if you are men of the Way who depend on nothing, then you are the mother of the buddhas. Therefore the buddhas are born from the realm that leans on nothing. If you can waken to this leaning on nothing, then there will be no Buddha to get hold of. If you can see things in this way, this is a true and proper understanding.

"But students don't push through to the end. Because they seize on words and phrases and let words like *common mortal* or *sage* obstruct them, this blinds their eyes to the Way and they cannot perceive it clearly. Things like the twelve divisions of the scriptures all speak of surface or external matters. But students don't realize this and immediately form their understanding on the basis of such surface and external words and phrases. All this is just depending on something, and whoever does that falls into the realm of cause and effect and hasn't yet escaped the threefold world of birth and death.

"If you want to be free to be born or die, to go or stay as one would put on or take off a garment, then you must understand right now that the person here listening to the Dharma has no form, no characteristics, no root, no beginning, no place he abides, yet he is vibrantly alive. All the ten thousand kinds of contrived happenings operate in a place that is in fact no place. Therefore the more you search the farther away you get, the harder you hunt the wider astray you go. This is what I call the secret of the matter.

"Followers of the Way, don't take up with some dream or phantom for a companion. Sooner or later you're headed for the impermanence that awaits us all. While you are in this world, what sort of thing do you look to for emancipation? Instead of just looking for a mouthful of food and spending time patching up your robe, you should go around hunting for a teacher. Don't just drift along, always trying to take the easy way. Time is precious, moment by moment impermanence draws nearer! The elements of earth, water, fire, and air are waiting to get the coarser part of you; the four phases of birth, continuation, change, and extinction press on your subtler side. Followers of the Way, now is the time to understand the four types of environment that are without characteristics. Don't just let the environment batter you around." . . .

The Master was standing in attendance at Te-shan's side. Te-shan said, "I'm tired today!"

The Master said, "What's this old fellow doing talking in his sleep?"

Te-shan struck the Master a blow.

The Master grabbed the chair Te-shan was sitting on and turned it over.

Te-shan let the matter end there.

The Master was out working with the other monks hoeing the fields when he saw Huang-po coming. Using his grub hoe for a staff, he stood leaning on it.

Huang-po said, "This fellow's tired, eh?"

The Master said, "I haven't even lifted up my hoe—why should I be tired?"

Huang-po struck him a blow. The Master grabbed hold of Huang-po's stick and gave it a shove, knocking him over.

Huang-po called to the *wei-na*, "*Wei-na*, help me up!"

The *wei-na* came forward to help him. "Reverend," he said, "why do you put up with such rudeness from this raving idiot?"

As soon as Huang-po got to his feet, he struck the *wei-na* a blow.

The Master, hoeing the ground, said, "Other places they cremate them, but at our place we bury them all alive!"

Later Wei-shan asked Yang-shan, "When Huang-po hit the *wei-na*, what was that about?"

Yang-shan said, "When the real thief runs away, the man who was chasing him gets walloped."

One day the Master was sitting in meditation in front of the monks' hall when he saw Huang-po coming. Immediately he shut his eyes. Huang-po made as though he were frightened and then returned to his living quarters.

The Master followed him to his quarters and apologized. The head monk was standing in attendance at Huang-po's side.

Huang-po said, "This monk may be young, but he understands about this business!"

The head monk said, "Old Reverend, you must not have your feet on the ground if you give your approval to this young fellow!"

Huang-po gave himself a slap on the mouth.

The head monk said, "As long as you understand, it's all right."

Source: *The Zen Teachings of Master Lin-chi,* translated by Burton Watson (New York: Columbia University Press, 1993), 12–16, 29–37, 109–110.

20

Japanese Buddhist Tradition

The collected writings in this chapter include selections from some of the most enduring and influential figures in Japanese religious history. Three of these figures are from the Pure Land religious tradition: Hōnen (1133–1212), Shinran (1173–1262), and the prophetic Nichiren (1222–1282). The final two figures represent the Zen Buddhist tradition: Dōgen (1200–1253) is a major figure in the Sōtō branch of Zen, whereas Hakuin (c. 1685–1768) is a revitalizer of the Rinzai Zen tradition. With the exception of Hakuin, the other four figures lived during periods of tumultuous political and social upheavals in Japan.

Hōnen founded the Jōdo (Pure Land) sect after he read a text by the Chinese Pure Land monk Shan-tao at age forty-three. Never intending to establish a separate sect, Hōnen nonetheless created a new religious paradigm whereby every believer accepted his or her status as an ordinary person. The radical aspect of this new paradigm was connected with the rejection of the prior Buddhist assumption that the path to liberation must be grounded on difficult forms of practice. Due to the theory of the decline of the Buddhist law (*mappo*) and the weakness of human beings, there was an urgency to find a more rapid and easier path to salvation. The religious paradigm shift involved relying on the power of another's strength, which meant in practical terms throwing oneself at the mercy of the Buddha Amida and waiting for his grace. The chances for this act of salvific grace could be enhanced by chanting the name of Amida (*nembutsu*), which embodied a saving power. The selections from the works of Hōnen reflect his ideas about the benefits of chanting, which he supports by referring to other texts that support his notion, and also reflects the role of images in devotional Buddhism.

The most significant disciple of Hōnen was Shinran, who established the Jōdo Shinshu (True Pure Land) sect. Shinran was convinced that it was impossible for a person to perform a single positive action that could bring salvation during the current degenerate age, when actions tend to be involved with self-centeredness and passion. Under these circumstances,what alternative does a person have? Shinran's answer was that one must throw oneself on the mercy of Amida and rely solely on his saving grace. The selections from the works of Shinran in this anthology include his commentary on other Buddhist texts. His own postion evolves from his interpretation of these texts, in which he makes some interesting comments about faith, the path to salvation, Pure Land, and nirvāṇa.

Unlike Shinran and Hōnen, Nichiren relied on a single text, namely, the *Lotus Sūtra,* as the source of his inspiration. He even advocated chanting the title of the text. Viewing himself as messenger of the Buddha, Nichiren was so deeply convinced of the correctness of his religious position that he attacked other sects and political leaders. The selections from the works of Nichiren included here show him commentating on other Buddhist texts and connecting them to the *Lotus Sūtra,* a source of all Buddhist wisdom, from his perspective.

In contrast to the devotional path of these three figures, Dōgen Kigen advocated the difficult path to liberation that involved monastic discipline and meditation. Besides distinguishing his position from that of devotional sects, Dōgen also intended to expunge elements of esoteric Buddhism common in both the Tendai and Shingon schools of Japanese Buddhism. Selections from the works of Dōgen for this volume are taken from his major publication the seventy-five-volume *Shōbōgenzō* (The Eye and Treasury of the True Law), which was composed at the end of his life and represents his mature position. Selections from this work are confined to two fundamental notions in his philosophy: seated meditation (*zazen*) and Buddha-nature. Seated meditation is the best method, he said, because it permits liberation even when a person sits for the first time. This claim reflects Dōgen's nondualistic view of his method.

It is important to keep this nondualistic stance in mind when reading his writings. It not unusual to find him making some strange-sounding comments that can upset a reader's common sense, such as referring to mountains moving. Such remarks make perfect sense from the perspective of nondualism, however. A reader can understand this nondualistic position by grasping what he means by Buddha-nature in the second selection from the *Shōbōgenzō*. Dōgen interprets the Buddha-nature in a radical way by equating it with all existence, which includes not only sentient beings but also plant life, animals, and even the inanimate objects of the world, like rocks. Dōgen's inclusive understanding of Buddha-nature includes being, nonbeing, and emptiness. Moreover, the dynamic and creative aspects of Buddha-nature are equated with its impermanence.

Dōgen accorded a secondary importance to kōans (enigmatic statements made by past masters used in meditation) in his practice, but this was not true for Hakuin, a Zen philosopher, author, painter, and poet. In fact, Hakuin devised one of the most famous kōans: What is the sound of one hand clapping? It is precisely this type of kōan that gives rise to the great ball of doubt. If you doubted fully, you could become completely enlightened. In the selection from his works for this anthology, one finds Hakuin writing in an autobiographical manner that is very instructive about problems associated with arduously meditating for long periods of time. Hakuin identified such a problem as Zen sickness, and he shares a remedy with his readers. He also shares his enlightenment experience.

PURE LAND BUDDHISM

Selections from Hōnen's *Senchakushū*

Passages on the Benefit of the Nembutsu

Now let us consider the "one nembutsu." It refers, on the one hand, to the "one nembutsu" mentioned in the above passage regarding the fulfillment of the vow of the nembutsu. On the other hand, it refers to the "one nembutsu" that is spoken of in the passage concerning the lower class. Although, in the passage regarding the fulfillment of the vow, "one nembutsu" was also spoken of, the great benefit of its merits has not yet been explained. Likewise, the "one nembutsu" was mentioned in the passage on the lower class, but the great benefit of its merits was not explained.

When expounding this "one nembutsu," the sūtra here declare its great benefit and praises it as unsurpassed. It should be understood that this is intended to include the various examples of "one nembutsu" referred to earlier.

"Great benefit" is the opposite of "small benefit." Hence, the manifold practices of the awakening of the *bodhicitta* and the rest are of small benefit. "Even one nembutsu" is of great benefit. Further, the words "unsurpassed merit" are the opposite of "merit that can be surpassed." The remaining practices, then, are regarded as surpassable. The nembutsu is said to be unsurpassed. It has already been declared that "one nembutsu" contains an unsurpassed quantity of merit. Hence, it ought to be understood clearly that ten nembutsu contain ten unsurpassed quantities of merit, that a hundred nembutsu contain a hundred, and a thousand contain a thousand unsurpassed quantities of merit. In this manner, merit evolves and expands from few to many. If the nembutsu becomes as great in number as the sands of the Ganges, then the unsurpassed quantities of merit too will be as numerous as the sands of the Ganges. One should surely understand it in this manner. If this is the case, then why should people who desire birth abandon the nembutsu with its unsurpassed great benefits and strive to perform the other practices with their small and surpassable benefits?

Passages Relating That the Light of Amida Does Not Illuminate Those Who Engage in the Other Practices, but Embraces Only Those Who Practice the Nembutsu

Question: "If people engage in various practices and are careful to dedicate their merits toward birth, they all can attain it; then why does the light of the Buddha, which shines everywhere, embrace only those who practice the *nien-fo*? What is the meaning of this?"

Answer: There are three meanings. The first clarifies the intimate karmic relations [with A-mi-t'o Fo]. When sentient beings arouse themselves to practice and always recite with their lips the name of the Buddha, the Buddha will hear them. When they constantly and reverently prostrate themselves before the Buddha with their bodies, the Buddha will see them. When they constantly think of the Buddha in their hearts, the Buddha will know them. When sentient beings remember the Buddha, the Buddha will also remember them. In these three kinds of karmic acts, the Buddha and sentient beings are not separate from each other. Hence, they are called intimate karmic relations.

The second meaning clarifies the close karmic relations. When sentient beings desire to see the Buddha, he, in response to their desire, will appear before their very eyes. Hence, this is called close karmic relations.

The third clarifies the superior karmic relations. Sentient beings who recite [the name of A-mi-t'o Fo] and think of [the Buddha] are rid of the accumulated sins of many kalpas. When they are at the point of death, the Buddha together with the holy assembly will come in person to welcome them. Their evil karma cannot obstruct his coming. That is why this is called superior karmic relations.

The remaining manifold practices, even though they are called "good," cannot even be compared with the *nien-fo*. That is why in many passages of various sūtras the virtue of the nembutsu is widely praised. For example, in the forty-eight vows of the *Wu-liang-shou ching* (Sūtra of Immeasurable Life) it is explained that only by wholeheartedly reciting the name of A-mi-t'o Fo can one be born. Further, in the *A-mi-t'o ching* (Amida Sūtra) one reads that by reciting the name of A-mi-t'o Fo wholeheartedly from one to seven days, one can attain birth. Moreover, the testimony of the many buddhas of the ten directions as countless as the sands of the Ganges is not false. Also, in the passage of the sūtra [*Kuan wu-liang-shou ching*] concerning the contemplative and noncontemplative practices, it is revealed that by simply reciting the name wholeheartedly, one can be born. There are numerous other examples like these. This ends the discussion from various angles of the *nien-fo samādhi*. . . .

The following is my own opinion. Question: "What meaning is there in the fact that the Buddha's light illuminates only practitioners of the nembutsu but does not those who perform other practices?"

Answer: There are two ways to understand this. The first pertains to the three types of karmic relations, such as the intimate karmic relations shown in the above quotation. The second pertains to the original vow. Because the other practices are not in accord with the original vows, this light does not illuminate and embrace those who practice them, but it does illuminate and embrace those who practice the nembutsu, because it is in accord with the original vow. . . .

The nembutsu is the refined practice that was long ago adopted from among twenty-one billion practices. The manifold practices are the coarse ones that were, among the twenty-one billion, already rejected. This is why it is said that they "cannot even be compared [with the *nien-fo*]." Further, the nembutsu is the practice specified in the original vow [of Amida Buddha]. The manifold practices are not. That is why it is said that they "cannot even be compared [with the *nien-fo*]."

Passages Relating How Practitioners
Should Practice the Four Cultivations

Shan-tao says in his *Wang-sheng li-tsan* (Hymns in Praise of Birth):

> Further, I wish to urge that you practice the four modes of practice. What are these four? The first is the cultivation with reverence: for example, to prostrate oneself with reverence before that buddha as well as all holy beings. For this reason, it is called the cultivation with reverence. When one never ceases it as long as one lives, it is called the "long-term cultivation." The second is called the "exclusive cultivation." It is to recite fervently the name of that buddha and devotedly to think of, meditate on, wholeheartedly offer prostration, and praise that buddha and all the other holy beings, but never to mix any other practices with these. For this reason, it is called the exclusive cultivation. When one never ceases it throughout one's life, it is called the "long-term cultivation."
>
> The third is called the "uninterrupted cultivation." It is unceasingly to offer prostration with reverence, to recite his name and praise him, to think of and contemplate him, and to dedicate [one's merits toward one's birth in the Pure Land] and resolve [to be born there]. It is to continue in these practices with total concentration and without interruption, allowing no room for other practices to come and interfere. This is why it is called the uninterrupted cultivation. Further, there is no room for either greed, anger, or the deluding passions to come and interfere. As soon as one commits such an offense, one should repent without allowing a moment to pass, much less an hour or a day. Always to maintain such purity is also called the uninterrupted cultivation. When one never ceases this throughout one's life, it is known as "long-term cultivation."

The *Hsi-fang yao-chüeh* (Essentials for Birth in the Western Land) says:

One should perform only the four modes of practice as the right practice. The first of these is the long-term cultivation: from the first awakening of the aspiration for enlightenment until the actual attainment of its realization, one should continually perform the pure karmic deeds and never regress.

The second is the cultivation with reverence. It has five aspects. The first is to venerate the holy beings [A-mi-t'o Fo, and so on] with whom one has a karmic relationship; whether moving or standing still, sitting or lying down, one should never turn one's back on the west; and one should never blow one's nose, spit, or relieve oneself while facing the west.

The second aspect is to venerate the images and holy scriptures of those with whom one has a karmic relationship. For the former, one should make images and pictures of A-mi-t'o Fo in the Western [Pure Land]. If one should be unable to create many images, then only that buddha and the two bodhisattvas are enough. As for venerating the holy scriptures, one should place the *A-mi-t'o ching* (Amida Sūtra) and the other Pure Land sūtras in a covering of the five colors and read them oneself and have others read them too. One should enshrine these images and sūtras in a room, and there one should come at the six specified times of the day and bow to them, repent one's sins before them, and, offering flowers and incense, specially esteem them.

The third is to venerate the religious teachers with whom one has a karmic relationship. That is, if there is such a person who propagates the Pure Land teachings, even if he should be a hundred or a thousand miles away or more, still one should go to him, associate intimately with him, honor him, and make offerings to him. One should also cultivate a respectful attitude toward all people who follow different teachings and should show deep respect for those who do not agree with one's views. Once one gives way to scorn and pride, the resulting sins will have no bounds. Therefore one should show respect to all people, for this eliminates obstacles that would impede one's practice.

The fourth is to respect the fellows with whom one shares the same karmic relationship, that is, those who engage in the same practice. Even those who are not able to practice alone because of heavy hindrances will certainly be able to practice well by relying on good friends. Thus they will be rescued from danger and saved from misfortune. Thus they are able to help and assist each other. People should deeply appreciate and esteem the good karmic relationship they have with their fellows.

The fifth is to reverence the three treasures. One should deeply reverence them whether taken as identical to the essence [of truth] or as separate categories. [Interpretations regarding these two aspects of the three treasures] will not be treated here in detail because people [of today], capable of only shallow effort, are unable to put these teachings into practice.

Nevertheless, the three treasures in their represented forms produce great favorable karma in today's people of shallow understanding, and so I will now briefly consider this matter.

As regards the Buddha treasure [in its represented forms], this refers to those images carved in sandalwood, embroidered in brocade, made of unadorned materials, gold-leafed, inlaid with precious stones, painted on silk, sculpted of stone, or molded from clay. One should give special reverence to these hallowed images. If anyone but briefly contemplates these forms, his or her sins will vanish and his or her merit will increase. If one succumbs to even the slightest pride [and does not revere these images], his or her evil will increase and his or her goodness will vanish. Thus, one should wholeheartedly contemplate these venerable images as if one saw the real Buddha.

The Dharma treasure [in its represented forms] is the teaching of the three vehicles expressed in words and phrases that flow out of the *dharmadhātu*. It is the condition that gives birth to our emancipation. Therefore it deserves exceptional reverence. It is the basis that gives rise to wisdom. [Accordingly] one should copy the sacred sūtras. They should always be placed in consecrated rooms, stored there in special boxes, and deeply revered. When they are read or recited, one's body and hands should be clean. The Sangha treasure includes holy monks, bodhisattvas, and those who break the precepts. One should arouse an equal respect for them all. Do not give rise to arrogant thoughts.

The third [of the four modes of practice] is the uninterrupted cultivation. This is to think of the Buddha always and to maintain a mind desirous of birth. At all times one should keep these things in mind. As an illustration, let us imagine a person who is seized and taken [to a foreign country] and who, being reduced to a lowly state, is undergoing various sufferings. Suddenly he thinks of his parents and wants to rush back to his home but lacks the means to equip himself for the journey. While he is in that foreign land, he broods day and night on his plight, and his pain is too great to endure. Not even for a single moment can he get rid of the thoughts of his parents. At last he is able to make the necessary preparations and actually returns [to his home]. There he rejoices in being close to his father and mother and is ecstatic with joy.

The same is true of the practitioner. The goodness of his heart and mind has long ago been spoiled by deluding passions, and the treasures of virtue and wisdom are all lost. For long ages he has been swept along in the stream of birth and death, and is not free to control [his deluding passions]. Always as a servant of the devil king, he runs here and there among the six paths and suffers from torments of body and mind. But now he encounters favorable karmic conditions; thus he hears that A-mi-t'o Fo, the compassionate father, will save the multitude of beings, never deviating from his universal [original] vow. Day and night, he hastens to cultivate the aspiration for enlightenment and longs for birth. Therefore, one should practice diligently and untiringly. One should ponder one's debt to the Buddha and throughout life think of how one can repay it.

The fourth is the exclusive cultivation. It is to seek wholeheartedly after the Land of Perfect Bliss while revering and thinking of A-mi-t'o Fo. One should not engage in the exercise or performance of any miscellaneous practices. The practice that one should engage in every day is the nembutsu and the recitation of the sūtras. Other practices should be cast aside.

The following is my own opinion: I hope one should simply read the above passage concerning the four modes of practice. I shall not explain it further for fear of repetition. However, in the first of the above quotations, it was stated that there are four modes of practice, while only three were discussed. Has part of the text been omitted accidentally? Or is there a reason for such an omission? Without question no part of the text has been omitted. There is a deep meaning behind this. How do we know this? Of the four modes of practice, the first is the long-term cultivation, the second is the cultivation with reverence, the third is the exclusive cultivation, and the fourth is the uninterrupted cultivation; and the first long-term cultivation pervades the other three.

That is, if one were to cease to continue the cultivation with reverence [and therefore did not practice that cultivation for a long period of time], then one would be unable to complete that cultivation. If one were to cease to continue the exclusive cultivation, then one would be unable to complete that cultivation. And if one were to cease to continue the uninterrupted cultivation, then one would not complete that cultivation.

The long-term cultivation accompanies the other three in order to fulfill them. It pervades them and causes them to be carried out. For this reason, one finds at the end of the three passages concerning the cultivations the following words: "When one never ceases it until the end of one's life, this is called the 'long-term cultivation.'" If we look at the six *pāramitās*, we find the same thing; the [*pāramitā* of] zeal pervades the other five *pāramitās*.

Source: *Hōnen's Senchakushū*, translated and edited by Senchakushū English Translation Project (Honolulu: University of Hawaii Press, 1998), 90–91, 96–98, 113–117.

Selection from Shinran's "Notes on 'Essentials of Faith Alone'"

In the title, *Essentials of Faith Alone,* Alone means "this one thing only," expressing a rejection of two things standing together. It also means "by itself."

Faith is the heart and mind without doubt; it is shinjin, which is true and real. It is the heart and mind free of that which is empty and transitory. "Empty" means vain; "transitory" means provisional. "Empty" means not real, not sincere; "transitory" means not true. To be free of self-power, having entrusted oneself to the Other Power of the Primal Vow—this is *faith alone.*

Essentials indicates the selecting and gathering together of significant passages from the scriptures. Thus the title, *Essentials of Faith Alone.*

Faith alone also means that nothing is placed equal with this shinjin of Other Power, for it is the working of the universal Primal Vow. . . .

> The sacred Name of the Tathagata is exceedingly distinct and clear
> Throughout the worlds in the ten quarters it prevails
> Solely those who say the Name all attain birth
> Avalokiteśvara and Mahāsthāmaprāpta come of themselves to welcome
> them

The sacred Name of the Tathagata is exceedingly distinct and clear
The Tathagata is the Tathagata of unhindered light. *The sacred name* is Namu-amida-butsu.

Sacred means holy, excellent.

Name (*gō*) indicates the name of a Buddha after the attainment of Buddha-hood; another term (*myō*) indicates the name before this attainment. The sacred Name of the Tathagata surpasses measure, description, and conceptual understanding; it is the Name of the Vow embodying great love and great compassion, which brings all sentient beings into the supreme nirvana.

The Name of this Buddha surpasses the names of all the other Tathagatas, for it is based on the Vow to save all beings.

Exceedingly distinct and clear
Exceedingly here means utterly, unsurpassed.

Distinct implies "to distinguish"; here it means to distinguish each sentient being.

Clear means evident. It is evident that Amida, distinguishing every sentient being in the ten quarters, guides each to salvation; thus the Buddha's compassionate concern for us is unsurpassed.

Throughout the worlds in the ten quarters it prevails
Throughout means universally, extensively, boundlessly.

Prevails means that the Name spreads universally throughout the worlds in the ten quarters, countless as minute particles, and guides all to the practice of the Buddha's teaching. This means that, since there is no one—whether among the wise of the Mahayana or the Hinayana, or the ignorant, good or evil—who can attain supreme nirvana through his or her own self-cultivated wisdom, we are encouraged to enter the ocean of the wisdom-Vow of the Buddha of unhindered light, for the Buddha's form is the light of wisdom. This form comprehends the wisdom of all the Buddhas. It should be understood that light is none other than wisdom.

Solely those who say the Name all attain birth
Solely those who means that only those who say the Name single-heartedly attain birth in the Pure Land of bliss; this is the meaning of "Those who say the Name all attain birth.". . .

Avalokiteśvara and Mahāsthāmaprāpta come of themselves to welcome them
Namu-amida-butsu is the Name embodying wisdom; hence, when persons accept and entrust themselves to this Name of the Buddha of inconceivable wisdom-light, holding it in mindfulness, Avalokiteśvara and Mahāsthāmaprāpta accompany them constantly, as shadows do things. The Buddha of unhindered light appears as Avalokiteśvara, and becomes manifest as Mahāsthāmaprāpta. A sutra states that Avalokiteśvara, with the name Bodhisattva Treasure-response, reveals himself as the god of the sun and dispels the pitch darkness of ignorance in all beings; and Mahāsthāmaprāpta, with the name Bodhisattva Treasure-happiness, reveals himself as the god of the moon and illuminates the long night of birth-and-death. Together they bring forth wisdom in all beings.

Come of themselves to welcome: of themselves (*ji*) means "in person." Amida and a vast and numberless saintly host, consisting of innumerable manifestation-bodies of Buddhas, of Avalokiteśvara, and of Mahāsthāmaprāpta, appear in person to be alongside and always protect those who have realized true and real shinjin, at all times and in all places; hence the word "themselves."

Ji also means of itself. "Of itself" is a synonym for *jinen,* which means to be made to become so. "To be made to become so" means that without the practicer's calculating in any way whatsoever, all that practicer's past, present, and future evil karma is transformed into the highest good. "To be transformed" means that evil karma, without being nullified or eradicated, is made into the highest good, just as all waters, upon entering the great ocean, immediately become ocean water. We are made to acquire the Tathagata's virtues through entrusting ourselves to the Vow-power; hence the expression, "made to become so." Since there is no contriving in any way to gain such virtues, it is called *jinen.* Those persons who have attained true and real shinjin are taken into and protected by this Vow that grasps never to abandon; therefore, they realize the diamondlike mind without any calculation on their own part, and thus dwell in the stage of the truly settled. Because of this, constant mindfulness of the Primal Vow arises in them naturally (by *jinen*). Even with the arising of this shinjin, it is written that supreme shinjin is made to awaken in us through me compassionate guidance of Śākyamuni, the kind father, and Amida, the mother of loving care. Know that this is the benefit of the working of *jinen.*

Come to welcome: come means to cause to come to the Pure Land; it is a word which expresses the actualizing of Amida's Vow, "If any should not be born in my land, may I not attain the supreme enlightenment." It indicates that a person is made to reject the defiled world and come to the true and real fulfilled land. In short, the word indicates the working of Other Power.

Come also means to return. To return is to attain the supreme nirvana without fail because one has already entered the ocean of the Vow; this is called "returning to the city of dharma-nature." The city of dharma-nature is none other than the enlightenment of Tathagata, called dharma-body, unfolded naturally. When persons become enlightened, we say they "return to the city of dharma-nature." It is also called realizing true reality or suchness, realizing the uncreated or dharma-body, attaining emancipation, realizing the eternal bliss of dharma-nature, and attaining the supreme enlightenment. When persons attain this enlightenment, with great love and great compassion immediately reaching their fullness in them, they return to the ocean of birth-and-death to save all sentient beings; this is known as attaining the virtue of Bodhisattva Samantabhadra. To attain this benefit is *come;* that is, "to return to the city of dharma-nature."

To welcome means that Amida receives us, awaits us. Hearing the inconceivable selected Primal Vow and the holy Name of supreme wisdom without a single doubt is called true and real shinjin; it is also called the diamondlike mind. When sentient beings realize this shinjin, they attain the equal of perfect enlightenment and will ultimately attain the supreme enlightenment, being of the same stage as Maitreya, the future Buddha. That is, they become established in the stage of the truly settled. Hence shinjin is like a diamond, never breaking, or degenerating, or becoming fragmented; thus, we speak of "diamondlike shinjin." This is the meaning of *to welcome.*

The *Larger Sutra of the Buddha of Immeasurable Life* states:

> All sentient beings aspire to be born in that land; they then attain birth and dwell in the stage of nonretrogression.

Aspire to be born in that land is a command: All beings should aspire to be born in that land!

They then attain birth means that when a person realizes shinjin, he or she is born immediately. "To be born immediately" is to dwell in the stage of nonretrogression. To dwell in the stage of nonretrogression is to become established in the stage of the truly settled. This is also called the attainment of the equal of perfect enlightenment. Such is the meaning of *they then attain birth.*

Then means immediately; "immediately" means without any passage of time and without any passage of days.

That the Name spreads universally throughout the worlds in the ten quarters is due to the fulfillment of the Vow embodying the ocean of the One-Vehicle wisdom, the Seventeenth Vow of Bodhisattva Dharmākara's Forty-eight great Vows, which states, "My Name shall be praised and pronounced by the countless Buddhas in the ten quarters." This is evident from the description of the Buddhas' witness and protection in the *Smaller Sutra.* The Buddhas' intention in their witness and protection is also expressed in the *Larger Sutra.* Thus, this Vow of compassion already shows that the Primal Vow, which encourages the saying of the Name, is the true cause of birth selected by Amida. . . .

> That Buddha, in the causal stage, made the universal Vow:
> When beings hear my Name and think on me, I will come to welcome
>   each of them,
> Not discriminating at all between the poor and the rich and wellborn,

Not discriminating between the inferior and the highly gifted,

Not choosing the learned and those upholding pure precepts,

Nor rejecting those who break precepts and whose evil karma is
profound.

Solely making beings turn about and abundantly say the nembutsu,

I can make bits of rubble change into gold.

That Buddha, in the causal stage, made the universal Vow
That Buddha refers to Amida Buddha.

In the causal stage indicates the time when Amida Buddha was Bodhisattva Dharmākara.

Universal means wide, to spread. Bhikṣu Dharmākara established the supreme, unexcelled Vow and spread it widely. "Supreme" means that it goes beyond the vows of other Buddhas. It connotes transcendent, unequalled. The Tathagata's establishing of the universal Vow is explained in detail in *Essentials of Faith Alone.*

When beings hear my Name and think on me
Hear is a word indicating shinjin.

Name refers to the Name embodying the Tathagata's Vow.

Think on me instructs us, Hold this Name in mindfulness! This is implied in the compassionate Vow that all the Buddhas pronounce the Name. "Hold in mindfulness" means that people of true shinjin constantly recall the Primal Vow without interruption.

I will come to welcome each of them
Each of them means all inclusive, everyone. *Welcome* means to receive, to await, expressing Other Power. *Come* means to return, to be made to come. Thus, we are made to come and return to the city of dharma-nature. Since there is coming from the city of dharma-nature into this Sahā world to benefit sentient beings, *come* has the sense of "to arrive from"; since there is attainment of the enlightenment of dharma-nature, it means "to return."

Not discriminating at all between the poor and the rich and wellborn
Not discriminating means not choosing, not rejecting.

Poor means impoverished and in need. *At all* is for emphasis, meaning "not at all"; it also means "with" and to lead. *Rich and wellborn* indicates the wealthy and the people of rank. Thus, without in the least differentiating among such people, Amida leads each and every person to the Pure Land.

Not discriminating between the inferior and the highly gifted
Inferior refers to those whose knowledge is shallow, limited, and slight.

Highly gifted indicates those with great ability for learning. Amida does not choose between the two.

Not choosing the learned and those who uphold pure precepts
Learned means to hear and believe in numerous and diverse sacred teachings.

Upholding means to maintain. "To maintain" means not to lose or dissipate what we learn.

Pure precepts indicates all the various Hinayana and Mahayana precepts—the five precepts, the eight precepts, the ten precepts of morality, all the Hinayana codes of precepts, the three-thousand regulations of deportment, the sixty-thousand regulatory practices, the diamondlike one-mind precepts of the Mahayana, the threefold pure precept, the fifty-eight precepts expounded in the *Brahma-net Sutra,* and so on—all the precepts for monks and for laypeople. To maintain these is "to uphold" and to violate them is "to break." Even saintly people who observe these various Mahayana and Hinayana precepts can attain birth in the true fulfilled land only after they realize the true and real shinjin of Other Power. Know that it is impossible to be born in the true, fulfilled Pure Land by simply observing precepts, or by self-willed conviction, or by self-cultivated good.

Nor rejecting those who break precepts and whose evil karma is profound
Break precepts applies to people who, having received the precepts for monks or laymen mentioned earlier, break and abandon them; such people are not rejected.

Evil karma is profound: evil people who have committed the ten transgressions or the five grave offenses, people of evil karma who have reviled the teaching or who lack seeds for Buddhahood, those of scant roots of good, those of massive karmic evil, those of shallow inclination to good, those of profound attachment to evil—such wretched men as these, profound in various kinds of evil karma, are described by the word *profound. Profound* means bottomless. Good people, bad people, noble and low, are not differentiated in the Vow of the Buddha of unhindered light, in which the guiding of each person is primary and fundamental. Know that the true essence of the Pure Land teaching (*Jōdo shinshū*) is that when we realize true and real shinjin, we are born in the true fulfilled land.

Come and welcome each of them means making all beings of true and real shinjin return to the Pure Land by welcoming and leading them there.

Solely making beings turn about and abundantly say the nembutsu
Solely making beings turn about instructs us, Singleheartedly make your heart turn about!

Turn about means to overturn and discard the mind of self-power. Since those people who are to be born in the true fulfilled land are without fail taken into the heart of the Buddha of unhindered light, they realize diamondlike shinjin. Thus, they "abundantly say the Name."

Abundant means "great" in the sense of great in number, "exceeding" and "supreme" in the sense of excelling and surpassing all good acts. This is because nothing excels the Primal Vow embodying Other Power.

"To abandon the mind of self-power" admonishes the various and diverse kinds of people—masters of Hinayana or Mahayana, ignorant beings good or evil—to abandon the conviction that one is good, to cease relying on the self; to stop reflecting knowingly on one's evil heart, and further to abandon the judging of people as good and bad. When such shackled foolish beings—the lowly who are hunters and peddlers—thus wholly entrust themselves to the Name embodying great wisdom, the inconceivable Vow of the Buddha of unhindered light, then while burdened as they are with blind passion, they attain the supreme nirvana. "Shackled" describes us, who are bound by all our various blind passions. Blind passions refers to pains which torment the body and afflictions which distress the heart and mind. The hunter is one who slaughters many kinds of living things; this is the huntsman. The peddler is one who buys and sells things; this is the trader. They are called "low." Such peddlers, hunters, and others are none other than we, who are like stones and tiles and pebbles.

I can make bits of nibble change into gold
This is a metaphor. When we entrust ourselves to the Tathagata's Primal Vow, we, who are like bits of tile and pebbles, are turned into gold. Peddlers and hunters, who are like stones and tiles and pebbles, are grasped and never abandoned by the Tathagata's light. Know that this comes about solely through true shinjin. We

speak of the light that grasps because we are taken into the heart of the Buddha of unhindered light; thus, shinjin is said to be diamondlike.

Although I have not set forth the meaning of this passage as fully as I would like, I have presented a rough explanation. I hope the reader will ask good teachers about its profound implications.

The passage is the exposition of Tz'u-min, master of the Tripitaka, who studied in India. In China he is known as Hui-jih.

> The land of bliss is the realm of nirvana, the uncreated;
> I fear it is hard to be born there by doing sundry good acts according to
>   our diverse conditions.
> Hence, the Tathagata selected the essential dharma,
> Instructing beings to say Amida's Name with singleness, again singleness.

The land of bliss is the realm of nirvana, the uncreated
The land of bliss is that Pure Land of happiness, where there are always countless joys and never any suffering mingled with them. It is known as the land of peace. It was Master T'an-luan who praised it and called it "Land of Peace." Also, the *Treatise on the Pure Land* describes it as "the lotus repository world" and as the uncreated.

The realm of nirvana refers to the place where one overturns the delusion of ignorance and realizes the supreme enlightenment.

Realm means "place"; know it as the place of attaining enlightenment.

Nirvana has innumerable names. It is impossible to give them in detail; I will list only a few. Nirvana is called extinction of passions, the uncreated, peaceful happiness, eternal bliss, true reality, dharma-body, dharma-nature, suchness, oneness, and Buddha-nature. Buddha-nature is none other than Tathagata. This Tathagata pervades the countless worlds; it fills the hearts and minds of the ocean of all beings. Thus, plants, trees, and land all attain Buddhahood.

Since it is with this heart and mind of all sentient beings that they entrust themselves to the Vow of the dharma-body as compassionate means, this shinjin is none other than Buddha-nature. This Buddha-nature is dharma-nature. Dharma-nature is dharma-body. For this reason there are two kinds of dharma-body with regard to the Buddha. The first is called dharma-body as suchness and the second, dharma-body as compassionate means. Dharma-body as suchness has neither color nor form; thus, the mind cannot grasp it nor words describe it. From this oneness was manifested form, called dharma-body as compassionate means.

Taking this form, the Buddha announced the name Bhikṣu Dharmākara and established the Forty-eight great Vows that surpass conceptual understanding. Among these Vows are the Primal Vow of immeasurable light and the universal Vow of immeasurable life, and to the form manifesting these two Vows Bodhisattva Vasubandhu gave the title, "Tathagata of unhindered light filling the ten quarters." This Tathagata has fulfilled the Vows, which are the cause of that Buddhahood, and thus is called "Tathagata of the fulfilled body." This is none other than Amida Tathagata.

"Fulfilled" means that the cause for enlightenment has been fulfilled. From the fulfilled body innumerable personified and accommodated bodies are manifested, radiating the unhindered light of wisdom throughout the countless worlds. Thus appearing in the form of light called "Tathagata of unhindered light filling the ten quarters," it is without color and without form; that is, it is identical with the dharma-body as suchness, dispelling the darkness of ignorance and unobstructed by karmic evil. For this reason it is called "unhindered light." "Unhindered" means that it is not obstructed by the karmic evil and blind passions of beings Know therefore, that Amida Buddha is light, and that light is the form taken by wisdom.

I fear it is hard to be born there by doing sundry good acts accords to our diverse conditions
According to our diverse conditions refers to directing the merit of practicing various good acts, which one performs according one's own particular circumstances and opportunities, toward birth in the land of bliss. There are 84,000 gates of dharma. Since they are all good practices done in self-power, they are rejected as not leading to birth in the true fulfilled land. Thus, *I fear it is hard to be born.*

Fear means to be apprehensive; that is, apprehensive about whether a person can be born in the true fulfilled land through the adulterated good practices, the good practices characterized by self-power.

Hard to be born means that it is difficult to attain birth in the Pure Land.

Hence, the Tathagata selected the essential dharma
Know that Śākyamuni Buddha selected the Name of Amida from among all the various goods and gave it to the evil beings, possessing wrong views and lacking faith, and living in this evil world of the five defilements. This is called selected, meaning "to pick out from among many."

Essential means wholly, to seek, to promise.

Dharma indicates the Name.

Instructing beings to say Amida's Name with singleness, again singleness

Instructing means to preach, the teaching. Here it refers to the instruction of Śākyamuni.

To say Amida's Name means to make a decision and not to calculate in any way. Thus, these words instruct us, Be wholehearted in the single practice of saying the Name embodying the selected Primal Vow!

With singleness, again singleness: the first *singleness* means that we should perform the single practice.

Again means furthermore; it means to repeat. Hence *with singleness* furthermore means "Be of one-mind!" That is, Be wholly of single practice and of one mind! Moreover, *singleness* means "one." *Wholly* implies, Do not be of two minds! Thus not wavering in any way is one mind. Amida grasps, never to abandon, such a person of this single practice and one mind, and therefore is called Amida. This is stated by Shan-tao, the Master of Kuang-ming temple.

This one mind is the shinjin of *leaping crosswise.*

Crosswise means across; *leaping* means "going beyond." This way surpasses all other teachings, and through it one quickly goes beyond the great ocean of birth-and-death and attains supreme enlightenment; therefore the term leaping is used. It is made possible by the power of the Vow that embodies the Tathagata's great compassion.

The shinjin becomes the diamondlike mind because of Amida's grasp. This is the threefold shinjin of the Primal Vow of birth through the nembutsu and not the three minds of the *Contemplation Sutra.* Bodhisattva Vasubandhu declares that this true and real shinjin is none other than the aspiration to become a Buddha. This is the great thought of enlightenment of the Pure Land. This aspiration for Buddhahood is none other than the wish to save all beings. The wish to save all beings is the wish to carry all beings across the great ocean of birth-and-death. This shinjin is the aspiration to bring all beings to the attainment of supreme nirvana; it is the heart of great love and great compassion. This shinjin is Buddha-nature and Buddha-nature is Tathagata. To realize this shinjin is to *rejoice and be glad.* People who rejoice and are glad are called "people equal to the Buddhas."

To rejoice means to be joyous after being assured of attaining what one shall attain; it is rejoicing after realizing shinjin.

To be glad means to always have joy uninterruptedly in one's heart and constantly keep it in mind. It means *to leap and jump,* expressing boundless joy:

To leap is to dance to the heavens, *to jump* is to dance on the earth. The person who has realized shinjin is also likened to the white lotus flower.

The difficulty of realizing this shinjin is taught in the *Larger Sutra:* "The most difficult of all difficulties is to hear this sutra and accept it in shinjin; nothing surpasses this difficulty"; and in the *Smaller Sutra* we find, "It is the dharma that is most difficult to accept." But Śākyamuni Tathagata, appearing in this evil world of five defilements, put this dharma that is difficult to accept into practice and attained the supreme nirvana. He then gave this Name embodying wisdom to the sentient beings living in defilement. The witness of the Buddhas throughout the ten quarters and the protection of the Tathagatas as numberless as the sands of the Ganges are solely for the sake of people of true and real shinjin. Know that Śākyamuni, our loving father, and Amida, our compassionate mother, guide us to shinjin as our own parents.

For vast ages in the past, under Buddhas who appeared in this world three times the sands of the Ganges in number, we awakened the great thought of enlightenment of self-power. Having performed good practices numerous as the sands of the Ganges, we are now able to encounter the karmic power of the great Vow. Those who have realized the threefold shinjin of Other Power must never disparage the other good practices or malign the other Buddhas and bodhisattvas.

The person with the three minds will be born without fail in that land
This means that because a person has the three minds he or she will be born without fail in that land. Thus Shan-tao states:

> If one possesses these three minds, one will necessarily attain birth. If the one mind is lacking, then birth is not attained.

If one possesses these three minds means that we must have the threefold mind.

If the one mind is lacking means that no one can be born when this one mind is lacking. To lack the one mind is to lack shinjin. To lack shinjin is to lack the true and real threefold shinjin of the Primal Vow. To realize the three minds of the *Contemplation Sutra* and then the threefold shinjin of the *Larger Sutra* is to realize the one mind. When this one mind is lacking, one is not born in the real fulfilled land. The three minds of the *Contemplation Sutra* are parts of the mind of self-power of a person who pursues meditative and nonmeditative practice. Know that the deep mind and sincere mind, which are means, are intended to bring the two goods—meditative and nonmeditative—into the aspiration for the threefold shinjin of the *Larger Sutra*. When one has not attained the true and real threefold shinjin, one is not born in the true fulfilled land. Since one is not born, it is said *then birth is not attained.*

Then means immediately.

Birth is not attained means that the person is not born. Those of meditative and nonmeditative good acts—performing sundry practices, undergoing disciplines, and lacking threefold shinjin—will be born in the true and real fulfilled land, after countless lives in vast ages, after they have realized the threefold shinjin of the *Larger Sutra*. Thus, the person is not born. The sutras state that even if such a person attains birth in the palace of womb or the borderland, he or she must pass five hundred years there; furthermore, out of millions upon millions of beings, scarcely a single one will advance to the true fulfilled land. Thus, we must carefully understand the importance of threefold shinjin and aspire for its realization.

We should not express outwardly signs of wisdom, goodness, or diligence
People who aspire for the Pure Land must not behave outwardly as though wise or good, nor should they act as though diligent. The reason is stated, *for inwardly we are possessed of falsity* (literally, *that which is empty and transitory*).

Inwardly means "within"; since the mind is filled with blind passions, it is empty and transitory.

Empty means vain, not real, not sincere.

Transitory means provisional, not true.

For this reason, in the Tathagata's teaching this world is called the defiled world of the corrupt dharma. All beings lack a true and sincere heart, mock teachers and elders, disrespect their parents, distrust their companions, and favor only evil; hence, it is taught that everyone, both in secular and religious worlds, is possessed of "Heart and tongue at odds," and "Words and thoughts both insincere." The former means that what is in the heart and what is said are at variance, and the latter means that what is spoken and what is thought are not real. Real means "sincere." People of this world have only thoughts that are not real, and those who wish to be born in the Pure Land have only thoughts of deceiving and flattering. Even those who renounce this world have nothing but thoughts of fame and profit. Hence, know that we are not good persons, nor persons of wisdom; that we have no diligence, but only indolence, and within, the heart is ever empty, deceptive, vainglorious, and flattering. We do not have a heart that is true and real.

Reflect on this means that a person must understand this in accordance with the way things truly are.

Nor rejecting those who break precepts and whose evil karma is profound
This means that men who break the various precepts and whose evil karma is deep are not rejected. This was explained fully above. Please read the explanation carefully.

If sentient beings, saying my Name perhaps even ten times, should not be born there, may I not attain the supreme enlightenment
This is from the text of the selected Primal Vow. It means that if the people who say the Name as stated in the Vow, "up to ten times," are not born in my land, may I not become a Buddha.

Perhaps even contains all the meanings of upper or lower limit, more or less, near or far, long continued. This is the Vow that Bodhisattva Dharmākara made in advance out of compassion for beings of later ages, seeking to end attachment to either many-calling or once-calling. We should be truly happy about this, and take delight and rejoice.

Neither accommodated nor real
This is a teaching of the Tendai school. It has nothing to do with Shin Buddhism, and expresses the thought of the Path of Sages. It is not the way of easy practice, so please ask people of the Tendai school about it.

If you cannot think on Amida
This is the teaching which urges the person guilty of the five grave offenses and ten transgressions and of engaging in defiled expositions of the dharma, "If you are tormented by suffering due to illness and cannot think on Amida, then simply say Namu-amida-butsu with your lips." This demonstrates that Amida made verbal utterance the essence of the Primal Vow. The expression *say the Name of the Buddha of immeasurable life* refers to this fact, and *say* instructs us to utter the Name.

> When you say *Namu-muryōju-butsu* [Namu-amida-butsu] ten times, because
> you say the Buddha's Name, with each utterance the evil karma of eight bil-
> lion kalpas of birth-and-death is eliminated.

Those who commit the five grave offenses are burdened with evil karma, in fact, tenfold eight billion kalpas of evil karma; hence, they are urged to say

Namu-amida-butsu ten times. It is not that the evil karma of tenfold eight billion kalpas cannot be extinguished in a single utterance; but in this way, we are made to realize the seriousness of the evil karma of the five grave offenses.

Ten times means that we should simply say the Name ten times with the lips. Thus, Shan-tao rephrases the selected Primal Vow,

If, when I attain Buddhahood, the sentient beings of the ten quarters say my Name even ten times but do not attain birth, may I not attain the supreme enlightenment.

Here, in Amida's Primal Vow, *even* includes "few" in contrast to "many," teaching us that sentient beings who say the Name as few as ten times will without fail attain birth. Know that "thinking" and "voicing" have the same meaning; no voicing exists separate from thinking, and no thinking separate from voicing.

Source: Shinran, "Notes on 'Essentials of Faith Alone'" in *The Collected Works of Shinran*, volume 1, *The Writings*, translated by the Shin Buddhism Translation Series (Kyoto: Jōdo Shinshū Hong-wanji-ha, 1997), 451–468.

Selections from Nichiren

And the Nirvana Sutra says, "In this way, those who believe in the Nirvana Sutra will take up no more land than can be placed on top of a fingernail. . . . Those who do not believe in the sutra will occupy all the lands in the ten directions."

These passages from the scriptures arc extremely apt, considering the times we live in, and they are deeply etched in my mind. Nowadays in Japan one hears people everywhere declaring, "I believe in the Lotus Sutra," and "I, too, believe in the Lotus Sutra." If we took them at their word, we would have to conclude that there is not a soul who slanders the Law. But the passage from the sutra which I have just quoted says that in the Latter Day, the slanderers of the Law will occupy all the lands in the ten directions, while those who uphold the True Law will take up no more land than can be placed on top of a fingernail. What the sutra says and what the people of the world today say are as different as fire is from water. People these days say that in Japan, Nichiren is the only one who slanders the Law. But the sutra says that there will be more slanderers of the Law than the great earth itself can hold.

The *Hōmetsujin* Sutra says that there will be only one or two good persons, and the Nirvana Sutra says that the believers can fit into the space of a fingernail. If we accept what the sutras say, then in Japan Nichiren is the only good person, the one who fits into the space of a fingernail. Therefore I hope that people who are seriously concerned about the matter will consider carefully whether they want to accept what the sutras say, or what the world says.

Someone might object that the passage in the Nirvana Sutra speaks about the votaries of the Nirvana Sutra being so few that they can fit into the space of a fingernail, while I am talking about the Lotus Sutra. I would reply to this as follows.

The Nirvana Sutra defines itself as being contained in the Lotus Sutra. The Great Teacher Miao-lo says, "The great sutra is itself pointing to the Lotus Sutra and saying that it is the ultimate." The words "the great sutra" here refer to the Nirvana Sutra. The Nirvana Sutra is calling the Lotus Sutra the ultimate. Therefore, when followers of the Nirvana school state that the Nirvana Sutra is superior to the Lotus Sutra, it is the same as calling a retainer a lord or a servant a master.

To read the Nirvana Sutra means to read the Lotus Sutra. For the Nirvana Sutra is like a worthy man who rejoices to see another holding his sovereign in esteem even when he himself is treated with contempt. Thus the Nirvana Sutra would despise and regard as its enemy anyone who tried to demote the Lotus Sutra and praise the Nirvana Sutra instead.

With this example in mind, one must understand the following point. If there are likewise those who read the *Kegon* Sutra, the *Kammuryōju* Sutra, the *Dainichi* Sutra, or some other sutra, and they do so thinking that the Lotus Sutra is inferior to those sutras. then they are doing violence to the very heart of those sutras! One must also understand the following point. Even though one reads the Lotus Sutra and appears to believe in it, if he thinks that he may also attain enlightenment through any other sutra as well, then he is not really reading the Lotus Sutra!

For example, the Great Teacher Chia-hsiang wrote a work in ten volumes entitled the *Hokke Genron* in which he praised the Lotus Sutra. But Miao-lo criticized the work, saying, "There are slanders in it—how can it be regarded as true propagation and praise?"

Chia-hsiang was in fact an offender against the Lotus Sutra. Thus, when he was defeated by the Great Teacher T'ien-t'ai and served him, he no longer lectured on the Lotus Sutra. "If I were to lecture on it," he said, "I could not avoid falling back into the paths of evil."

And for seven years, he made his own body a bridge for T'ien-t'ai to walk on.

Similarly, the Great Teacher Tz'u-en wrote a work in ten volumes entitled the *Hokke Genzan* in which he praised the Lotus Sutra, but the Great Teacher Dengyō criticized it, saying, "Even though he praises the Lotus Sutra, he destroys its heart."

If we consider these examples carefully, we will realize that, among those who read the Lotus Sutra and sing its praises, there are many who are destined for the hell of incessant suffering. Even men like Chia-hsiang and Tz'u-en were actually slanderers of the one vehicle of the Lotus Sutra. And if such can be said of them, it applies even more to men like Kōbō, Jikaku, and Chishō, who displayed open contempt for the Lotus Sutra.

There are those like Chia-hsiang, who ceased giving lectures, dispersed the group of disciples that had gathered around him, and became a disciple of T'ien-t'ai, even making his body into a bridge for his teacher. But in spite of these actions, the offense of his earlier slanders of the Lotus Sutra was not, I expect, so easily wiped out. The crowd of people who despised and attacked Bodhisattva Fukyō, although they later came to believe in his teachings and became his followers, still carried the burden of their former actions and had to spend a thousand kalpas in the Avīci Hell as a result.

Accordingly, if men like Kōbō, Jikaku, and Chishō had lectured on the Lotus Sutra, even if they had repented of their errors, they would still have had difficulty making up for their former grave offenses. And of course, as we know, they never had any such change of heart. On the contrary, they completely ignored the Lotus Sutra and spent day and night carrying out Shingon practices and morning and evening preaching Shingon doctrine.

The bodhisattvas Vasubandhu and Aśvaghoṣa were both on the point of cutting out their tongues because of the offense they had committed [in their younger days] by adhering to Hinayana doctrines and criticizing Mahayana. Vasubandhu declared that, although the *Agon* sutras of the Hinayana were the words of the Buddha, he would not let his tongue utter them even in jest. And Aśvaghoṣa, as an act of penance, wrote the *Kishin Ron* in which he refuted the Hinayana teachings.

Chia-hsiang in time went to the Great Teacher T'ien-t'ai and begged for his lectures. In the presence of a hundred or more distinguished Buddhists, he threw himself on the ground, and, with sweat pouring from every part of his body and tears of blood streaming from his eyes, he declared that from then on he would not see his disciples any more and would no longer lecture on the Lotus Sutra. For, as he said, "If I were to go on facing my disciples and lecturing on the Lotus Sutra, they might suppose that I have the ability to understand the sutra correctly, when in fact I do not."

Chia-hsiang was both older and more eminent than T'ien-t'ai, and yet, in the presence of others, he deliberately put his teacher T'ien-t'ai on his back and carried him across a river. Whenever T'ien-t'ai was about to ascend the lecture plat-form, Chia-hsiang would take him on his back and carry him up to the platform. After T'ien-t'ai's death, when Chia-hsiang was summoned into the presence of the emperor of the Sui dynasty, he is said to have wept and dragged his feet like a little child whose mother has just died.

When one examines the work entitled *Hokke Genron* by Chia-hsiang, one finds that it is not the kind of commentary that speaks slanderously of the Lotus Sutra. It merely says that, although the Lotus Sutra and the other Mahayana sutras differ in the profundity of their teachings, they are at heart one and the same. Is this statement perhaps the source of the charge that the work slanders the Law?

Both Ch'eng-kuan of the Kegon school and Shan-wu-wei of the Shingon school declared that the Lotus Sutra and the *Dainichi* Sutra reveal the same prin-ciple. Therefore, if Chia-hsiang is to be blamed for the statement I have just referred to, then Shan-wu-wei can hardly escape being blamed as well.

Shan-wu-wei in his youth was the ruler of a kingdom in central India. But he abdicated the throne and traveled to other lands, where he met two men named Shushō and Shōdai from whom he received instruction in the Lotus Sutra. He built a hundred thousand stone stupas, and appeared to be a votary of the Lotus Sutra. Later, however, after he had received instruction in the *Dainichi* Sutra, he seems to have concluded that the Lotus Sutra is inferior to the *Dainichi* Sutra. He did not insist on this opinion at first, but came to do so later when he went to China and became a teacher to Emperor Hsüan-tsung of the T'ang dynasty.

Perhaps because he was consumed by jealousy of the Tendai school, he died very suddenly and found himself bound with seven cords of iron and dragged by two guardians of hell to the court of Emma, the king of hell. But he was told that his life span had not reached its conclusion and therefore was sent back to the world of men.

While in hell, he suspected that he had been brought before Emma because he had slandered the Lotus Sutra, and he therefore quickly set aside all his Shin-gon mudras, mantras, and methods of concentration and instead chanted the passage from the Lotus Sutra that begins, "Now this threefold world is all my [the Buddha's] domain," whereupon the cords that bound him fell away and he was returned to life.

On another occasion, he was ordered by the imperial court to recite prayers for rain and rain did in fact suddenly begin to fall, but a huge wind also rose up and did great damage to the country.

Later, when he really did die, his disciples gathered around his deathbed and praised the remarkable way in which he died, but in fact he fell into the great citadel of the hell of incessant suffering. You may ask how I know that this is so. I would reply that, if you examine his biography, you will find it stated, "Looking now at Shan-wu-wei's remains, one can see that they are gradually shrinking, the skin is turning blackish and the bones are exposed."

Shan-wu-wei's disciples perhaps did not realize that this was a sign that after his death he had been reborn in hell, but supposed that it was a manifestation of his virtue. Yet in describing it, the author of the biography exposed Shan-wu-wei's guilt, recording that after his death his body gradually shrank, the skin turned black, and the bones began to show. . . .

Pu-k'ung, too, was ordered by the emperor to pray for rain, and within three days, rain did in fact fall. The emperor was pleased and dispensed rewards with his own hand. But shortly after, a huge wind descended from the sky, buffeting and damaging the imperial palace and toppling the quarters of the upper noblemen and high ministers until it seemed that not a building would be left standing. The emperor, astounded, issued an imperial command for prayers that the wind be stopped. But though it would stop for a little, it would start blowing again and again, until in the end it blew uninterrupted for a space of several days. Eventually, messengers were dispatched to drive Pu-k'ung out of the country, and then at last the wind subsided.

The evil winds of these three men have become the huge wind of the Shingon leaders that blows throughout all of China and Japan! And if that is so, then the great gale that arose on the twelfth day of the fourth month in the eleventh year of Bun'ei (1274) must have been an adverse wind brought about by Kaga Hōin of the Amida Hall, one of the most eminent monks of Tō-ji, when he was praying for rain. We must conclude that the evil teachings of Shan-wu-wei, Chin-kang-chih, and Pu-k'ung have been transmitted without the slightest alteration. What a strange coincidence indeed!

Let us turn now to the Great Teacher Kōbō. At the time of the great drought in the second month of the first year of Tenchō (824), the emperor first ordered Shubin to pray for rain, and within seven days Shubin was able to make rain fall. But the rain fell only in the capital and did not extend to the countryside.

Kōbō was then ordered to take over the prayers for rain, but seven days passed and there was no sign of it. Another seven days passed and there still were no clouds. After seven more days had passed, the emperor ordered Wake no Matsuna to go and present offerings in the Shinsen-en garden, whereupon rain fell from the sky for a period of three days. Kōbō and his disciples thereupon proceeded to appropriate this rain and claim it as their own, and for more than four hundred years now, it has been known as "Kōbō's rain."

Jikaku said he had a dream in which he shot down the sun. And Kōbō told a great falsehood, claiming that, in the spring of the ninth year of the Kōnin era (818), when he was praying for an end to the great epidemic, the sun came out in the middle of the night.

Since the Kalpa of Formation, when the earth took shape, down to the ninth kalpa of decrease in the Kalpa of Continuance, twenty-nine kalpas have passed by, but in all that time, the sun has never been known to come out at night! And as to Jikaku's dream of the sun, where in all the five thousand or seven thousand volumes of the Buddhist scriptures or the three thousand or more volumes of the secular classics is it recorded that to dream of shooting the sun is auspicious? The king of the *asuras,* angered at the deity Taishaku, shot an arrow at the sun god, but the arrow came back and struck the king himself in the eye. Chou, the last ruler of the Yin dynasty, used the sun as a target for his arrows, and in the end he was destroyed.

In Japan, in the reign of Emperor Jimmu, the emperor's elder brother Itsuse no Mikoto engaged in battle with the chieftain of Tomi, Nagasunebiko, and Itsuse no Mikoto was wounded in the hand by an arrow. He said, "I am a descendant of the sun deity. But because I have drawn my bow while facing the sun, I have incurred this punishment from the sun deity."

In India, King Ajātaśatru renounced his earlier mistaken views and became a follower of the Buddha. He returned to his palace and lay down to sleep, but later rose up in alarm and said to his ministers, "I have dreamed that the sun has left the sky and fallen to the earth!"

His ministers said, "Perhaps this means the passing away of the Buddha." Subhadra also had the same kind of dream just before the Buddha passed away.

It would be particularly inauspicious to dream, [as Jikaku claims he did,] of shooting the sun in Japan, since the supreme deity in Japan is Amaterasu, the Sun Goddess, and the name of the country, Japan, means "the Land of the Rising Sun." In addition, Shakyamuni Buddha is called the "Sun Seed" because his mother Queen Māyā dreamed that she conceived the sun and in time gave birth to this child, the crown prince, [who later became the Buddha].

The Great Teacher Jikaku established Dainichi Buddha as the object of worship on Mount Hiei and rejected Shakyamuni Buddha. He paid honor to the three Shingon sutras and acted as an enemy to the Lotus Sutra and its two companion sutras. That was no doubt the reason why he dreamed this dream of shooting the sun.

On the subject of dreams, there is also the case of the priest Shan-tao in China. In his youth he met a priest named Ming-sheng of Mi-chou and received instruction in the Lotus Sutra. Later, however, when he met Tao-ch'o, he threw aside his trust in the *Kammuryōju* Sutra. He even wrote a commentary on the sutra, which asserted that with the Lotus Sutra, not one person in a thousand can be saved, whereas the Nembutsu practice insures that ten persons out of ten or a hundred persons out of a hundred will be reborn in the Pure Land. In order to prove his point, he prayed before Amida Buddha to confirm whether or not his views accorded with the Buddha's intent. . . .

Again in the work entitled *Kujakkyō Ongi*, or Annotations on the Peacock Sutra, we read: "After the Great Teacher Kōbō returned from China, he desired to establish the Shingon sect in Japan, and representatives of all the various sects were summoned to the imperial court. But many of them had doubts about the Shingon doctrine of the attaining of Buddhahood in one's present form. The Great Teacher Kōbō thereupon formed his hands in the wisdom mudra and faced south. Suddenly his mouth opened and he turned into the golden-colored Buddha Maha-vairocana—that is, he reverted to his original form. In this way he demonstrated that the Buddha is present in the individual and that the individual is present in the Buddha, and that one can immediately attain Buddhahood in this very existence. On that day, all doubts concerning the matter were completely resolved, and from that time the Shingon or Yuga sect with its doctrines of secret mandalas was established."

The same work also says, "At this time the leaders of the other sects all bowed to the opinion of the Great Teacher Kōbō and for the first time received instruction in Shingon, sought its benefit and practiced it. Dōshō of the Sanron sect, Gennin of the Hossō sect, Dōō of the Kegon set, and Enchō of the Tendai sect were all among those who did so."

In addition, the biography of the Great Teacher Kōbō states: "On the day when he set out by ship from China, he voiced a prayer, saying, 'If there is a spot that is particularly suitable for the teaching of these doctrines that I have learned, may this three-pronged vajra implement land there!'" Then he faced in the direction of Japan and threw the implement up into the air. It sailed far away and disappeared among the clouds. In the tenth month, he returned to Japan.

The same work states, "He journeyed to the foot of Mount Kōya and determined to establish his place of meditation there . . . and later it was discovered that the three-pronged vajra implement which he had thrown out over the sea was there on the mountain."

It is clear from these two or three incidents that the Great Teacher Kōbō was a person of inestimable power and virtue. Since he was a person of such great power, why do you say that one should not believe in his teachings, and that anyone who does so will fall into the Avīci hell?

Answer: I, too, admire and believe in these various accomplishments of his. There are other men of old who possessed such uncanny powers. But the possession of such power does not indicate whether that person's understanding of the Buddhist Law is correct or not. Among the Brahman believers of India there have been men who could pour the water of the Ganges River into their ear and keep it there for twelve years, who could drink the ocean dry, grasp the sun and moon in their hands, or change the disciples of Shakyamuni Buddha into oxen or sheep. But such powers only made them more arrogant than ever and caused them to create further karma to suffer in the realm of birth and death. It is men like these whom T'ien-t'ai is referring to when he says, "They seek after fame and profit and increase their illusions of thought and desire."

The Chinese priest Fa-yün of Kuang-che-ssu could make it rain suddenly or cause flowers to bloom immediately, but Miao-lo writes of him, "Though he could bring about a response in this way, his understanding still did not accord with the truth [of the Lotus Sutra]." When the Great Teacher T'ien-t'ai read the Lotus Sutra, soft rain began to fall in an instant, and the Great Teacher Dengyō caused the rain of amṛta to fall within the space of three days. However, they did not say that because of such powers their understanding of the truth coincided with that of the Buddha.

Regardless of what unusual powers Kōbō may have had, he described the Lotus Sutra as a doctrine of childish theory, and wrote that Shakyamuni Buddha was still in the region of darkness. Men of wisdom and understanding should have nothing to do with such writings!

Say what you may, there are surely doubtful points in the accounts of Kōbō's powers you have just cited. The text says, "In the spring of the ninth year of Kōnin (818), the empire was troubled by a great plague." But spring is ninety days long. On which day of which month of spring did this happen? This is the first doubtful point.

Secondly, was there in fact an outbreak of plague in the ninth year of Kōnin?

Thirdly, the text says, "When night came, the sun continued to shine bright and red." If it really did so, then this is an occurrence of major importance. During the ninth year of Kōnin, Emperor Saga reigned. But did the court historians of the left and right record any such event?

Even if they had, it would be difficult to believe. During the twenty kalpas of the Kalpa of Formation, as well as nine kalpas of the Kalpa of Continuance, a total of twenty-nine kalpas, never once has such a thing occurred. What then is this about the sun appearing in the middle of the night? In all the teachings expounded by Shakyamuni Buddha during his lifetime, there is no mention of any such thing. And in the *Three Records* and *Five Canons* of China which describe the three sovereigns and five emperors of antiquity, there is no prediction that at some future date the sun will come out in the middle of the night. In the scriptures of Buddhism, we are told that in the Kalpa of Decline, two suns, three suns, or even seven suns will appear, but these will appear in the daytime, not at night. And if the sun should appear at night in our own region, the continent of Jambudvīpa in the south, then what about the other three regions of the east, west, and north?

Regardless of what the Buddhist scriptures or the secular works may have to say about such an event, if in fact there were some entry in the diaries of the courtiers, the other families of the capital, or the priests of Mount Hiei saying that in the spring of the ninth year of Kōnin, in such and such a month, on such and such a day, at such an hour of the night the sun appeared, then we might perhaps believe it. [But no such record exists.]

Later, the text says, "I was present long ago at Eagle Peak when the Buddha preached the Heart Sutra, and I personally heard him expound its profound doctrines." This is surely a wild falsehood that is intended to make people have faith in his commentary. If not, are we to believe that at Eagle Peak the Buddha announced that the Lotus Sutra was a piece of "childish theory" and that the *Dainichi* Sutra represented the truth, and that Ānanda and Monju were simply mistaken in saying that the Lotus Sutra represents the truth?

As for making it rain, even a promiscuous woman and a breaker of the precepts were able by their poems to cause rain to fall. Yet Kōbō prayed for twenty-one days and still it did not rain, so what sort of powers could he have possessed? This is the fourth doubtful point.

Source: Nichiren, *Selected Writings of Nichiren,* translated by Burton Watson (New York: Columbia University Press, 1990), 289–299.

ZEN BUDDHISM

Selection from Dōgen's "The Actualization of Enlightenment"
(*Genjōkōan*)

When all things are the Buddha-dharma, there is enlightenment, illusion, practice, life, death, Buddhas, and sentient beings. When all things are seen not to
have any substance, there is no illusion or enlightenment, no Buddhas or sentient
beings, no birth or destruction. Originally the Buddhist Way transcends itself and
any idea of abundance or lack—still there is birth and destruction, illusion and
enlightenment, sentient beings and Buddhas. Yet people hate to see flowers fall
and do not like weeds to grow.

It is an illusion to try to carry out our practice and enlightenment through
ourselves, but to have practice and enlightenment through phenomena, that is
enlightenment. To have great enlightenment about illusion is to be a Buddha. To
have great illusion about enlightenment is to be a sentient being. Further, some
are continually enlightened beyond enlightenment but some add more and more
illusion.

When Buddhas become Buddhas, it is not necessary for them to be aware
they are Buddhas. However, they are still enlightened Buddhas and continually
realize Buddha. Through body and mind we can comprehend the form and sound
of things. They work together as one. However, it is not like the reflection of a
shadow in a mirror, or the moon reflected in the water. If you look at only one
side, the other is dark.

To learn the Buddhist Way is to learn about oneself. To learn about oneself is
to forget oneself. To forget oneself is to perceive oneself as all things. To realize
this is to cast off the body and mind of self and others. When you have reached
this stage you will be detached even from enlightenment but will practice it continually without thinking about it.

When people begin to seek the Dharma [outside themselves] they are immediately far removed from its true location. When the Dharma has been received
through the right transmission, one's real self immediately appears.

If you are in a boat, and you only look at the riverbank, you will think that the
riverbank is moving; but if you look at the boat, you will discover that the boat
itself is actually moving. Similarly, if you try to understand the nature of phenomena only through your own confused perception you will mistakenly think
that your nature is eternal. Furthermore, if you have right practice and return to
your origin then you will clearly see that all things have no permanent self.

Once firewood is reduced to ashes, it cannot return to firewood; but we should not think of ashes as the potential state of firewood or vice-versa. Ash is completely ash and firewood is firewood. They have their own past, future, and independent existence.

Similarly, when human beings die, they cannot return to life; but in Buddhist teaching we never say life changes into death. This is an established teaching of the Buddhist Dharma. We call it "non-becoming." Likewise, death cannot change into life. This is another principle of Buddha's Law. This is called "non-destruction." Life and death have absolute existence, like the relationship of winter and spring. But do not think of winter changing into spring or spring to summer.

When human beings attain enlightenment, it is like the moon reflected in the water. The moon appears in the water but does not get wet nor is the water disturbed by the moon. Furthermore, the light of the moon covers the earth and yet it can be contained in a small pool of water, a tiny dewdrop, or even one miniscule drop of water.

Just as the moon does not trouble the water in any way, do not think enlightenment causes people difficulty. Do not consider enlightenment an obstacle in your life. The depths of the dewdrop can contain the heights of the moon and sky.

When the True Law is not totally attained, both physically and mentally, there is a tendency to think that we possess the complete Law and our work is finished. If the Dharma is completely present, there is a realization of one's insufficiencies.

For example, if you take a boat to the middle of the ocean, beyond the sight of any mountains, and look in all four directions, the ocean appears round. However, the ocean is not round, and its virtue is limitless. It is like a palace, or an adornment of precious jewels. But to us, the ocean seems to be one large circle of water.

So we see that this can be said of all things. Depending on the viewpoint we see things in different ways. Correct perception depends upon the amount of one's study and practice. In order to understand various types of viewpoints we must study the numerous aspects and virtues of mountains and oceans, rather than just circles. We should know that it is not only so all around us but also within us—even in a single drop of water.

Fish in the ocean find the water endless and birds think the sky is without limits. However, neither fish nor birds have been separated from their element. When their need is great, their utilization is great, when it is small, the utilization is small. They fully utilize every aspect to its utmost—freely, limitlessly. However, we should know that if birds are separated from their own element they will die. We should know that water is life for fish and the sky is life for birds. In the sky, birds are life; and in the water, fish are life. Many more conclusions can be drawn like this. There is practice and enlightenment [like the above relationships of sky and birds, and fish and water]. However, after the clarification of water and sky, we can see that if there are birds or fish that try to enter the sky or water, they cannot find either a way or a place. If we understand this point, there is actualization of enlightenment in our daily life. If we attain this Way, all our actions are the actualization of enlightenment. This Way, this place, is not great or small, self or others, neither past or present—it exists just as it is.

Like this, if we practice and realize the Buddhist Way we can master and penetrate each dharma; and we can confront and master any one practice. There is a place where we can penetrate the Way and find the extent of knowable perceptions. This happens because our knowledge co-exists simultaneously with the ultimate fulfillment of the Buddhist Dharma.

After this fulfillment becomes the basis of our perception do not think that our perception is necessarily understood by the intellect. Although enlightenment is actualized quickly, it is not always totally manifested because [it is too profound and inexhaustible for our limited intellect].

One day, when Zen Master Hōtetsu of Mt. Mayoku was fanning himself, a monk approached and asked, "The nature of the wind never changes and blows everywhere, so why are you using a fan?"

The master replied, "Although you know that the nature of the wind never changes you do not know the meaning of blowing everywhere." The monk then said, "Well, what does it mean?" Hōtetsu did not speak but only continued to fan himself. Finally the monk understood and bowed deeply before him.

The experience, the realization, and the living, right transmission of the Buddhist Dharma is like this. To say it is not necessary to use a fan because the nature of the wind never changes and there will be wind even without one means that he does not know the real meaning of "never changes" or the wind's nature. Just as the wind's nature never changes, the wind of Buddhism makes the earth golden and causes the rivers to flow with sweet, fermented milk.

Selections from Dōgen's "Buddha-nature"

Shakyamuni Buddha said, "All sentient beings totally possess Buddha-nature. The Tathāgata is permanently abiding, not subject to change."

Although this is the turning of the Wheel of the Law of the Great Teacher Sha-kyamuni, it is also the essence and enlightened vision of all the Buddhas and Patri-archs. This teaching has been studied for 2,190 years, having been directly handed down through fifty generations (up to my late master Tendō Nyojō)—twenty-eight generations in India, and twenty-three in China (including Nyojō). All the Bud-dhas and Patriarchs of the ten directions possess and maintain this teaching.

What is the meaning of "All sentient beings totally possess Buddha-nature?" It is the turning of the wheel of the Law of "What has come?" Sometimes, it is called "sentient beings," "animate beings," "living things," "living species," "totally," equals sentient beings, all living things. "Totally possess" is Buddha-nature; One part of possessing is sentient beings. At the proper time, inside and outside of sentient beings is Buddha-nature totally. It is not only valid for trans-mission of skin, flesh, bones, and marrow, but for all transmissions of "you pos-sess my skin, flesh, bones and marrow."

We must know that the "possess" of "totally possess" is not related to posses-sion or non-possession. "Totally possess" is the word and tongue of Buddha, the enlightened vision of the Buddhas and Patriarchs, and the nostrils of Zen monks. "Totally possess" does not mean initial, original, miraculous or any other kind of possession. It is, of course, not attained as a result of karma or delusion, and has nothing to do with mind, circumstance, nature, form, etc.

Therefore, that is why the correct understanding of "sentient beings totally possess" does not occur through the influence of karma, does not arise by illusory causation, does not occur naturally, and is not developed through the miraculous power of practice and enlightenment. If the "totally possess" of sentient beings depended upon karma, causation, or nature and so forth, so would the realization of saints, the awakening of the Buddhas, and the enlightened vision of the Bud-dhas and Patriarchs. But, that is not the case.

The entire world is free of dust, and here there can be no second person. This is because we are unaware that the root of illusion is cut off and there is no way for the disturbed flow of karma to cease. It has not been bred by deluded causa-tion since nothing in the relative world has ever been concealed. "Nothing has been concealed" does not necessarily mean that all worlds exist. That the relative world is self existent is an erroneous view of non-believers. Existence is not orig-inal being because it is not confined to past or present. It is not an initial occur-rence because it contains nothing extra. . . .

Some say that Buddha-nature is similar to the seed of a plant; when it receives the nourishing rain of the Dharma, it naturally sprouts—leaves, flowers, and fruit appear, and the fruit contains its own seeds. This is the view of ordinary, unenlightened people. Those holding such a view should learn that the seed, flowers and fruit each and at the same time have the pure mind [of Buddha-nature]. Within the fruit there are seeds. Although the seeds are not visible, still the roots, stem, and the rest grow. Without outside assistance the branches multiply and a large tree appears. This procedure is not outside or inside; it is true for any time of the past or present. Therefore, even though we have an unenlightened view, the root, stem, branches, and leaves all live, die, "totally possess," and become and are Buddha-nature simultaneously.

Buddha said, "In order to know the principle of Buddha-nature watch for the proper time and circumstance. When the time comes, Buddha-nature will be manifest." "In order to understand the principle of Buddha-nature" does not mean simply "knowing," but means also practicing, enlightening, clarifying, and ultimately forgetting. This explaining, practicing, enlightening, and mistaking or not mistaking are all "proper time and circumstance." The way to watch for proper time and circumstance is through proper time. Watch for proper time with a fly whisk, a staff, and so on. Original enlightenment, initial enlightenment, nonenlightenment, right enlightenment, and their wisdom cannot be seen through either worldly or sacred knowledge.

"Watch for" is neither related to the watcher or the watched, nor to true or false watching. It is just watching. It is pure watching—not one own's perception nor others. It is to "watch" beyond proper time. It is Buddha-Buddha, nature-nature.

Many people in the past and present have taken "the proper time and circumstance" to mean "wait for a time in the future for Buddha-nature to appear." They say, "If we practice like that, Buddha-nature will naturally appear at the proper time. Even if we study under a master and seek the Dharma, if it is not the proper time, Buddha-nature will not appear. People with such views are worldings who expect good things to fall directly from heaven. Such people are like the nonbelievers who hold that everything occurs by chance.

"In order to know the principle of Buddha-nature" means "directly knowing the principle of Buddha-nature." "Watch for the proper time" and circumstance means directly knowing the proper time. That is, if we want to know Buddha-nature, we must seek the proper time and circumstance.

The expression "when the time comes" means the "time has already come." Even if we doubt it, still Buddha-nature has emerged in us.

You should know that "when the time comes" is manifest in each hour of the day. "When it comes" is as if it has already come." "When the time comes," Buddha-nature has not come. Therefore, that is why "the time has already come" is the manifestation of Buddha-nature. In other words, the truth is self-evident. "There has never been a time that has not come right now and an actualization of Buddha-nature that has not appeared right here." . . .

We should know this. "Sentient beings possess Buddha-nature; Sentient beings do not possess Buddha-nature." Realize, actualization of Buddha-nature and attainment of Buddhahood occur simultaneously. This is the Buddhist Dharma. Had this principle not been studied, the Dharma would not exist today. If we fail to clarify this principle we will neither clarify attainment of Buddhahood nor realize it. Thus the Fifth Patriarch said to the Sixth Patriarch "People of Renan have no Buddha-nature."

"Sentient beings do not possess Buddha-nature." To a man who has just encountered a Buddha and heard the Dharma for the first time, this is the most incomprehensible, most taxing statement of all. Later, whether through having followed a good master or through having studied the sutras, this statement is the most joy giving of all. If we do not totally feel the truth of "sentient beings do not possess Buddha-nature," then we have not yet experienced Buddha-nature.

When the Sixth Patriarch, a sincere seeker of Buddhahood, met the Fifth Patriarch, the latter said, "People of Renan have no Buddha-nature." He said nothing more than this and used no other method.

Thus we realize, the very questioning and studying of "no-Buddha-nature" is itself the direct path to Buddhahood. At the right time of "no-Buddha-nature" there is Buddhahood. If we have neither experienced nor clarified no-Buddha-nature, then we have not yet attained Buddhahood.

The Sixth Patriarch said, "Although men differ from north to south, Buddha-nature does not." Think about this very carefully; it has great significance. What does he mean "north and south"? Seek to clarify these words, for they too are a profound teaching. This statement implies that while man can attain Buddhahood, Buddha-nature cannot. I wonder whether the Sixth Patriarch intended to imply this.

The words "no-Buddha-nature" used by the Fifth and Sixth Patriarchs express the entire truth, they are absolute detachment. In the same spirit, when past Buddhas such as Shakyamuni and Kāśyapa turned the wheel of the Law they said with full conviction, "All sentient beings possess Buddha-nature." If there is a "possess" in "possess Buddha-nature" how could there be no transmission of "no-Buddha-nature." . . .

The Sixth Patriarch's understanding of impermanence is very different from that of non-Buddhists or Hinayānists. Even though the latter teach impermanence, they do not fully realize its implication. . . .

"Impermanence is itself Buddha-nature"; thus both saints and ordinary men are impermanent. Only in the eyes of small minded, ignorant people is this not so. If this latter view were correct, the body of the Buddha would be very small indeed. Hence the Sixth Patriarch's statement: "Impermanence itself is Buddha-nature." Permanence is "not turning." In other words is something that is uneffected by attachment—detachment, coming—going, and so forth. In this sense it [Buddha-nature] has permanency.

Therefore, since grasses, trees, and bushes are impermanent, they are Buddha-nature. The very impermanence of man's body and mind is Buddha-nature. Supreme enlightenment and parinirvāna, because they are impermanent, are Buddha-nature. Hinayānists and scholars of the abidharma and sutras must be surprised and puzzled by this; truly they are no better than devils. . . .

Manifesting a round full moon is actualization of all the Buddhas. Since all the Buddhas are actualized, the form of a full moon appears. Therefore, we must study all the forms of long, short, square, and round body. If we fail to grasp the meaning of "body" and "manifesting," the full moon will not be understood; consequently the bodies of all the Buddhas will not appear. Fools think, "He is expressing his form as a full moon." A ridiculous idea, proof that these people have not inherited the Buddhist Way. How, and at what place and time can he express his form in a body other than his own. Nāgārjuna was simply sitting on the dias—his form no different to anyone else who is just sitting. Realize that the body is an actualization of the full moon.

The actualized body is not square, round, existent or non-existent, hidden or revealed, or is it limitless form—it is just actualization of form. Here the moon is full, but know it can either full or quarter. Since the actualized body does not relate to the self, it is not Nāgārjuna—it is the body of all the Buddhas. Furthermore, because of its nature it transcends all the Buddha bodies. That is to say it is beyond the body of Buddha itself.

Buddha-nature is a radiant full moon. This is true, but it is not limited to this form; much less can it be put into words, or actualized as body or mind. It cannot be found in the world of phenomena, yet it appears in the phenomenal world as the body of all the Buddhas. It is characteristic of proclaiming the Dharma with no form. When no form becomes formless samadhi, the body is actualized. . . .

The actual body of Nāgārjuna clarifies Buddha-nature—it is clear and bright, perfect emptiness. Therefore, the body that is clarifying Buddha-nature expresses the body of all Buddhas. There is not one Buddha not actualizing Buddha-nature in the form of Buddha. Buddha-form is the actualized body. The actualized body is Buddha-nature.

Therefore, the Buddha-form and Patriarch form are actualized in the four elements and five *skhandas.* All virtue of the Buddha is contained in this virtue. The virtue of Buddha is completely formed and actualized in our body. The unlimited, boundless activity of virtue is one part of the body's actualization. The words of Nāgārjuna and Kāṇadeva are the ultimate in Buddhist wisdom, the like of which has not since been heard anywhere. How many scholars of the sūtras and abhidharmas have mistaken the Way of the Buddhas and Patriarchs? . . .

The moon has a round shape; the round shape is the body's complete actualization. When you consider a round shape, do not think of a small coin or rice cake. The body's form is that of a full moon, the shape is that of a full moon. With proper understanding of roundness, even a coin or rice cake can be studied. . . .

A thing that is unpaintable is best left unpainted; or if we must, then at least do so correctly. The body in the form of a round moon is one such unpaintable thing.

When they have failed to realize that Buddha-nature is not perceived by mental cognition, they cannot hope to grasp the meaning of "Buddha-nature" and "no Buddha-nature." It is rare, in fact, that any even try to clarify these terms. Truly there is lack of earnest concentration on the Way.

There are many abbots of various Zen temples who do not even mention "Buddha-nature" throughout their entire life. Some say, "Those who study Buddhism talk about Buddha-nature, but those who practice don't." These people are worse than beasts—just evil beings that defile the Way of the Buddhas and Patriarchs. Both study and practice [zazen] is the Way of the Buddhas and Tathāgatas, is it not? Realize that in Buddhism there is no distinction between study and practice.

National Teacher Saian of Enkan prefecture in Koshu was one of Baso Dōitsu's foremost disciples. Once he said to an assembly of monks: "All sentient beings possess Buddha-nature."

Consider these words carefully. What does he mean, "all sentient beings"— what is "a sentient being"? Firstly, there is no one kind of sentient being, each being differs according to circumstantial and personal karma. Thus, each has different views and perception. There are unenlightened, non-believers, the three vehicles, the five vehicles, and so forth. In Buddhism, a sentient is a being that possesses a mind. That is to say, mind means sentient being. In the sense that mind means sentient being, things without mind are sentient beings. Therefore, mind is sentient being. Sentient beings are Buddha-nature. Grass, trees, and lands are mind; thus they are sentient beings. Because they are sentient beings they are Buddha-nature. Sun, moon, and stars are mind; thus they are sentient beings; thus they are Buddha-nature.

The National Teacher's words "possesses Buddha-nature" is like this. If this were not so it would not be Buddhism. The National Teacher's statement simply means "all sentient beings possess Buddha-nature." That is, no sentient being— no Buddha-nature. "Do all Buddhas possess Buddha-nature?" Think about this question and ask the National Teacher. Why is it said that "sentient beings *possess* Buddha-nature," rather than "sentient beings *equal* Buddha-nature"? This question too deserves careful consideration. Drop off the possess in "possess Buddha-nature." Here, "drop off" captures the essence; that is to say is ultimate freedom. Thus we have "all Buddha-natures possess sentient beings." In this truism, both sentient beings and Buddha-nature are dropped off.

Although the National Teacher's words were beyond his level of understanding, there will come a time when they will be equal.

"His words were beyond his level of understanding—do not take this to mean his words are unreliable, a misinterpretation of the truth. On the contrary, even though he himself does not understand the truth, he embodies it. That is to say, there is still the four elements, five *skhandas,* skin, flesh, bone, and marrow [of Buddha-nature]. Just like this, it may take a life time to understand the Truth and another life time to express it.

Zen Master Dai'e of Mount Daien said to the assembled monks: "All sentient beings have no Buddha-nature." Among the men and gods who heard this, some were overjoyed, others confused. Shakyamuni taught "All sentient beings have Buddha-nature," yet Dai'e said: "All sentient beings have no Buddha-nature." "Have" and "have no" are totally different; "which is correct?" is a question that has been asked by many. "Sentient beings have no Buddha-nature" is, however, the ultimate in the Buddhist Way. Reason would argue Enkan's "have Buddha-nature" supports Shakyamuni, but opposes Dai'e, yet the latter and the former's words are not essentially different. Enkan was the first generation disciple of Baso and Dai'e the second. In this case the second generation surpasses the first and even the Old Master himself [Baso].

Dai'e's "all sentient beings have no Buddha-nature" is the ultimate truth. It is the boundless universe. Ask yourself, "How can sentient beings have Buddha-nature?" If sentients had Buddha-nature, they would be ranked as demons: a demon in the form of a sentient. Buddha-nature is Buddha-nature and sentient beings are sentient beings. Realize that sentient beings do not from the beginning have Buddha-nature; yet you also cannot endow yourself with it since it is not something that appears now for the first time.

"Chang drinks, and Li gets drunk"—it is not like this. A sentient being that originally has Buddha-nature is not a sentient being. As there are sentient beings, then there is no Buddha-nature.

Hence Hyakujō's words: If we teach that sentient beings possess Buddha-nature, we slander the Buddha, Dharma, and Sangha. If we teach that sentient beings possess no Buddha-nature, we slander the Buddha, Dharma, and Sangha. Even though both "have Buddha-nature" and "have not Buddha-nature" are slanderous to the Three Treasures, we cannot just remain silent [on the subject]. Ask Dai'e and Hyakujō: "you both taught about Buddha-nature, did you not? Was that not slanderous? Even given that you did, wouldn't such a teaching confuse more than clarify. Teaching and listening are contingent on each other: each must occur together." Turning to Dai'e: "You said 'all sentient beings have no Buddha-nature,' but you did not say all Buddha-nature has no sentient beings,' or 'all Buddha-nature has no Buddha-nature,' much less could you realize, or even dream, that 'all Buddhas have no Buddha-nature.' What have you to say about this?" . . .

Ōbaku was sitting in Nansen's tea room. Nansen said: "[It says in the *Nirvāna-Sūtra*] if we practice samadhi and prajñā equally, we will clearly see Buddha-nature. What is your understanding of this?" Ōbaku replied, "We gain essential understanding through being non attached at all times." Nansen replied, "You've realized this for yourself, haven't you?" Ōbaku replied, "Oh no, not really." Nansen said, "Money for drinking water may be set aside, but who can return the money used for straw sandals?" Ōbaku made no reply.

"Practice samadhi and prajñā equally." Do not take this to mean Buddha-nature is clearly seen when neither practice takes precedence over the other. Rather, understand that when Buddha-nature is clearly seen, samadhi and prajñā are practiced equally. Nansen said, "What is your understanding of this?" In other words, "Who is it that is clearly seeing Buddha-nature?" All of the expressions in this dialogue are sayings of the Way.

Ōbaku's words: "We gain essential understanding through being non-attached at all times." That is to say: "At all times, everywhere there is no clinging to anything. Not clinging to anything occurs at all times." Therefore we clearly see Buddha-nature. As for time: when will time fail to be? In what land will it not exist? Think about "time." Does it mean "time" as we know it, "time" in some other world, or "time" in the Radiant Pure Land? Whichever it might be, the point is "do not be attached to anything." This is a fundamental truth; it does not change according to circumstances.

"You've realized this for yourself, haven't you?" That is: "this is your own utterance, your own understanding isn't it?" Do not take this to mean this understanding is limited to Ōbaku. Ōbaku was the vessel from which the words came, but the essence of his words is a universal truth.

Ōbaku said: "Oh no, not really. "In Sung China this was a more or less standard reply to questions asked about one's ability. Even if one had the ability [in question], this is the reply given [out of modesty]. Don't, therefore take "Oh no, not really" to literally mean "Oh no, not really": the overall meaning transcends the words themselves. . . .

Jōshū said "*Mu.*" *Mu* is the way to practice. The self-named *Mu* of Buddha-nature, of the dog, of the observer is like this *mu.* Thus *Mu* is all-powerful, rock-melting *Mu.*

The monk asked: "All sentient beings have Buddha-nature, why doesn't the dog?" This is explained as: "If there are no sentient beings, there can be no sentient beings, and of course no dog. This is the meaning of 'what lives?'" Why is it necessary to a ascribe *Mu* to the dog or Buddha-nature?

Jōshū said, "It [the dog] is bound by karma." That is, it is karma. There is karma, therefore there is a dog—no dog, no Buddha-nature. Karma has no "meeting" with the dog, so how can the dog encounter Buddha-nature? All such functions are bound with karma.

Another monk asked Jōshū: "Does a dog have Buddha-nature or not?" Clearly this monk was familiar with Jōshū's thought. Questions about Buddha-nature are the every day occurrences of eating rice and taking tea of the Buddhas and Patriarchs.

Jōshū said: "It has." Here, "it has" is not the existence [u] of the Abhidharmists of Sarvāstivāda school." It has should be understood in the context of Buddhism. Buddha's "it has" is Jōshū "it has," is the same as the dog's "it has," which is the same as Buddha-nature's it has.

A monk asked: "Given it has Buddha-nature, what is the purpose of the [physical] body?" What does he mean by "has"? Is it in the present, in the past, or already possessed? Although "has" seems to be related to all other forms of existence, this "has" alone shines brightly. Is "has" something that can be put somewhere or not? The practice of trying to put it somewhere is not entirely correct, but not totally useless.

Jōshū said, "Knowingly and deliberately it sinned." These words are common and widely used, but take on special significance as Jōshū's saying of the Way. The meaning of "knowingly it sinned" is doubted by many. The word "put" is difficult to comprehend here, and in fact is not necessary. There is a saying, "If you want to know the undying fellow in his heritage, don't separate yourself from your bag of skin." The undying man cannot be separated from this bag of skin. "Knowingly sinned" is not equal to "put into a skin bag" and vice versa. "Knowingly" is deliberately sinning. Know that "deliberately sinning" is hidden within the daily activities of the liberated body. This is the meaning of "put in." When the liberated body of practice is correctly hidden, self and others are truly concealed. Do not, then, say you are still confined with a bunch of louts. There's more: The High Patriarch Ummon said, "By learning everything about the Buddha-Dharma, you become confused." Even halfway through such study, there has been a long period of confusion and mistakes. Days and months on end nothing more than repeated failures to push something into the dog's bag of skin. "Knowingly and deliberately it sinned" is "has Buddha-nature."

Source: Dōgen, *Shōbōgenzō,* translated by Kōsen Nishiyama (Tokyo: Nakayama Shobo, 1975–1983), 1: 1–4; 4: 120–139.

Selections from the Zen Master Hakuin's "Oratengama"

Yesterday I received your letter, delivered to me from afar. It must be a great relief to have successfully brought to a finish your entertainment of the Koreans. Thank you for inquiring about my health: I am well as usual and you need not worry about me. I was most pleased to hear that you are devoting yourself unceasingly to koan meditation in both its active and quietistic aspects. As for the other matters you touch upon in your letter, I find myself in complete agreement. You cannot imagine how delighted I am at your many accomplishments.

If their motivation is bad, virtually all Zen practitioners find themselves blocked in both the active and quietistic approaches to their practice of koan meditation. They fall into a state of severe depression and distraction; the fire mounts to the heart, the metal element in the lungs shrinks painfully, the health generally declines, and quite frequently they develop an illness most difficult to cure. Yet if they polish and perfect themselves in the true practice of introspection, they will conform to the secret methods for the ultimate nourishment, their bodies and minds will become strong, their vitality great, and they will readily attain to enlightenment in all things. . . .

Even though I am past seventy now my vitality is ten times as great as it was when I was thirty or forty. My mind and body are strong and I never have the feeling that I absolutely must lie down to rest. Should I want to I find no difficulty in refraining from sleep for two, three, or even seven days, without suffering any decline in my mental powers. I am surrounded by three-to five-hundred demanding students, and even though I lecture on the scriptures or on the collections of the Masters' sayings for thirty to fifty days in a row, it does not exhaust me. I am quite convinced that all this is owing to the power gained from practicing this method of introspection.

Initially emphasis must be placed on the care of the body. Then, during your practice of introspection, without your seeking it and quite unconsciously, you will attain, how many times I cannot tell, the benefits of enlightenment experiences. It is essential that you neither despise nor grasp for either the realm of activity or that of quietude, and that you continue your practice assiduously.

Frequently you may feel that you are getting nowhere with practice in the midst of activity, whereas the quietistic approach brings unexpected results. Yet rest assured that those who use the quietistic approach can never hope to enter into meditation in the midst of activity. Should by chance a person who uses this approach enter into the dusts and confusions of the world of activity, even the power of ordinary understanding which he had seemingly attained will be entirely lost. Drained of all vitality, he will be inferior to any mediocre, talentless person. The most trivial matters will upset him, an inordinate cowardice will afflict his mind, and he will frequently behave in a mean and base manner. What can you call accomplished about a man like this?

The Zen Master Ta-hui has said that meditation in the midst of activity is immeasurably superior to the quietistic approach. Po-shan has said that if one does not attain to this meditation within activity, one's practice is like trying to cross a mountain ridge as narrow as a sheep's skull with a hundred-and-twenty-pound load on one's back.

I am not trying to tell you to discard completely quietistic meditation and to seek specifically for a place of activity in which to carry out your practice. What is most worthy of respect is a pure koan meditation that neither knows nor is conscious of the two aspects, the quiet and the active. This why it has been said that the true practicing monk walks but does not know he is walking, sits but does not know he is sitting.

For penetrating to the depths of one's own true self-nature, and for attaining a vitality valid on all occasions, nothing can surpass meditation in the midst of activity. Supposing that you owned several hundred *ryō* of gold and you wanted to hire someone to guard it. One candidate shuts up the room, seals the door, and just sits there. True, he does not allow the money to be stolen, but the method he adopts does not show him to be a man with much vitality. His practice may best be compared with that of the Hinayana follower, who is intent only on his own personal enlightenment. . . .

I cannot emphasize enough that the true practice of introspection is an absolute essential that must never be neglected. The true practice of introspection (*naikan*) consists of [this contemplation]: "the area below my navel down to my loins and the soles of my feet is all Chao-chou's *Mu*. What principle can this *Mu* possibly have! The area below my navel down to my loins and the soles of my feet is all my own original face. Where can there be nostrils in this original face! The area below my navel down to my loins and the soles of my feet is all the Pure Land of my own mind. With what can this Pure Land be adorned! The area below my navel down to my loins and the soles of my feet is all the Buddha Amida in my own body. What truth can this Amida preach! The area below my navel down to my loins and the soles of my feet is all the village where I was born. What news can there be from this native village!"

If at all times even when coughing, swallowing, waving the arms, when asleep or awake, the practitioner accomplishes everything he decides to do and attains everything that he attempts to attain and, displaying a great, unconquerable determination, he moves forward ceaselessly, he will transcend the emotions and sentiments of ordinary life. His heart will be filled with an extraordinary purity and clarity, as though he were standing on a sheet of ice stretching for thousands of miles. Even if he were to enter the midst of a battlefield or to attend a place of song, dance, and revelry, it would be as though he were where no other person was. His great capacity, like that of Yün-men with his kingly pride, will make its appearance without being sought.

At this time all Buddhas and sentient beings will be like illusions, "birth and death and Nirvana like last night's dreams." This man sees through both heaven and hell; Buddha worlds and demon's palaces melt away. He strikes blind the True

Eye of the Buddhas and the Patriarchs. To his own content he expounds the hundred thousand uncountable teachings and the mysterious principle in all its ramifications. He brings benefit to all sentient beings, and passes through innumerable kalpas without becoming wearied. For endless time he spreads the teachings of Buddhism without being once in error. He makes clear all the countless activities [of a bodhisattva] and establishes a teaching of wide influence. Attaching to his arm the supernatural talisman that wrests life from death, he lets reverberate in his mouth the talons and teeth of the Cave of the Dharma, smashes the brains of monks everywhere, and pulls out the nails and knocks out the wedges. Without the least human feeling he produces an unsurpassedly evil, stupid, blind oaf, be it one person or merely half a person, with teeth sharp as the sword-trees of hell, and a gaping mouth like a tray of blood. Thus will he recompense his deep obligation to the Buddhas and the Patriarchs. The status he has achieved is known as the causal conditions for a Buddha-realm or for the dignities of a bodhisattva. He is a great man, far excelling all ordinary people, who has accomplished his cherished desire.

There are some blind, bald idiots who stand in a calm, unperturbed, untouchable place and consider that the state of mind produced in this atmosphere comprises seeing into their own natures. They think that to polish and perfect purity is sufficient, but have never even in a dream achieved the state [of the person described above]. People of this sort spend all day practicing non-action and end up by having practiced action all the while; spend all day practicing non-creating and end up by having practiced creating all the while. Why is this so? It is because their insight into the Way is not clear, because they cannot arrive at the truth of the Dharma-nature.

What a shame it is that they spend in vain this one birth as a human being, a birth so difficult to obtain. They are like blind turtles wandering pointlessly in empty valleys, like demons who guard the wood used for coffins. That they return unreformed in suffering to their old homes in the three evil ways is because their practice was badly guided, and from the outset they had not truly seen their own natures. They have exhausted the strength of their minds in vain and have in the end been able to gain no benefit at all. This is regrettable indeed. . . .

Again I say, do not discard the essentials of introspection but train and nurture them. The true practice of introspection is the most important ingredient in the nourishment of one's own health. This conforms with the basic alchemistic principles of the hermits. These first began with Shakamuni Buddha; later they were described in detail by Chih-i of the Tendai school in his *Mo-ho chih-kuan.* In my middle years I learned them from the Taoist teacher Hakuyū. Hakuyū lived in a cave at Shirakawa in Yamashiro. He is said to have been two-hundred and forty years old and the local inhabitants referred to him as the hermit Hakuyū. It is reported that he was the teacher of the late Ishikawa Jōzan. . . .

But above all, one must realize that this elixir is by no means something outside one's own body. For example, there are jewel fields and there are millet fields. The jewel fields produce jewels; the millet fields produce crops. In man there are the *kikai* and the *tanden*. The *kikai* is the treasure house where the vital energy is accumulated and nurtured; the *tanden* is the castle town where the divine elixir is distilled and the life span preserved. A man of old has said: "The reason the great rivers and seas attained to sovereignty over the hundred other streams was that they had the virtue of being lower than the others." The oceans from the outset occupy geographically a position lower than all other waters; thus they receive all these waters but never increase or lessen. The *kikai* is situated in the body at a position lower than that of the five internal organs and ceaselessly stores up the true energy. Eventually the divine elixir is perfected and the status of an immortal is achieved.

The *tanden* is located in three places in the body, but the one to which I refer is the lower *tanden*. The *kikai* and the *tanden* are both located below, the navel; they are in actuality one thing although they have two names. The *tanden* is situated two inches below the navel, the kikai an inch and a half below it, and it is in this area that the true energy always accumulates. When the body and mind are attuned, they say that even if one is a hundred years old, the hair does not turn white, the teeth remain firm, the eyesight is clearer than ever before, and the skin acquires a luster. This is the efficacy of nurturing the primal energy and bringing the divine elixir to maturity. There is no limit to the age to which one may live; it depends only on the effectiveness with which the energy is nurtured. The inspired doctors of old effected cures even before a disease made its appearance and enabled people to control the mind and nurture the energy. Quack doctors work in just the opposite way. After the disease has appeared they attempt to cure it with acupuncture, moxa treatment, and pills, with the result that many of their patients are lost. . . .

Do not say that worldly affairs and pressures of business leave you no time to study Zen under a Master, and that the confusions of daily life make it difficult for you to continue your meditation. Everyone must realize that for the true practicing monk there are no worldly cares or worries. Supposing a man accidentally drops two or three gold coins in a crowded street swarming with people. Does he forget about the money because all eyes are upon him? Does he stop looking for it because it will create a disturbance? Most people will push others out of the way, not resting until they get the money back into their own hands. Are not people who neglect the study of Zen because the press of mundane circumstances is too severe, or stop their meditation because they are troubled by worldly affairs, putting more value on two or three pieces of gold than on the unsurpassed mysterious way of the Buddhas? A person who concentrates solely on meditation amid the press and worries of everyday life will be like the man who has dropped the gold coins and devotes himself to seeking them. Who will not rejoice in such a person? . . .

When I talk about the similarities of the *Mu* koan and the calling of the Buddha's name, I do not mean that they are not without differences when it comes time to test the quality of the virtue gained and the depth or shallowness with which the Way is seen. In general, for the hero who would seek enlightenment, and would cut off the seepages of emotions and conceptions, and destroy the film of ignorance that covers the eye, nothing surpasses the *Mu* koan. . . .

To all intents and purposes, the study of Zen makes as its essential the resolution of the ball of doubt, That is why it is said: "At the bottom of great doubt lies great awakening. If you doubt fully you will awaken fully." Fo-kuo has said: "If you don't doubt the koans you suffer a grave disease." If those who study Zen are able to make the great doubt appear before them, a hundred out of a hundred, a thousand out of a thousand, will without fail attain awakening.

When a person faces the great doubt, before him there is in all directions only a vast and empty land without birth and without death, like a huge plain of ice extending ten thousand miles. As though seated within a vase of lapis lazuli surrounded by absolute purity, without his senses he sits and forgets to stand, stands and forgets to sit. Within his heart there is not the slightest thought or emotion, only the single word *Mu*. It is just as though he were standing in complete emptiness. At this time no fears arise, no thoughts creep in, and when he advances single-mindedly without retrogression, suddenly it will be as though a sheet of ice were broken or a jade tower had fallen. He will experience a great joy, one that never in forty years has he seen or heard. At this time "birth, death, and Nirvana will be like yesterday's dream, like the bubbles in the seas of the three thousand worlds, like the enlightened status of all the wise men and sages." This is known as the time of the great penetration of wondrous awakening, the state where the "Ka" is shouted. It cannot be handed down, it cannot be explained; it is just like knowing for yourself by drinking it whether the water is hot or cold. The ten directions melt before the eyes, the three periods are penetrated in an instant of thought, What joy is there in the realms of man and Heaven that can compare with this?

This power can be obtained in the space of three to five days, if the student will advance determinedly. You may ask how one can make this great doubt appear. Do not favor a quiet place, do not shun a busy place, but always set in the area below the navel Chao-chou's *Mu*. Then, asking what principle this *Mu* contains, if you discard all emotions, concepts, and thoughts and investigate single-mindedly, there is no one before whom the great doubt will not appear. When you call forth this great doubt before you in its pure and uninvolved form you may undergo an unpleasant and strange reaction. However, you must accept the fact that the realization of so felicitous a thing as the Great Matter, the trampling of the multi-tiered gate of birth and death that has come down through endless kalpas, the penetration of the inner understanding of the basic enlightenment of all the Tathāgatas of the ten directions, must involve a certain amount of suffering.

When you come to think about it, those who have investigated the *Mu* koan, brought before themselves the great doubt, experienced the Great Death, and attained the great joy, are countless in number. Of those who called the Buddha's name and gained a small measure of benefit from it, I have heard of no more than two or three. The abbot of Eshin-in has called it the benefits of wisdom or the power of faith in the mind. If you investigate the *Mu* or the Three Pounds of Flax or some other koan, to obtain True Reality in your own body should take from two or three months to a year or a year and a half. The efficacy gained from calling the Buddha's name or reciting the sutras will require forty years of strenuous effort. It is all a matter of raising or failing to raise this ball of doubt. It must be understood that this ball of doubt is like a pair of wings that advances you along the way. . . .

Five or six years ago I made up my mind to instruct everyone by saying, "Listen to the Sound of the Single Hand." I have come to realize that this koan is infinitely more effective in instructing people than any of the methods I had used before. It seems to raise the ball of doubt in people much more easily and the readiness with which progress in meditation is made has been as different as the clouds are from the earth. Thus I have come to encourage the meditation on the Single Hand exclusively.

What is the Sound of the Single Hand? When you clap together both hands a sharp sound is heard; when you raise the one hand there is neither sound nor smell. Is this the High Heaven of which Confucius speaks? Or is it the essentials of

what Yamamba describes in these words: "The echo of the completely empty valley bears tidings heard from the soundless sound?" This is something that can by
no means be heard with the ear. If conceptions and discriminations are not
mixed within it and it is quite apart from seeing, hearing, perceiving, and knowing, and if, while walking, standing, sitting, and reclining, you proceed straightforwardly without interruption in the study of this koan, then in the place where
reason is exhausted and words are ended, you will suddenly pluck out the karmic
root of birth and death and break down the cave of ignorance. Thus you will
attain to a peace in which the phoenix has left the golden net and the crane has
been set free of the basket. At this time the basis of mind, consciousness, and
emotion is suddenly shattered; the realm of illusion with its endless sinking in the
cycle of birth and death is overturned. The treasure accumulation of the Three
Bodies and the Four Wisdoms is taken away, and the miraculous realm of the Six
Supernatural Powers and Three Insights is transcended.

How worthy of veneration it is! When the [Sound of the] Single Hand enters
the ear to even the slightest degree, the sound of the Buddha, the sound of the
gods, the sound of the bodhisattvas, *śrāvakas, pratyeka-buddhas,* hungry ghosts,
fighting demons, the sound of beasts, of heaven and of hell, all sounds existing in
this world, are heard without exception. This is called "the pure supernatural
power of hearing any sound anywhere." When the [Sound of the] Single Hand
enters the ear to even the slightest degree, it is possible at a glance to see through
one's own world, other worlds, Buddha worlds, the demons' palaces, all Pure
Lands in the ten directions, and the filthy worlds of the six realms, as if one were
looking at the palm of one's hand. This is called "the pure supernatural power of
seeing anything anywhere." When the [Sound of the] Single Hand enters the ear
even to the slightest degree, all traces rising and falling through the endless cycle
of rebirth from the infinite kalpas of the past, all shadows revolving back and
forth from the infinite kalpas of the past, appear as clearly and brilliantly as
though they were placed before the treasure mirror. This is called "the pure
supernatural power of knowing of the former existence of one's self and others."
When the [Sound of the] Single Hand enters the ear even to the slightest degree,
you penetrate to the fact that eating gruel and rice, motion and action do not lie
in practice or study, but are the living *samādhi* with which all men are from the
outset endowed. . . .

Source: Hakuin, "Oratengama" in *The Zen Master Hakuin: Selected Writings,* translated by Philip B.
Yampolsky (New York: Columbia University Press Press, 1971), 29–30, 32–34, 38–41, 43–44, 49,
144–146, 163–165.

21

Mahāyāna
Hagiographic Literature

Hagiographic literature is common in virtually all religious traditions with a substantial body of literature. Hagiographic literature functions as a testimonial record
of a person undertaking a religious quest. These accounts are not neutral and
objective retelling of a religious life; such stories are often embellished with
extraordinary acts of piety, demonstrations of powers, or performance of miracles.
Hence, it is impossible to know for certain the extent of the truthfulness of the
narratives. Nonetheless, the ordinary portraits must be realistic in order for readers to feel familiar with and to be able to recognize the episodes depicted. In other
words, the narratives must represent the world of the audience in order to be
effective.

From a cross-cultural and comparative perspective, hagiography serves as a
model of a particular type of religious figure. The hagiographic narratives also function didactically in the sense of demonstrating paradigms of religious life. They
accomplish this by setting the cosmologies and doctrines of the sacred scriptures
or treatises within a specific local context of particular persons and reactions to
them by observers. In summary, hagiographic literature combines paradigmatic
thinking that provides a system of categories and concepts with narrative thinking
that depicts experience by locating it in particular times and places. If paradigmatic
thought produces a whole system, narrative thought generates particular stories.
Although their results are different, these two types of thinking are complemen-
tary ways of knowing. Moreover, they reinforce and legitimate each other.

The selection from Chinese hagiographical literature depicts a renowned scholar and monk named Aśvaghoṣa (second century c.e.), who was attached to the court of the Kusāna king Kaniṣka. According to the Mahāyāna Buddhist tradition, Aśvaghoṣa composed the following works: *Buddhacarita* (The Acts of the Buddha), *Saundarananda* (Nanda the Fair), *Śāriputraprakaraṇa* (Story of Śāriputra), and *Mahāyānaśraddhotpāda-śastra* (Awakening of Faith in Mahāyāna). His life serves as a paradigm for the pious scholarly monk. It is not unusual to find hagiographical literature using an antiparadigm to make a very different point. The Japanese monk Ikkyū Sōjun (1294–1481) is not only considered the antithesis of a Zen monk because of his violation of monastic rules by drinking wine and visiting brothels, but he was also considered a madman by his contemporaries for his unusual behavior.

CHINESE HAGIOGRAPHIC LITERATURE

The Master, who was named Aśvaghoṣa Bodhisattva, was a disciple of Elder Pārśva. When Elder Pārśva, being deeply concerned about the Buddha-Dharma, entered *samādhi* in order to contemplate who was competent to renounce the world and widely propogate the teachings of the Way so as to enlighten living beings, he had a vision of a hermit heretic in central India who was well versed in worldly wisdom, eloquent in debate, and good at argumentation. The hermit announced, "If there is any *bhikṣu* who can hold debate with me, let him strike the *ghaṇṭā* (bell). If he cannot, he is not qualified to strike the *ghaṇṭā* in public and receive offerings from the people."

Elder Pārśva then set out from Northern India with the intention of traveling to the city of Śākya in Madhyadeśa. On his way, he met some *śrāmaṇeras* who joked with him, saying, "Virtuous Elder, let us carry your books for you." Then they took away his books and teased him in various ways for no reason. Elder Pārśva's countenance did not change and, with a placid mind, he took no notice of their mischievous tricks.

One of the *śrāmaṇeras*, who was a well-learned person, discerned that the elder was a great and farsighted man and suspected that he was no ordinary person. He questioned the elder and observed his behavior, and found that he never ceased in his spiritual progress. [Elder Pārśva's] being was settled, his mind was deep and far-reaching, and he never thought of trivial matters.

When all the *śrāmaṇeras* realized that the elder was a man of great virtue and unfathomable magnanimity, they treated him with doubled respect and served as his attendants in order to help send him on his way.

Then Elder Pārśva disappeared by supernatural power. Upon arriving in Central India, he stayed in a monastery. He asked the *bhikṣus,* "Why do you not strike the *ghaṇṭā* according to the Dharma?"

The *bhikṣus* said, "Elder Mahallaka has a reason for not striking it."

"What is the reason?" asked Pārśva.

The *bhikṣus* replied, "There is a heretical recluse who is good at argumentation. He announced that if none of the Buddhist *śrāmaṇeras* in the country can debate with him, they should not strike the *ghaṇṭā* in public to receive offerings from the people. Because of this, we do not strike the *ghaṇṭā.*"

Elder Pārśva said, "Just strike the *ghaṇṭā.* If he comes, I will deal with him."

Surprised at these words, the old *bhikṣus* were doubtful and could not come to a decision. After assembling and discussing the matter, they said, "Let us strike the *ghaṇṭā.* If the heretic comes, we will ask the elder to do whatever he pleases." Thus they struck the *ghaṇṭā.*

The heretic appeared and asked, "Why do you strike this piece of wood today?"

The *bhikṣu* replied, "An elder *śrāmaṇa* came from the north and struck the *ghaṇṭā.* It was not we who struck it."

The heretic said, "Ask him to come." Then Elder [Pārśva] came and met the heretic, who asked him, "Do you intend to hold a debate with me?"

"Yes," [Pārśva] replied.

The heretic said with a contemptuous smile, "This elder *bhikṣu* looks quite old and his words are nothing unusual. How can he hope to hold a debate with me?"

They then agreed to hold a debate in seven days' time at that spot, in the presence of the king, ministers, other great masters of the Dharma, *śrāmaṇas,* and heretics.

On the night of the sixth day, Elder Pārśva entered *samādhi* to contemplate what he should do. At dawn on the seventh day, a great congregation assembled. [Pārśva] arrived first and ascended the high seat, looking more cheerful and pleasant than usual. The heretic arrived later and took a seat at the front. He observed that the *śrāmaṇa* had a peaceful countenance and a quiet and calm demeanor and that his physical body possessed all the characteristics of a debater. He thought, "Is this not a saintly *bhikṣu,* with such a calm and pleasant presence and a physical body that has all the characteristics of a debater? Today we shall have a splendid debate."

They first discussed what punishment should be meted out to the loser. The heretic said, "The defeated person should have his tongue cut off."

Elder Pārśva said, "We must not do that. Let the defeated man become the disciple of the victor. That would be a fair enough agreement."

"Yes," replied the heretic, who then asked, "Who will speak first?"

Elder Pārśva said, "As I am advanced in age, have come from a distant place, and took my seat here before you, I should speak first."

The heretic said, "That is agreeable to me. I will refute whatever you may say."

The Elder Pārśva said, "We should make the country be at peace, the great king enjoy a long life, and the land rich and happy without any calamity."

The heretic remained silent, not knowing what to say. According to the rule, the one who was unable to respond lost the debate. He submitted to becoming the elder's disciple, had his head and beard shaved, became a śrāmaṇera, and received full ordination. Sitting alone at another place, he pondered, "My brilliant talents and deep knowledge have won me worldwide fame. How is it that by a few words I was defeated and made a disciple?" Thinking of this, he was unhappy.

Elder [Pārśva] understood the heretic's mind, and asked him to come to his room. He demonstrated his supernatural power, performing various kinds of transformations. Then the heretic realized that his teacher was no ordinary person and was happy to be subdued by him, thinking, "It befits me to be his disciple."

The teacher said to him, "It was not easy for you to have [developed] such brilliant talents, but you have not achieved the truth. If you learn the Dharmas I have acquired, the [five] organs (indriya), the [five] powers (bala), the [seven factors of] enlightenment (bodhyanga), and the [eightfold] path, and become endowed with profound and elucidative eloquence and a clear understanding of the meaning of all doctrines, you will be unrivaled in all the world."

Elder [Pārśva] then returned to his own country, while his disciple remained in central India, where he became well versed in various sutras and thoroughly mastered both Buddhist and non-Buddhist teachings. His matchless talents in debate won him the respect and admiration of the four groups of Buddhist followers (monks, nuns, laymen, and laywomen), and the king of India held him in great esteem.

Later on, the king of Minor Yuezhi in Northern India attacked Central India and beseiged it for a long time. The king of Central India dispatched a letter that

read, "If you want anything from me, I will give it to you. Why should you surround and aggravate my people by staying here for such a long time?"

The [Yuezhi king] replied, "If you intend to surrender, send me three crores
of golden coins and I will spare you."

The king replied, "I do not have even one crore of golden coins in the whole
of my country. How can I acquire three crores of golden coins?"

The [Yuezhi king] replied, "You have two great treasures in your country: one
is the Buddha's almsbowl, and the other is an eloquent *bhikṣu*. Give these to me,
and they may be reckoned as equivalent to two crores of golden coins."

The king said, "I value these two treasures highly. I cannot surrender them."

Then the *bhikṣu* preached the Dharma to the king, saying, "Nothing in the
world is comparable to the edification of living beings. The Way of the Buddha is
deep and broad. It is meant to save both oneself and others. Among the virtues of
a great person, the salvation of others is the greatest. Worldwide edification is difficult; a king can rule but one country. If you dismantle the Way of the Buddha,
you will be a king of the Dharma across the four seas. That a *bhikṣu* should save
his people is not objectionable. Merits exist in the mind, whether one is far or
near. Be magnanimous and farsighted. Why should you look only at what is before
your eyes?"

Because the king had always venerated the *bhikṣu*, he respectfully accepted
his advice and handed him over to the envoy. After the envoy of the king of Yuezhi
returned to this own country, the courtiers discussed the matter and said, "It
befits the king to venerate the Buddha's almsbowl. But it is too much to accept
that a *bhikṣu* is worth a crore of golden coins, when there are so many *bhikṣus*
everywhere under the sky."

The king ascertained that the *bhikṣu* was a well-learned person of superior
ability and understanding who taught and benefited the people in a broad and
profound manner, and whose eloquent preaching could edify even nonhuman
beings. In order to remove his courtiers' doubts, he ordered that seven horses not
be fed for six days. On the morning of the sixth day, he assembled all Buddhist and
non-Bhuddist *śrāmaṇas* of different schools and invited the *bhikṣu* to preach the
Dharma to them. All those who listened to him became enlightened. The king
tethered the horses in front of the assembly and placed grass before them. Betel,
which horses like, was also placed in the fodder. With tears flowing, the horses listened to the [*bhikṣu's*] preaching without any thought of eating the fodder.

Thus everyone knew that the *bhikṣu* was no ordinary person. Because even
horses could understand his words, he was named Aśvaghoṣa ("Horse Cry") Bod-

hisattva. He propagated Buddhism widely in Northern India to teach and benefit all living things. As he knew well how to use expedient [means] to help people achieve merit, he won the respect of the four groups of Buddhist followers. All acclaimed that day as a day of merit.

Source: "The Life of Aśvaghoṣa Bodhisattva" in *Lives of Great Monks and Nuns,* translated by Li Ringxi (Berkeley: Numata Center for Buddhist Translation and Research, 2002), 9–13.

JAPANESE ZEN HAGIOGRAPHIC LITERATURE OF THE MONK IKKYŪ

A Dialogue about Hell

Once Ikkyū was spending a few days in the province of Kai. There was a mountain there called "Hell" on which were located a number of ruins, and he decided to have a look. But the Lord of a nearby manor had heard that Ikkyū was a witty talker and so arranged to encounter him on the trail while attended by only a handful of retainers. Pretending not to know who he was, the Lord asked Ikkyū,

"Your Reverence, please tell me about Heaven and Hell."

"Oh, shit!" Ikkyū replied.

Now the Lord was thoroughly outraged at "this foul-mouthed priest" and told his attendants, "Tie him up, and see that he learns to keep his mouth shut!"

In obedience to this command his young worthies rushed to pummel Ikkyū to the ground and tied his arms behind his back.

But Ikkyū with complete self-possession turned to the Lord and said, "Now you see what is meant by 'Hell.'"

At these words the Lord of the manor realized what had been going on and got off his horse in a flurry and undid Ikkyū's bonds with his own hands. Then he insisted that Ikkyū mount the horse and accompany him to the manor where he laid out all sorts of delicacies and obliged Ikkyū to spend the entire day feasting with him. After which Ikkyū is said to have told the Lord,

"And this is what I call Heaven."

Funeral for a Cat

There was a small wine shop in a section of Kyoto called something like Tatsumi Otobahashi. It was run by a loving couple who made their way through life harmoniously working together, so that at a fairly early age they had established a good business and were even able to employ a few servants. From the time they

got up in the morning to when they went to bed at night, this couple lived cheer-
fully together. But in spite of the fact that they were in their twenties and were
very close, their marriage was still childless. They finally decided that they would
have to ask for the blessings of the Buddhas and gods, and they proceeded to visit
all the auspicious shrines and temples and to repeat wholeheartedly their earnest
desire. But their situation remained just as before, and they seemed fated to be
childless. It seemed that the gods and Buddhas were not willing to hear their plea.
But the couple did not revile the deities for this; for they felt that if their hopes
for children were failing to blossom in this life, it must be because they had themselves failed to plant the seeds of good karma in former lives, and they simply
resigned themselves to the situation.

They say that people without children always devote their love to a cat, and
true enough this young couple soon got themselves a fine pussycat on whom they
showered all their affections. In the daytime they took turns holding her in their
robes, and at night they made her sleep in their bed snuggled between them.
People came to say, "If they had a child, that's how they'd be with it." The man
and wife always fed the cat the best quality fish with the bones already removed.
In short, they made caring for the cat their chief pleasure. Though she was only a
dumb animal, they placed her above human beings and showered her with undue
affections. Perhaps it was the law of karma acting against these excesses, but
there came a time when the cat did not eat for two or three days in a row and
began to meow piteously. Finally, on the fourth morning of her illness, her paws
started to quiver, her hair stood on end, and after turning two or three circles, she
gave the couple a plaintive mew as a final memento and died. The man and his
wife were extraordinarily distressed—even more than if they had lost a true
child—and they took it into their minds to call in Ikkyū, the famous priest of
Murasakkino, to perform rites for the departed.

After hearing the whole story, Ikkyū, who would have taken his own good
time answering a call to an ordinary human funeral, was caught up by the idea
that it was a cat, and hurried back with the couple's messenger.

They were naturally overjoyed and repeating the whole story of the cat with
tears streaming down their faces they asked Ikkyū, "Please conduct a service to
help her become a Buddha in the next life, and see that she won't just be a four-
footed creature again."

"Don't worry," said Ikkyū, still fascinated by the strangeness of their request,
"I'll do a fine service and see that she gets the seed of Buddhahood. You just stand
over there and listen." And he began to chant:

While you were alive,

You caught many mice

And reaped human kindness as a reward

And lived a contented life.

Now, whatever you're born as,

Be sure to catch a Buddha.

Amen.

As Ikkyū was about to leave, the couple stopped him and said, "Your words just now have led us to enlightenment. No longer will we talk of afterlife except in true piety."

Some time later Ikkyū explained this. "When that couple who had asked about salvation in the afterlife heard me say 'Whatever you are born as, be sure to catch a Buddha,' in my service for their cat, they were struck by those unusual words and moved from the realm of desire to the realm of enlightenment." And with a broad grin he added, "Even those ordinary people were able to see that to pray to become a golden-skinned Buddha sitting on one of the nine grades of lotus, free from hunger and cold like a gilded statue, is itself an even greater than ordinary greed, since it extends earthly avarice even into the unseen next world. And they saw then that, better than to foolishly pray for a good rebirth, one should hope for that mental state which is beyond all thoughts and desires."

For after all isn't it always best to cleave to the Middle Way in all things?

New Year's Day Celebration

"Now it is Gansan and the days, the months, and the year are all at their beginning. On this day everyone, the high and the low, the troubled, the carefree, the rich and the poor, all pass congratulations back and forth and decorate their houses. Still, if one were to substitute raw *sake* for the spiced New Year's wine, it would stick to his beard. And the man who carelessly carries out a plate of New Year's buns may slip and fall on his own. Nonetheless, everyone scurries about making festive preparations.

"In reality, of course, this day is no different from yesterday. The same fog spreads quietly across the landscape, past the pine boughs lining the roadside, and under the sacred ropes that mark men's hopes for longevity at every house. Still, men who ran helterskelter from house to house until midnight last, demanding this or that, have, with the dawning, become quite gentle-hearted and give no sign of the anxieties that beset them on the final day of the Old Year.

"Men have set out pines to signify long life; they wish each other many good years and give no heed to the fact that death will come to all. They pay deep respect to worldly things, covet profits that are as short-lived as the morning dew-drops, spend their evening years lost in concern only for their children and grand-children. Then, like ants trying to topple a stone tea-mortar, they mumble blessings of long life to one another, completely unaware of the fast-approaching Autumn winds.

"Yes, such are the mindless thoughts that fill mortal heads."

Thus pondered the monk Ikkyū as he considered the foolishness of men.

"They see the quick passage of the morning glory but consider it long-lived. They are like dayflies whose quick flight through the morning sky is too short even for joy. And, then, they cap their obscenely simple view of life with that cheerful New Year's greeting, 'O-medetō!'

"One glance is all it takes to see how soon they will all be reduced to smoke above a funeral pyre. How needful they are of some instruction in these matters."

Thus pondered the monk Ikkyū.

And straightaway Ikkyū went to the graveyard where he obtained a human skull which he fastened to the end of a bamboo pole. And from the early hours of New Year's morning onward he proceeded throughout the streets of Kyoto bang-ing on every door and shoving the skull at the people and shouting, "Beware, beware!" (Of course everyone was disgusted by this and slammed their doors shut, and it is from this incident that the practice of locking doors for the first three days of the New Year arose.) But one of the people who saw him said, "You're quite right to tell us to 'Beware!' For despite all our 'Medetais' and our decorations, that's the way we will all end up. Yes, you're quite right to replace the common custom of cheerful congratulations by introducing that hideous skull from door to door."

Ikkyū answered only, "But, I too am only offering New Year's congratulations as I go from door to door with this skull. What better way to make comprehen-sible the words 'O-me-deto!' Once, the Goddess Amaterasu let her light shine forth from the Cave, and that was the Beginning of things. And from that time on noth-ing has been more 'medetai' than a skull." And he added a poem:

Oh, this artless skull
Of all things it is most
"Medetai."

"Look at it, you people! 'Medetai!' here is spoken by its eyeless sockets! You should all be aware of that. From yesterday you are thoughtlessly carried into today. You fail to see that the world is as impermanent as the swirling depths of the Asuka River. Men unmoved by the sound of the passing winds, I tell you to 'Beware!' Unless you understand what I am saying *your 'medetai's!'* will be without substance."

Hearing this, they all knew that Ikkyū was a lofty saint, and there was none but that did him reverence.

Ikkyū Does Magic

Once Ikkyū was taking the Yodo no Kawase ferry on his way to Sakai. There was a *yamabushi* on board who began to question him.

"Hey, Your Reverence, what sect are you?"

"I belong to the Zen sect," replied Ikkyū.

"I don't suppose your sect has miracles the way our sect does?"

"No, actually we have lots of miracles. But if it's miracles, why don't you show the sort of miracles that your people have?"

"Well," said the *yamabushi,* "By virtue of my magic powers I can pray up Fudō before your very eyes and make him stand right there on the prow of the boat."

And, with the beads of his rosary the man began to invoke first Kongō and then Seitaka. At this all the passengers began to look back and forth wondering what was going to happen. Then, just as he had said, there on the prow of the boat, the form of Fudō appeared surrounded by a halo of dancing flames.

Then the *yamabushi* made a ferocious face and told them, "You'd all better offer him a prayer." This made the other passengers very uneasy—all, that is, but Ikkyū who was completely unruffled.

"Well," spat out the *yamabushi,* "How about you, Zen-monk? How are you going to deal with my miracle?"

"By producing a miracle of my own. From my very body I will cause water to issue forth and extinguish the flames of your Fudō. You'd better start up your prayers again." And Ikkyū began to pee mightily all over the flames until at last the *yamabushi*'s magic was counteracted, and the entire image melted away. There-upon the passengers on the boat all bowed to Ikkyū for this wonderful display.

Well, now, as the boat reached land and everyone was getting off, a really huge dog ran up at them barking so loudly that the riverside fairly rang with the noise.

"Well, Your Reverence," said the *yamabushi* to Ikkyū, "I admit you won our little contest of Dharma-magic back on the boat just now, but I'll bet you don't have the power to make that dog stop barking and come over to you, do you? Well, how about it?"

"Why that's as easy as can be," said Ikkyū, "but you go first. Then if he doesn't come for you I can take over."

The *yamabushi* pulled out his Ōirataka-redwood rosary and began to click it rapidly through his fingers until he had made a full round of the beads. But the dog was still barking as loudly as ever. And it did not show the least intention of coming over to them. The *yamabushi* then made a magical gesture in the air slashing up-and-down and then back-and-forth to calm the dog's wild expression. Then he chanted the *mantra*, "*Abira-unken sowaka! Abira-unken sowaka!*" But the dog just kept on barking.

Ikkyū was finding this all pretty silly, and at last he broke in, "Move over! This isn't the sort of business for either '*Abira-unken*'s' or '*Sowaka*'s.' I'll show you how to calm his anger and bring him right over here." And he pulled a lump of roasted rice out of his robes and let the dog see it. And, like any other dog, once it saw the food, it stopped barking and trotted over with its tail wagging—to the total amazement of the *yamabushi*. But all the others felt that somehow they had been part of a very special event, and they went off on their separate ways quite moved by the whole affair.

The Eye-Opening Ceremony

When the statue of Jizō was first built at Seki, the people gathered together and were talking about what sort of priest they ought to invite for the eye-opening ceremony when one of their number spoke out.

"When I was last in the capital doing some sightseeing, all the Kyotoites were saying that there is no one these days who can outdo the priest Ikkyū of Mura-sakino. Well now, as we've built such a fine Jizō here, I think that, rather than some ordinary everyday priest, we should ask this Ikkyū to come do the job."

Everyone agreed that that was the thing to do, and they quickly sent a deputation off to the capital. Ikkyū was then at the temple, and the men from Seki asked him to undertake the ceremony, making especially clear their willingness to pay him for his trouble. To this request Ikkyū responded that as he was, in fact, by a fortunate coincidence, about to make a pilgrimage to the Kantō region, he would be able to stop on his way and take care of the eye-opening.

Overjoyed, the petitioners ran back to Seki to tell everyone that Ikkyū himself would soon be with them. In a frenzy they got ready, turning everything upside down, sweeping non-existent dust from the walks and knocking themselves out in general. Then they ran out to meet him, their feet spinning like millwheels. For his part Ikkyū approached rather dispassionately, even as all the villagers ran out to greet him in a happy throng. Ikkyū asked where the Jizō was, and they showed him a fine statue, with the offerings all ready, flowers and incense laid out, and a full complement of subsidiary decorations. They asked if he would begin the ceremony, and after stepping all over each other to get up front, they stood on tiptoe to see just what he would do.

Without further ado, Ikkyū climbed right up the ladder, and from the level of Jizō's head he began to piss all over the place. It was like the waterfall of Lu Shan. Soon all the offerings were thoroughly soaked, and as this veritable flood ceased Ikkyū told them,

"So much for an eye-opening," and set off rapidly toward the east.

When the locals saw this, they proclaimed, "What kind of filthy outrage is this? That skinny priest is out of his mind. The gall of him, taking a leak on our important *bodhisattva;* it makes me boil. After him! Don't let him get away!" and they took out in chase each hoping to get hands on him first.

In the meantime, some lay-nuns gathered together and cursing "that damned Ikkyū" for his sacrilege, they began to wash the statue and replace the offerings, all the while asking Jizō to forgive them.

The young men who had started after Ikkyū soon fell exhausted on the road. But the women washing the statue somehow worked themselves up into a strange frenzy until at last, not even realizing the truth of their own words, they told one another,

"If the world-famous monk Ikkyū has chosen urination as his form of eye-opening, who are we to wash it off?"

And, to the utter shock of their families, they set off to catch Ikkyū and ask him to come back and repeat the ceremony. They finally caught up with him just as he was boarding the Kuwana Ferry and detailed their request. Ikkyū begged off pleading inconvenience, and in place of returning himself, he pulled out his own loincloth which he offered them saying it "was thought to be some eight hundred years old," and that "if you were to tie it around Jizō's head, it would cure ills instantly." The villagers torn between the fear of committing sacrilege on the one hand, or missing out on a miracle on the other, timidly accepted the cloth and hurried back to Seki as Ikkyū went off to the Kantō.

Back at the village they related what they had been told and gingerly tied the loincloth around Jizō's head. But no sooner had they accomplished this, than they began to feel that evil spirits were being driven off and that they had become the recipients of a unique honor. And any thought of removal of the cloth became a virtual impossibility.

On his way back to Kyoto, though, Ikkyū removed the loincloth, replaced it with a cloth-of-gold band, and went on to the capital. This is why the Buddhist and Shinto cloth-of-gold bands of today are the same length as a loincloth, six feet long. But then, the world is full of strange things.

Source: *The Zen Monk Ikkyū,* translated by James H. Sanford (Chico, Cal.: Scholars Press, 1981), 259, 268–274, 280–283, 291–295.

22

The Feminine Thread
in Mahāyāna Literature

In an important Mahāyāna text entitled the *Vimalakīrti-nirdeśa Sūtra,* there occurs a philosophical dialogue between the monk Śāriputra and a female, a twelve-year practitioner of meditation and student of Buddhist scriptures. During the course of the dialogue, the monk becomes impressed by her grasp of Buddhist thought and high level of spiritual attainment, and he impertinently asks her why she never exchanged her female sexuality for that of a male. She confidently replies that during her study and meditation she could not find any innate characteristics of the female sex, and she compares her femininity to a magically created illusion of a woman. The impressed monk agrees that her female sexuality could not be changed because it does not possess any innate determinative aspects. The woman proceeds to change Śāriputra into her own likeness and transforms herself into the monk. Having turned the table on a befuddled Śāriputra, she asks him why he does not change his female sexuality. Since the monk is confused, she gives him a lecture, saying essentially that if he could transform his female form, then all women could also change their sexuality, which is the rationale for the Buddha teaching that men and women are not what they appear to be. After regaining his male form, the monk confesses that he possesses a deeper grasp of emptiness. This type of dialogical exchange introduces a new spirit into the perspective about the nature of gender in Mahāyāna Buddhism. Nonetheless, a reader can find cultural bias against females in other Mahāyāna works.

A good example of prejudice toward females in Mahāyāna literature is found in the popular and influential *Lotus Sūtra*. The text contains a narrative about a young Nāga (serpent, dragon) princess, who possesses the face of a comely woman and a serpentine body–the first selection of this chapter. It helps a reader to know that these human/serpentine beings inhabit aquatic places, are known as guardians of the treasures of the ocean, protect the source of life symbolized by waters, and possess the power of self-rejuvenation. Within the context of Buddhist mythology, they are entrusted with the most precious teaching of the Buddha in the form of the Perfection of Wisdom. Besides being renowned for her beauty, wit, and charm, a Nāga princess carries a priceless jewel on her head, which is symbolically associated with her sexuality, because male Nāgas did not possess them. As the narrative unfolds, the princess offers her jewel to the Buddha after a monk reminds her that a woman cannot gain enlightenment. Her action represents both a sign of her commitment to the teachings of the Buddha and a message that she is willing to give up her female sexuality and thoughts to become a male in order to attain enlightenment. Although this narrative embodies a misogynist attitude, a more ambivalent attitude may also be discovered in Mahāyāna literature.

This ambivalent attitude toward women is evident in *Jātaka* tales translated into Chinese around the middle of the third century C.E. In comparison to tales of the Buddha's former births that originate within the Indian cultural context, many of which demonstrate strong misogynist attitudes (and among which there are no narratives that depict the Buddha as a female), the Chinese versions of these narratives include tales of the Buddha being reborn female. Moreover, within the Chinese canon and cultural context of strong prejudices toward women there are numerous biographies of accomplished Buddhist nuns. Biographies of selected nuns are included in this chapter. Many of these Chinese biographies manifest a similar pattern of which a reader should be aware. The narrative often begins with the nun's place of origin, family background, descriptions of strong character and intelligence, trials that the nun overcame, and attainment of her spiritual goal.

Selection from the *Lotus Sūtra*

Manjushri replied, "There is the daughter of the dragon king Sagara, who has just turned eight. Her wisdom has keen roots and she is good at understanding the root activities and deeds of living beings. She has mastered the dharanis, has been able to accept and embrace all the storehouse of profound secrets preached by the Buddhas, has entered deep into meditation, thoroughly grasped the doctrines, and in the space of an instant conceived the desire for bodhi and reached the level of no regression. Her eloquence knows no hindrance, and she thinks of living beings with compassion as though they were her own children. She is fully endowed with blessings, and when it comes to conceiving in mind and expounding by mouth, she is subtle, wonderful, comprehensive and great. Kind, compassionate, benevolent, yielding, she is gentle and refined in will, capable of attaining bodhi."

Bodhisattva Wisdom Accumulated said, "When I observe Shakyamuni Thus Come One, I see that for immeasurable kalpas he carried out harsh and difficult practices, accumulating merit, piling up virtue, seeking the way of the bodhisattva without ever resting. I observe that throughout the thousand-millionfold world, there is not a single spot tiny as a mustard seed where this bodhisattva failed to sacrifice body and life for the sake of living beings. Only after he had done that was he able to complete the bodhi way. I cannot believe that this girl in the space of an instant could actually achieve correct enlightenment."

Before his words had come to an end, the dragon king's daughter suddenly appeared before the Buddha, bowed her head in obeisance, and then retired to one side, reciting these verses of praise:

He profoundly understands the signs of guilt and good fortune
and illuminates the ten directions everywhere.
His subtle, wonderful pure Dharma body
is endowed with the thirty-two features;
the eighty characteristics adorn his Dharma body.
Heavenly and human beings gaze up in awe,
dragons and spirits all pay honor and respect;
among all living beings,
none who do not hold him in reverence.
And having heard his teachings, I have attained bodhi—
the Buddha alone can bear witness to this.
I unfold the doctrines of the Great Vehicle
to rescue living beings from suffering.

At that time Shariputra said to the dragon girl, "You suppose that in this short time you have been able to attain the unsurpassed way. But this is difficult to believe. Why? Because woman's body is soiled and defiled, not a vessel for the Law. How could you attain the unsurpassed bodhi? The road to Buddhahood is long and far-stretching. Only after one has spent immeasurable kalpas pursuing austerities, accumulating deeds, practicing all kinds of paramitas, can one finally achieve success. Moreover, a woman is subject to the five obstacles. First, she cannot become a Brahma heavenly king. Second, she cannot become the king Shakra. Third, she cannot become a devil king. Fourth, she cannot become a wheel-turning sage king. Fifth, she cannot become a Buddha. How then could a woman like you be able to attain Buddhahood so quickly?"

At that time the dragon girl had a precious jewel worth as much as the thousand-millionfold world which she presented to the Buddha. The Buddha immediately accepted it. The dragon girl said to Bodhisattva Wisdom Accumulated and to the venerable one, Shariputra, "I presented the precious jewel and the World-Honored One accepted it—was that not quickly done?"

They replied, "Very quickly!"

The girl said, "Employ your supernatural powers and watch me attain Buddhahood. It will be even quicker than that!"

At that time the members of the assembly all saw the dragon girl in the space of an instant change into a man and carry out all the practices of a bodhisattva, immediately proceeding to the Spotless World of the south, taking a seat on a jeweled lotus, and attaining impartial and correct enlightenment. With the thirty-two features and the eighty characteristics, he expounded the wonderful Law for all living beings everywhere in the ten directions.

Source: *Lotus Sūtra,* translated by Burton Watson (New York: Columbia University Press, 1993), 187–188.

Selections from "The Goddess of the Ganges"

Then a woman joined the assembly and sat down. Rising from her seat, she adjusted the upper part of her robe to her shoulder, saluted the Lord, and with folded hands she spoke: "Lord, I will not be afraid of such a position. No, I will not be frightened. Fearlessly, I will teach the Dharma to all beings."

At that very instant, the Lord smiled and radiated light upon the endless and limitless world spheres; it ascended to the realm of Brahma. The smile then returned and circumambulated around the Lord three times, disappearing into his head. Immediately after the Lord smiled, the woman gathered golden flowers and scattered them over the Lord. Standing free, these golden flowers remained suspended in space.

Then Ānanda, rising from his seat, adjusted the upper part of his robe to his shoulder, circumambulated the Lord, folding his hands, and spoke: "Why did you smile, Lord? The Tathāgata, Arhat, Enlightened One does not smile without a reason."

[The Lord replied:] "Ānanda, in the future this goddess of the Ganges will be the Tathāgata named Golden Flower, the Tathāgata, Arhat, Enlightened One, proficient in knowledge and practice, the Well-Gone, knower of the world, tamer of men, teacher of both gods and men, the Buddha, the Lord. That Buddha will appear in the world during the starlike era and will realize perfect enlightenment. This goddess of the Ganges, Ānanda, after her death, will change her sex from female to male and be born in the Buddha land called Delight, the Buddha-relam of Akṣobhya. Then he will observe the holy life in the presence of Akṣobhya. After his death, he will go from one Buddha realm to another, without ever separating from the sight of the Tathāgata. He will pass from one Buddha realm to another, without ever separating from the Buddhas. Ānanda, in the case of a universal monarch, he goes from palace to palace during his lifetime, yet the soles of his feet never touch the ground. Until his death, his feet never touch the ground. Likewise, this goddess of the Ganges will go from Buddha realm to Buddha realm, without ever separating from the Buddhas, the lords, until she realizes full enlightenment."

Ānanda [spoke]: "Those bodhisattvas, the great beings, who will be in the presence of the Tathāgata Akṣobhya, must be recognized as the assembly of the Tathāgata." Reading Ānanda's thoughts, the Lord spoke to him: "Yes, you are correct, Ānanda. Those bodhisattvas who have crossed over the quagmire observe the practice of holiness in the Buddha realm of Akṣobhya, the Tathāgata, Arhat, Perfectly Enlightened One should be recognized as having approached the culmination of enlightenment. Moreover, Ānanda, Buddha Golden Flower's assembly of disciples will be styled unlimited. Why? Because his disciples are so many they cannot be counted. They amount to such a high number they are immeasurable, numberless. Ānanda, at that time, in that Buddha realm, there will be no wastelands inhabited by beasts of prey or by robbers, no deserts, no disease, no famine. These and all other such offensive wastelands will absolutely neither exist nor he perceived at any time. So Ānanda, when the Tathāgata Golden Flower has realized the perfect enlightenment, then such places which instill fear and terror will absolutely neither exist nor be perceived at any time."

Ānanda [asked]: "Lord, in which Tathāgata's presence did the goddess of the Ganges nurture virtuous habits to cause the first awakening to the thought which leads to perfect enlightenment?"

[The Lord replied:] "Ānanda, in Dīpankara's presence the goddess of the Ganges nurtured virtuous habits to cause the first awakening to the thought which leads to the perfect enlightenment by throwing golden flowers upon her, when she desired perfect enlightenment.

"When I had strewed the five lotuses over the Buddha Dīpankara, I acquired the patience to understand nonarising phenomena, and Dīpankara predicted my future enlightenment: 'In the future, young man, you will be endowed with knowledge and practice, be a knower of the world, tamer of men, teacher of both gods and men, the Buddha.'"

When this goddess heard the prediction, she thought to herself: "Oh, I should certainly have a prediction for the full enlightenment like that young man." So Ānanda, in the presence of Dīpankara, the goddess planted virtuous habits that caused the first awakening to the thought which leads to full enlightenment.

Ānanda [spoke]: "Lord, this goddess of the Ganges who has received the prediction of full enlightenment has certainly been well prepared and is accomplished."

Source: "The Goddess of the Ganges" in the *Sūtra of the Perfection of Wisdom in Eight Thousand Lines,* edited by P. L. Vaidya (Darbhanga: Mithila Institute, 1960), 180–182.

Selections from the *Biographies of Buddhist Nuns*

Shi Huiqiong of Nan-an Nunnery

Huiqiong, originally surnamed Zhong, was a native of Guang-zhou. She devoted herself to the Way in a noble and unsullied manner and never tasted fish or meat. When she was nearly eighty, she was even more assiduous in performing religious deeds. She always wore ramie or hemp cloth and never used silk or floss silk. Besides taking charge of the nunnery, she engaged in preaching.

Originally Huiqiong lived at Nan-an Nunnery in Guang-ling. In the eighteenth year of Yuan-jia (441), Lady Wang, the mother of the heir apparent of the Prince of Jiang-xia of the Song dynasty, presented Huiqiong with a parcel of land on which she built a convent named Southern Yong-an Nunnery. Later, in the twenty-second year (445), Xiao Chengzhi of Lan-ling erected a stupa in a foreign style at the nunnery. In the fifteenth year of Yuan-jia (438), Huiqiong also constructed the Bodhi Nunnery, of which all the halls, shrines, and other buildings were grand and beautiful. She then went to live there and presented Southern Yong-an Nunnery to the Buddhist monk Huizhi.

In the twentieth year of Yuan-jia (443), while en route to Kuai-ji with Meng Yi, Huiqiong passed away at Po-kang. She had instructed her disciples, "After my death my body need not be buried. You may hire someone to cut it into pieces to feed to living creatures." But when she died, her disciples could not bear to carve up her remains. So they went to report the case to the magistrate of Ju-rong County, who ruled that the corpse should be carried to the mountains to allow birds and animals to feed on it by themselves.

For more than ten days, the body remained as it was before and did not change its complexion. The magistrate asked the villagers to scatter some raw rice around the corpse. The birds ate up all the rice at some distance from the body, but the grains near it were left untouched. Upon hearing about this matter in the capital, Huiqiong's disciple Huilang rushed to the spot. She brought the remains back and buried them on the hill in front of Gao-zuo Nunnery. A stupa was erected over the grave.

Sengguo of Guang-ling

Sengguo was originally surnamed Zhao and her given name was Fayou. She was a native of Xiu-wu in Ji Prefecture. She had instinctive piety and faith that had been cultivated in her previous lives, and her pure devotion was spontaneous. Even as a child at the breast, she would not eat after midday. For this her parents praised her and marveled at her. On reaching adulthood, she fixed her mind on one purpose. But because favorable circumstances were intermingled with obstacles, she was able to leave secular life only when she was twenty-seven years old.

Sengguo served as a teacher to the nun Huicong of Guang-ling. She observed the Vinaya rules with perseverance in a clear manner, and practiced meditation in a faultless way. Each time she entered *samādhi*, she would sit from dusk to dawn with her spirit dwelling in a state of mental purity and her body as motionless as a withered tree. Yet shallow-minded people still doubted her.

In the sixth year of Yuan-jia (428), a foreign shipowner named Nandi traveled from the Land of the Lion (Sri Lanka) with some nuns, who arrived in the capital of Song and stayed at Jing-fu Nunnery. Some time later, they inquired of Sengguo, "Have there been any foreign nuns in this country before?"

She replied, "No."

Then they asked, "Where did the Chinese nuns get both of the two sanghas from whom to receive the full ordination?"

Sengguo replied, "They received the full precepts only from the *bhikṣu* sangha, as an expedient means to arouse feelings of the great importance [of becoming ordained] in their minds. In this same way, Mahāprajāpatī received ordination through accepting the Eight Rules of Veneration. Thus the five hundred ladies of the Śākya clan could have Mahāprajāpatī as their preceptress. This was an eminent precedent."

Even though Sengguo replied thus [to the nuns' question], she still had doubts in her own mind. So she inquired about the whole matter from the Tripiṭaka master, who offered the same explanation. Then she asked further, "May one receive full ordination for a second time?"

The master said, "As *śīla, samādhi,* and *prajñā* are developed from imperceptibility to prominence, it would be even better for one to receive ordination again."

In the tenth year (433) the ship owner Nandi came again with eleven nuns, Devasārā and others, from the Land of the Lion. The nuns who arrived earlier had by now mastered the Chinese language. Saṃghavarman was asked to mark the boundaries of a chapter house at Nan-lin Monastery, in which more than three hundred persons were reordained, one after another.

In the eighteenth year (441), when Sengguo was thirty-four, she once sat in meditation for an entire day. The ceremonial leader touched her and announced that she was dead. The functionaries of the nunnery were surprised at the announcement, and they all came to look into the matter. They saw that Sengguo's body had become cold and her flesh stiff, but she was still breathing faintly. When they started to carry her away, she opened her eyes and talked to them, smiling as usual. Thus the ignorant were convinced of her spiritual attainment. It is not known what happened to her afterward.

Fayuan of Zeng-cheng in Dong-guan

Fayuan, originally surnamed Yu, was a native of Zeng-cheng in Dong-guan. In the ninth year of Yuan-jia (432) of the Song dynasty, she was ten years old and her younger sister Facai was nine. They knew nothing of Buddhist scriptures or the Dharma, [but both] suddenly disappeared on the eighth day of the second month. They returned home three days later. They said that they had been to the heavenly palace of the Pure Land, where they saw the Buddha and received edification from him.

On the fifteenth day of the ninth month, they went there again and returned after ten days. After that they could write and speak a foreign language and chant

Buddhist scriptures. When they saw people from the Western Region, they could talk and joke fluently with perfect mutual understanding.

On the fifteenth day of the first month in tenth year (433), [Fayuan and Facai] vanished once again. Some farmers working in the fields saw them drifting toward the sky in a gust of wind. Their parents were worried about them and offered sacrifices to the gods to seek blessing. After a month, the sisters returned in the form of nuns wearing religious robes, holding their own [shorn] hair in their hands.

They said that they had seen the Buddha and a nun, who said to them, "Due to causes in your previous lives, you are to be my disciples." Then she raised her hand to stroke their heads, and their hair fell off by itself. She gave the religious name Fayuan to the elder sister and Facai to the younger one. When they were sent back, the nun said to them, "You may construct a *vihāra* and I will give you the scriptures."

After returning home, Fayuan and her sister Facai demolished the household shrine for worshiping the gods and built a *vihāra* instead. There they lectured and chanted scriptures day and night. In the evenings, a ray of five colors often issued from the mountaintops, as if there were lamps or candles.

From that time on, [the sisters'] deportment was elegant and dignified, and their speech and rituals were perfect and correct. The chanting of scriptures in the capital could not surpass their recitations. Both of the two prefectural governors, Wei Lang and Kong Mo, made offerings to them. Upon hearing their utterances, the governors respected them all the more as extraordinary persons. Hence all the scholars believed in the right Dharma.

In the Jian-yuan period (479–482), Fayuan died at the age of fifty-six.

Senggai of Chan-ji Nunnery

Senggai, originally surnamed Tian, was a native of Jun-ren in the state of Zhao. Her father, named Hongliang, was the governor of Tian-shui. When she was young, she left home to become a disciple of the nun Sengzhi. She lived at Hua-lin Nunnery at Peng-cheng. She cared nothing for personal gain and was indifferent to praise or blame from others.

In the first year of Yuan-hui (473), when the Tuoba clan of the north invaded the state, Senggai traveled south to the capital with her fellow student Fajin and lived at Miao-xiang Nunnery. She attended numerous lectures on the scriptures and Vinaya texts, and made profound studies of their ultimate meanings. She practiced meditation exclusively and always felt that the days were not long enough [to practice as much as she would like]. Whether it was the cold or hot season, she never changed her garments. She never took seasonal food throughout the the four seasons, eating only one vegetarian dish for her midday meal.

Senggai studied under the two *dhyāna* masters Yin and Shen, both of whom praised her for her faculty of quick awakening. During the Yong-ming period of the Qi dynasty, she went to live at Chan-ji Nunnery with the intention of propagating the way of contemplation. Clergy and laypeople visited her for consultations, and this became so disruptive to her that she had to build a separate meditation room to the left of the nunnery in which she sat in silent contemplation. When she came out of her room, she instructed others earnestly without feeling tired.

Xiao Ziliang, Prince Wenxuan of Jing-ling of the Qi dynasty, provided her with all the requisites for the four seasons. In spite of her old age, she did not slacken in her aspirations. For a whole day she would reside in a state of unattached serenity and she would not lie down all through the night. In the eleventh year of Yong-ming (493), Senggai died at the age of sixty-four.

Zhixian of the Western Nunnery in Si-zhou

Zhixian, originally surnamed Zhao, was a native of Chang-shan. Her father, named Zhen, served as magistrate of Fu-liu County.

Since her childhood, Zhixian was refined in behavior and chaste in character. She donned the religious robe and perfectly observed the disciplinary rules with a spirit of rectitude and profundity, never cherishing any impure thought in her magnanimous mind.

The governor Du Ba, a devout believer in Taoism, hated the Buddhists. He wanted to diminish the number of Buddhist monks and nuns living in the monasteries and nunneries under his jurisdiction by putting them through an examination at a fixed date. The standard of the test was set so high that no ordinary person could possibly pass it. The young monks and nuns were so frightened that they fled in fear. Zhixian alone had no fear and lived with composure in her nunnery as usual.

On the day of the examination, all those assembled at the Archers' Hall outside the city were elderly people. Among the nuns, Zhixian was the only person who was in the prime of life. Du Ba first put some questions to Zhixian and found that she was well above the standard of the test. She was elegant in appearance and spoke in a polished and eloquent manner. Du Ba harbored evil intentions and forced Zhixian to stay alone with him. Having sensed his ill purpose, Zhixian vowed not to violate the disciplinary rules and resisted the governor with harsh words at the risk of her life. Du Ba became furious and struck her with a knife, inflicting more than twenty wounds on her body. She fainted and fell to the ground. When Du Ba had gone away, she recovered consciousness.

Since then Zhixian practiced Buddhism more strenuously and lived an austere life, taking only vegetarian food. She had over a hundred disciples, who were always in perfect harmony with her, like water mixed with milk.

When Fu Jian illegitimately established himself as ruler (in 331), he heard of Zhixian's fame and showed great respect for her. He had an embroidered brocade robe made for her. It took three years to complete the needlework, which was worth a million coins. Afterward she lived at the Western Nunnery in Si-zhou, propagating the right Dharma and spreading faith in and the practice of Buddhism.

During the Tai-he period (366–370), when Zhixian was over seventy years old, she still recited the *Saddharmapuṇḍarīka-Sūtra* once every day and night. At her living quarters many birds used to perch on the trees and whenever she took a walk in the open, they always followed her, chirping and singing.

Source: "Biographies of Buddhist Nuns" in *Lives of Great Monks and Nuns,* translated by Li Rongxi (Berkeley: Numata Center for Buddhist Translation and Research, 2002), 95–96, 103–104, 115–116, 123–124, 75–76.

INDEX

ABOUT THE AUTHOR

PROFESSOR CARL OLSON has taught at Allegheny College since 1981. The college has appointed him to the National Endowment for the Humanities Chair (1991–1994), Teacher-Scholar Professorship of the Humanities (2000–2003), and chairperson. During 2002, he was appointed to a Visiting Fellowship at Clare Hall, University of Cambridge, and was elected a Permanent Fellow of Clare Hall by its board of trustees.

Professor Olson has published over two hundred articles and reviews for various journals. He has served as review editor for the *International Journal of Hindu Studies* since 1996. He has also published the following books: *The Book of the Goddess Past and Present: An Introduction of Her Religion* (1983); *The Mysterious Play of Kali: An Interpretive Study of Ramakrishna* (1990); *The Theology and Philosophy of Eliade: A Search for the Centre* (1992); *The Indian Renouncer and Postmodern Poison: A Cross-Cultural Encounter* (1997); *Zen and the Art of Postmodern Philosophy: Two Paths of Liberation from the Representational Mode of Thinking* (2000); *Indian Philosophers and Postmodern Thinkers: Dialogues on the Margins of Culture* (2002).